LEUVEN GLOBAL GOVERNANCE

Series Editor: Jan Wouters, *KU Leuven, Belgium*

The Leuven Global Governance series comprises high-quality monographs and edited volumes dedicated to innovative research on global governance. The series focuses particularly on the following themes: European Union and global multilateral governance; trade and sustainable development; peace and security studies; human rights, democracy and the rule of law; space governance; and comparative federalism. In full recognition of the complex issues involved, the series favours studies approaching global governance from a multidisciplinary, multi-level and multi-actor perspective.

Titles in the series include:

China, the European Union and Global Governance
Edited by Jan Wouters, Tanguy de Wilde, Pierre Defraigne and Jean-Christophe Defraigne

Private Standards and Global Governance
Economic, Legal and Political Perspectives
Edited by Axel Marx, Miet Maertens, Johan Swinnen and Jan Wouters

The Governance of Climate Relations between Europe and Asia
Evidence from China and Vietnam as Key Emerging Economies
Edited by Hans Bruyninckx, Qi Ye, Nguyen Quang Thuan and David Belis

Indirect Expropriation in International Law
Sebastián López Escarcena

China, the European Union and the Developing World
A Triangular Relationship
Edited by Jan Wouters, Jean-Christophe Defraigne and Matthieu Burnay

Global Governance and Democracy
A Multidisciplinary Analysis
Edited by Jan Wouters, Antoon Braeckman, Matthias Lievens and Emilie Bécault

The Contribution of International and Supranational Courts to the Rule of Law
Edited by Geert De Baere and Jan Wouters

Global Governance of Labor Rights
Assessing the Effectiveness of Transnational Public and Private Policy Initiatives
Edited by Axel Marx, Jan Wouters, Glenn Rayp and Laura Beke

Global Governance through Trade
EU Policies and Approaches
Edited by Jan Wouters, Axel Marx, Dylan Geraets and Bregt Natens

Global Governance through Trade

Global Governance through Trade

EU Policies and Approaches

Edited by

Jan Wouters

Full Professor of International Law and International Organizations, Jean Monnet Chair ad personam *EU and Global Governance, and Director, Leuven Centre for Global Governance Studies and Institute for International Law, KU Leuven, Belgium*

Axel Marx

Deputy Director, Leuven Centre for Global Governance Studies, KU Leuven, Belgium

Dylan Geraets

Doctoral Researcher, Leuven Centre for Global Governance Studies, KU Leuven, Belgium

Bregt Natens

Associate, Sidley Austin LLP, Belgium

LEUVEN GLOBAL GOVERNANCE

Edward Elgar
PUBLISHING

Cheltenham, UK • Northampton, MA, USA

Published by
Edward Elgar Publishing Limited
The Lypiatts
15 Lansdown Road
Cheltenham
Glos GL50 2JA
UK

Edward Elgar Publishing, Inc.
William Pratt House
9 Dewey Court
Northampton
Massachusetts 01060
USA

A catalogue record for this book
is available from the British Library

Library of Congress Control Number: 2015943175

This book is available electronically in the **Elgar**online
Law subject collection
DOI 10.4337/9781783477760

MIX
Paper from
responsible sources
FSC® C013056
FSC
www.fsc.org

ISBN 978 1 78347 775 3 (cased)
ISBN 978 1 78347 776 0 (eBook)

Typeset by Columns Design XML Ltd, Reading
Printed and bound in Great Britain by TJ International Ltd, Padstow, Cornwall

Contents

Contributors

Lorand Bartels, University Senior Lecturer in Law in the Faculty of Law and Fellow of Trinity Hall, University of Cambridge, UK

Laura Beke, Doctoral Researcher at KU Leuven, Belgium

Nicolas A.J. Croquet, Associate with the Brussels office of McKenna Long & Aldridge LLP, Belgium

Chad Damro, Senior Lecturer, Jean Monnet Chair and Director of the Jean Monnet Centre of Excellence, and Co-Director of the Europa Institute at the University of Edinburgh, UK

Dylan Geraets, PhD Candidate at the Leuven Centre for Global Governance Studies, KU Leuven, Belgium

Nicolas Hachez, Project Manager and Researcher at the Leuven Centre for Global Governance Studies, KU Leuven, Belgium

Marieke Koekkoek, PhD Candidate at the Leuven Centre for Global Governance Studies, KU Leuven, Belgium

Joris Larik, Assistant Professor in Comparative, EU and International Law at Leiden University, the Netherlands, Senior Researcher with the Global Governance Program of The Hague Institute for Global Justice, and Associate Fellow, Leuven Centre for Global Governance Studies, KU Leuven, Belgium

Rafael Leal-Arcas, Professor of European and International Economic Law, Director of Research at the Centre for Commercial Law Studies (CCLS), Queen Mary University, UK; Editor-in-Chief of *Renewable Energy Law and Policy Review*

Axel Marx, Deputy Director of the Leuven Centre for Global Governance Studies, KU Leuven, Belgium

Petros C. Mavroidis, Edwin B. Parker Professor at Columbia Law School, New York, and Professor of Law at the University of Neuchâtel, Switzerland (on leave at the European University Institute, Florence)

Bregt Natens, Associate, Sidley Austin LLP, Brussels, Belgium

Cedric Ryngaert, Professor of Public International Law and Programme Leader of the Master of Public International Law, Utrecht University, the Netherlands

Jadir Soares, Associate Fellow at the Leuven Centre for Global Governance Studies, KU Leuven, Belgium

Geert van Calster, Professor and Head of the Department of European and International Law at KU Leuven, Belgium

Catherine M. Wilmarth, Associate with Kelley Drye & Warren LLP

Jan Wouters, Jean Monnet Chair *ad personam* EU and Global Governance, Full Professor of International Law and International Organizations, and founding Director of the Institute for International Law and of the Leuven Centre for Global Governance Studies, KU Leuven, Belgium

James Yap, International Human Rights Lawyer, Toronto

1. Global governance *through* trade: an introduction

Axel Marx, Bregt Natens, Dylan Geraets and Jan Wouters

1. MULTILATERALISM, MULTIPOLARITY AND GLOBAL GOVERNANCE

It has become a commonplace to say that the multilateral institutions which have been set up since the end of the Second World War are currently facing a severe crisis. After the end of the Cold War, everything had looked so promising: an era of international cooperation dawned, in which the United Nations (UN) received a new boost; a great number of multilateral treaties were concluded (from the 1992 UN Framework Convention on Climate Change to the 1997 Kyoto Protocol) and important new international institutions saw the light of day (from the World Trade Organization (WTO) to the International Criminal Court). In Europe, the European integration process yielded new highlights, with the Maastricht Treaty's creation of a European Union (EU or Union), which deepened the internal integration through the gradual implementation of an Economic and Monetary Union, and made the EU a more cohesive international actor, pursuing a set of norms and values on a global scale (Wouters et al., 2012). However, the optimism of the 1990s seems to have ceded to the pessimism of the new millennium. With the emergence of powerful new players with very specific characteristics like China, India and Brazil (Keukeleire and Hooijmaaijers, 2014), reinforced by the global financial crisis and the sovereign debt crisis in the euro area, we seem to have evolved from the bipolarity of the Cold War, over the unipolarity of the 1990s, to some kind of multipolarity or, according to some, interpolarity (Grevi, 2009), in which both Europe and multilateral organizations are confronted with significant challenges.

The multilateral system is facing severe challenges, with regard to the negotiation of new rules and the enforcement of existing rules. First, multilateral negotiations in several fields are at a stalemate. It appears increasingly difficult to conclude internationally binding agreements or to enforce them. Some observers stress the limits of the consensual structure of the international legal order, which relies on the sovereign equality of states in multilateral negotiation fora (for a discussion see Krisch (2014); for a whole set of case studies on the stagnation of international law see Pauwelyn, Wessel and Wouters (2012; 2014)). Examples include the climate change negotiations, multiple (failed) efforts to reach an agreement on global forest governance and combat deforestation, and the negotiations in the context of the multilateral trading system. The Doha Development Round, which commenced in 2001, has produced very few tangible results. Although the conclusion of the Bali Package in December 2013 resulted in renewed interest for the Round, many still question the ability of the WTO to serve nowadays as a successful forum for conducting trade negotiations (Cottier, 2015).

As a matter of fact, the Doha mandate has been overtaken by reality. The issues that were relevant at the start of the Round, almost 15 years ago, are no longer what is crucial for today's international business community. There is a need for a set of new rules to govern twenty-first century trade (Baldwin, 2014). Actors are now pursuing unilateral, bilateral or plurilateral strategies in order to create these new rules. The main pragmatic reason for this is that agreement will be more easily reached with a limited number of participants. A clear case in point is the proliferation of preferential trade agreements. The trend towards mega-regionalism in trade, exemplified by the US-led Trans-Pacific Partnership (TPP), the Transatlantic Trade and Investment Partnership Agreement (TTIP) and the China-Japan-Korea trilateral, points to the emergence of a multipolar – and no longer solely multilateral – world trading system.

International forest governance constitutes another example. The international forest community has for a long time demanded an international, multilateral, 'hard' law instrument for the governance of forests. This demand has been supported by several states – the EU, in particular, has fought for a global forest convention for more than two decades. Starting from the failure in Rio in 1992, where no agreement was reached on an international forest convention, over the establishment of the Intergovernmental Panel on Forests (1995–97) and the Intergovernmental Forum on Forests (1997–2000), to the formation of the UN Forum on Forests (UNFF), one can observe the failure of current multilateral initiatives with regard to forest governance. Dimitrov et al. (2007, p. 243) state that the UNFF is 'explicitly deprived of a policymaking mandate'. In the absence of such a global convention, forest governance remains highly fragmented and ineffective (Rayner, Buck and Katila,

2011), and pushes some actors to become what Scott (2013) calls 'contingent unilateralists', extending their own regulations extraterritorially.

Second, existing multilateral efforts are increasingly confronted with the limitations of enforcing agreed rules. Where multilateral efforts have resulted in a binding agreement, the absence of an international enforcement mechanism often results in lax implementation of these standards. In the field of labour rights, for example, efforts within the International Labour Organization (ILO) have led to numerous conventions and core labour standards. In the absence of an international enforcement mechanism, it is difficult to ensure that these standards are also applied in practice (for a full discussion, see Hendrickx et al., 2015 forthcoming).

This impasse on the multilateral level coincides with an increasing call to further pursue an international good governance agenda (Wouters and Ryngaert, 2004) and an agenda for the protection of global public goods. As Inge Kaul, then Director of the Office of Development Studies at the UN Development Programme (UNDP), and colleagues noted in 2003, 'Open borders and the free flow of private economic activity are one side of globalization. Concerted cross-border public policy action must be the other side if globalization is to serve as a means of improving people's lives rather than wreaking havoc on them' (Kaul et al., 2003, pp. 2–3). This focus on global public goods and good governance is increasingly gaining attention. In its latest 'Development Co-operation Report 2014 – Mobilising Resources for Sustainable Development' the Organisation for Economic Co-operation and Development (OECD) (2014, p. 10) also emphasizes the need for international action to 'deliver much-needed global public goods such as stable and efficient international financial markets, peace and security, a healthy environment and climate, fair international trade [...] and global knowledge for development'. However, the report also notes that 'international consensus and concrete collective action on global public goods have been elusive up to now' (OECD, 2014, p. 10).

Given the stagnation of international action through multilateral channels, one sees a turn to informal lawmaking (Pauwelyn, Wessel and Wouters, 2012; 2014), non-consensual transnational lawmaking (Krisch, 2014), unilateral action (Scott, 2013), and governance *through* trade (this volume). The latter strategy is especially pursued in relation to global public goods by international actors with a strong normative international agenda. The EU qualifies as such an actor. The norms and values which the Union is pursuing are enshrined in EU primary law, most notably the Treaty of Lisbon. They include respect for human dignity, freedom, democracy, equality, the rule of law and respect for human rights (Article 2 Treaty on European Union (TEU)). In addition, under Article 21 TEU, the Union must pursue international policies and actions *inter alia* to consolidate democracy, the rule of law and human rights, and to preserve and improve the quality of the environment and the sustainable management of global natural resources. These objectives apply also to the Common Commercial Policy (Article 205 Treaty on the Functioning of European Union (TFEU)), an exclusive competence of the EU (Article 3 TFEU). However, what does this governance *through* trade, the focus of the present volume, entail?

2. TRADE AS A TRANSNATIONAL GOVERNANCE INSTRUMENT

As noted above, in the absence of multilateral progress, actors seek other mechanisms by which to pursue their international agenda. Savaresi (2012) documents how the EU aims to support forest governance via its Forest Law Enforcement, Governance and Trade (FLEGT) Action Plan. In order to promote the verification of the legality of timber through this Plan, the Union has shifted from an approach of trying to achieve a multilateral solution to bilateral strategies with willing third countries. By conditioning access to its market, the EU made use of its weight as a trading partner, inducing timber exporting countries to introduce forest management strategies.

The example of FLEGT illustrates a wider trend to pursue international strategies *through* trade, especially by the EU. This shift to the use of trade as a foreign policy instrument has received scholarly attention in recent times. In an early contribution, Meunier and Nicolaïdis (2006) distinguish between exercising power *in* trade and *through* trade with reference to EU policies. On the one hand, power *in* trade refers to the trade relation in which access to an actor's domestic market is granted conditionally on access to export markets. This is an emanation of the concept of reciprocity in trade. Power *through* trade, on the other hand, refers to the fact that the Union uses market access power and its market size to 'export' its laws, standards, values and norms. When exercising power *through* trade, the EU uses the size of its domestic market as an asymmetric bargaining chip to 'force' domestic changes within the territory of its trading partner on issues such as good governance, environmental policy and human rights (see also Hafner-Burton, 2005; Zwagemakers, 2012).

The use of trade as a governance instrument is becoming increasingly important in a world that has witnessed a tremendous growth in international commerce and an increasing dependency of countries on exports. As Hoekman (2014) documents, the growth of international trade over the last half century has been spectacular. With an almost thirty-fold increase over 50 years it has truly transnationalized economic activity. The value of global trade in goods and services constitutes 59 per cent of global GDP in 2013, compared with 39 per cent of GDP in 1990. As a region, the Union is the largest importer (€2188 billion in 2013) and exporter (€2415 billion in 2013) of trade in goods and commercial services in the world (European Commission, 2014). This is reflected in the share of trade in the EU's GDP: in 2013, trade in goods and services constituted a whopping 80.5 per cent of EU GDP (World Bank, 2015).

Undoubtedly, economic globalization and the consequences thereof on trade, in their own right, impact upon the provision of specific public goods, such as environmental and social protection. This book, however, does not engage in the debate on whether global trade, if left unregulated, contributes to, or rather worsens, the protection of, for example, environmental and social standards. The research on this is long standing and the debates on the trade and environment conflict, or the interplay between trade and human rights, have been discussed before. Such debates on trade and public goods have often been posited in terms of races to the bottom and races to the top. Research shows that trade liberalization can have a negative effect on environmental protection (Esty, 1994) but also a positive effect on environmental standards (Vogel, 1995), and a negative effect on the protection of specific human rights such as labour rights (see Levi et al., 2012; Mosley, 2011) but also a positive effect on the protection of human rights more in general (Potrafke, 2014). As Aaronson and Zimmerman (2007) argue in the context of the human rights and trade debate, but is in our view applicable more generally, it is true that very little is known about the specific mechanisms that determine the way in which trade does or does not influence the protection of public goods. Many different dynamics can unfold and the subject matter is a moving target. Indeed, the recent burgeoning literature on global value chains shows empirically that in certain cases economic upgrading, spurred by greater trade openness and increased international trade, leads to social upgrading (Barrientos, Gereffi and Rossi, 2011). This, however, is not an automatic mechanism and there are, once again, also several case studies that show social downgrading and pressures on the protection of specific rights (for an elaboration on these issues see Marx et al. (2015)).

Notwithstanding these contentions regarding the impact of trade liberalization on the provision of public goods, there is increasing recognition that, by means of the governance of trade flows, one can also govern social and environmental issues, as exemplified by Meunier and Nicolaïdis' concept of power *through* trade. This governance *through* trade can be executed either directly, by making compliance with specific standards mandatory for market access, or indirectly, by providing additional preferences as an incentive to ratify and effectively implement a series of international human rights, labour, environmental and good governance instruments (such as in the case of GSP+).[1] As a result, several policy initiatives, unilaterally as well as bilaterally, which link trade governance with the governance of non-trade issues, have been developed. How this is done and the results of these initiatives are the focus of the present volume.

This book aims to provide an extensive analysis of both unilateral and bilateral 'new generation' EU governance-*through*-trade policies, in the context of which we seek to understand two key issues. First, we focus on the institutional design of these new instruments. What does it actually entail to link trade with non-trade objectives? How can this be achieved? How is this translated in policy instruments and legal texts? How compatible are these initiatives with international trade law? Second, we aim to understand the impact of these initiatives. For this purpose, contributions to this book elaborate on specific case studies and present original empirical data. In this way our book aims to contribute to the broader study of non-traditional forms of international lawmaking and global governance.

3. OUTLINE OF THE BOOK

The first part of this volume combines insights from political science and legal studies to frame the role of the EU as an actor in the field of international trade. The concept of 'governance through trade' is explored in order to determine why, how and on what legal basis the Union pursues other societal objectives through its trade policy. Following an introductory chapter, the 'new generation' EU governance *through* trade policies is contextualized in Chapter 2 by Chad Damro, who elaborates on the idea of power *through* trade and his concept of 'Market Power

[1] The importance of the link between trade and the governance of non-trade issues is not confined to the actions of state actors, but also to non-state actors. Indeed, the literature on non-state market regulation has for a long time recognized the increasing non-state regulation of transnational supply chains on a set of social and environmental criteria (see, for example, Cashore et al., 2004; Vogel, 2008; Marx et al., 2012).

Europe' (MPE) (Damro, 2012). MPE posits that the Union should be seen as exercising power 'through the externalization of its social and economic agendas' (Damro, 2012, p. 696). Damro introduces the debate on the 'EU as a Power' and conceptualizes MPE. The author discusses the centrality of trade policy and the ways in which new generation trade policies provide MPE with an additional tool to externalize the EU's market-related policies and regulatory measures. He clarifies the contentious nature of the efforts of MPE to externalize different types of new generation trade policy and the ways in which the three characteristics of MPE (market size, institutional features and interest contestation) help to inform the analysis. Damro elaborates upon and extensively discusses issues of inconsistency which emerge out of the application of power *through* trade. The core of the problem with inconsistency is that any action that appears to be the promotion of one general non-trade objective may at the same time contradict or be inconsistent with the promotion of other general non-trade objectives. Damro offers several suggestions to overcome problems of inconsistency. In Chapter 3, Joris Larik addresses the linkages between the EU Common Commercial Policy and the Union's contribution to 'good global governance' in the TEU. Pursuing 'good global governance' in its external actions, including its trade policy, is an obligation of constitutional rank for the Union – regardless of the instructive character of this obligation. Larik concludes that 'the trade policy of the EU is certainly no end in itself, but a powerful means to ends now prominently enshrined in the highest laws of the EU'.

In Part II of this volume (on 'exporting' social and environmental compliance through bilateral conditional market access), the new generation of EU free trade agreements (FTAs) is addressed. The authors analyse the types of mechanism to manage and leverage global public goods, such as the environment and human rights, that are set out in these FTAs, and how these mechanisms are subsequently implemented (for an early analysis, see Dimopoulos, 2009). In Chapter 4, Lorand Bartels addresses the extent to which human rights and sustainable development obligations in EU FTAs give the EU the means of implementing its obligations under the TEU and TFEU. Bartels finds that the human rights clauses in these FTAs are effective in the sense that they allow the Union to fulfil its constitutional objective of respecting human rights in its external action by withdrawing from a commitment that may jeopardize that objective. The same cannot be said for the sustainable development clauses, which do not leave such leeway. This may be explained by the language of the objective of promoting sustainable development, which is less obligatory than the language on human rights in Article 21 TEU.

Moreover, the internal coherence of both objectives in EU FTAs is lacking, as a result of differences in implementation and remedies. These differences may be difficult to sustain.

In Chapter 5, Rafael Leal-Arcas and Catherine Wilmarth focus further on sustainable development in FTAs by conducting a comparative analysis of the negotiations on sustainable development for the Pacific Rim Trans-Pacific Partnership (TPP) and for the EU–US Transatlantic Trade and Investment Partnership (TTIP). The authors argue that mega-regional FTAs, such as the TPP and TTIP, can be more efficient vehicles for the promotion of sustainable development than multilateral environmental agreements. The question is whether that potential appears to be fulfilled in the negotiations for the TPP and TTIP. After assessing relevant issues related to sustainable development in both negotiations, the authors compare the available relevant information on scope, enforcement, dispute resolution, implementation and constraints on regulatory autonomy in the TPP and TTIP negotiations. For now, the conclusion is that the TPP does not appear to live up to its potential as an efficient agreement promoting sustainable development, while it remains to be seen whether the EU and the US will make the TTIP an exemplary agreement in this regard.

Chapter 6 by Nicolas Croquet turns to a specific case study and assesses the climate change provisions in the EU-Korea FTA from the perspective of hard and soft law, based on legal scholarship and the direct effect doctrine of the Court of Justice of the European Union (CJEU). The provisions that deal directly with climate change are characterized by generality, looseness, and policy-oriented and conditional language. They contain a low degree of clarity, detail and self-sufficiency, and reflect in essence best-efforts legal obligations rather than result-based obligations. They can best be characterized as soft law obligations. In comparison, the indirect climate change provisions can be characterized as hard law. These provisions do not deal with climate change directly, but touch upon this issue as they, for example, include the general exceptions clause of Article XX of the General Agreement on Tariffs and Trade (GATT) 1994 which is incorporated through *renvoi*. However, there is merit in the provisions that deal with climate change directly: the normative interactions with the indirect climate change provisions of the EU-Korea FTA urge the signatory states to interpret the FTA's trade-furthering and trade-restricting provisions in the most environmental law-friendly way. This includes triggering good administration principles and defence rights that supplement the direct climate change chapter's embryonic transparency provision. Consequently, the 'direct climate change provisions' provide normative context for the 'hard law' obligations that are found in the 'indirect climate change provisions'. Whereas the former merely reflect best-efforts obligations rather than result-based obligations, the latter may be interpreted from a climate change perspective. Essentially, this means that the issue of climate change becomes a societal concern that can be addressed through hard law clauses such as the general exceptions clause, whereas this exceptions clause historically did not foresee climate change as one of the objectives that could be legitimately pursued.

In Chapter 7, Axel Marx and Jadir Soares provide an explorative empirical assessment of the potential impact of the inclusion of labour rights in FTAs. Based on original data-gathering and a time series, the authors assess the degree to which two specific labour rights – namely freedom of association and collective bargaining (FACB) rights – have been protected effectively in a selected number of countries with which the EU has concluded a free trade agreement which includes strong provisions on the protection of labour rights. The authors construct a FACB rights index based on several components and measured through a screening of different sources. This index is subsequently used for an empirical analysis of 13 countries with which the EU has concluded a trade agreement which includes strong provisions on labour rights: Antigua and Barbuda, the Bahamas, Barbados, Belize, Chile, Colombia, Costa Rica, Dominica, Dominican Republic, Ecuador, South Korea, Panama and Peru. The authors show that these rights are slightly less protected over time, which indicates a limited impact in including such provisions in trade agreements.

In Part III (on 'exporting' social and environmental compliance through unilateral conditional market access), this book provides an in-depth analysis of a selection of new 'autonomous' EU normative initiatives which focus on imports as a way of encouraging development or reform in countries seeking to export to the EU. Two chapters focus on the Generalised System of Preferences (GSP) of the EU, which makes preferential market access conditional upon adherence to specific norms. GSP is a set of rules granting preferential EU market access to exporters from developing countries through lower duties on some or all of their exports to the EU, thereby contributing to the growth of their economies. In October 2012, EU Regulation 978/2012 updated the Union's GSP Scheme with the following objectives: (i) to focus help on those countries truly in need; (ii) to strengthen the incentives for good governance and sustainable development (known as 'GSP+'); and (iii) to make the scheme more transparent, stable and predictable. Each chapter contains a country-specific case study that examines different aspects of the EU GSP.

In Chapter 8, Laura Beke and Nicolas Hachez focus on the stringency of the conditions for the suspension of preferences in the EU GSP scheme and further examine this issue through a case study on Myanmar. They start from the observation that the unilateral and non-reciprocal nature of the GSP instrument stands in contrast to the bilateral instruments discussed in the other chapters whereby conditionality clauses are subject to negotiation. In practice, the suspension of GSP preferences has been applied on only three occasions: against Myanmar in 1997, against Belarus in 2007, and against Sri Lanka in 2010. The authors then focus on the case study of Myanmar, in which the preferences were reinstated in 2013, leaving many unconvinced as to whether Burma, as it was still called in 1997, was complying with GSP conditions. They discuss the reasons underpinning the EU's decision to withdraw Burma/Myanmar's GSP preferences in 1997 and to subsequently reinstate them in 2013. The authors conclude with reflections on what this case might show in terms of balancing trade and non-trade objectives.

James Yap, in Chapter 9, provides a case study of the impact of GSP on fostering labour rights in the Bangladeshi garment industry, in the aftermath of the 2013 Rana Plaza tragedy in which over 1100 garment workers died. Bangladesh is a beneficiary of the most beneficial GSP scheme, 'Everything But Arms', which is *inter alia* conditional upon respect for core labour standards. The GSP scheme contains two tools for the promotion of labour rights: (i) the withdrawal of benefits (GSP); and (ii) the granting of additional preferences contingent upon ratification and effective implementation of certain international instruments (GSP+). Acting under international pressure from non-governmental organizations (NGOs), the EU and Bangladesh, together with the ILO, agreed on the introduction of a 'sustainability compact' in July 2013. The author extensively reviews preliminary evidence regarding the implementation of the compact, concluding that there has been 'modest but clear' progress for the protection of labour rights. The threat of revoking GSP status appears to have played a significant role, especially considering that the US had already terminated preferences for Bangladeshi exports. Yap also analyses whether the GSP trade preferences may have contributed to the unsatisfactory implementation of labour standards in the first place. In suggesting further reform of the GSP, the author argues in favour of earlier intervention through a larger range of tools to promote labour rights and avoid violations of such rights.

The book then goes on to provide an in-depth analysis of new regulations which put conditions on the importation of certain goods, thereby limiting access to the economically important EU market. Examples of such measures include Regulation 1007/2009 on the trade in seal products and Regulation 1005/2008 on the prevention of illegal fishing. Although generally applicable equally to domestic and imported products, these regulations have extraterritorial effects; this raises several questions as to their legitimacy and their compatibility with international (trade) law (see, for example, Ankersmit, Lawrence and Davies, 2012).

In Chapter 10, Cedric Ryngaert and Marieke Koekkoek analyse the extraterritorial regulation of natural resources and human rights from a legal perspective. They explore the merits of this new approach to the international governance of natural resources. In the face of prolonged and widespread difficulties in reaching multilateral agreement on global challenges and problems, they argue that unilateral action – although susceptible to protectionist interests – may be a second best alternative, even where it may have an extraterritorial impact resulting from the need to guarantee the effectiveness of internal regulation. Cognizant, however, of the inherent risks associated with a return to unilateralist policies, the authors suggest that common ground has to be found between the two strict approaches. Their approach involves a determination of the 'function' of the extraterritorial aspects contained in the measure. The larger the extent to which this 'function' is grounded in international norms or interests (the authors argue that an interest-based approach may be more appropriate than a 'slavish norm-based' approach), the more likely it is that the measure could be considered to be 'presumptively permissible'. They apply this approach to three EU legal instruments aimed at the pursuit of natural resource objectives – the EU Timber Regulation, the EU Renewable Energy Directive (RED) and the EU Seals Regulation. The authors assess the extent to which the three instruments are 'embedded in international norms or interests'. In doing so they find that the concerns addressed by the Timber Regulation appear to be embedded in international norms or interests, rendering this measure to be the most legitimate out of the three, whereas the legitimacy of the RED and the Seals Regulation is more questionable, given the lack of international norms on the issues in question.

Chapters 11 to 13 return again to the multilateral dimension in order to assess these regulatory approaches from the perspective of the law of the World Trade Organization (WTO). Chapter 11, by Dylan Geraets and Bregt Natens, contains an in-depth analysis of the EU Timber Regulation. This Regulation aims to prevent illegally logged timber, and timber products containing such timber, from entering the European market. The result is the 'export' of environmental governance by imposing on the import of products conditions relating to the way in which natural resources are governed in the country of origin. The underlying rationale is that the depletion of natural resources is partially the result of state failure and the lack of enforcement of local and international rules and commitments. In order to provide incentives for the strengthening of state capacity, the EU links good environmental governance with trade. Such regulatory incentives nonetheless need to comply with international trade rules, foremost being those obligations that are applicable to the EU as a Member of the WTO. The EU Timber Regulation is assessed from the perspective of compliance with WTO disciplines, with a focus on developing WTO-compliant regulations that further good global governance objectives.

In Chapter 12, Petros Mavroidis addresses the extraterritoriality of domestic environmental, or green, policies from the perspective of the law of the WTO, with a focus on the question of jurisdiction. Mavroidis notes that the relevant case law has 'implicitly embraced the principle that WTO Members have the right to regulate the conditions under which they grant market access, irrespective of adverse effects for their trading partners'. Because the WTO agreements do not address the issue squarely, Mavroidis relies on public international law rules on jurisdiction before turning to the Report of the Working Party on Border Tax Adjustments and case law under the GATT 1947 and the WTO. The author's conclusion based on the case law analysis is that, so far, there has been little clarification on the legal relevance of 'default' public international law rules since parties to the disputes, as well as the panels adjudicating these disputes, appear to be hesitant in addressing this jurisdictional question.

In Chapter 13, Geert van Calster elaborates on the methods of integration of regulatory priorities and compares the approaches taken by the EU and the WTO in this regard. The author distinguishes between positive and negative harmonization and argues that there is little room for positive harmonization within the framework of the WTO. He then compares the different approaches to negative harmonization adopted by the CJEU and the WTO's Dispute Settlement Body. Van Calster concludes by partially holding the lack of unity in the international regulatory community responsible for the current status quo. Blaming the 'Trade and …' conundrum solely on the approach adopted by WTO Panels and the Appellate Body is wrong in his view.

In the concluding chapter, Jan Wouters, Axel Marx, Dylan Geraets and Bregt Natens offer perspectives on the potential of these trade instruments to act as effective policy tools for the achievement of normative objectives such as the protection of human rights or sustainable development. They bring together the main insights from the various contributions on the potential and limitations of governance *through* trade measures structured along three dimensions: (i) legality; (ii) consistency; and (iii) effectiveness.

REFERENCES

Aaronson, S. and J.M. Zimmerman (2007), *Trade Imbalance: The Struggle to Weigh Human Rights Concerns in Trade Policymaking*, Cambridge: Cambridge University Press.

Ankersmit, L.J., J.C. Lawrence and G.T. Davies (2012), 'Diverging EU and WTO Perspectives on Extraterritorial Process Regulation', *Minnesota Journal of International Law*, **21**, 14–94.

Baldwin, R. (2014), 'WTO 2.0: Governance of 21st Century Trade', *The Review of International Organizations*, **9** (2), 261–83.

Barrientos, S., G. Gereffi and A. Rossi (2011), 'Economic and Social Upgrading in Global Production Networks: A New Paradigm for a Changing World', *International Labour Review*, **150** (3–4), 319–40.

Cashore, B., G. Auld and D. Newsom (2004), *Governing Through Markets. Forest Certification and the Emergence of Non-state Authority*, New Haven, CT: Yale University Press.

Charnovitz, S. (2002), *Trade Law and Global Governance*, Nottingham: Cameron May.

Choudhury, B. (2012), *Public Services and International Trade Liberalization: Human Rights and Gender Implications*, Cambridge: Cambridge University Press.

Cottier, T. (2015), 'The Common Law of International Trade and the Future of the World Trade Organization', *Journal of International Economic Law*, **18** (1), 3–20.

Damro, C. (2012), 'Market Power Europe', *Journal of European Public Policy*, **19** (5), 682–99.

Dimitrov, R.S., D.F. Sprinz, G. DiGuisto and A. Kelle (2007), 'International Non-Regimes: A Research Agenda', *International Studies Review*, **9** (2), 230–58.

Dimopoulos, A. (2009), 'EC Free Trade Agreements: An Alternative Model for Addressing Human Rights in Foreign Investment Regulation and Dispute Settlement?', in P.-M. Dupuy, E.-U. Petersmann and F. Francioni (eds), *Human Rights in International Investment Law and Arbitration*, Oxford: Oxford University Press, pp. 565–94.

Esty, D.C. (1994), *Greening the GATT: Trade Environment and the Future*, Washington, DC: Peterson Institute for International Economics.

European Commission (2014), 'EU Position in World Trade', accessed 14 January 2015 at http://ec.europa.eu/trade/policy/eu-position-in-world-trade.

Francioni, F. (ed.) (2001), *Environment, Human Rights, and International Trade*, Oxford: Hart Publishing.

Grevi, G. (2009), 'The Interpolar World: A New Scenario', Occasional Paper No. 79, EU Institute of Security Studies.

Hafner-Burton, E. (2005), 'Trading Human Rights: How Preferential Trade Agreements Influence Government Repression', *International Organization*, **59** (3), 593–629.

Hendrickx, F., A. Marx, G. Rayp and J. Wouters (2015), 'The Architecture of Global Labour Governance', *International Labor Review* (forthcoming).

Hoekman, B. (2014), *Supply Chains, Mega-Regionals and Multilateralism: A Road Map for the WTO*, London: CEPR Press.

Kaul, I., P. Conceição, K. Le Goulven and R. Mendoza (2003), 'Why Do Global Public Goods Matter Today', in I. Kaul, P. Conceição, K. Le Goulven and R.U. Mendoza (eds), *Providing Global Public Goods: Managing Globalization*, Oxford: Oxford University Press, pp. 2–20.

Keukeleire, S. and B. Hooijmaaijers (2014), 'The BRICS and Other Emerging Power Alliances and Multilateral Organizations in the Asia-Pacific and the Global South: Challenges for the European Union and its Views on Multilateralism', *Journal of Common Market Studies,* **52** (3), 582–99.

Krisch, N. (2014), 'The Decay of Consent: International Law in an Age of Global Public Goods', *The American Journal of International Law*, **108** (1), 1–40.

Levi, M. et al. (2012), 'Aligning Rights and Interests: Why, When and How to Uphold Labor Standards', Background Paper for the World Development Report 2013.

Manner, I. (2002), 'Normative Power Europe: A Contradiction in Terms?', *Journal of Common Market Studies*, **40** (2), 235–58.

Marx, A., M. Maertens, J. Swinnen and J. Wouters (eds) (2012), *Private Standards and Global Governance*, Cheltenham, UK and Northampton, MA, USA: Edward Elgar Publishing.

Marx, A., J. Wouters, L. Beke and G. Rayp (eds) (2015), *Global Governance of Labour Rights*, Cheltenham, UK and Northampton, MA, USA: Edward Elgar Publishing.

Meunier, S. and K. Nicolaïdis (2006), 'The European Union as a Conflicted Trade Power', *Journal of European Public Policy*, **13**, 906–25.

Mosley, L. (2011), *Labour Rights and Multinational Production*, Cambridge: Cambridge University Press.

OECD (2014), *Development Co-operation Report 2014 – Mobilising Resources for Sustainable Development*, Paris: OECD.

Pauwelyn, J., R. Wessel and J. Wouters (eds) (2012), *Informal International Lawmaking*, Oxford: Oxford University Press.

Pauwelyn, J., R. Wessel and J. Wouters (eds) (2014), 'When Structures Become Shackles: Stagnation and Dynamics in International Lawmaking', *European Journal of International Law*, **25**, 733–63.

Potrafke, N. (2014), 'The Evidence on Globalisation', *World Economy*, **38** (3), 509–52, doi: 10.1111/twec.12174.

Rayner, J., A. Buck and P. Katila (2011), *Embracing Complexity: Meeting the Challenges of International Forest Governance. A Global Assessment Report by the Global Forest Expert Panel on the International Forest Regime*, Vienna: International Union of Forest Research Organizations.

Savaresi, A. (2012), 'EU External Action on Forests: FLEGT and the Development of International Law', in E. Morgera (ed.), *The External Environmental Policy of the European Union*, Cambridge: Cambridge University Press, pp. 149–73.

Scharma, R. (2012), *Breakout Nations: In Pursuit of the Next Economic Miracles*, New York: W.W. Norton and Company.

Scott, J. (2013), 'Contingent Unilateralism – International Aviation in the European Emissions Trading Scheme', in B. van Vooren, S. Blockmans and J. Wouters (eds), *The EU's Role in Global Governance: The Legal Dimension*, Oxford: Oxford University Press, pp. 209–223.

Vogel, D. (1995), *Trading Up: Consumer and Environmental Regulation in a Global Economy*, Cambridge, MA: Harvard University Press.

Vogel, D. (2008), 'Private Global Business Regulation', *Annual Review of Political Science*, **11**, 261–82.

World Bank (2015), 'Trade (% of GDP)', accessed 14 January 2015 at http://data.worldbank.org/indicator/NE.TRD.GNFS.ZS/countries/1W-EU?display=graph.

Wouters, J. and C. Ryngaert (2004), 'Good Governance: Lessons from International Organizations', in D.M. Curtin and R.A. Wessel (eds), *Good Governance in the European Union: Lessons from National and International Law*, Antwerp and Oxford: Intersentia, pp. 69–104.

Wouters, J., H. Bruyninckx, S. Basu and S. Schunz (eds) (2012), *The European Union and Multilateral Governance: Assessing EU Participation in United Nations Human Rights and Environmental Fora*, Basingstoke: Palgrave.

Zwagemakers, F. (2012), 'The EU's Conditionality Policy: A New Strategy to Achieve Compliance', IAI Working Paper 12|03.

PART I

Defining 'governance *through* trade'

2. Market Power Europe and new EU trade policies

Chad Damro

1. INTRODUCTION

It would be difficult to argue that the European Union (EU) is not a trade power. By comparative economic figures, the EU is a leading actor in today's global economy and the 'world's largest presence in international trade' (McGuire and Lindeque, 2010, p. 1330). The sheer size of the EU as a single market with a common external tariff ensures its centrality in the international trading system. Yet this is not merely a recent development. While the Common Commercial Policy (CCP), dating from the 1957 Treaty of Rome, and subsequent treaty revisions provided the basis for the EU to develop into a trade power, the importance of the EU's CCP today is amplified further through its operation as 'a unique tool for forwarding policy priorities that extended beyond pure trade considerations' (Dimopoulos, 2010, p. 153).

While the EU must be taken seriously as a *trade* power, this status and its capacity to use the CCP to forward non-trade policy priorities speak to a broader conceptualization of the EU as a power in the international system. More specifically, the historical and contemporary development of its trade policies helps to inform the conceptualization of the EU as Market Power Europe (MPE) (Damro, 2012). According to this conceptualization, three central characteristics of the EU's identity – market size, institutional features and interest contestation – may contribute to the drive and capacity to externalize its social and economic agendas. From this perspective, the exercise of power both within and beyond trade has been enhanced by the establishment of new generation trade policies, or legislation which attaches conditions for market entry (see Chapter 1, this volume). As the EU strives to externalize its economic and social market-related policies and regulatory measures via free trade agreements and autonomous initiatives, new generation trade policies provide important tools to influence the behaviour of various non-EU actors. The themes and contributions of this edited volume, therefore, provide an excellent context in which to explore MPE, externalization and the three characteristics that inform its identity.

The conditions associated with new generation trade policies help to draw a distinction between trade and non-trade objectives and reflect Meunier and Nicolaïdis' understanding of the EU as a 'conflicted trade power'. While the EU is clearly a power *in* trade, they argue that the EU is becoming a power *through* trade by using market access to promote policy changes abroad, such as environmental protection, higher labour standards, greater respect for human rights and 'more generally to shape new patterns of global governance' (Meunier and Nicolaïdis, 2006, p. 907). These non-trade objectives that arise in new generation trade policies are based in EU primary and secondary legislation, but they also appear in clauses of free trade agreements and requirements and conditions of autonomous initiatives. Taken together, the trade and non-trade objectives can be seen as part of the economic and social market-related policies and regulatory measures that MPE attempts to externalize both in and through trade.

A central issue that arises in the analysis of new generation trade policies and the EU as a power is the problem of inconsistency between and among its trade and non-trade objectives. Long the focus of policymakers, the EU has sought to overcome this problem in practice with successive policy and institutional reforms. On the theoretical side, legal scholars have usefully focused on the codification of measures to ensure consistency, while political scientists tend to analyse empirically the extent to which the EU is consistent in its external relations. This difference in approach may reflect each discipline's objectives, but the differences are not insurmountable.[1] As Wouters and his co-authors put it, '[f]or legal scholars, the main challenge is giving empirical research methods a chance, whereas political scientists specialized in international relations need, above all, to overcome their treatment of international and EU law as merely an outcome of political processes and to engage more thoroughly in its interpretation' (Wouters et al., 2008, p. 54). Drawing from the contributions of legal scholars in this volume and the empirical treatment of the EU as a power, this chapter aims to provide insights into

---

[1] Regarding disciplinary objectives, political science can often be seen as pursuing an explanatory agenda, whereas 'doctrinal law is normative perforce' (Engel and Héritier, 2003, p. 11).

the understandings held by both disciplines of the challenges related to inconsistency that may arise in the pursuit of new generation trade policies.

For analytical purposes, the core of the problem with inconsistency is that any action that appears to be the promotion of one general non-trade objective may at the same time contradict or be inconsistent with the promotion of other general non-trade objectives. The analytical uncertainty about what exactly is being promoted and the inability to disentangle empirically what the EU is doing as a power leaves little room for scholars to generate with confidence any precise statements about what kind of power the EU really is or to judge what the EU says and does as a power. This inability to provide assurances that the EU is promoting a single broad or general objective at any given time is most problematic for conceptualizations of the EU as a power that depends on the EU promoting imprecise objectives such as 'civilian ends' or 'norms'.[2] However, these problems may be overcome with an MPE-based approach that emphasizes a narrower and more empirical tracing of the EU's externalization of trade and non-trade objectives. As such, this chapter contributes to discussions about the legal and political bases, and ways in which and the extent to which the EU is able to externalize various market-related policies and regulatory measures (trade and non-trade objectives) with a particular tool (new generation trade policies), regardless of the potential for inconsistency.

The remainder of the chapter proceeds in the following manner. The next section introduces the so-called 'EU as a Power' debates and elaborates upon the Market Power Europe conceptualization and the

---

[2] The differences between law and political science are not always clearly drawn, which can lead to confusion in the use of terms like 'civilian ends' or the more widely used 'norms'. While there may be connections in understanding the meaning of 'norms' in these two disciplines, the approaches undertaken and ultimate analytical objectives are often different. A crucial difference for political scientists working on international relations (IR) is their tendency to view norms as having ideational causal effects. According to Finnemore and Sikkink, '[t]here is general agreement on the definition of a norm as a standard of appropriate behavior for actors with a given identity' (1998, p. 891). These norms, which often fall into different categories (regulative, evaluative and prescriptive), can affect and change the interests and identity of actors. However, while 'customary international law *is* norms', international law 'has been ignored by IR scholars for decades' (Finnemore and Sikkink, 1998, p. 916). For an excellent discussion of the similarities and differences between political science and international law treatments of norms, see Hafner-Burton et al. (2012).

importance of trade policy as a tool to externalize the EU's market-related policies and regulatory measures. The chapter then clarifies the contentious nature of EU efforts to externalize different types of new generation trade policy and the ways in which the three characteristics of MPE help to inform the analysis. The following section highlights different disciplinary understandings and approaches to the issue of inconsistency as it relates to the 'EU as a Power' debates and the treatment of specific and general, as well as trade and non-trade, objectives. The section also provides an exploration of how the empirical approach of MPE may help to overcome the analytical pitfall of inconsistency when investigating new generation trade policies. The chapter concludes with a summary of the findings.

2. MARKET POWER EUROPE AND THE IMPORTANCE OF TRADE POLICY

For legal scholars, the relationship between EU external relations and international law is a growing area of inquiry in which prominent contributions have shown that the EU is a significant international legal actor which often attempts to export its legal framework on a multilateral basis (Van Vooren and Wessel, 2014; Kuijper et al., 2013; Eeckhout, 2011; Wessel, 2011) and contributes to the international rule of law across various policy areas (Bradford, 2012; Scott, 2014; Van Vooren, Blockmans and Wouters, 2013). The literature's focus on legal dimensions, while understandable, tends to neglect the concept of power as a central analytical tool for understanding the way in which and the extent to which the EU may influence other actors in the international system. In contrast, the concept of power has been 'eternally fundamental to political science' (Hafner-Burton et al., 2012, p. 51). By considering power in the context of the EU's external relations, we can ascertain the conditions under which international law may enable or constrain the ability of this actor to determine its own circumstances.

In the social sciences, and especially political science, the study of the EU in international affairs has resulted in a proliferation of competing conceptualizations of the EU as a power. These 'EU as a Power' debates often focus on the EU's particular characteristics and prioritize questions about what kind of power the EU is, what the EU says as a power and what the EU does as a power (Damro, 2012). Starting in 1972, Duchêne argued that the EU's unique characteristics made it a different kind of actor for which military power has been supplanted by civilian power. While the EU is now certainly understood as an influential global actor of some sort, it still compares uncomfortably with other traditional and legally recognised actors like individual states and international organizations. This has helped to reinforce scholarly understandings of the EU as a unique or *sui generis* actor. According to these debates, the particular characteristics that provide the basis for the EU to be a power now range from the strategically constrained Small Power (Toje, 2011), to the disjointed Fragmented Power (Sapir, 2007), to the generally cautious Risk-Averse Power (Laïdi, 2010), to, perhaps the most prominent, the ideationally influential Normative Power Europe (Manners, 2002) and the Transformative Power of Europe project.[3]

Another contribution to these debates – the conceptualization of the EU as Market Power Europe (MPE) – was not designed to explain the dynamics of trade policy alone. However, if the EU is conceptualized as MPE, it is important to explore the ways in which this perspective sheds light on the EU's external trade relations. To do so, it is useful to provide a brief recapitulation of the conceptualization.

As Market Power Europe, the EU's identity, both historically and presently, is crucially linked to its experience with market integration. However, the conceptualization does not require analysts to study the EU as a *sui generis* actor. Rather, using general insights from leading contributions to the comparative and international political economy literature, the EU as a power may be understood as a combination of three broad characteristics that contribute to any market power's identity: (i) material existence in terms of market size (Drezner, 2007); (ii) institutional features such as regulatory capacity (Bach and Newman, 2007); and (iii) interest contestation (Dür and De Bièvre, 2007). While these three characteristics are often treated as competing explanations, the MPE conceptualization considers them inter-related and mutually reinforcing, which encourages us to explore the connections and relationships among the characteristics in order to generate a more complete understanding of the EU's identity and actions as a power (Damro, 2015).

MPE focuses on the EU's capacity to exercise its power through the externalization of a wide array of market-related policies and regulatory measures. These policies and measures cover both economic and social regulation, some of which liberalizes the market and some of which constrains market actors. Such externalization can be considered to have taken place when another state or non-state actor adheres to a level of

[3] For the Transformative Power of Europe project, see http://www.polsoz.fu-berlin.de/en/v/transformeurope, (accessed 29 January 2015).

regulation similar to that in effect in the European single market or behaves in a way that generally satisfies or conforms to the EU's market-related policies and regulatory measures (Damro, 2012, p. 690).

In terms of the three characteristics of MPE, externalization may be driven by the large size of the Single European Market, high levels of regulatory capacity and the pressure exerted by pro-externalization coalitions of domestic groups in society. Such an exercise of power, which may occur (both coercively and persuasively) as intentional or unintentional action, suggests that the EU is fully capable of influencing international affairs through a wide range of means and tools – for example, the use of positive and negative conditionality, multilateral and bilateral legal instruments, formal and informal networks, internal regulatory measures – in its relations with both states and non-state actors. Many of these tools are often recognized in the EU studies and international legal literature, and many feature prominently in the area of trade policy.

Trade policy holds a prominent place in relation to the conceptualization of MPE. In its historical development, the common market and the CCP served as original and essential building blocks of European integration and EU identity. Highlighting further the importance of trade, Meunier and Nicolaïdis argue that '[h]istorically, internal trade liberalization and external trade policy served as the glue to bind together the former enemies within Europe' (2006, pp. 906–7).[4] The fundamental nature of trade policy for the EU is also witnessed in its constitutional prerogatives and placement. Indeed, the inclusion of trade policy within the EU's constitutional treaties underlines the importance of this policy area and encourages linkages with other external policies. So important is trade policy to the EU that, as Larik notes through comparison, 'it seems to be rather rare for a constitution to address specifically trade policy and its goals, much less to link it to a wider constitutionally entrenched foreign policy agenda. Hence, the latter remains a speciality of the EU' (Larik, Chapter 3, this volume).

This specialty of the EU contributes to the importance of trade policy for MPE because the CCP is cross-cutting in the sense that it touches upon various other policy areas. As a result, MPE's understanding of 'economic and social market-related policies and regulatory measures' can be broadly interpreted to cover all types of EU legislation and instrument (including standards set by private bodies) across a wide

[4] On the importance of trade, see also Young and Peterson (2014).

variety of policy areas and, conceivably, the entire *acquis*.[5] With the advent of new generation trade policies, the CCP is now a tool that may help to increase the EU's externalization of various trade and non-trade objectives, both of which may be seen as the market-related policies and regulatory measures that are central to the MPE conceptualization.

3. MPE AND THE CONTENTIOUS NATURE OF NEW GENERATION TRADE POLICIES

As measures which attach conditions for market entry, new generation trade policies are intimately related to EU efforts to externalize its market-related policies and regulatory measures. However, the conditions attached to the new generation trade policies can be highly contentious because they include a variety of often sensitive, non-trade objectives.[6] So, what exactly are these non-trade objectives that the EU externalizes through trade policy?

Article 3.5 of the Treaty on European Union (TEU)[7] lists the more general principles and goals, including trade and non-trade objectives, which will guide the EU's external action.[8] For the list of objectives more specific to external action, we turn to Article 21 TEU.[9] This article is

[5] For a discussion of the purview of MPE's market-related policies and regulatory measures, see Damro (2015).

[6] These non-trade objectives may also be thought of as 'global public goods' (see Marx et al., Chapter 1, this volume), 'WTO-Extra' issues (Horn, Mavroidis and Sapir, 2010) or linked to what Kerremans and Orbie (2009) refer to as the 'social dimension' of EU trade policies. Similarly, the 'normative' component of these objectives has led some to label them as 'civilian ends' or 'norms' that are often ascribed to the EU (Smith, 2005; Manners, 2002). To avoid confusion, this section refers to these various labels as 'non-trade objectives'.

[7] Consolidated Version of the Treaty on European Union [2008] OJ C 115/13.

[8] http://www.lisbon-treaty.org/wcm/the-lisbon-treaty/treaty-on-european-union-and-comments/title-1-common-provisions/4-article-3.html (accessed 22 January 2015).

[9] Article 21 TEU reads, in full:

> 1. The Union's action on the international scene shall be guided by the principles which have inspired its own creation, development and enlargement, and which it seeks to advance in the wider world: democracy, the rule of law, the universality and indivisibility of human rights and fundamental freedoms, respect for human dignity, the principles of equality and solidarity, and respect for the principles of the United Nations Charter and international law.

based on Article 3 (Dimopoulos, 2010) and includes an array of objectives for EU external action. While Article 21(2)(e) deals more directly with trade, non-trade objectives appear prominently throughout the remainder of the clauses. Dimopoulos (2010) classifies these Article 21 non-trade objectives into three categories: (i) democracy, rule of law, and respect for human rights, as well as the security and integrity of the

---

The Union shall seek to develop relations and build partnerships with third countries, and international, regional or global organisations which share the principles referred to in the first subparagraph. It shall promote multilateral solutions to common problems, in particular in the framework of the United Nations.

2. The Union shall define and pursue common policies and actions, and shall work for a high degree of cooperation in all fields of international relations, in order to:

(a) safeguard its values, fundamental interests, security, independence and integrity;
(b) consolidate and support democracy, the rule of law, human rights and the principles of international law;
(c) preserve peace, prevent conflicts and strengthen international security, in accordance with the purposes and principles of the United Nations Charter, with the principles of the Helsinki Final Act and with the aims of the Charter of Paris, including those relating to external borders;
(d) foster the sustainable economic, social and environmental development of developing countries, with the primary aim of eradicating poverty;
(e) encourage the integration of all countries into the world economy, including through the progressive abolition of restrictions on international trade;
(f) help develop international measures to preserve and improve the quality of the environment and the sustainable management of global natural resources, in order to ensure sustainable development;
(g) assist populations, countries and regions confronting natural or man-made disasters; and
(h) promote an international system based on stronger multilateral cooperation and good global governance.

3. The Union shall respect the principles and pursue the objectives set out in paragraphs 1 and 2 in the development and implementation of the different areas of the Union's external action covered by this Title and by Part Five of the Treaty on the Functioning of the European Union, and of the external aspects of its other policies.

The Union shall ensure consistency between the different areas of its external action and between these and its other policies. The Council and the Commission, assisted by the High Representative of the Union for Foreign Affairs and Security Policy, shall ensure that consistency and shall cooperate to that effect.

EU and the preservation of international peace and security; (ii) quality of the environment and the sustainable management of global natural resources, as well as sustainable economic, social, and environmental development of developing countries; and (iii) multilateralism and good governance.

Article 21(3) places responsibility for ensuring consistency among these various trade and non-trade objectives with the Council, the Commission and the High Representative of the Union for Foreign Affairs and Security Policy. While this is a clear indication of the priority placed on the need for consistency, it does not clarify the exact meaning of the non-trade objectives contained in the article.

Given this rather ambiguous nature of non-trade objectives, it is hardly surprising that their pursuit in both types of new generation policy – free trade agreements (FTAs) and autonomous initiatives – can be highly contentious for EU trade partners. In addition to this ambiguity, an important reason for the EU's non-trade objectives being so contentious is that the extent to which they are universally held is debatable. Furthermore, even if they were universally held, different trading partners understand them differently and do not always prioritize them in equal measure.

With regard to FTAs, the European Commission acknowledges that the negotiation of trade and non-trade objectives presents a 'significant and highly challenging' trade agenda for the EU (European Commission, 2010, p. 9). However, given the requirements of primary legislation (Articles 3 and 21 TEU), the EU's approach to FTAs focuses on the inclusion of mechanisms and provisions for a variety of non-trade objectives: for example, EU FTAs include provisions which aim to protect the environment, consumers, workers and the public at large via human rights and democratic principles as well as labour and environmental standards (Bartels, Chapter 4, this volume). As Croquet (Chapter 6, this volume) shows, the EU-Korea FTA includes non-trade objectives on climate change and corporate social responsibility. Leal-Arcas and Wilmarth (Chapter 5, this volume) also show that the EU promotes various components of sustainable development in its pursuit of regional trade agreements.

The inclusion of such non-trade objectives in FTAs can be legally complex and raises important questions about ensuring consistency with other objectives, although their inclusion can also be politically sensitive during the negotiation of this type of new generation trade policy. Indeed, as Khorana and Garcia argue, the negotiation of non-trade objectives is often so contentious that they can serve as 'deal breakers' (2013, p. 694). Despite the Article 21 requirement, such obstacles may help to explain why the EU has negotiated certain bilateral agreements that lack human rights clauses. For example, more narrow sectoral agreements, such as textiles, can lack human rights clauses; similarly, fisheries agreements can lack comprehensive non-trade objectives, and bilateral agreements on trade in steel products also can lack binding human rights clauses.[10]

Beyond the new generation of FTAs, the EU's autonomous initiatives focus on incoming trade as a way to encourage development or reform in countries seeking to import goods into the EU. These initiatives can be thought of in two ways: (i) the Generalised System of Preferences (GSP) and GSP+, and (ii) legislation that puts restrictions on the import of certain goods, thereby limiting access to the lucrative EU market. For both types of autonomous initiative, MPE can use trade policy to externalize non-trade objectives based in the EU's market-related policies and regulatory measures. Under the first types of autonomous initiative, the enhanced trade preferences that are offered through the GSP+ are clearly linked to a variety of non-trade objectives. More specifically,

---

[10] For bilateral textile agreements that lack human rights clauses, see Agreement between the European Community and the Kingdom of Cambodia, on trade in textile products, [2002] OJ L 349 (24/12/2002); Agreement on trade in textile products between the European Community and the Lao People's Democratic Republic, [2003] OJ L 16 (22/01/2003); Agreement between the European Community and the Kingdom of Nepal on trade in textile products, [2000] OJ L 326 (22/12/2000); Memorandum of Understanding between the European Community and the Democratic Socialist Republic of Sri Lanka on arrangements in the area of market access for textile and clothing products, initialled in Brussels on 5 December 2000, [2001] OJ L 80 (20/03/2001); Agreement between the European Community and the Republic of Serbia on trade in textile products, [2005] OJ L 90 (08/04/2005). It should be noted that this agreement with Serbia specifies in its preamble that it joins only within the framework of the Stabilisation and Association process; however, a Stabilisation and Association Agreement between the EU and Serbia, which contains a human rights clause, came into force in September 2013 ([2013] OJ L 278 (18/10/2013). For fisheries agreements, see http://ec.europa.eu/fisheries/cfp/international/agreements/index_en.htm (accessed 2 February 2015). Steel product agreements may refer to partnership and cooperation agreements, which include human rights clauses. However, such references are typically mentioned in the preamble and have no binding power. Two examples are the Agreement between the European Community and the Russian Federation on trade in certain steel products, [2007] OJ L 300 (17/11/2007); and the Agreement between the European Community and the Government of Ukraine on trade in certain steel products, [2007] OJ L 178 (06/07/2007). The author is indebted to Katia Rochereuil (Paris Sorbonne University, Abu Dhabi) for these insights; see also Rochereuil (2013).

these preferences are granted to countries which ratify and implement international conventions relating to human and labour rights, environment and good governance (EU Regulation 978/2012).[11]

The second type of autonomous initiative covers a variety of new regulations and directives that may also act as tools for externalizing non-trade objectives, especially in relation to the activity of private actors. For example, Ryngaert and Koekkoek (Chapter 10, this volume) show the potential to externalize EU environmental objectives and the protection of natural resources through the Timber Regulation (see also Geraets and Natens, Chapter 11, this volume), the Renewable Energy Directive and the Seals Regulation. The Regulation on the prevention of illegal, unreported and unregulated fishing also provides a tool through which the EU can use an autonomous initiative to externalize related non-trade objectives like the protection of natural resources (Miller, Bush and Mol, 2014). While both types of autonomous initiative can be used by the EU, such attempts at externalization can be as contentious as efforts to negotiate non-trade objectives into FTAs.

Because of the sensitive nature of non-trade objectives, the EU's use of its trade power to externalize them may not always be successful, but this would not undermine an understanding of the EU as MPE. Rather, any (in)decision to include such objectives in new generation trade policies should be broadly determined by the three characteristics of MPE. In short, the EU's large market size may create a strong but not completely irresistible incentive for other countries to engage with the EU's new generation trade policies and to consider abiding by the associated non-trade objectives. A variety of actors and institutional decision-making rules and capabilities (such as regulatory capacity) may influence the EU's externalization but do not always determine that externalization is the best course of action. The institutional features of the EU also help to clarify the avenues through which interest groups and civil society actors may influence externalization in such sensitive matters. Therefore, the existence of the three characteristics helps us to understand when and perhaps why, despite their highly contentious nature, the EU is likely to pursue non-trade objectives in new generation trade policies.

---

[11] Regulation (EU) No. 978/2012 of 25 October 2012 applying a scheme of generalised tariff preferences. See also Larik (Chapter 3, this volume); Beke and Hachez (Chapter 8, this volume); Yap (Chapter 9, this volume); Orbie and Tortell (2009).

4. THE EU AS A POWER AND THE ANALYTICAL PITFALL OF INCONSISTENCY

There are important practical reasons for EU policy makers to worry about inconsistency: the EU's power in the international system can be seriously undermined when its external relations are inconsistent.[12] As Nuttall (2005) argues, such inconsistency can lead to serious failures of foreign policy and an inability to attain fundamental objectives.[13] In effect, it can increase confusion, undermine credibility and decrease legitimacy in internal and external perceptions of the EU as a global actor. In addition to these practical pitfalls, scholars working in the 'EU as a Power' debates can run into an analytical problem, or pitfall, related to the issue of consistency. This pitfall becomes particularly apparent in the context of new generation trade policies. As the EU increasingly becomes a power *through* trade, the scope for such inconsistencies between and among trade and non-trade objectives increases significantly and demands further attention and engagement from legal scholars and political scientists alike.

4.1 Engaging Inconsistency

From a legal perspective, the problem of inconsistency does not necessarily create an analytical pitfall for understanding the EU as a power. Essentially, this is so because legal scholars give less priority to generating general explanations about the EU's identity as a power and why it acts like a power. However, this does not mean that legal scholars are not interested in issues surrounding consistency; rather, they often engage the issues by exploring the codification and interpretation of law as ways to avoid or overcome the practical problem of inconsistency. Much of this work starts by identifying the legal potential for inconsistency and the legal instruments that may increase the likelihood of consistency.

For example, as Larik (Chapter 3, this volume) shows, there is potential for inconsistency between the EU's *general* treaty objectives

[12] While a number of scholars have identified different types of practical or policy inconsistency in EU external action, the discussion herein focuses upon what might be called 'internal' and 'horizontal' inconsistency within, between or among different policies (Gebhard, 2011).

[13] For a discussion of how coherence relates to EU external effectiveness in global trade governance, see da Conceição-Heldt (2014).

and other more *specific* policy-based objectives, such as trade policy.[14] Article 207(1) of the Treaty on the Functioning of the European Union (TFEU) states that the CCP 'shall be conducted in the context of the principles and objectives of the Union's external action', which makes clear that trade policy is part of external action and should, therefore, be conducted in line with the general objectives of external action (especially Article 21 TEU). According to Krajewski, however, there is no hierarchy between the specific CCP and the more general objectives of Article 21. Rather, all objectives are of equal relevance (2012, p. 294).[15] Larik agrees, adding that:

> the weak binding force of such objectives makes discussion about any strict hierarchies between them a rather idle exercise. In view of the various evocations of the principle of 'coherence' and 'consistency' between different policies, all of the EU's external objectives have to be pursued as an ensemble, geared towards its overall vision of 'good global governance' (Larik, Chapter 3, section 4.1, this volume).

Of course, the pursuit of this ensemble is not always consistent in practice, which creates the analytical pitfall that will be discussed shortly. The primary complications for such pursuit can be seen as a mix of legal and political obstacles. As Dimopoulos argues, the legal and mandatory nature in the Lisbon Treaty of such objectives may be

> softened … by their broad formulation [which] leaves a great degree of discretion to the policy-making institutions to assess the means of action and the content of the chosen action. Articles 3(5) and 21 TEU impose arguably a justiciable obligation upon the EU institutions to pursue these objectives in the field of the CCP as well, but it leaves them a wide margin of appreciation to determine when, whether, and how these objectives can be pursued (2010, p. 165).

Larik lends credence to the general point, arguing that 'the width of these goals and their weak binding force limit their obligatory and prohibitive force, not least for adjudicatory purposes' (Larik, Chapter 3, this volume). Institutional discretion – which may become politicized and may reflect different political priorities at different times – to interpret the legal provisions, therefore, increases the potential for inconsistencies in

---

14 See also Larik (Chapter 3, this volume) for two excellent legal arguments on why broadly worded norms (e.g., general objectives) are loose and have limited legal force.

15 For a similar argument, see Croquet (Chapter 6, this volume).

the practical pursuit of general and specific objectives. In short, the pursuit of consistency depends upon political will (Van Elsuwege, 2010).

For political science contributions to the 'EU as a Power' debates, the problem of inconsistency becomes an analytical pitfall when categorizing the EU's 'guiding principles' or general objectives in broad terms, such as civilian ends, values, principles and/or norms. These broad and rather imprecise labels are frequently employed as ways to engage with the EU's objectives and to describe and understand their causal effect in (and beyond) prominent contributions to the 'EU as a Power' debates.[16]

For example, from a Civilian Power perspective, the EU can be seen to pursue civilian ends as its objectives (Orbie, 2008). While there is disagreement on exactly what are these civilian ends, Smith has noted that they tend to include such lofty goals as international cooperation, solidarity, domestication of international relations (or strengthening the rule of law), responsibility for the global environment, and diffusion of equality, justice and tolerance (2005, p. 66). While these goals seem to fit within the scope of the Article 21 general objectives and may be normatively appealing, Smith argues that 'the problem here is that these "civilian ends" are still quite fuzzily defined (for example, what does "solidarity" mean in terms of policy practice?)' (2005, p. 67).

From another prominent contribution to these debates we learn that the EU's objectives can be similarly thought of as 'norms' instead of civilian ends. In his formulation of Normative Power Europe (NPE), Manners argues for consideration of five core norms – peace, liberty, democracy, rule of law, and respect for human rights and fundamental freedoms – and four minor norms – social solidarity, anti-discrimination, sustainable development and good governance (Manners, 2002). Again, these objectives remind us of the Article 21 general objectives and may be viewed as normatively 'good'. Although these objectives are not identical to civilian ends, their rather broad and imprecise formulation remains the same. As a result, the analytical pitfall of inconsistency raises cautionary flags for

[16] This is not the place to engage in the social science debate about the causality of norms/ideas v. interests or institutions, nor in the extent to which the EU's norms are perhaps applied instrumentally. However, it is worth pointing out that while this chapter takes a decidedly MPE perspective, the conceptualization is not diametrically opposed to an understanding of such objectives as civilian ends or norms. Rather, if civilian ends and norms can be reliably linked to certain internal market-related policies and regulations, MPE can be used to test empirically the factors (market size, institutional features and interest contestation) that contribute to externalization and the extent to which those norms are externalized.

work that understands objectives as these broad civilian ends and/or norms (Damro, 2015; Sjursen, 2006).

Going back to the legal distinction between general and specific objectives, we see the likelihood and importance of this potential for inconsistency. For trade policy, the EU is bound by the Lisbon Treaty to pursue specific CCP objectives (Article 207 TFEU) as well as the more general objectives of external action (Article 21 TEU). Yet this legal requirement creates a situation in which inconsistencies are likely to arise. As Dimopoulos notes, the drafters of the Lisbon Treaty included the Article 21 general objectives for external action in order to enhance consistency (2010, p. 161). Yet, in a sense, inconsistency is built into the system because these general objectives are extremely broad and there is no hierarchy established between them and the more specific policy objectives. Similarly, there is no hierarchy established among the various general objectives. In addition, discretion is given to political actors to interpret and pursue these imprecise general objectives while also pursuing the more precise and specific policy objectives. Therefore, while the Lisbon Treaty provides legal and institutional foundations for consistency (Article 21(3)), it does not eliminate the potential for inconsistencies to occur. Only the political actors can do that, which is why, in practice, the EU remains open to criticism over its perceived and/or real inconsistency.

In effect, the EU's general objectives – which may be seen as rather imprecise civilian ends or norms – are best seen not as strict rules, but as guidance for EU external policy-making (see Larik, Chapter 3, this volume). Therefore, instead of assessing the extent to which the EU externalizes these broad, imprecise and potentially inconsistent general objectives, an MPE-based approach tends to focus the analysis on the externalization of specific objectives, all of which are (operationally) reflected in and may be considered part of the EU's market-related policies and regulatory measures. How precisely linked these specific objectives are to market-related policies and regulatory measures is a question deserving of empirical attention from legal scholars and political scientists; this will be explored in the next section.

4.2 Overcoming Inconsistency

In the context of this chapter, it is important to reiterate that while general non-trade objectives are based in EU primary legislation (especially Article 21 TEU), exactly what they mean and include is not so clear. This, again, is where and why we encounter the analytical pitfall of inconsistency. However, if these general non-trade objectives can be made more precise and linked to less fuzzy market-related policies and regulatory measures, then we can trace, and determine empirically with more confidence, the extent to which the EU actually externalizes them.

This is not to say that MPE eliminates the problem of inconsistency *in practice*. It is only to say that it removes the complications that arise from trying to *analyse* the externalization of general non-trade objectives. MPE does so by focusing on specific objectives that are reflected in market-related policies and regulatory measures. In other words, MPE encourages the use of more precise targets of analysis, which may include but are not analytically dependent upon or constrained by the broad and imprecise principles (civilian ends and norms) equated with general non-trade objectives. An MPE-based analysis that finds evidence of the EU externalizing a specific market-related policy or regulatory measure could, therefore, provide empirical support for the notion that a certain civilian end or norm has been exported. However, the MPE approach and conceptualization is concerned only with the externalization of the specific market-related policy or regulatory measure (regardless of whether it is trade or non-trade) and not the export of the fuzzy civilian end or norm.

An investigation of new generation trade policies helps to illustrate how the empirical approach of MPE can overcome the analytical pitfall of inconsistency. In particular, empirically linking together the two different types of new generation trade policy – a free trade agreement (FTA) and an autonomous initiative – allows MPE to scrutinize the externalization of trade and non-trade objectives (all of which are part of the EU's market-related policies and regulatory measures), while also avoiding the analytical pitfall of inconsistency.

To see this more clearly, it is useful to look at the EU's first of a new generation of FTAs – that concluded with South Korea (see also Croquet, Chapter 6). This agreement has 15 chapters, several annexes and appendices, three protocols and four understandings.[17] Chapters 1–12 and 14–15 are what might be considered traditional and more specific trade and trade-related objectives.[18] Chapter 13 is the crucial chapter for our purposes because it covers 'Trade and Sustainable Development'. At first glance, it may seem that this FTA does not fit with the MPE approach because it includes the imprecise non-trade objective of sustainable

[17] http://trade.ec.europa.eu/doclib/docs/2011/october/tradoc_148303.pdf, p. 3 (accessed 22 January 2015).

[18] Chapters 1–11 cover traditional, specific trade objectives. Understood as specific 'trade-related' objectives, Chapter 12 covers 'Transparency', Chapter 14 covers 'Dispute Settlement', and Chapter 15 covers 'Institutional, General and Final Provisions'.

development. A closer look shows the ways in which this chapter can be understood and analysed, without fear of inconsistency, through an MPE approach.

First, as Croquet mentions (Chapter 6), Chapter 13 does not provide detailed provisions on how to implement effectively the various and general non-trade objectives included in the agreement under the label of 'sustainable development'. Rather, it sets broad and collective goals, the operationalization and implementation of which require further *inter-governmental negotiation*. The extent to which these non-trade objectives will be externalized and will link with EU market-related policies and regulatory measures will be determined to a large extent via such inter-governmental negotiation, which, in turn, will be conditioned by the size of the EU's market and institutional features.[19] Simply agreeing them as collective goals in the actual FTA is not a guarantee of seamless adoption and implementation by South Korea.

The agreement also creates new avenues for other actors – in particular, civil society – to contribute to the inter-governmental negotiations. Article 13.12 creates an institutional mechanism to establish so-called Domestic Advisory Groups 'on sustainable development (environment and labour) with the task of advising on the implementation of this Chapter' (Article 13.12.4). These groups will comprise 'independent representative organisations of civil society in a balanced representation of environment, labour and business organisations as well as other relevant stakeholders' (Article 13.12.5). These Domestic Advisory Groups, following the logic of MPE's third characteristic of interest contestation, will input regularly into the ongoing process of inter-governmental negotiation and possible externalization.[20]

Second, an even closer look at the EU-Korea FTA reveals how the two different types of new generation trade policy can be empirically linked to one another with an MPE approach to assess externalization, while avoiding the analytical pitfall of inconsistency. To show how this can be done, I take the example of an autonomous initiative discussed in this volume: EU Regulation 995/2010 on illegal timber (see Ryngaert and Koekkoek, Chapter 10, this volume; and Geraets and Natens, Chapter 11).

[19] To clarify the inter-governmental interaction and negotiation, Article 13.14 establishes the institutional procedures for government consultation.

[20] Their input will also be considered through their contributions to an annual Civil Society Forum that will meet 'to conduct a dialogue encompassing sustainable development aspects of trade relations between the Parties' (Article 13.13.1).

Again, Chapter 13 of the FTA suggests the presence of an imprecise and fuzzy non-trade objective: that of sustainable development. But in Article 13.11, the Parties recognize 'the importance of cooperating on the more specific trade-related aspects of social and environmental policies in order to achieve the objectives of this Agreement'.[21] This clause also commits the Parties to 13 cooperative activities listed in Annex 13.[22]

---

[21] On the scope of sustainable development in Chapter 13, Article 13.2 says: 'Except as otherwise provided in this Chapter, this Chapter applies to measures adopted or maintained by the Parties affecting trade-related aspects of labour and environmental issues …' The Chapter includes multilateral labour standards and agreements (Art. 13.4) and environmental agreements (Art. 13.5), and mentions that the Parties 'highlight the value of greater policy coherence between trade policies, on the one hand, and employment and labour policies on the other' (Art. 13.6).

[22] Annex 13 of the EU-Korea FTA states:

Cooperation on Trade and Sustainable Development

1. In order to promote the achievement of the objectives of Chapter Thirteen and to assist in the fulfilment of their obligations pursuant to it, the Parties have established the following indicative list of areas of cooperation:

(a) exchange of views on the positive and negative impacts of this Agreement on sustainable development and ways to enhance, prevent or mitigate them, taking into account sustainability impact assessments carried out by the Parties;

(b) cooperation in international fora responsible for social or environmental aspects of trade and sustainable development, including in particular the WTO, the ILO, the United Nations Environment Programme and multilateral environmental agreements;

(c) cooperation with a view to promoting the ratification of fundamental and other ILO Conventions and multilateral environmental agreements with an impact on trade;

(d) exchange of information and cooperation on corporate social responsibility and accountability, including on the effective implementation and follow-up of internationally agreed guidelines, fair and ethical trade, private and public certification and labelling schemes including eco-labelling and green public procurement;

(e) exchange of views on the trade impact of environmental regulations, norms and standards;

(f) cooperation on trade-related aspects of the current and future international climate change regime, including issues relating to global carbon markets, ways to address adverse effects of trade on climate, as well as means to promote low-carbon technologies and energy efficiency;

(g) cooperation on trade-related aspects of biodiversity including in relation to biofuels;

Annex 13 clarifies more precisely what is included in the non-trade objective of sustainable development, what needs to be done to achieve the objectives of Chapter 13, and the various areas in which cooperation will occur. For example, Annex 13(i) mentions trade-related measures to tackle deforestation and illegal logging as an area of cooperation. This would contribute to the broad non-trade objective of sustainable development, but deforestation and illegal logging are usefully more specific than the general concept of sustainable development, and they can also be linked to a more specific EU regulatory measure, which increases their analytical precision. The inter-governmental negotiations (with input from the Domestic Advisory Groups) over future implementation in this area of cooperation may be persuasive or coercive, but the EU's position will reflect what it has already agreed in a relevant regulatory measure – the autonomous initiative Regulation 995/2010 on illegal timber.

To assess the EU's externalization via the FTA and autonomous initiative, careful empirical tracing would help to determine the extent to which South Korea: (i) adjusts its own regulations and/or behaviour related to illegal timber in ways that conform with or generally satisfy the EU regulation; and (ii) has made such adjustments as a result of the EU-Korea inter-governmental negotiation and other cooperation taking place under this Chapter and Annex of the FTA. One might find that the South Korean government and/or timber exporting firms have adjusted, and now make legality verification arrangements and document the legality of their products. While sufficient evidence of this may be difficult to find, if such connections can be established empirically, then

---

(h) cooperation on trade-related measures to promote sustainable fishing practices;
(i) cooperation on trade-related measures to tackle the deforestation including by addressing problems regarding illegal logging;
(j) cooperation on trade-related aspects of multilateral environmental agreements, including customs cooperation;
(k) cooperation on trade-related aspects of the ILO Decent Work Agenda, including on the interlinkages between trade and full and productive employment, labour market adjustment, core labour standards, labour statistics, human resources development and life-long learning, social protection and social inclusion, social dialogue and gender equality;
(l) exchange of views on the relationship between multilateral environmental agreements and international trade rules; or
(m) other forms of environmental cooperation as the Parties may deem appropriate.

2. The Parties agree that it would be desirable if cooperative activities developed by them could have as broad an application and benefit as possible.

the EU may be said to have externalized its market-related regulatory measures on illegal timber via the tool of new generation trade policies. Empirical work can also reveal the ways in which and extent to which the three characteristics of MPE – market size, institutional features and interest contestation – influence and condition the externalization of EU timber regulatory measures as established in a new generation trade policy (the autonomous initiative) to South Korea via another new generation trade policy (the FTA).

While this illustration may also be seen as an instance of the EU seemingly externalizing the general objective of sustainable development, for analytical purposes it does not matter whether this particular outcome is consistent or inconsistent with, for example, the various other non-trade objectives listed in Annex 13(k). The EU certainly has market-related policies and regulatory measures linked to the general objective of sustainable development and other Annex 13(k) non-trade objectives such as employment, labour standards, social protection and gender equality, but whether the EU pursues them consistently or inconsistently has no direct analytical implications for MPE. All that matters is whether the EU does or does not externalize the specific (timber) market-related policy or regulatory measure. If it does, then the EU has exercised its power of externalization and South Korea – regardless of the extent to which it is consistent with other EU objectives – now adheres to a level of (timber) regulation similar to that in effect in the European single market, or behaves in a way that generally satisfies or conforms with the EU's (timber) market-related policies and regulatory measures.

Unlike MPE, the possibility of inconsistency in this case raises clear pitfalls for other contributions to the 'EU as a Power' debates that rely upon civilian ends and norms. For example, if the EU exports its timber standards via EU Regulation 995/2010, it may then be seen as promoting sustainable development. However, the provisions of that regulation may not be consistent with the trade objective of liberalization or the EU's general objective of poverty eradication. Similarly, the provisions could be inconsistent – depending on how one chooses to interpret their fuzzy broadness – with a whole host of other general non-trade objectives associated with civilian power (such as international cooperation, solidarity, equality, tolerance) and normative power (such as peace, liberty, human rights, social solidarity, anti-discrimination). In such a case, the single instance of the EU promoting sustainable development may, in effect, seem to support civilian and normative conceptualizations. In the bigger picture, however, it would be difficult to judge such a finding as convincing evidence of either conceptualization when the EU is simultaneously undermining so many other civilian ends and norms that are integral to these other conceptualizations of the EU as a power. As a result, the above illustration of moving away from general non-trade objectives towards the more specific market-related policies and regulatory measures demonstrates two benefits of taking an MPE approach: (i) as the analysis becomes more specific, the evaluation of externalization becomes more methodologically and diagnostically precise and reliable; and (ii) consistency with other general or specific objectives, whether trade or non-trade, matters less for analysing and understanding what the EU says, does, and is as a power.

5. CONCLUSIONS

Trade policy is one of the EU's most prominent tools for externalization of its internal economic and social market-related policies and regulatory measures. With the emergence of new generation trade policies (both trade agreements and autonomous initiatives), this tool may be used increasingly to externalize the trade and non-trade objectives that are reflected in these EU policies and measures. Such developments help to inform and reinforce a conceptualization of the EU as Market Power Europe. At the same time, the inclusion of non-trade objectives in the EU's trade policies can be a politically sensitive matter that complicates trade negotiations. However, despite the contentious nature and practical problems that may arise from such actions, the existence of the three characteristics of MPE – market size, institutional features and interest contestation – helps us to understand when and perhaps why the EU is likely to pursue non-trade objectives in new generation trade policies.

The MPE conceptualization also helps to identify and overcome more analytical problems that arise when studying the externalization of trade and non-trade objectives. In particular, the exploration of new generation trade policies brings to the fore the issue of consistency in EU external relations. Considerable legal and political science scholarship – while taking different approaches and focusing on different aspects – has grappled with this issue. Drawing together their disciplinary insights and viewing the issue within the context of the 'EU as a Power' debates helps to demonstrate the problems that can be associated with this issue.

The analytical pitfall of inconsistency, however, can be overcome with an MPE-based approach that emphasizes a narrower and more empirical tracing of the EU's externalization of trade and non-trade objectives. In order to understand the EU as a power, MPE does not depend upon consistency across the EU's general or specific objectives, whether they be trade or non-trade. Rather, it provides an analytical framework through which the EU's externalization of its internal policies and regulatory measures can be clearly understood and evaluated. It also helps to narrow and make more empirically manageable the analysis of the extent to which the EU's market size, institutional features and interest contestation contribute to the likelihood of externalization. Such an approach is useful because it helps to show more clearly what the EU does as a power, it helps us to judge what the EU says as a power, and helps to clarify what kind of power the EU really is.

REFERENCES

Bach, D. and L. Newman (2007), 'The European Regulatory State and Global Public Policy: Micro-Institutions, Macro-Influence', *Journal of European Public Policy*, **14** (6), 827–46.

Bradford, A. (2012), 'The Brussels Effect', *Northwestern University Law Review*, **107** (1), 1–68.

da Conceição-Heldt, E. (2014), 'When Speaking with a Single Voice Isn't Enough: Bargaining Power (A)symmetry and EU External Effectiveness in Global Trade Governance', *Journal of European Public Policy*, **21** (7), 980–85.

Damro, C. (2012), 'Market Power Europe', *Journal of European Public Policy*, **19** (5), 682–99.

Damro, C. (2015), 'Market Power Europe: Exploring a Dynamic Conceptual Framework', *Journal of European Public Policy*, **22** (9), 1336–54.

Dimopoulos, A. (2010), 'The Effects of the Lisbon Treaty on the Principles and Objectives of the Common Commercial Policy', *European Foreign Affairs Review*, **15** (2), 153–70.

Drezner, D. (2007), *All Politics is Global: Explaining International Regulatory Regimes*, Princeton, NJ: Princeton University Press.

Duchêne, F. (1972), 'Europe's Role in World Peace', in R. Mayne (ed.), *Europe Tomorrow*, London: Fontana, pp. 32–47.

Dür, A. and D. de Bièvre (2007), 'The Question of Interest Group Influence', *Journal of Public Policy*, **27** (1), 1–12.

Eeckhout, P. (2011), *EU External Relations Law*, 2nd edn, Oxford: Oxford University Press.

Engel, C. and A. Héritier (2003), *Linking Politics and Law*, Baden-Baden: Nomos.

European Commission (2010), 'Trade, Growth and World Affairs: Trade Policy as a Core Component of the EU's 2020 Strategy', Directorate General Trade, COM(2010) 612, Brussels (Belgium), http://trade.ec.europa.eu/doclib/docs/2010/november/tradoc_146955.pdf.

Finnemore, M. and K. Sikkink (1998), 'International Norm Dynamics and Political Change', *International Organization*, **52** (4), 887–917.

Gebhard, C. (2011), 'Coherence', in C. Hill and M. Smith (eds), *International Relations and the European Union*, 2nd edn, Oxford: Oxford University Press, pp. 101–27.

Hafner-Burton, E., D. Victor and Y. Lupu (2012), 'Political Science Research on International Law: The State of the Field', *The American Journal of International Law*, **106** (1), 47–96.

Horn, H., P. Mavroidis and A. Sapir (2010), 'Beyond the WTO? An Anatomy of EU and US Preferential Trade Agreements', *World Economy*, **33** (11), 1565–88.

Kerremans, B. and J. Orbie (2009), 'The Social Dimension of European Union Trade Policies', *European Foreign Affairs Review*, **14** (5), 629–41.

Khorana, S. and M. Garcia (2013), 'European Union–India Trade Negotiations: One Step Forward, One Back?', *Journal of Common Market Studies*, **51** (4), 684–700.

Krajewski, M. (2012), 'The Reform of the Common Commercial Policy', in A. Biondi, P. Eeckhout and S. Ripley (eds), *EU Law after Lisbon*, Oxford: Oxford University Press, pp. 292–311.

Kuijper, P.J., J. Wouters, F. Hoffmeister, G. de Baere and T. Ramopoulos (2013), *The Law of EU External Relations: Cases, Materials and Commentary on the EU as an International Legal Actor*, Oxford: Oxford University Press.

Laïdi, Z. (2010), 'Is Europe a Risk-Averse Power: A Hypothesis', Garnet Policy Brief 11, February.

Manners, I. (2002), 'Normative Power Europe: A Contradiction in Terms?', *Journal of Common Market Studies*, **40** (2), 235–58.

McGuire, S. and J. Lindeque (2010), 'The Diminishing Returns to Trade Policy in the European Union', *Journal of Common Market Studies*, **48** (5), 1329–49.

Meunier, S. and K. Nicolaïdis (2006), 'The European Union as a Conflicted Trade Power', *Journal of European Public Policy*, **13** (6), 906–25.

Miller, A.M.M., S.R. Bush and A.P.J. Mol (2014), 'Power Europe: EU and the Illegal, Unreported and Unregulated Tuna Fisheries Regulation in the West and Central Pacific Ocean', *Marine Policy*, **45** (March), 138–45.

Nuttall, S. (2005), 'Coherence and Consistency', in C. Hill and M. Smith (eds), *International Relations and the European Union*, Oxford: Oxford University Press, pp. 91–112.

Orbie, J. (2008), 'Civilian Power in the World? Instruments and Objectives in European Union External Policies', in J. Orbie (ed.), *Europe's Global Role: External Policies of the European Union*, Farnham: Ashgate, pp. 1–34.

Orbie, J. and L. Tortell (2009), 'The New GSP+ Beneficiaries: Ticking the Box or Truly Consistent with ILO Findings?', *European Foreign Affairs Review*, **14** (5), 663–81.

Rochereuil, K. (2013), 'The Bilateral Agreements of the European Union', PhD thesis, Paris: University Paris-Descartes.

Sapir, A. (ed.) (2007), *Fragmented Power*, Brussels: Bruegel.

Scott, J. (2014), 'Extraterritoriality and Territorial Extension in EU Law', *American Journal of Comparative Law*, **62** (1), 87–126.

Sjursen, H. (2006), 'The EU as a "Normative" Power: How Can This Be?', *Journal of European Public Policy*, **13** (2), 235–51.

Smith, K.E. (2005), 'Beyond the Civilian Power Debate', London: LSE Research Online, available at: http://eprints.lse.ac.uk/812.

Toje, A. (2011), 'The European Union as a Small Power', *Journal of Common Market Studies*, **49** (1), 43–60.

Van Elsuwege, P. (2010), 'EU External Action after the Collapse of the Pillar Structure: In Search of a New Balance between Delimitation and Consistency', *Common Market Law Review*, **47** (4), 987–1019.

Van Vooren, B. and R. Wessel (2014), *EU External Relations Law: Texts, Cases and Materials*, Cambridge: Cambridge University Press.

Van Vooren, B., S. Blockmans and J. Wouters (eds) (2013), *The EU's Role in Global Governance: The Legal Dimension*, Oxford: Oxford University Press.

Wessel, R. (2011), 'The Legal Framework for the Participation of the European Union in International Institutions', *European Integration*, **33** (6), 621–35.

Wouters, J., H. Bruyninckx, S. Keukeleire, T. Corthaut, S. Basu and S. Schunz (2008), 'The European Union and Global Multilateral Governance – An Interdisciplinary Research Project: Research Notes (Part 1)', *Journal of Contemporary European Research*, **4** (1), 52–5.

Young, A.R. and J. Peterson (2014), *Parochial Global Europe: 21st Century Trade Politics*, Oxford: Oxford University Press.

3. Good global governance through trade: constitutional moorings

Joris Larik

1. INTRODUCTION

Ensuring good global governance through trade is not just a powerful idea,[1] or a global 'strategy';[2] it is also firmly anchored in the highest laws of the European Union (EU or Union) – its 'constitutional charter'.[3] According to the Treaty on European Union (TEU),[4] the EU is to 'promote an international system based on stronger multilateral cooperation and good global governance' (Article 21(2)(h)) and 'uphold and promote its values and interests' (Article 3(5)) in its external relations. One crucial means to these lofty ends is the EU's Common Commercial Policy (CCP). This policy is concerned *a priori* with the pursuit of goals at the heart of international trade, such as 'free and fair trade' (Article 3(5) TEU) and 'the harmonious development of world trade, the progressive abolition of restrictions on international trade and on foreign direct investment' (Article 206 Treaty on the Functioning of

[1] See Chapters 1 and 2, this volume.

[2] European Commission, 'Global Europe: Competing in the World: A Contribution to the EU's Growth and Jobs Strategy', COM(2006) 567 final, Brussels, 4 October 2006, 2: 'Through our trade policies, we also seek to contribute to a range of the Union's external goals, in particular development and neighbourhood objectives.'

[3] Case 294/83 *Parti écologiste 'Les Verts'* [1986] ECR 1339, para 23.

[4] Throughout this chapter 'TEU' and 'TFEU' refer to the consolidated versions of the Treaty on European Union and the Treaty on the Functioning of the European Union [2012] OJ C 326/1. The consolidated text of the TEU post-Nice, but pre-Lisbon (Treaty on European Union (consolidated text) [2002] OJ C 325/5) is referred to 'TEU (Nice version)'. Unless otherwise indicated, 'TEC' refers to the Treaty establishing the European Community in the consolidated version following the Nice revision, i.e. the Treaty establishing the European Community (consolidated text) [2002] OJ C 325/33.

the European Union (TFEU); see also Article 21(2)(e) TEU). However, as a textual innovation through the Lisbon Treaty reform, the CCP is henceforth to 'be conducted in the context of the principles and objectives of the Union's external action' (Article 207(1) TFEU). Among these, we find now a plethora of foreign policy objectives – a 'wish list for a better world',[5] if you will – which can be placed under the general conceptual umbrella of 'good global governance'.[6] 'Global governance' can be defined as 'the management of global problems and the pursuit of global objectives through concerted efforts of states and other international actors'.[7] 'Good', as an overtly normative statement, is to be interpreted, then, as a vision of global governance informed by the pursuit of global objectives according to the values and principles set out in the EU Treaties. The latter reflects a constitutionally entrenched 'sanguine world view',[8] representing the external dimension of what can be called 'the conscience of the Constitution'.[9]

Promoting 'good global governance' through trade policy brings together two of the hallmarks of the EU as an international actor. On the one hand, it concerns the area of the EU's most obvious asset, its economic clout. Despite tectonic shifts at work in the distribution of global economic power, the EU, for the foreseeable future, stands its ground as one of the world's foremost trade powers, being 'the world's largest economy', 'the world's largest trading block [sic]' and 'the world's second-largest investor'.[10] On the other hand, the EU is not only

---

[5] Wiebke Drescher, 'Ziele und Zuständigkeiten', in Andreas Marchetti and Claire Demesmay (eds), *Der Vertrag von Lissabon: Analyse und Bewertung* (Nomos 2010) 59–71, 68 (in the original: 'Wunschzettel für eine bessere Welt').

[6] Eleftheria Neframi, 'Vertical Division of Competences and the Objectives of the European Union's External' in Marise Cremona and Anne Thies (eds), *The European Court of Justice and External Relations: Constitutional Challenges* (Hart 2014), 73–94, 73.

[7] Martin Ortega, 'Building the Future: The EU's Contribution to Global Governance', EUISS Chaillot Paper No. 100, April 2007, 46 (italics omitted).

[8] Joris Larik, 'Entrenching Global Governance: The EU's Constitutional Objectives caught between a Sanguine World View and a Daunting Reality', in Bart Van Vooren, Steven Blockmans and Jan Wouters (eds), *The EU's Role in Global Governance: The Legal Dimension* (Oxford University Press 2013) 7–22.

[9] To borrow an expression used in Indian constitutional law: Granville Austin, *The Indian Constitution: Cornerstone of a Nation* (Clarendon 1966) 50.

[10] European Commission, Directorate-General for Trade, *European Union Trade and Investment 2014* (Publications Office of the European Union 2014); see also Marise Cremona, 'The External Dimension of the Internal Market', in

a 'formidable power *in* trade' but also 'a power *through* trade'.[11] In other words, trade power 'can be used to attain other, non-economic objectives'.[12] This relates to the idea of the EU not only as a 'civilian power',[13] but indeed as a 'normative power'[14] which shapes the world around it by harnessing its economic strength according to a larger vision and based on values which go beyond the strictly economic realm.

In order to capture the constitutional moorings of the mandate to pursue 'good global governance' through trade and to elucidate its implications, the present chapter shines the spotlights on this issue through three different lenses: historical, comparative and legal-institutional. First, it retraces the evolution of this idea and its progressive codification in the course of time. Second, it puts the EU's constitutional 'conscience' as a trade power into a comparative context. Against this double backdrop, the chapter then turns to the legal significance of such norms, addressing what they can – and cannot – achieve as norms of EU constitutional law.

2. THE EU'S EVOLVING CONSTITUTIONAL CONSCIENCE

The EU did not grow a 'constitutional conscience' with regard to the exercise of its trade power overnight. Just as national constitutions are 'more deeply rooted in a nation's history and culture' and more 'political

---

Catherine Barnard and Joanne Scott (eds), *The Law of the Single European Market* (Hart 2002) 351–94.

[11] Sophie Meunier and Kalypso Nicolaïdis, 'The European Union as a Trade Power', in Christopher Hill and Michael Smith (eds), *International Relations and the European Union* (2nd edn, Oxford University Press 2011) 275–98, 294 (emphasis in the original).

[12] Marise Cremona, 'The Union's External Action: Constitutional Perspectives', in Giuliano Amato, Hervé Bribosia and Bruno de Witte (eds), *Genesis and Destiny of the European Constitution* (Bruylant 2007) 1173–217, 1213; also Angelos Dimopoulos, 'The Effects of the Lisbon Treaty on the Principles and Objectives of the Common Commercial Policy' (2010) 15(2) *European Foreign Affairs Review* 153–70, 153.

[13] François Duchêne, 'Europe's Role in World Peace', in Richard Mayne (ed.), *Europe Tomorrow: Sixteen Europeans Look Ahead* (Fontana 1972) 32–47.

[14] Ian Manners, 'Normative Power Europe: A Contradiction in Terms?' (2002) 40(2) *Journal of Common Market Studies* 235, 245 (referring to trade policy as norm diffusion through 'transference'). See also Bartels (Chapter 4, this volume) for an account of the EU's treaty-making practice in this respect.

in nature' than other sources of law,[15] EU constitutional law, as it stands today, has absorbed and entrenched policy priorities and, more generally, a world outlook shaped by the founders of the European project and six decades of integration history. This becomes evident when retracing the linkages of trade policy with a wider foreign policy agenda in the Treaties over the course of time. The various norms on which this chapter focuses are the result of an evolution which commenced with the inception of European integration itself, and which received a new impetus with the Convention on the Future of Europe of 2002–03. The results of the latter eventually spilled over into the Lisbon Treaty, and thus into the primary law in force today.

2.1 From the Communities to the Union

The Treaty establishing the European Coal and Steel Community (ECSC) of 1951 already reveals a 'bigger picture' into which economic integration could be situated. It states in its preamble 'that *world peace* can be safeguarded only by creative efforts commensurate with the dangers that threaten it'.[16] The operative part includes objectives pertaining to international trade as a corollary of the common market. The ECSC is mandated to 'see that the common market [for coal and steel] is regularly supplied, taking account of the needs of third countries'[17] and to 'further the development of international trade and see that equitable limits are observed in prices charged on external markets'.[18] However, 'grand vision' and trade objectives are not yet explicitly linked to each other.

The Treaty establishing the European Economic Community (EEC Treaty), in its original 1957 version, expresses the desire of the contracting parties to contribute 'to the progressive abolition of restrictions on international trade'[19] by virtue of a Common Commercial Policy. While the 'task' of the EEC is centred on the Common Market,[20] the 'activities' of the Community include 'the establishment of a common customs tariff

---

[15] Monica Claes and Maartje de Visser, 'Reflections on Comparative Method in European Constitutional Law', in Maurice Adams and Jacco Bomhoff (eds), *Practice and Theory in Comparative Law* (Cambridge University Press 2012) 143–69, 157.

[16] First recital of the preamble, Treaty establishing the European Coal and Steel Community (ECSC Treaty), Paris, signed 18 April 1951 (emphasis added).

[17] Art 3(a) ECSC Treaty.

[18] Art 3(f) ECSC Treaty.

[19] Sixth recital of the preamble, Treaty establishing the European Economic Community (EEC Treaty), Rome, signed 25 March 1957.

[20] Art 2 EEC Treaty.

and of a common commercial policy toward third countries'[21] as well as 'the association of overseas countries and territories in order to increase trade and to promote jointly economic and social development'.[22] The CCP is furthermore given specific objectives: 'the harmonious development of world trade' and the 'progressive abolition of restriction on international trade and the lowering of customs barriers'.[23] From these various provisions, it becomes apparent that both the internal (intra-Community) and external economic spheres are conceived of as intertwined and, furthermore, that trade policy is not to be conducted in clinical isolation from other policies, such as development cooperation.

In the following decades, as European integration progressed, the scope of activities of the Communities and later of the Union widened, including those pertaining to what is now called 'good global governance'. Through the Single European Act (SEA) of 1986, European Political Cooperation in the area of 'foreign policy' acquired a treaty basis.[24] The SEA also extended the policies of the EEC to other fields with an external dimension, including environmental protection.[25]

The Treaty on European Union of 1993 introduced the rather complex pillar structure.[26] The newly established Union included the Communities as one of the three pillars next to the inter-governmental Common Foreign and Security Policy (CFSP) and Justice and Home Affairs (JHA), which was later narrowed down to Police and Judicial Cooperation in Criminal Matters. The emergence of the CFSP is a watershed in EU external relations law as it legally codifies and institutionalizes European cooperation in this area.

The original Maastricht TEU included the objective for the Union 'to assert its identity on the international scene'.[27] What this international identity would consist of more specifically, however, was left open. Nevertheless, Maastricht and the subsequent reforms at Amsterdam and

---

[21] Art 3(b) EEC Treaty.

[22] Art 3(k) EEC Treaty; see also Arts 131 and 132 EEC Treaty.

[23] Art 110(1) EEC Treaty.

[24] Art 1(3) Single European Act (SEA) [1987] OJ L 169/1. Note also the fifth recital of the preamble to the SEA, which refers to the principles of democracy, the rule of law and human rights, as well as to contributing to international peace and security in external relations.

[25] Art 25 SEA, introducing then Art 130r TEC (subsequently Art 174 TEC).

[26] See Marise Cremona, 'The Common Foreign and Security Policy of the European Union and the External Relations Powers of the European Community', in David O'Keeffe and Patrick Twomey (eds), *Legal Issues of the Maastricht Treaty* (Wiley Chancery 1994) 247–58.

[27] Art 2 TEU (Nice version).

Nice added a number of provisions, both in the TEU and the amended TEC, from which the basic features of such an identity could be gleaned. These include the codification of 'values' on which the Union was founded,[28] the general objectives of the Union according to Article 2 TEU (Nice version) and the specific objectives of each policy area to the extent that these had an external dimension. The latter consisted of the CFSP, which had its own set of goals spelled out in the TEU,[29] and the external policies of the Community, which now also comprised, next to the traditional CCP, development cooperation,[30] and economic, financial and technical assistance to third countries.[31]

The list of activities of the European Community (with the adjective 'Economic' having been omitted from its name) was extended to include development cooperation.[32] This policy area was endowed with its own set of specific objectives, which were to foster:

- the sustainable economic and social development of the developing countries, and more particularly the most disadvantaged among them;
- the smooth and gradual integration of the developing countries into the world economy; and
- the campaign against poverty in the developing countries.[33]

Moreover, Community development policy was to 'contribute to the general objective of developing and consolidating democracy and the rule of law, and to that of respecting human rights and fundamental freedoms'.[34] Crucially for good global governance through trade, the amended TEC also obliged the Community to 'take account of the objectives referred to in Article 177 [on development cooperation] in the policies that it implements which are likely to affect developing countries',[35] which include trade policy as well as internal policies such as the Common Agricultural Policy and the Internal Market.

28 Art 6 TEU (Nice version).
29 Art 11 TEU (Nice version).
30 Arts 177–81 TEC.
31 This policy was codified only by the Nice Treaty (Art 181a TEC).
32 Art 3(r) TEC.
33 Art 177(1) TEC.
34 Art 177(2) TEC.
35 Art 178 TEC.

2.2 The Convention on the Future of Europe

Shortly after the Nice Treaty and with the enlargement of the Union to the east and south looming, another major recasting of the basic structure of the EU was launched. This marks the beginning of a decade-long treaty reform process culminating in the Lisbon Treaty.[36] However, the main conceptual work, also and especially with regard to the codification of the EU's foreign policy agenda and the orientation of trade policy, was done at the Convention on the Future of Europe of 2002–03.

Kicking off the reform process, the Laeken Declaration of 2001 publicly asked whether 'Europe [does] not, now that is finally unified, have a leading role to play in a new world order, that of a power able both to play a stabilising role worldwide and to point the way ahead for many countries and peoples'.[37] In providing the answer itself, the Declaration stated that 'Europe needs to shoulder its responsibilities in the governance of globalisation'.[38] In doing so, the EU was to become 'a power wanting to change the course of world affairs in such a way as to benefit not just the rich countries but also the poorest' and a 'power seeking to set globalisation within a moral framework'.[39]

The Laeken Declaration represents another leap in terms of global ambition for the EU, now linking comprehensive international engagement with overt normativity and an 'active paradigm',[40] which eventually found its way into the primary law by virtue of the Lisbon Treaty.

The Convention on the Future of Europe started its work in February 2002 and concluded in July 2003 by presenting to the European Council

---

[36] See, for instance, Paul Berman, 'From Laeken to Lisbon: The Origins and Negotiation of the Lisbon Treaty', in Andrea Biondi, Piet Eeckhout and Stephanie Ripley (eds), *EU Law after Lisbon* (Oxford University Press 2012) 3–39; Paul Craig, *The Lisbon Treaty: Law Politics and Treaty Reform* (Oxford University Press 2010) 1–31; Jean-Claude Piris, *The Lisbon Treaty: A Legal and Political Analysis* (Cambridge University Press 2010) 7–63.

[37] Presidency Conclusions, European Council meeting, Laeken, 14–15 December 2001, Annex I, Laeken Declaration on the Future of the European Union, 20.

[38] Ibid.

[39] Ibid.

[40] Fabian Amtenbrink and Dimitry Kochenov, 'The Active Paradigm of the Study of the EU's Place in the World: An Introduction', in Fabian Amtenbrink and Dimitry Kochenov (eds), *The European Union's Shaping of the International Legal Order* (Cambridge University Press 2013) 1–18.

a Draft Treaty establishing a Constitution for Europe.[41] During the general debate at the Convention on external action in July 2002, '[m]any stressed that the values which were at the heart of the Union were themselves an argument for a greater role globally, and that these values should underpin and inform the Union's external policies'.[42] Subsequently, the idea to formulate – and *constitutionally* codify – a comprehensive normative foreign policy agenda that would guide the Union's external action, including trade policy, was born at the Convention.

The Præsidium of the Convention drafted what would later become Article 3 TEU on the general objectives of the Union, which included a paragraph on relations with the rest of the world. After a first draft had been circulated in February 2003,[43] several amendments called for the inclusion of 'free and fair trade' as a goal,[44] which was taken up by the Convention in its final draft.[45] The Working Group on External Action also perceived 'the need to define more clearly *in a future Treaty* the underlying objectives of EU external action'.[46] According to the Convention Secretariat, 'Working Group VII [on External Action] opted for the approach of defining the principles and objectives of all external action in a single Article, therefore deleting the lists of specific objectives of each policy area concerned in existing Articles'.[47]

---

[41] For a detailed account see Peter Norman, *The Accidental Constitution: The Story of the European Convention* (2nd edn, EuroComment 2005).

[42] Secretariat of the European Convention, Summary Report of the Plenary Session – Brussels, 11 and 12 July 2002, Brussels, 16 July 2002, CONV 200/02, 3.

[43] Secretariat of the European Convention, Draft of Articles 1 to 16 of the Constitutional Treaty, Brussels, 6 February 2003, CONV 528/03, Annex I: Draft Text of the Articles of the Treaty Establishing a Constitution for Europe, 3.

[44] See Secretariat of the European Convention, Suggestion for Amendment by the Earl of Stockton MEP, http://european-convention.europa.eu/docs/Treaty/pdf/3/Art%203a%20Stockton.pdf (accessed 22 June 2015) (proposing to add 'the promotion of free and fair trade in the wider world' to the article on Union objectives); and Secretariat of the European Convention, Suggestion for Amendment by Elmar Brok and others, http://european-convention.europa.eu/docs/Treaty/pdf/3/Art%203%20EPP.pdf (accessed 22 June 2015) (proposing to add 'free trade', but sans 'fair').

[45] Art 3(4) Draft Treaty establishing a Constitution for Europe, Brussels, 18 July 2003, CONV 850/03.

[46] Secretariat of the European Convention, Working Group VII on External Action, Summary of the Meeting held on 8 October 2002, Brussels, 11 October 2002, CONV 342/02, 6 (emphasis added).

[47] Secretariat of the European Convention, Draft Articles on External Action in the Constitutional Treaty, 23 April 2003, CONV 685/03, 25.

This would have constituted a major shift in the way in which Union policies had been organized in the Treaties. However, this streamlining exercise succeeded only in part. On the one hand, the draft text submitted by the working group to the Convention on EU external action had indeed omitted the individual objectives for the CFSP, development cooperation and economic, financial and technical aid. On the other hand, the CCP had retained objectives of its own and the newly inserted section on humanitarian aid even included new policy-specific goals. With regard to trade policy in particular, the text proposed by Working Group VII and endorsed by the Præsidium reproduced most of the language of former Articles 131 and 133(1) TEC, but added references to foreign direct investment as well as – importantly for the explicit linkage of trade and 'good global governance' – to the general principles and objectives of external action (that is, to what is now Article 21 TEU).[48]

It was also during the work of the working group on external action that the reference 'to promote an international system based on stronger multilateral cooperation and good global governance'[49] was added to what would later become Article 21 TEU. There were, furthermore, calls to include explicit references to contribute to the preservation and promotion of 'global public goods'.[50] These were not successful, and the concept of a 'global public good' thus remains absent from the EU Treaties. Nonetheless, even if not labelled this way, many of the ideas enshrined in Articles 3(5) and 21 TEU undoubtedly fit the usual definition of 'global public goods'.[51]

---

[48] Ibid 52–4.

[49] Secretariat of the European Convention, Working Group VII on External Action, Final Report of Working Group VII on External Action, Brussels, 16 December 2002, CONV 459/02, 3.

[50] For example, Secretariat of the European Convention, Suggestion for Amendment by Mr Voggenhuber and others, http://european-convention.europa.eu/docs/Treaty/pdf/861/Art%20III%20188%20Voggenhuber%20EN.pdf (accessed 22 June 2015); Secretariat of the European Convention, Suggestion for Amendment by Mr Brok and others, http://european-convention.europa.eu/docs/Treaty/pdf/861/Art1Brok%20EN.pdf (accessed 22 June 2015); and Secretariat of the European Convention, Suggestion for Amendment by Mr Ingvar Svensonn, http://european-convention.europa.eu/docs/Treaty/pdf/861/Art1Svensson%20EN.pdf (accessed 22 June 2015), who names as examples in the explanatory note 'biodiversity, preservation of the atmosphere, access to fresh water, and effective prevention of HIV/AIDS'.

[51] Cf. Daniel Bodansky, 'What's in a Concept? Global Public Goods, International Law, and Legitimacy' (2012) 23(3) *European Journal of International Law* 651, 652–4.

The text agreed by the Convention and transmitted to the President of the European Council,[52] compared with the situation of the Nice Treaty and what preceded it, certainly shows progress in terms of codifying the foreign policy agenda of the EU.[53] However, by using former Article 11 TEU (Nice version) on CFSP objectives as the template for the general article on EU external action (now Article 21 TEU), and without replacing it in the section on the CFSP, the latter policy is deprived of its own set of specific objectives, as is the section on economic, financial and technical aid. In contrast, the external policies not only on trade, but also on development and the newly codified section on humanitarian aid, all received a set of policy-specific objectives. A distinction thus remains between the overall objectives of EU external action – its contribution to 'good global governance' – and the specific goals of its trade policy.

2.3 The Lisbon Treaty

The Treaty establishing a Constitution for Europe was signed by the Member States in Rome in October 2004. However, after the failed referendums in France and the Netherlands in 2005, a subsequent 'period of reflection' led to the drafting of a 'reform treaty' that would not replace the existing treaties but would amend them.[54] The 'constitutional concept', pushed by the Convention, was officially dropped by the Council.[55] However, this should not be confused with depriving the legal order of the Union of its constitutional features.[56] The resulting Lisbon

---

[52] Draft Treaty establishing a Constitution for Europe, Brussels, 18 July 2003, CONV 850/03.

[53] See Marise Cremona, 'The Draft Constitutional Treaty: External Relations and External Action' (2003) 40 *Common Market Law Review* 1347, 1348–9.

[54] Treaty of Lisbon amending the Treaty on European Union and the Treaty establishing the European Community, signed at Lisbon, 13 December 2007 (Lisbon Treaty) [2007] OJ C 306/1. See further Gráinne de Búrca, 'The EU on the Road from the Constitutional Treaty to the Lisbon Treaty' (2008) Jean Monnet Working Paper 03/08.

[55] Presidency Conclusions of the Brussels European Council, 21 and 22 June 2007, 20 July 2007, 11177/1/07 REV 1, Annex I: IGC Mandate, 15.

[56] See, in particular, Stefan Griller, 'Is this a Constitution? Remarks on a Contested Concept', in Stefan Griller and Jacques Ziller (eds), *The Lisbon Treaty: EU Constitutionalism without a Constitutional Treaty?* (Springer 2008) 21–56 (arguing in favour of the constitutional credentials of the EU after Lisbon).

Treaty, after going through some ratification troubles of its own, entered into force on 1 December 2009.[57]

The Lisbon Treaty incorporated virtually all of the reforms proposed by the Constitutional Treaty, leaving aside mostly symbolic provisions such as those on the flag, the anthem, the motto and the term 'Union Foreign Minister'.[58] The reformed codified foreign policy agenda of the EU had not been abandoned or rolled back in the Lisbon Treaty. In terms of the basic structure – which, under Lisbon, comprises two treaties (the TEU and TFEU) – a relocation of the articles on the general objectives of EU external action took place. In the Constitutional Treaty, one article introduced a comprehensive part on EU 'External Action' containing all the external policies of the Union. Under the Lisbon Treaty, by contrast, this article (Article 21 TEU) was situated in the TEU at the start of its Title V on 'General Provisions on the Union's External Action and Specific Provisions on the Common Foreign and Security Policy'. This title contains merely the external policy area of the CFSP/CSDP, while the others, including trade policy, are now to be found in Part V of the TFEU on 'External Action by the Union'. Nonetheless, Article 205 TFEU, which introduces Part V, refers back to Article 21 TEU.

In the primary law now in force, the idea of ensuring good governance through trade has become a constitutional mandate for the EU. On the one hand, the Union is to continue to pursue goals intimately connected with trade (that is, to promote 'free and fair trade')[59] and 'contribute, in the common interest, to the harmonious development of world trade, the progressive abolition of restrictions on international trade and on foreign direct investment, and the lowering of customs and other barriers'.[60] On the other hand – and this is the novelty post-Lisbon[61] – its trade policy 'shall be conducted in the context of the principles and objectives of the Union's external action' at large (that is, all the objectives listed in Articles 3(5) and 21 TEU). These include the promotion of the Union's values and interests, and contributing also to peace, democracy, the rule of law, security, sustainable development, eradication of poverty, human rights and respect for international law – a kaleidoscope of aspects of what the EU considers to be 'good global governance'.

57 See Piris (n 36) 49–63.
58 Ibid 34.
59 Art 3(5) TEU.
60 Art 206 TFEU, similarly also Art 21(2)(e) TEU.
61 Dimopoulos (n 12) 161–3.

3. TRADE AND GOOD GOVERNANCE: A COMPARATIVE PERSPECTIVE

The EU now boasts in its primary law a very ambitious foreign policy agenda. With regard to trade policy, the Treaties also provide policy-specific goals but these are explicitly put under the umbrella of this wider agenda. Given the prominence of this agenda in the current primary law, it is worthwhile to survey other constitutions, in order to determine how 'special' the EU is in this respect. Are other trade powers endowed with such a 'constitutional conscience'? To this end, the following paragraphs will elaborate upon two points. First, in general, many contemporary constitutions address 'global governance' at least in abstract terms, for instance, through calls for a more 'just' world order. Second, it seems to be rather rare for a constitution to address specifically trade policy and its goals, much less to link it to a wider constitutionally entrenched foreign policy agenda. Hence, the latter remains a speciality of the EU.

3.1 'Good Global Governance': Constitutional Acknowledgements

There is a wider trend in constitutional design, which earlier I termed 'dynamic internationalization'[62] – the progressive codification of foreign policy goals, in many cases with idealistic underpinnings. For instance, the German Basic Law acknowledges, in a clearly universalist tone, 'inviolable and inalienable human rights as the foundation of every community, of peace and justice in the world'.[63] The Portuguese Constitution, furthermore, stresses that Portugal's international relations will be governed, *inter alia*, by the overarching objectives of 'the emancipation and progress of humanity'[64] and 'the creation of an international order capable of safeguarding peace and justice in relations between peoples'.[65] The Bulgarian Constitution, in a similar vein, makes 'the promotion of a just international order'[66] an objective of the state.

---

[62] Joris Larik, 'Shaping the International Order as an EU Objective', in Fabian Amtenbrink and Dimitry Kochenov (eds), *The European Union's Shaping of the International Legal Order* (Cambridge University Press 2013) 62–87, 64.

[63] Art 1(2), German Constitution.

[64] Art 7(1), Portuguese Constitution; on Portuguese constitutional foreign policy objectives in this provision see Paulo Jorge Canelas de Castro, 'Portugal's World Outlook in the Constitution of 1976' (1995) 71 *Boletim da Faculdade de Direito da Universidade de Coimbra* 489.

[65] Art 7(2), Portuguese Constitution.

[66] Art 24(2), Bulgarian Constitution.

Beyond Europe, similar constitutional language can be found. The preamble to the Constitution of the People's Republic of China, today undeniably one of the world's leading economic and trade powers,[67] contains a number of guidelines for its foreign policy. It stresses that

> China adheres to an independent foreign policy as well as to the five principles of mutual respect for sovereignty and territorial integrity, mutual non-aggression, non-interference in each other's internal affairs, equality and mutual benefit, and peaceful coexistence in developing diplomatic relations and economic and cultural exchanges with other countries; China consistently opposes imperialism, hegemonism and colonialism, works to strengthen unity with the people of other countries, supports the oppressed nations and the developing countries in their just struggle to win and preserve national independence and develop their national economies, and strives to safeguard world peace and promote the cause of human progress.[68]

This language can be seen as less proactive in exporting and promoting normative standards around the world.[69] Nonetheless, the preamble does exhibit the parameters of what China would consider not to be 'good global governance' – for instance, interference and imperialism.

The Japanese Constitution, too, exhibits references concerning the 'global common good'. It expresses the determination 'to preserve [Japan's] security and existence, trusting in the justice and faith of the peace-loving peoples of the world' as well as the belief 'that no nation is responsible to itself alone, but that laws of political morality are universal'.[70] The Constitution of Brazil, moreover, enumerates 'fundamental principles' governing the country's foreign policy; next to 'national independence' these include 'cooperation among people for the progress of humanity'.[71] While certainly verbose, from a comparative point of view the EU Treaties are by no means unique in expressing a desire for their constitutional organs to contribute to 'good global governance' or similar notions such as 'a just international order'.

---

[67] Hanns Günther Hilpert, *China's Trade Policy: Dominance without the Will to Lead*, SWP Research Paper No. 1, January 2014, 7–10.

[68] Preamble, Constitution of the People's Republic of China.

[69] The 'five principles' originate from a treaty between China and India in 1954 and have since been the cornerstones of Chinese foreign policy: see Anu Bradford and Eric Posner, 'Universal Exceptionalism in International Law' (2011) 52 *Harvard International Law Journal* 3, 26.

[70] Preamble, Japanese Constitution.

[71] Art 4, Brazilian Constitution.

3.2 Good Governance through Trade: an EU Speciality

Regardless of more general references that fit the theme of 'good global governance', only a few constitutions address trade policy in terms of its substantive goals.[72] The presence of specific trade goals can be explained through the particular historical trajectory of the EU, as outlined in the previous section, which started out with an emphasis on economic integration and the corresponding formulation of a common trade policy. However, linking trade policy with a wider normative agenda is a distinctive feature of the EU – one which cannot be explained by its original nature as a functional international organization.

A notable exception to this general rule is the Swiss Constitution, which is similar to the EU Treaties, albeit to a limited degree. Next to general references in the realm of 'good global governance' – such as its commitment 'to an enduring conservation of the natural resources and to a peaceful and just international order',[73] to 'the alleviation of need and poverty in the world, and to the respect for human rights [...]'[74] – the Swiss Constitution contains an article devoted specifically to 'foreign trade', which reads:

1. The Confederation safeguards the interests of the Swiss economy abroad.
2. In special cases, it may take measures to protect the domestic economy. It may, if necessary, depart from the principle of economic freedom.[75]

On the one hand, this is similar to the EU Treaties in that both a constitutional call for 'good global governance' and an external trade policy geared towards certain ends are present in Swiss constitutional law. On the other hand, what is missing is a clear link between the two elements – that is, an instruction to use trade policy for the benefit of the wider normative agenda. In the Swiss case, the constitutional mandate, as

---

[72] Foreign trade is sometimes explicitly made a federal competence in federal systems (e.g. Art 8(3), United States constitution). This is then simply a matter of allocating power between different levels of government, rather than of guiding trade policy towards certain normative ends.

[73] Art 2(4), Swiss Constitution.

[74] Art 54(2), Swiss Constitution.

[75] Art 101, Swiss Constitution. On the proliferation of 'programmatic' norms in general in Swiss constitutional law see Ulrich Häferlin, Walter Haller and Helen Keller, *Schweizerisches Bundesstaatsrecht* (8th edn, Schulthess 2012) 57.

far as foreign policy is concerned, is 'good global governance' *and* an economically oriented, assertive trade policy, rather than 'good global governance' *through* trade policy in the fashion of the EU Treaties.

4. LEGAL SIGNIFICANCE: MANDATE, INSTITUTIONS AND IMPLEMENTATION

As the previous sections have demonstrated, the idea of promoting good global governance through trade as a constitutional mandate for the EU has grown over decades and is now firmly established in the primary law. Such a constitutional mandate, moreover, is rather rare from a comparative perspective. While many constitutions today give a nod to 'good global governance' at large, making the explicit connection between trade policy and global governance is a speciality of the EU. In this section, the legal significance of such constitutional provisions will be analysed. What force do they have as legal norms, what do they entail for the institutions called upon in the Treaties to pursue this normative agenda through the CCP, and how are they being implemented? To shed light on these aspects of the constitutional moorings of 'good global governance through trade' in the EU, the following paragraphs will address first the general legal significance of such externally oriented constitutional objectives, followed by their role in the institutional architecture of the EU, and lastly an illustration of how they are implemented in EU legislation with a trade dimension.

4.1 'Good Global Governance' as a Constitutional Mandate

As part of the EU Treaties – understood as the 'constitutional charter'[76] of the EU – the contents of Articles 3(5) and 21 TEU, as well as Articles 205–207(1) TFEU, are legally binding norms of primary law. Hence, based on the principle of primacy, they reign supreme over any secondary EU legislation as well as over the law of the Member States.[77] Even if by

---

76 *Parti écologiste 'Les Verts'* (n 3); also Joined Cases C-402/05 P and C-415/05 P *Kadi and Al Barakaat* [2008] ECR I-6351, para 281. Further, Paul Craig, 'Constitutions, Constitutionalism, and the European Union' (2001) 7 *European Law Journal* 125 (arguing that the EU legal order exhibits 'thick' constitutional features); and Griller (n 56).

77 The principle of primacy does not feature in the EU Treaties, but see Declaration No. 17 concerning Primacy, attached to the Lisbon Treaty. Further, Piris (n 36) 79–82.

certain commentators their content is ridiculed as 'redolent of motherhood and apple pie',[78] their content and status are the result of the drafting and ratification process of the primary law as it stands today. In other words, to contribute to good global governance through trade is the stated and entrenched intention of the Union's constitutional legislator (*pouvoir constituant*).[79]

That being said, this constitutional mandate is not endowed with either a particularly strong obligatory or prohibitive force, at least in any immediate sense. In an early judgment, the Court of Justice of the European Union (CJEU) ruled that 'it will always be necessary to reconcile to a certain degree the various objectives of Article 3 [ECSC Treaty] since it is clearly impossible to attain them all fully and simultaneously as those objectives constitute general principles which must be observed and harmonized as far as possible'.[80]

Even though the Court noted that the objectives enshrined in the Treaties have 'obligatory force',[81] their 'normativity'[82] is thus rather limited in at least two ways. First, these provisions by no means establish individual rights: no individual may address the CJEU and claim that the Treaties were violated by adopting (or failing to adopt) a particular trade measure that does not sufficiently advance the cause of, for instance, promoting the rule of law or democracy. As the CJEU has ruled regarding the objectives of the former Community, these 'cannot have the effect either of imposing legal obligations on the Member States or of conferring rights on individuals'.[83]

Second, even aside from individual standing, failure to fully live up to constitutional objectives, especially those of such a broadly defined and ambitious nature, is in itself unlikely to amount to an infringement of the Treaties to be invoked by the EU institutions and Member States before the CJEU. Only in the most extreme cases of manifest disregard would this become arguable. Regarding the objectives of the CCP in particular,

---

[78] Alan Dashwood and others, *Wyatt & Dashwood's European Union Law* (6th edn, Hart 2011) 903, referring to Art 21 TEU.

[79] Larik (n 8) 19–21.

[80] Case 8/57 *Groupement des hauts fourneaux et aciéries belges v High Authority* [1958] ECR English special edition 245, 253.

[81] Case 6/72 *Continental Can* [1973] ECR 215, para 25.

[82] On the *normativité limitée* of constitutional objectives in general, Pierre de Montalivet, *Les objectifs de valeur constitutionnelle* (Dalloz 2006) 563.

[83] Case C-339/89 *Alsthom Atlantique* [1991] ECR 1991 I-107, para 9. Note also Case C-181/06 *Deutsche Lufthansa* [2007] ECR I-5903, para 31 (stating that the codified objectives and activities of the former Community 'do not lay down obligations on Member States or public or private bodies').

the Court made clear in the *Dürbeck* case that the '"aim to contribute, in the common interest, to the harmonious development of world trade, the progressive abolition of restrictions on international trade [...]", cannot be interpreted as prohibiting the Community from enacting, upon pain of committing an infringement of the Treaty, any measure liable to affect trade'.[84]

This limited legal force also finds confirmation in the long-standing case law of the Court of Justice regarding the position of World Trade Organization law within the Union legal order, according to which both individuals and Member States are generally barred from invoking violations of these rules before EU courts. The CJEU denied this with a reference to the necessary 'scope for manoeuvre' for the EU institutions in conducting trade negotiations,[85] and allowed derogations from this rule only in the case of narrowly defined exceptions.[86]

Hence, for all practical purposes, these norms are not to be seen as strict rules which can be either respected or violated. Rather, it is more appropriate to conceive of them as 'optimization requirements' in the sense of Robert Alexy: 'norms that require that something be realised to the greatest extent possible given the legal and factual possibilities'.[87]

The slight changes in wording brought about in the Lisbon Treaty regarding trade objectives do not alter this general finding. Pre-Lisbon, the CCP was to '*aim to contribute*, in the common interest, to the harmonious development of world trade, the progressive abolition of restrictions on international trade and the lowering of customs barriers'.[88] Under current Article 206 TFEU, the 'Union *shall contribute*' to these goals.[89] For one commentator this signifies a shift from 'the aspirational

---

[84] Case 112/80 *Dürbeck* [1981] ECR 1095, para 44.

[85] Case C-149/96 *Portugal v Council* [1999] ECR I-8395, para 46; and Case C-280/93 *Germany v Council* [1994] ECR I-0973; see further Antonello Tancredi, 'EC Practice in the WTO: How Wide is the "Scope for Manoeuvre"?' (2004) 15(5) *European Journal of International Law* 933.

[86] Joris Larik, 'Much More Than Trade: The Common Commercial Policy in a Global Context', in Malcolm Evans and Panos Koutrakos (eds), *Beyond the Established Legal Orders: Policy Interconnections between the EU and the Rest of the World* (Hart 2011) 13–46, 37–40; and Panos Koutrakos, *EU International Relations Law* (2nd edn, Hart 2015) 301–7.

[87] Robert Alexy, *A Theory of Constitutional Rights* (Oxford University Press 2002) 47. Note also Karl-Peter Sommermann, *Staatsziele und Staatszielbestimmungen* (Mohr Siebeck 1997) 361 (calling objectives of the state optimization requirements '*par excellence*').

[88] Art 131(1) TEC (emphasis added).

[89] Art 206 TFEU (emphasis added).

character of the liberalization objective' to one of a 'mandatory nature'.[90] However, this in itself would not make trade liberalization a more 'binding' goal than the other external relations objectives of the Union, including its global governance agenda. The language employed with regard to these objectives is essentially the same.[91]

Moreover, the various cross-references between the general external action objectives and the policy-specific objectives, as well as the principle of coherence, militate against any strict hierarchies among objectives. According to Article 21(3) TEU, '[t]he Union shall respect the principles and pursue the objectives' that inspire its external action in all its external policies as well as in the 'external aspects of its other policies'. The CCP, as the Treaties clearly state, 'shall be conducted in the context of the principles and objectives of the Union's external action' (Article 207(1) TFEU). In addition, the weak binding force of such objectives makes discussion about any strict hierarchies between them a rather idle exercise. In view of the various evocations of the principle of 'coherence' and 'consistency' between different policies,[92] all of the EU's external objectives have to be pursued as an ensemble, geared towards its overall vision of 'good global governance'.

4.2 Institutional Architecture: Legal Basis and Exclusivity

While there are various examples of EU measures which harness trade policy for 'good global governance', a central question is which institution is responsible, and of which prerogatives it can avail itself. Here, the constitutional moorings of 'good global governance' play an important role, with their most palpable legal effect being a lens for constitutional interpretation.[93]

This has two related institutional implications regarding the use of trade policy for the benefit of 'good global governance'. First, in the

---

[90] Dimopoulos (n 12) 160.

[91] Cf Art 3(5) TEU: '[The EU] *shall contribute* to peace, security, the sustainable development of the Earth [...]' (emphasis added); Art 208(1), 2nd subpara TFEU: 'Union development cooperation policy *shall have as its primary objective* the reduction and, in the long term, the eradication of poverty' (emphasis added).

[92] Art 16(6), 3rd subpara TEU; Art 21(3), 2nd subpara TEU; Art 7 TFEU.

[93] Larik (n 62) 82–5; generally for EU objectives, Koen Lenaerts and Piet Van Nuffel, *European Union Law* (2nd edn, Sweet & Maxwell 2011) 111; and Christian Calliess, 'Kollektive Ziele und Prinzipien im Verfassungsrecht der EU – Bestandsaufnahme, Wirkungen und Perspektiven' (2003) 92 *Archiv für Rechts- und Sozialphilosophie-Beihefte* 85, 92.

horizontal relationship, concerning the determination of the correct legal basis and the applicable institutional procedures; second, in the vertical dimension, regarding the scope of permissible action of the Member States on the international stage, and also in terms of the pursuit of their own respective visions of 'good global governance'.[94]

These aspects are of particular importance regarding the CCP, the scope and nature of which as a matter of competence have seen drastic changes in the course of time.[95] Moreover, as the EU legal order has matured over the decades – coupled with the introduction of more policies and competences, as well as value statements and fundamental rights catalogues – Union competences and objectives have parted ways and exist now as two distinct norm categories in EU constitutional law.[96] However, through interpretation, the latter is still capable of shaping the outer limits of the former.

The CCP, being rather narrowly defined in the beginning and intimately connected with the fledgling Common Market, kindled the idea of an *a priori* exclusive external EU competence in the case law of the CJEU, which, in the words of the Court, was 'incompatible with the freedom to which the Member States could lay claim by invoking a concurrent power'.[97] Nevertheless, for want of other suitable legal bases for external action in the Treaties, the Court accepted trade policy to be used also for development cooperation and humanitarian aid,[98] until those became endowed with their proper legal bases through subsequent treaty reform. This codification of additional policies with their own legal bases and procedures 'had a significant impact on the use of the CCP for

---

[94] The two dimensions are intricately linked in the institutional set-up of the EU, as 'the "vertical" interests of the Member States will be felt horizontally through the Council': Bart Van Vooren, *EU External Relations Law and the European Neighbourhood Policy: A Paradigm for Coherence* (Routledge 2012) 71.

[95] Piet Eeckhout, *EU External Relations Law* (2nd edn, Oxford University Press 2011) 11–69.

[96] Joris Larik, 'From Speciality to a Constitutional Sense of Purpose: On the Changing Role of the Objectives of the European Union' (2014) 63 *International & Comparative Law Quarterly* 935.

[97] *Opinion 1/75* [1975] ECR 1355.

[98] Case C-54/86 *Commission v Council (GSP)* [1987] ECR I-1493; also Dimopoulos (n 12) 157–8; and Panos Koutrakos, 'Legal Basis and Delimitation of Competence in EU External Relations', in Marise Cremona and Bruno de Witte (eds), *EU Foreign Relations Law: Constitutional Fundamentals* (Hart 2008) 171–98.

pursuing non-trade objectives'.[99] So did the changing scope of the CCP itself, as it represented a moving target in the course of time in terms of using it as a legal basis. Because of the widening of the trade agenda in view of the founding of the WTO in 1995, the CCP came to be considered a partly shared competence.[100]

The pre-Lisbon era hence saw a number of high-profile cases in which different EU institutions fought over whether or not a certain measure or action fell within the scope of the CCP. Typically, the Commission, as the institution with a more powerful position in CCP matters than in policy areas of a shared character (such as environmental protection), would argue for a legal basis in the CCP, while the Council would argue for the proper legal basis being outside the CCP.[101]

After Lisbon, the CCP is again entirely exclusive,[102] and covers a wider field than ever before. It now includes trade in services (including of the cultural and audio-visual kind), commercial aspects of intellectual property, as well as foreign direct investment.[103] Being now both entirely exclusive in nature and broader than ever before in scope, using the post-Lisbon CCP as a vehicle for promoting 'good global governance' has important legal consequences. According to the TFEU, in such areas 'only the Union may legislate and adopt legally binding acts, the Member States being able to do so themselves only if so empowered by the Union or for the implementation of Union acts' (Article 2(1) TFEU). Moreover, the Commission would be the obvious 'Union negotiator' for international trade agreements (Article 218(3) TFEU), while the Member States would be barred from acting on their own behalf internationally in this area.

---

[99] Dimopoulos (n 12) 157.

[100] *Opinion 1/94* [1995] ECR I-05267; and later *Opinion 1/08* [2009] ECR I-11129; see also Christoph Herrmann, 'Common Commercial Policy after Nice: Sisyphus would have done a Better Job' (2002) 39 *Common Market Law Review* 7.

[101] See Case C-281/01 *Commission v Council* (*Energy Star Agreement*) [2002] I-12049; Case C-94/03 *Commission v Council* (*Rotterdam Convention*) [2006] ECR I-1; Case C-178/03 *Commission v Parliament and Council* [2006] ECR I-107; and Case C-411/06 *Commission v Parliament and Council* (*Waste shipments*) [2009] ECR I-7585.

[102] Art 3(1)(e) TFEU. Note, however, the caveat concerning the area of transport in Art 207(5) TFEU.

[103] Art 207 TFEU. While the exact delimitation of trade in services, commercial aspects of intellectual property and foreign direct investment may be difficult, they would seem to match the scope of the relevant WTO agreements: Eeckhout (n 95) 59.

In this respect, there exists an inherent tension in the idea of a 'global' or 'comprehensive approach',[104] which advances a broader normative agenda, and the 'constitutional'[105] requirement to identify the proper legal basis, which is an expression of the principle of conferred powers in the EU.[106] The TEU makes it abundantly clear, however desirable the objectives pursued may be, that the EU shall pursue them 'by appropriate means commensurate with the competences which are conferred upon it in the Treaties'.[107] In this context, regardless of any overarching normative 'vision', policy-specific goals become a key tool that can be utilized in determining within which area of EU policy a particular measure, in view of its aim and content, fits best.[108]

While today the CFSP is deprived of specific objectives in the Treaties, which have to be ascertained instead through judicial interpretation,[109] the CCP can rely on the objectives of Article 206 TFEU to this end. However, this does not mean that as soon as a non-trade related 'global governance' goal enters the picture, the CCP cannot be used as the sole legal basis of a measure.

In the emerging post-Lisbon case law, promoting a wide notion of 'global governance' – for instance, by exporting certain rules and standards beyond the borders of the EU through the CCP – has received judicial endorsement. In 2013, the CJEU interpreted the reference in Article 207(1) TFEU to the general EU external action objectives in the following manner:

> [I]t follows from Article 207(1) TFEU – and, in particular, from the second sentence of that provision, in the words of which the common commercial policy belongs within the context of 'the Union's external action' – that the common commercial policy relates to trade with non-member countries, not to trade in the internal market.[110]

---

[104] From the vantage point of international crisis management, see European Commission and the High Representative of the European Union for Foreign Affairs and Security Policy, 'The EU's Comprehensive Approach to External Conflict and Crises', JOIN(2013), 30 final Brussels, 11 December 2013.

[105] *Opinion 2/00* (*Cartagena Protocol*) [2001] ECR I-09713, para 5.

[106] Art 5(1) and (2) TEU.

[107] Art 3(6) TEU.

[108] Dimopoulos (n 12) 166.

[109] See Case C-130/10 *Parliament v Council*, EU:C:2012:472, para 62; and Case C-220/14 P, *Ahmed Abdelaziz Ezz*, EU:C:2015:147, para 46.

[110] Case C-137/12 *Commission v Council* (*European Convention on the legal protection of services based on, or consisting of, conditional access*),

Hence, it was used here as a way to distinguish the CCP from the Internal Market. In this case this was a response to the Council, which had used Article 114 TFEU on the approximation of laws (together with Article 218(5) TFEU) as the legal basis for concluding an international agreement, rather than the CCP with Article 207(4) TFEU. The further reasoning of the Court reveals a wide understanding of the CCP, which is well able to capture a wider agenda of 'global governance': 'An EU act falls within that policy if it relates specifically to international trade in that it is essentially intended to promote, facilitate or govern trade and has direct and immediate effects on trade.'[111]

The CJEU noted further that the signing of the international agreement at issue in the case 'on behalf of the European Union, which the contested decision is intended to authorise, is undertaken with a view to encouraging broader ratification of the Convention by Member States of the Council of Europe'.[112] The goal was to extend EU regulation 'beyond the borders of the European Union'.[113] The Court stressed that this goal, 'which can be seen [...] to be the primary objective of that decision, therefore has a specific connection with international trade in those services, by dint of which it can legitimately be linked to the common commercial policy'.[114]

This continues the string of case law of the CJEU from before the Lisbon Treaty, according to which trade measures which also contain non-trade components can be comfortably placed on a CCP legal basis.[115] While this favours the institutional position of the Commission after Lisbon, it also brings the European Parliament to the forefront since, as far as international agreements are concerned, its consent is required now before trade agreements may be concluded by the EU.[116] The position of these institutions is thus strengthened, but they are also

EU:C:2013:675, para 56; also Case C-414/11 *Daiichi Sankyo and Sanofi Aventis Deutschland*, EU:C:2013:520, para 50.

111 *Commission v Council* (n 110) para 57; *Daiichi Sankyo and Sanofi Aventis Deutschland* (n 110) para 51.

112 *Commission v Council* (n 110) para 57.

113 Ibid, para 63.

114 Ibid, para 65.

115 Dimopoulos (n 12) 158–9. However, the trade component must be seen as predominant in such cases. In the case of a twofold trade and non-trade purpose which are both equally important and inextricably linked, a dual legal basis may be necessary; cf *Commission v Council* (*Rotterdam Convention*) (n 101). Further, Koutrakos (n 98).

116 Art 207(2) and (3) TFEU together with Art 218(6)(a)(v) TFEU; Eeckhout (n 95) 459.

called upon to be protagonists in advancing 'good global governance' through trade.

The Council retains important supervisory powers in trade policy under Article 207 TFEU, including through the Trade Policy Committee (formerly known as the 'Article 133 Committee'), preserving its role in promoting the wider normative agenda through the CCP. However, the implications for its constituents, the Member States, are drastic. Given the exclusive nature of the entirety of the CCP, Member States are barred from acting on their own behalf on the international stage. This means also that they can no longer pursue their own visions of 'good global governance', constitutionally codified or otherwise, in the international arena as far as the CCP is concerned: for them in such cases it is henceforth 'good global governance' *through* the EU and *its* trade policy. In this sense, EU external action becomes less 'polyphonic'.[117] In the CCP, the Union speaks with one voice on the international stage, and the message it is constitutionally mandated to spread globally is to be found in Articles 21 and 3(5) TEU.

4.3 Implementing 'Good Global Governance' through Trade

Union objectives are to guide the exercise of EU powers, and their pursuit is to resonate through the secondary legislation and other acts of the Union.[118] This corresponds with a view of coherence as goal-oriented 'complementarity'[119] and 'positive synergy'.[120] As Bart van Vooren rightly argues, 'coherence thus implies that norms, actors and instruments are positively aligned towards *EU Treaty objectives*'.[121] Despite the weak legal force and the width of the EU's constitutional mandate to foster good global governance, including through its trade policy, there are a number of examples of trade or trade-related measures through which the EU seeks to implement this overarching vision. Two recent initiatives of

---

[117] Christophe Hillion, 'Mixity and Coherence in EU External Relations: The Significance of the "Duty of Cooperation"', in Christophe Hillion and Panos Koutrakos (eds), *Mixed Agreements Revisited: The EU and its Member States in the World* (Hart 2010) 87–115, 87.

[118] Calliess (n 93) 90. See, for example, Geraets and Natens (Chapter 11, this volume).

[119] Marise Cremona, 'Coherence in European Union Foreign Relations Law', in Panos Koutrakos (ed), *European Foreign Policy: Legal and Political Perspectives* (Edward Elgar Publishing 2011) 55–92, 89.

[120] Bart Van Vooren (n 94) 69.

[121] Ibid 71 (emphasis added).

the EU can serve to illustrate this: one is squarely a CCP measure; the other is not.

First, the EU's Generalised System of Preferences (GSP), in its revised legal framework,[122] is arguably the most obvious example. It is formalized as a measure with a CCP legal basis but which clearly pursues a wider agenda.[123] Regulation (EU) No. 978/2012 is based on Article 207 TFEU (CCP), but its preamble also recalls that '[t]he Union's common commercial policy shall be guided by the principles and pursue the objectives set out in the general provisions on the Union's external action, laid down in Article 21 of the Treaty on European Union (TEU)' (second recital). More specifically, the Regulation notes in the fourth recital that

> [t]he Union's common commercial policy is to be consistent with and to consolidate the objectives of the Union policy in the field of development cooperation, laid down in Article 208 of the Treaty on the Functioning of the European Union (TFEU), in particular the eradication of poverty and the promotion of sustainable development and good governance in the developing countries.

Among the various ways to obtain preferences through this scheme, the 'special incentive arrangement for sustainable development and good governance' (GSP+) stands out as the prime illustration of harnessing trade policy for the benefit of a wider normative agenda. Under GSP+, developing countries eligible for the general scheme can gain additional preferences on the condition that they ratify a number of conventions listed in an annex and effectively implement them (Article 9(1) of Regulation (EU) No. 978/2012). These include international treaties on human rights, international labour rights, environmental protection and good governance, as listed in Annex VIII of the Regulation. To this end, the respective third countries also submit themselves to being monitored by the European Commission (Article 13). In the event of non-compliance with these conventions, benefits may be withdrawn (Article 15).

However, such measures are not always required to have their legal basis, or 'centre of gravity', in the CCP, but can still harness trade policy to advance the EU's entrenched global normative agenda. An example of

---

[122] Regulation (EU) No. 978/2012 of 25 October 2012 applying a scheme of generalised tariff preferences and repealing Council Regulation (EC) No 732/2008 [2012] OJ L 303/1.

[123] See further Chapters 8 and 9, this volume by Laura Beke and Nicolas Hachez, and James Yap respectively.

this is Regulation (EU) No. 995/2010 on timber and timber products,[124] which, by contrast, is based on Article 192 TFEU – the EU's environmental policy. This is because the rationale of this measure is environmental protection in terms of 'maintaining biodiversity and ecosystem functions and protecting the climate system' (first recital) and a contribution 'to the Union's climate change mitigation efforts' (third recital). The commercial dimension of the Regulation, however, is apparent in the fact that it 'lays down the obligations of operators who place timber and timber products on the internal market for the first time, as well as the obligations of traders' (Article 1). It does so by establishing various duties on operators and traders with a view to ensuring, through tracing and due diligence, that the timber and timber products introduced into the EU market comply with the exporting state's (timber) legislation.

Whatever their legal basis or the institutional and procedural setting, the basic idea behind these and other EU measures is the same: compliance with internationally recognized rules and standards which accord with the EU's vision of 'good global governance' lowers the barriers to accessing the EU internal market. This is one of the EU's most important instruments – if not *the* most important instrument – for leverage which it has at its disposal. In doing so, the EU and its institutions breathe life into the constitutionally entrenched goals of EU external action and respond to the constitutional mandate they entail.

5. CONCLUSION

This chapter has sought to elucidate the notion of 'good global governance though trade' as a constitutional matter for the EU. It has done so through a combined historical, comparative and legal-institutional analysis, which yields the following main conclusions. First, from the outset of European integration, both the centrality of the CCP in the external relations of the EU, as well as a wider normative agenda, found expression in the primary law. Over the course of several decades the latter became more clearly articulated, with the Convention on the Future of Europe devising the EU's comprehensive 'mission statement',[125] now

---

[124] Regulation (EU) No. 995/2010 of 20 October 2010 laying down the obligations of operators who place timber and timber products on the market [2010] OJ L 295/23. See further Chapter 11, this volume by Dylan Geraets and Bregt Natens.

[125] Bart Van Vooren, Steven Blockmans and Jan Wouters, 'The Legal Dimension of Global Governance: What Role for the EU? An Introduction', in

to be found in Articles 3(5) and 21 TEU and its explicit link to trade policy through Article 207(1) TFEU.

Second, such an explicit constitutional linkage between trade policy and general contributions to 'good global governance' represents a peculiarity from a comparative perspective. Only few constitutions address trade policy from a substantive point of view. The EU does so for historical reasons, and even after Lisbon the CCP retains objectives of its own. However, a general constitutional mandate to utilize trade policy to advance this wider global normative agenda is a veritable novelty in constitutional language.

Third, from a legal-institutional point of view, the introduction of Articles 3(5) and 21 TEU makes the pursuit of 'good global governance' along the lines expressed in these provisions an obligation of constitutional rank, which is to guide the exercise of EU powers in its external action. However, the width of these goals and their weak bindingness limit their obligatory and prohibitive force, not least for adjudicatory purposes. Rather, they serve for constitutional interpretation. As the emerging post-Lisbon case law affirms, the CCP – now wider in scope than ever and entirely exclusive – can serve as the legal basis (or at least one of the legal bases) for a broad range of measures which advance a wider agenda. As a consequence, this strengthens not only the institutional position of the Commission in EU external action, but also that of the Parliament as far as international agreements are concerned. The Member States, by contrast, will have to pursue their own ideas of 'good global governance' through the Council as far as matters pertaining to the post-Lisbon CCP are concerned. Regardless of the legal basis and the institutional procedures to be followed, the only way to live up to this constitutional mandate is through specific measures. Post-Lisbon, there is evidence of trade measures that explicitly acknowledge the link with the wider normative agenda of Article 21 TEU, and also of other measures, for instance in the environmental domain, with a clear trade dimension. Both types, their different legal bases notwithstanding, must be considered as steps which harness the EU's commercial clout in the interest of promoting 'good global governance' and the coherence between different policy domains.

In sum, the primary law post-Lisbon is abundantly clear: 'good global governance' through trade not just a (fleeting) policy preference; it is a constitutional duty firmly moored in the Treaties. Consequently, the trade

---

Bart Van Vooren, Steven Blockmans and Jan Wouters (eds), *The EU's Role in Global Governance: The Legal Dimension* (Oxford University Press 2013) 1.

policy of the EU is certainly no end in itself, but a powerful means to 'higher ends'[126] now prominently enshrined in the highest laws of the EU.

[126] *From War to Peace: A European Tale*, Nobel Peace Prize Lecture on behalf of the European Union by Herman Van Rompuy, President of the European Council, and José Manuel Durão Barroso, President of the European Commission, Oslo, 10 December 2012, in which then Commission President Barroso noted that European unity 'is not an end in itself, but a means to higher ends'.

PART II

'Exporting' social and environmental compliance through bilateral conditional market access

4. Human rights and sustainable development obligations in EU free trade agreements

Lorand Bartels

1. INTRODUCTION

Since the early 1990s, trade agreements entered into by the European Union (EU) have included a 'human rights clause' requiring the parties to respect human rights and democratic principles. More recently, beginning with the 2008 EU-Cariforum Economic Partnership Agreement,[1] they have also included 'sustainable development' chapters, which contain obligations to respect labour and environmental standards. These sets of provisions are a central means by which the EU achieves its 'ethical' foreign policy objectives.[2] This chapter considers a slightly different question, which is the extent to which, legally, these two sets of provisions give the EU the means of implementing its obligations to ensure that its external activities respect human rights and pursue the objective of promoting sustainable development. It also considers the differences in the EU's approach to human rights and democratic principles, on the one hand, and labour and environmental standards, on the other, and the extent to which these different approaches risk undermining the EU's obligation to respect the indivisibility of all human rights.

1 EU-Cariforum Economic Partnership Agreement [2008] OJ L 289/I/3.

2 Urfan Khaliq, *Ethical Dimensions of the Foreign Policy of the European Union: A Legal Appraisal* (Cambridge: Cambridge University Press, 2008).

2. HUMAN RIGHTS CLAUSES IN TRADE AGREEMENTS

2.1 Origins

The EU has long insisted that accession countries comply with human rights and democratic principles, a notable instance being its rebuff in 1962 of Spain's desire for accession on the basis that a non-democratic country could not be considered a 'European country'.[3] However, it was only later that the EU made this a condition of its external relations with non-accession countries. An important catalyst occurred in 1977, when the EU sought to terminate Stabex payments to Uganda in response to human rights obligations, and discovered that this was not technically possible under the African, Caribbean and Pacific (ACP)-EU Lomé Convention.[4] This situation was resolved informally, but it led the EU to attempt to persuade its ACP partners to introduce a clause into the Lomé Convention that would enable the suspension or termination of the agreement in the event of human rights abuses. For a variety of reasons, the EU's efforts in this regard were essentially unsuccessful, and even a much lauded human rights clause finally introduced into the Lomé IV Convention 1989 was of little operative value.[5]

Other countries, however, have proved to be more receptive to the EU's policy goals. A properly effective human rights clause appeared in the 1990 Argentina-EU Cooperation Agreement, interestingly, at the behest of Argentina,[6] itself newly emerged from dictatorship; and, over the next few years, similar clauses were included in new cooperation agreements with other countries.[7] This development was paralleled closer to home, where, following the collapse of communism in 1989, the EU was busy

---

[3] Agustín José Menéndez, 'Exporting Rights: The Charter of Fundamental Rights, Membership and Foreign Policy of the European Union,' ARENA Working Papers WP 02/18, 2002, referring to *Rapport de la Commission Politique de l'Assemblée Parlementaire Européenne sur les aspects politiques et institutionnels*, 15 January 1962, Document 122 (Archives of the European Communities, 07.515:32;X3.075.15), especially para 25; and Bruno Olivi, *L'Europe Difficile* (Paris: Gallimard, 2001), 303.

[4] Lomé Convention [1976] OJ L 25/1. See Lorand Bartels, *Human Rights Conditionality in the EU's International Agreements* (Oxford: Oxford University Press, 2005), 8–11.

[5] Ibid., 11–15.

[6] Commission Answer to Written Question No. 617/93 [1993] OJ C 264/42.

[7] Bartels, n. 4 above, 16–17.

building relations with its central and eastern European neighbours. The EU adopted a formal external human rights policy in 1991[8] and set about including operative human rights clauses in new cooperation and association agreements with these countries and others around the world. It was against this background that in 1995, after almost two decades of negotiations, the revised Lomé IV Convention finally included an operative human rights clause, a more elaborate version of the model developed in agreements with other countries,[9] which now exists as Articles 9 and 96 of the 2000 Cotonou Agreement.[10]

The year 1995 also saw the formal adoption by the EU Council of a concrete policy of adopting operative human rights clauses in all future cooperation and trade agreements.[11] The EU has adhered to this policy ever since, although in more recent cases it has done so by cross-referencing (sometimes by implication)[12] human rights clauses in existing agreements between the parties.[13] In addition, the EU has expanded its external human rights conditionality policies to its autonomous instruments granting trade preferences (including the EU's Generalised

---

8 Commission Communication on Human Rights, Democracy and Development Cooperation Policy, SEC (91) 6; Resolution of the Council and of the Member States Meeting in the Council on Human Rights, Democracy and Development, 28 November 1991, reported in *EC Bulletin* 1991–11, 122.

9 Articles 5(1)(3) and 366a of the revised Lomé IV Agreement (commonly known as the Lomé IV*bis* Agreement), introduced by the Agreement amending the Fourth ACP-EC Convention of Lomé [1998] OJ L 156/3.

10 Partnership Agreement between the members of the African, Caribbean and Pacific Group of States of the one part and the European Community and its Member States of the other part, signed in Cotonou on 23 June 2000 (hereinafter Cotonou Agreement) [2000] OJ L 317/3, amended in 2005 and 2010. Article 8, establishing a political dialogue, is also relevant.

11 Commission Communication on the Inclusion of Respect for Democratic Principles and Human Rights in Agreements between the Community and Third Countries', COM(95) 216, and EU Council Conclusions of 29 May 1995 (reported in *EU Bulletin* 1995–5, point 1.2.3).

12 Article 15.14, EU-Korea Free Trade Agreement [2011] OJ L 127/6, states that '[u]nless specified otherwise, previous agreements between the Member States of the European Union and/or the European Community and/or the European Union and Korea are not superseded or terminated by this Agreement'.

13 This policy is understood to be set out in the confidential EU documents 7008/09, 7008/09 COR 1 and 10491/1/09 REV 1 (RESTREINT UE). See EU Council Document 12450/11 rejecting an application for public access to these documents.

System of Preferences (GSP) programme)[14] as well as to financing agreements with developing countries.[15]

2.2 Obligations

2.2.1 The 'essential elements' clause

The core of all human rights clauses is an 'essential elements' clause, which is in relatively standard wording. The following, from the 2012 EU-Central America agreement, is a good example:

> Respect for democratic principles and fundamental human rights, as laid down in the Universal Declaration of Human Rights, and for the principle of the rule of law, underpins the internal and international policies of both Parties and constitutes an essential element of this Agreement.[16]

The EU's early agreements contain little else; it is unfortunate, in some respects, that it was one of these agreements – the 1993 EU-India cooperation agreement – that is the best known, thanks to an ECJ case in 1996 on the human rights clause in this agreement.[17] In fact, the human rights clause at issue is not representative of later human rights clauses, which have quite different forms and legal effects, and much of what the Court said about this clause is of limited relevance to these clauses.[18]

---

[14] Regulation 732/2008 [2008] OJ L 211/1.

[15] For example, Annex I of the 2012 Model General Conditions to Financing Agreements, available at http://ec.europa.eu/europeaid/funding/procedures-beneficiary-countries-and-partners/financing-agreements_en. Note, however, that unlike their 2006 predecessor instruments, the current European Neighbourhood and Partnership Instrument (Regulation 232/2014 [2014] OJ L 77/27) and the Partnership Instrument (Regulation 234/2014 [2014] OJ L 77/77) no longer contain an express provision permitting human rights conditionality. The European Parliament appended statements to both new instruments reserving its rights should a decision be taken to suspend financial aid under these agreements.

[16] Article 1, EU-Central America Association Agreement [2012] OJ L 346/3, signed 29 June 2012.

[17] Cooperation Agreement between the European Community and the Republic of India on Partnership and Development [1994] OJ L 223/24, signed 20 December 1993. Case C-268/94, *Portugal v Council* [1996] ECR I-6177.

[18] To take an example, Article 60 of the Vienna Convention on the Law of Treaties, referred to by the Advocate-General and the parties to the case, is, by its own terms, only a default clause and therefore not applicable to later versions of the human rights clause, which expressly regulate the consequences of violations of the norms in the essential elements clause. Of course, strictly speaking, Article 60 would not be relevant anyway, given that the EU is not a party to the Vienna

One of these later changes, now a standard feature of human rights clauses, is the inclusion of an 'implementation' clause, which states that '[t]he Parties shall adopt any general or specific measures required for them to fulfil their obligations under this Agreement'.[19] This clause derives from what is now Article 4(3) of the Treaty on European Union (TEU), which, in the context of EU law, has been interpreted as imposing a variety of additional obligations on the EU Member States, including the obligation to take steps to ensure the effective application of EU law.[20] This is not to say that an 'implementation clause' in an international agreement should be read in exactly the same way as it is in EU law. On the other hand, such a clause must have some meaning beyond redundantly restating the principle *pacta sunt servanda*.[21] Quite what it might mean is difficult to say outside the context of a specific case, but it could have the effect of imposing on the parties not only a duty to ensure that human rights and democratic principles are *respected* but also a positive duty to ensure that these norms are *fulfilled*.[22] Such an interpretation could, of course, also arise from an interpretation of the human rights and democratic principles at issue in any case.

2.2.2 Monitoring

To date, the agreements containing human rights clauses have not established any specific organs for monitoring the implementation of the clauses. This contrasts with the many other subject-specific organs, including those with a sustainable development mandate, established by these agreements. On the other hand, in some agreements subcommittees on human rights and democratic principles have been established on an ad hoc basis.[23]

Convention 1969, and the Vienna Convention 1986 is not in force. It is the customary international law rule reflected in this provision that would be relevant. Invariably, the academic commentary misses this point – e.g., recently, Khaliq, n. 2 above, 112–13.

19 For example, Article 355(1), EU-Central America Association Agreement, n. 16 above.

20 For a useful summary, see Christophe Hillion and Ramses Wessel, 'Restraining External Competences of EU Member States under CFSP', in Marise Cremona and Bruno de Witte (eds), *EU Foreign Relations Law* (Oxford: Hart, 2008), 92, with further references.

21 Jan Klabbers, *An Introduction to International Institutional Law* (Cambridge: Cambridge University Press, 2002), 195.

22 Bartels, n. 4 above, 147–9.

23 The first of these was established in the EU-Morocco Association Agreement, by Association Council Decision No. 1/2003 [2003] OJ L 79/14, Annex 1.

However, even in the absence of specific organs, issues arising under human rights clauses can be discussed within some of the organs established under the agreement. Most obviously, these would include the primary bilateral organ – namely, the Association Council or Joint Council (the names differ). Indeed, in many of the human rights clauses (although not in the relevant clause in the 2012 EU-Colombia/Peru agreement),[24] it is mandatory – except in cases of special urgency, which require the adoption of 'appropriate measures' – 'to submit to the Association Council within thirty days all relevant information required for a thorough examination of the situation with a view to seeking a solution acceptable to the Parties'.[25] Human rights and democracy issues may also be raised with other generic organs, where these exist, such as bilateral parliamentary committees and, depending on their mandate, civil society consultative committees.

2.2.3 Bilateral implementation

In most cases, an issue arising under a human rights clause should be resolved by one of the parties acting at the domestic level, but there may also be cases in which the issue arises as a result of the agreement itself. One could envisage market access commitments that encourage deforestation (to use the earlier example), or intellectual property obligations that are unduly restrictive of free speech or other human rights, or non-discrimination obligations that prevent a party from legislating in favour of minority groups. Even in these cases, there may be a unilateral resolution of the problem. In other cases it may be necessary to suspend or amend certain provisions of the agreement.

The question is whether this can be achieved without the need for a renegotiation of the treaty. This depends on the existence of any amendment procedures under the agreement, and, failing these (which do not exist in the relevant agreements), the powers of the organs established under the agreement to revise the agreement. The widest of such powers belong to the Joint Council established under the EU-Cariforum agreement, which enjoys 'the power to take decisions in respect of all matters covered by the Agreement'.[26] By contrast, the Association Council under

---

[24] Article 8(3), EU-Colombia/Peru Trade Agreement [2012] OJ L 354/3, signed 26 June 2012.

[25] For example, Article 355(2), EU-Central America Association Agreement, n. 16 above.

[26] Article 229(1), EU-Cariforum Economic Partnership Agreement, n. 1 above. The revision clause in Article 246 of this agreement also implies that the Joint Council has the power to revise the agreement.

the EU-Central America agreement has the more limited power 'to take decisions in the cases provided for in this Agreement'.[27] In the absence of any such 'cases' in the agreement relevant to human rights issues, the Association Council does not appear to have the power to revise the agreement to ensure that the parties are able to comply with their human rights obligations, should this prove necessary.

2.2.4 Unilateral enforcement

The cases just mentioned are the exception. In fact, human rights violations most commonly occur when a state fails to take action that it has the legal power to take. It is for these cases that human rights clauses are designed, insofar as they authorize the other party to respond by means of unilateral 'appropriate measures'. In most cases, this may be done without even the need for prior consultation.

This is achieved in most of the post-1996 agreements in a somewhat unwieldy way. A violation of the essential elements of the agreement is deemed to be a 'material breach' of the agreement, which is in turn deemed to be a 'case of special urgency',[28] automatically entitling the other party to adopt 'appropriate measures' under a so-called 'non-execution' clause.[29] More efficiently, the 2012 EU-Peru/Colombia agreement states that 'any Party may immediately adopt appropriate measures in accordance with international law in case of violation by another Party of the essential elements referred to in Articles 1 and 2 of this Agreement'.[30]

Conditions are imposed on the adoption of 'appropriate measures'. The measures must be taken in accordance with international law; priority must be given to measures that least disrupt the functioning of the agreement;[31] it is usually agreed that 'suspension would be a measure of last resort';[32] and it is sometimes also said that the measures must be

---

27 Article 6(1), EU-Central America Association Agreement, n. 16 above.

28 The wording is unfortunate. The phrase 'special urgency' implies temporal urgency, not material gravity.

29 For example, Article 355(2)–(5), EU-Central America Association Agreement, n. 16 above.

30 Article 8, EU-Colombia/Peru Trade Agreement, n. 24 above.

31 This second condition is entirely counterintuitive insofar as an appropriate measure under a human rights clause is adopted specifically to disrupt the normal implementation of the agreement. The explanation is that the condition originates in safeguards clauses, where the measures chosen are defensive, not offensive. In this original context, it makes perfect sense to oblige parties imposing restrictive measures to adopt measures that least affect the other party: see Bartels, n. 4, 24.

32 But not in the EU-Colombia/Peru Trade Agreement, n. 24 above.

revoked as soon as the reasons for their adoption have ceased to exist.[33] As to the nature of such measures, these conditions clearly indicate that a wide range of measures is envisaged, including the suspension of the agreement in whole or in part. This corresponds with the purpose of these clauses, which list a range of measures including trade sanctions.[34]

It is worth noting that non-execution clauses that mention 'appropriate measures' also permit the suspension not only of the agreement containing the clause, but also other agreements between the parties (and presumably also obligations between the parties under customary international law). This means that, for example, free trade agreements which do not themselves contain an operative human rights clause, or cross-refer to an existing human rights clause, are still subject to any otherwise binding human rights clause with a non-execution clause. Here, however, it is relevant to note that the 1993 EU-India cooperation agreement, predating the 1996 model, contains an essential elements clause but no 'non-execution' clause. Any EU-India free trade agreement would therefore have to contain its own non-execution clause to ensure that the human rights clause will have full effect.

2.2.5 Dispute settlement

While the post-1996 human rights clauses are relatively similar in substance, they differ significantly in the extent to which they, or 'appropriate measures', are subject to dispute settlement under the agreement. The Cotonou Agreement and all of the Euro-Mediterranean association agreements in force provide for dispute settlement in relation to the interpretation and application of their human rights clauses, including appropriate measures adopted under these clauses. By contrast, certain others – including, most recently, the EU-Central America agreement, only permit an affected party to 'ask that an urgent meeting be called to bring the Parties together within 15 days for a thorough examination of the situation with a view to seeking a solution acceptable to the Parties'.[35]

The 2012 agreement concluded with Peru/Colombia presents something of a puzzle in this regard. The normal rule (expressed as a jurisdiction clause in Article 299(1) and as an exclusive jurisdiction clause in Article 8(2)) is that the dispute settlement system established under the agreement applies to all disputes relating to the interpretation

---

33 Article 8(3), EU-Colombia/Peru Trade Agreement, ibid. This wording derives from Article 96(2)(a), Cotonou Agreement, n. 10 above.

34 Annex 2, Commission Communication COM(95) 216, n. 11 above.

35 Article 355(5), EU-Central America Association Agreement, n. 16 above.

and application of the agreement. However, Article 8(3) provides for an urgent meeting in the same terms as that in the Central America agreement. The question is whether, without more, this should operate as a carve out from dispute settlement. On balance, the answer is that it probably does not. The 'urgent meeting' by no means displaces or renders redundant the otherwise applicable consultation or dispute settlement proceedings in the event of appropriate measures. Indeed, a party calling such a meeting might have an interest in having these measures subjected to formal dispute settlement. It would therefore appear that, in contrast to the situation in certain of the EU's free trade agreements, in these agreements disputes relating to the human rights clause are fully subject to dispute settlement proceedings.

2.3 The EU's Practice

Over the past 20 years, human rights clauses have been applied on numerous occasions. In terms of the countries and conduct that has triggered a reaction, the EU's practice has been limited in a number of respects. First, there has never been any action under a human rights clause in an agreement other than the Cotonou Agreement except for the suspension of technical meetings under the Uzbekistan Partnership and Cooperation Agreement – a measure taken in response to the Andijan massacre in 2005.[36] Second, the occasions on which the clause has been invoked have involved political coups or other violations of democratic principles, in some cases along with human rights abuses. As to the types of measure applied, these have been rather extensive in scope, including delays in and suspension of financial cooperation. The effectiveness of these measures has recently been subject to a lengthy examination.[37] Of greater importance for present purposes (as will be discussed below), the practice of the EU falls far short in virtually all respects of what is legally possible under these clauses.

---

[36] Article 4, Council Common Position 2005/792/CFSP concerning restrictive measures against Uzbekistan [2005] OJ L 299/72; this, however, does not cite the human rights clause.

[37] Clara Portela, *European Union Sanctions and Foreign Policy: When and Why Do They Work?* (Abingdon: Routledge, 2010).

3. SUSTAINABLE DEVELOPMENT CHAPTERS

3.1 Origins

The EU's practice of including 'sustainable development chapters' in its free trade agreements has more recent origins. The principle of sustainable development is commonly attributed to the 1987 Brundtland Report,[38] and has been an important element of EU policy since the European Commission's 2001 Communication, 'A Sustainable Europe for a Better World: A European Union Strategy for Sustainable Development'.[39] The emphasis in this Communication (adopted at the 2001 Göteborg European Council) was on the internal dimensions of EU strategy. The external dimensions were then expanded in the Commission's 2002 Communication, 'Towards a Global Partnership for Sustainable Development', issued prior to the 2002 UN World Summit on Sustainable Development held in Johannesburg.[40] The principle of sustainable development also featured prominently in the 2005 European Consensus on Development, which defined common principles for the development policies of the EU and the Member States,[41] and stated that 'the primary and overarching objective of EU development cooperation is the eradication of poverty in the context of sustainable development'. More recently, since the 2009 Lisbon Treaty, the EU's external policies must pursue the objective of 'foster[ing] sustainable economic, social and environmental development of developing countries, with the primary aim of eradicating poverty'.[42]

The first of the EU's free trade agreements to make reference to the principle of 'sustainable development' was the 1993 EU-Hungary Europe

---

[38] For a full discussion, see Virginie Barral, 'Sustainable Development in International Law: Nature and Operation of an Evolutive Legal Norm' (2012) 23 *European Journal of International Law* 377. She notes (at 379, n. 9), that '[a]lthough the term 'sustainable development' is fully articulated and disseminated by the Brundtland Report, the expression was borrowed from the 1980 World Conservation Strategy (a joint IUCN/WWF/ UNEP document)'.

[39] COM(2001) 264.

[40] COM(2002) 82.

[41] Joint Statement by the Council and the representatives of the governments of the Member States meeting within the Council, the European Parliament and the Commission on European Union Development Policy [2006] OJ C 46/1.

[42] Article 21(3), referring to Article 21(2)(d) TEU.

Agreement,[43] and the principle has appeared regularly as an objective, or in an incidental or interpretive context, in agreements since then. The principle was given an unusually broad definition in the 2000 Cotonou Agreement, which states that '[r]espect for all human rights and fundamental freedoms, including respect for fundamental social rights, democracy based on the rule of law and transparent and accountable governance are an integral part of sustainable development'.[44] More conventionally, the EU-Central America agreement states that '[t]he Parties reaffirm their commitment to achieving sustainable development, whose pillars – economic development, social development and environmental protection – are interdependent and mutually reinforcing'.

It is notable that the principle of sustainable development has never been treated as a concrete obligation in itself: none of the agreements admit the possibility of violating the 'principle of sustainable development'.[45] Rather, in the context of this principle and sometimes under its banner, the agreements contain provisions on cooperation as well as, relevantly, concrete obligations to respect and 'strive' to improve multilateral and domestic labour and environmental standards.[46] Such chapters are now found in the 2008 EU-Cariforum agreement, the 2010 EU-Korea agreement, and the 2012 EU-Central America and EU-Peru/Colombia agreements, and are reportedly being included in agreements still under negotiation. The EU is now seemingly committed, as a matter of policy, to including these provisions in future free trade agreements. Yet questions remain as to what value this brings, and, for reasons to be explained, how these chapters relate to the EU's existing policy on human rights clauses.

---

43 The principle of 'sustainable development' first appeared in an international trade instrument in the EU-Hungary Europe Agreement [1993] OJ L 347/2.

44 Article 9, Cotonou Agreement, n. 10 above.

45 This is quite common: Barral, n. 38 above, 385.

46 These are not new clauses: in fact, they originate in the NAFTA labour and environment side agreements, and have since become common in North and South American trade agreements. For an account of their evolution, see Lorand Bartels, 'Social Issues: Labour, Environment and Human Rights', in Simon Lester, Bryan Mercurio and Lorand Bartels (eds), *Bilateral and Regional Trade Agreements: Commentary, Analysis and Case Studies*, 2nd edition (Cambridge: Cambridge University Press, 2015).

3.2 Obligations

As noted, the sustainable development chapters contain provisions on labour standards and environmental standards. In both cases, the obligations are of two types: (i) minimum obligations to implement certain multilateral obligations and, above this; (ii) a set of other obligations requiring the parties not to reduce their levels of protection, and encouraging them to raise such levels of protection, subject to a proviso that this is not undertaken for protectionist purposes.

The sustainable development chapter in the EU-Central America agreement is typical. The parties affirm their commitments to the core labour principles of the International Labour Organization (ILO)[47] and to certain multilateral environmental agreements;[48] and also undertake to 'effectively implement' the fundamental ILO Conventions referred to in the ILO Declaration on Fundamental Principles and Rights at Work of 1998.[49]

---

[47] Article 286(1), EU-Central America Association Agreement, n. 16 above. These core labour standards are: (a) freedom of association and the effective recognition of the right to collective bargaining; (b) the elimination of all forms of forced or compulsory labour; (c) the effective abolition of child labour; and (d) the elimination of discrimination in respect of employment and occupation.

[48] Article EU-Central America Association Agreement, n. 16 above. These are: (a) Montreal Protocol on Substances that Deplete the Ozone Layer; (b) Basel Convention on the Control of Transboundary Movements of Hazardous Wastes and their Disposal; (c) Stockholm Convention on Persistent Organic Pollutants; (d) Convention on International Trade in Endangered Species of Wild Fauna and Flora (CITES); (e) Convention on Biological Diversity; (f) Cartagena Protocol on Biosafety to the Convention on Biological Diversity; and (g) Kyoto Protocol to the United Nations Framework Convention on Climate Change. Article 287(3) and (4) provide that the Amendment to Article XXI of CITES must be ratified, and the Rotterdam Convention on the Prior Informed Consent Procedure for Certain Hazardous Chemicals and Pesticides in International Trade must be ratified and implemented.

[49] ILO, Declaration on Fundamental Principles and Rights at Work, adopted in 1998, 86th International Labour Conference; Article 286(2), EU-Central America Association Agreement, n. 16 above. These are: (a) Convention 138 concerning Minimum Age for Admission to Employment; (b) Convention 182 concerning the Prohibition and Immediate Action for the Elimination of the Worst Forms of Child Labour; (c) Convention 105 concerning the Abolition of Forced Labour; (d) Convention 29 concerning Forced or Compulsory Labour; (e) Convention 100 concerning Equal Remuneration for Men and Women Workers for Work of Equal Value; (f) Convention 111 concerning Discrimination in Respect of Employment and Occupation; (g) Convention 87 concerning Freedom of Association and Protection of the Right to Organise; and (h) Convention 98

Beyond this, the parties undertake (i) not to lower their levels of protection to encourage trade or investment, and (ii) not to fail in effectively enforcing their labour and environmental legislation in a manner that affects trade and investment between the parties;[50] they also undertake to 'strive to ensure' that their laws and policies provide for and encourage appropriate but high levels of labour and environmental protection and to 'strive to improve' these laws and policies.[51] The first of these obligations is an effective guarantee against retrogression, when this relates to trade or investment under the agreement. The second is weaker, in the sense that it is only a 'best endeavours' provision, but broader in scope in that it applies to labour and environmental standards even when trade and investment is not affected. Although weak, however, it is not meaningless: an overt weakening of existing legislative protection could hardly be said to be consistent with striving to improve these standards.

The sustainable development chapters also contain clauses to prevent abuse: for example, the EU-Central America agreement states that 'labour standards should never be invoked or otherwise used for protectionist trade purposes and … the comparative advantage of any Party should not be questioned'.[52] Interestingly, sometimes (as in this example) there is only such a clause in relation to labour standards, while in the Korea and Cariforum agreements there is an equivalent clause for environmental standards. It is likely, however, that any such standards would need to be justified under the general exceptions to the agreement, which contain provisions to prevent this type of abuse.

Unlike the other agreements so far concluded that contain sustainable development chapters, the EU-Cariforum agreement regulates investment in goods, and in this part of the agreement includes additional sustainable development obligations. The parties are required: (i) to act in accordance with core labour standards; (ii) not to operate their investments in a manner that circumvents international labour or environmental obligations; and (iii) to ensure that foreign direct investment is not encouraged by lowering domestic environmental, labour or occupational health and safety legislation and standards, or by relaxing core labour standards or

concerning the Application of the Principles of the Right to Organise and to Bargain Collectively.

[50] Article 291, EU-Central America Association Agreement, n. 16 above.

[51] Article 285, ibid.

[52] Article 286(4), ibid.

laws aimed at protecting and promoting cultural diversity.[53] These provisions reiterate the obligations set out in the sustainable development chapter, and their existence is probably explained in terms of a complicated negotiating dynamic. However, the fact that these provisions are located outside the usual chapter raises interesting questions (discussed below) as to their implementation and enforcement.

How, then, do these provisions relate to the parties' existing obligations, including those under the human rights clause? In terms of the applicable standards (as opposed to implementation and remedies), their novelty concerns the provisions that require the parties not to undermine their existing labour and environmental standards. It is quite conceivable that a measure may reduce the level of domestic protection in these areas without this amounting to a violation of the norms set out in the human rights clause, or indeed in any applicable multilateral environmental agreement. On the other hand, the provisions based on multilateral standards add nothing substantively new. As far as the ILO core labour standards are concerned, these are already binding on the parties by virtue of their membership of the ILO. In addition, as mentioned, all of these standards are, as the European Commission has itself acknowledged, covered by the human rights clause. The situation with the multilateral environmental agreements is a little different: the obligation to implement these agreements amounts to no more than a reaffirmation of obligations already binding on the parties under those agreements. It seems, then, that the provisions are not as original as they first appear. The question (addressed below) is whether such duplication comes at a cost.

3.3 Monitoring

The sustainable development obligations are specifically monitored by a variety of organs established under the agreements. Most important are the bilateral committees established specifically to deal with sustainable development issues. These committees have mandates of varying breadth. The Trade and Development Committee established by the EU-Cariforum agreement has a broad mandate to discuss sustainable development issues,[54] and is not therefore limited to discussing issues only

[53] Articles 72 and 73, EU-Cariforum Economic Partnership Agreement, n. 1 above.

[54] Article 230(3)(a), EU-Cariforum Economic Partnership Agreement, n. 1 above.

insofar as they concern the implementation of the sustainable development chapter. More narrowly, the Trade and Sustainable Development Board under the EU-Central America agreement has a mandate to oversee the implementation of the sustainable development chapter, but may otherwise have a limited jurisdiction.

These bilateral meetings and organs are accompanied by civil society mechanisms, in various forms, ranging from unilateral advisory groups to bilateral meetings of civil society groups – in the case of the EU-Cariforum agreement these meetings take place within a civil society consultative committee specifically designed for this purpose. Interestingly, the mandate of these groups is described in terms of 'trade-related aspects of sustainable development'. Bearing in mind the wide definition of sustainable development, it is not inconceivable that these organs might legitimately discuss certain issues relating to these matters. Indeed, this could include matters falling within the human rights clause if the broad definition of 'sustainable development' adopted in the Cotonou Agreement is applied.[55] There may ordinarily be no warrant for such a reading, but in the case of the Cariforum agreement this would be entirely proper, given that its parties are also parties to the Cotonou Agreement.

3.4 Bilateral Implementation

As mentioned in the context of the human rights clause, it may be that the agreement itself stands in the way of sustainable development principles. For example, a party may have adopted high labour standards, consistent with its right to do so, which have a disproportionate effect on products from the other party. The question would be whether such standards would thereby violate the national treatment obligation in the agreement to ensure that those products must not be granted less favourable treatment than domestic products. It may be that the problem can be resolved by means of interpretation: it may be that there is a violation, and the most appropriate solution is for the parties to agree bilaterally on a solution that permits such standards in the name of sustainable development. Again, the powers of the organs established under the agreement will determine whether such a course of action is possible, and this depends on the agreement.

---

[55] Article 9, n. 10 above.

3.5 Dispute Settlement

None of the sustainable development chapters give the parties the right of unilateral enforcement of the sustainable development obligations; nor (except in the EU-Cariforum agreement, on which see below) is it permissible to resort to the normal dispute settlement procedures established under the agreements. Rather, disputes on these matters are to be resolved by way of a self-contained system of dispute settlement involving consultations, followed by referral to a Panel of Experts.

Such a Panel has the power to examine whether there has been a failure to comply with the relevant obligations, to draw up a report and to make non-binding recommendations for the resolution of the matter. The next steps vary according to the agreement at issue. Under the terms of the EU-Korea agreement, the report goes to the parties, which 'shall make their best efforts to accommodate advice or recommendations … on the implementation of [the sustainable development] chapter', and to the Domestic Advisory Group.[56] Under the EU-Central America agreement, the report is published, and the relevant party must respond with an appropriate action plan, implementation of which is then monitored by the Trade and Sustainable Development Board.[57]

Once again, the EU-Cariforum agreement differs from this model. In this agreement, the normal dispute settlement procedures apply, but the suspension of concessions is ruled out.[58] This remedial 'carve out' applies only to violations of obligations set out in the sustainable development chapter; it does not apply to violations of the sustainable development obligations set out in the chapter on investment in goods. Perhaps by oversight, these obligations are subject not only to dispute settlement but also to the usual remedies available under the agreement.

---

[56] Article 13.15(2), EU-Korea Free Trade Agreement, n. 12 above.

[57] Article 301, EU-Central America Association Agreement, n. 16 above.

[58] Article 213(2), EU-Cariforum Economic Partnership Agreement, n. 1 above.

4. ASSESSMENT

4.1 EU Obligations

It is important to place the EU's treaty practice, as here described, in its proper legal context. Since the Treaty of Lisbon,[59] the EU's external policies must respect the principles of 'democracy, the rule of law, the universality and indivisibility of human rights and fundamental freedoms, respect for human dignity, the principles of equality and solidarity, and … the principles of the United Nations Charter and international law'.[60] The EU must also, in its external relations, pursue a set of further objectives, which include, as mentioned, '[the fostering of] sustainable economic, social and environmental development of developing countries, with the primary aim of eradicating poverty'.[61] Seen from this perspective, the EU's human rights clauses and sustainable development chapters are not simply a matter of discretionary foreign policy. They are mechanisms which, in theory, enable the EU to comply with its obligations under the EU Treaty. But are these mechanisms effective?

In the case of the EU's obligations with respect to human rights and democratic principles, the answer is that they are. Despite certain infelicities in wording, the human rights clause is sufficiently robust and flexible to enable the EU to ensure that it may withdraw from any commitment that would imperil its obligation to respect human rights and democratic principles in its external relations. It is more difficult to answer this question in the context of the EU's commitment to sustainable development and the eradication of poverty. What would happen if the agreement turned out to have negative effects on sustainable development or poverty? To be sure, it is not certain that this would be a violation of an EU obligation, given that the EU is only obliged to 'pursue' the objective of, *inter alia*, reducing poverty. However, assuming that the obligation does have a stricter meaning, the EU would have little power to withdraw from commitments that contribute to this situation; nor could it take coercive steps with a view to enforcing the other country's own obligations in this regard.

---

59 Article 21(3) TEU and Articles 205 and 208(1), Treaty on the Functioning of the European Union.

60 These principles are set out in Article 21(1) TEU. See, further, Lorand Bartels, 'The EU's Human Rights Obligations in Relation to Policies with Extraterritorial Effects' (2014) 25 *European Journal of International Law* 1071.

61 These objectives are set out in Article 21(2) TEU.

4.2 Internal Coherence

What, then, of the question of internal coherence? Here the situation appears to be more mixed. In some respects, of course, the two sets of provisions are indeed different. There is no equivalent of 'democratic principles' in the sustainability chapter; nor does the human rights clause necessarily prevent a treaty party from reducing the level of protection offered by domestic labour and environment legislation.[62] However, from a substantive point of view there are also significant areas of overlap between the human rights clause and the provisions concerning labour and environmental standards. The core labour standards of the ILO are also human rights;[63] and, as the European Commission has itself said, core labour standards are covered by the standard human rights clauses.[64] Similarly, there is an increasing overlap between human rights and environmental protection, particularly in the context of indigenous rights and transboundary pollution,[65] which is also ignored in the EU's model clauses.

The question, then, is whether in such cases it makes sense for such different provisions on implementation and remedies to apply to the same state conduct. Arguably, it is not sensible that, if seen as a violation of core labour standards, state conduct cannot be subjected to dispute settlement or counteracted by a suspension of trade concessions, but it can if it is seen as a violation of human rights. Arguably, it is equally lacking in the sense that such conduct would be subject to a dedicated monitoring mechanism if it is seen in terms of labour standards, but not if it is seen in human rights terms. Nor is the issue theoretical: US administrators once rejected a petition under the US Generalized System of Preferences in relation to the murder of a trade union leader on the

---

[62] Human rights law provides limited guarantees against 'retrogression'. See, for a relevant discussion, Gillian Moon, 'Fair in Form, but Discriminatory in Operation – WTO Law's Discriminatory Effects on Human Rights in Developing Countries' (2011) 14 *Journal of International Economic Law* 553.

[63] Philip Alston, '"Core Labour Standards" and the Transformation of the International Labour Rights Regime (2004) 14 *European Journal of International Law* 457, at 476. Alston also discusses the political and institutional dimensions of this issue, as does Virginia Mantouvalou, 'Are Labour Rights Human Rights?' (2012) 3 *European Labour Law Journal* 151.

[64] European Commission, Communication on Promoting Core Labour Standards and Improving Social Governance in the Context of Globalisation, COM(2001) 416, at 12.

[65] Alan Boyle, 'Human Rights and the Environment: Where Next?' (2012) 23 *European Journal of International Law* 613.

basis that this constituted a violation of 'human rights' rather than of 'worker rights'.[66] As a matter of policy, and perhaps even of law,[67] the EU should ensure that there is internal coherence in its external protection of human rights, labour and environmental standards, especially when this protection exists in the very same international agreement.

In sum, in terms of its obligation to conduct an ethical foreign policy, the EU's practice with respect to the regulation of social standards in its free trade agreements is a success. However, in terms of internal coherence, which is also in some respects legally required, it leaves much to be desired.

[66] US General Accounting Office, 'International Trade: Assessment of the Generalized System of Preferences', GAO/GGD-95–9, November 1994, 109, available at: http://www.gao.gov/assets/160/154744.pdf, cited in Bob Hepple, *Labour Laws and Global Trade* (Oxford: Hart, 2005), 96.

[67] Article 21 TEU requires the EU to treat all human rights as indivisible. If the EU treats human rights of varying types so differently, depending on how they are categorized, at the outside it might find itself in violation of this obligation also.

5. Strengthening sustainable development through regional trade agreements

Rafael Leal-Arcas and Catherine M. Wilmarth

1. INTRODUCTION

Sustainable development has been defined in various ways. The landmark definition is the following, which first appeared in 1987: 'Development that meets the needs of the present without compromising the ability of the future generations to meet their own needs'.[1] Following the premise that regional trade agreements (RTAs) are the building blocks of multilateralism,[2] creating RTAs with sustainable growth mechanisms is a key contemporary challenge. As things stand, RTAs can either contribute or undermine sustainable development efforts. Factors such as greater negotiating power, greater regulatory cooperation and smaller numbers of parties help in regional negotiations. For example, a state that aims to include sustainable development in all its policy aspects would find greater success in pursuing it through an RTA rather than multilaterally.[3] Furthermore, RTAs with environmental standards may help to level the playing field. They can nullify competitive advantages gained from weaker environmental legislation, help in environmental capacity building, and enable better understanding of environmental problems.

[1] The World Commission on Environment and Development, *Our Common Future* (Oxford University Press, 1987).

[2] See, for instance, R. Leal-Arcas, 'Proliferation of Regional Trade Agreements: Complementing or Supplanting Multilateralism?' (2011) 11(2) *Chicago Journal of International Law* 597–629.

[3] New Zealand Ministry of Foreign Affairs & Trade, 'Framework for Integrating Environment Issues into Free Trade Agreements', available at: http://www.mfat.govt.nz/Trade-and-Economic-Relations/NZ-and-the-WTO/Trade-Issues/0-environment-framework.php.

Arguendo, RTAs can ensure greater environmental protection than multilateral environmental agreements (MEAs).[4] Concessions granted while negotiating a trade deal may address sustainable development concerns.[5] As a result, RTAs can effectively fulfil many objectives of MEAs. Most importantly, RTAs often contain binding dispute resolution clauses, which can prove to be very effective in dealing with environmental disputes. If, indeed, RTAs are to become the building blocks for ensuring climate change mitigation and meet sustainable development objectives under MEAs,[6] negotiations would need to carefully balance trade, development and sustainable growth.[7] Further, the design of strategic RTAs is vital for sustainable development. This would require them to be of a relatively large size and be composed of some prominent economies, given that major economies are major greenhouse gas (GHG) emitters and therefore play a major role in climate change mitigation efforts. The Transatlantic Trade and Investment Partnership (TTIP) and Trans-Pacific Partnership (TPP) both fit this bill well.

This chapter provides an analysis of two mega-regional trade agreements currently under negotiation in the context of sustainable development: the TTIP and the TPP. Although neither agreement has been concluded at the time of writing this chapter, it is relevant to address the main issues in these agreements in the context of sustainable development as an overarching policy objective of the international community. For the reasons noted above, these RTAs may present a more efficient vehicle by which to promote sustainable development than the multilateral trading platform. The chapter discusses sustainable development and energy within the proposed TTIP and TPP. The TTIP aims to further economic growth, investment and trade between the United States (US) and the European Union (EU), and could potentially have a (very) large impact as the US-EU trade and investment flows are sizeable and a critical element in global commerce. The chapter argues that the TTIP has the potential to foster sustainable development, energy efficiency and energy security.

---

[4] Organisation for Economic Co-operation and Development (OECD), *Environment and Regional Trade Agreements* (OECD, 2007), p. 42.

[5] Ibid.

[6] R. Leal-Arcas, 'Climate Change Mitigation from the Bottom Up: Using Preferential Trade Agreements to Promote Climate Change Mitigation' (2013) 7(1) *Carbon and Climate Law Rev* 34–42.

[7] For proposals in this respect, see R. Leal-Arcas, 'Trade Proposals for Climate Action' (2014) 6(1) *Trade, Law and Development* 11–54.

Trade has already proved to be a powerful tool towards achieving environmental goals. For example, the Montreal Protocol on Substances that Deplete the Ozone Layer[8] restricted its parties from trading in ozone-depleting substances with non-parties. This served the dual purpose of encouraging wide participation (the Montreal Protocol now has 197 parties[9]) and removing any competitive advantage that a non-party might enjoy (that is, preventing leakage[10] to non-participating jurisdictions).[11] Moreover, the success of the Montreal Protocol lies in the fact that trade was not actually restricted.[12] Climate change, however, is a far more complex issue, both connected with and giving rise to a host of other issues and areas, including GHG emissions, clean energy technology, knowledge transfer, investment in low-carbon economies, development assistance, carbon capture and storage, and adaptation. While this makes it all the more challenging to harness trade policy towards climate change mitigation, it also presents a range of potential areas of cooperation, across different regimes and disciplines.

'Green industrial policy', as Aaron Cosbey dubs it,[13] is the crossroads for trade and climate, where we have the opportunity to purposefully shape policies in various sectors in order to promote environmental protection. According to Cosbey,

> green industrial policy … is any [such] policy that supports the development of industries that produce 'green' goods, or goods that: have better environmental performance in operation than their competitors (e.g., electric vehicles,

---

[8] (1987) 26 ILM 1550.

[9] http://ozone.unep.org/new_site/en/montreal_protocol.php.

[10] According to Patrick Low and his co-authors, 'carbon leakage may arise where countries implement asymmetric climate policies. When an industry in one country assumes additional costs in order to reduce greenhouse gas (GHG) emissions and those same industries in other countries incur lesser (or zero) costs, this may affect geographical patterns of investment, production and trade': see P. Low, G. Marceau and J. Renaud, 'The Interface between the Trade and Climate Change Regimes: Scoping the Issues', Staff Working Paper ERSD-2011-1, available at http://www.wto.org/english/res_e/reser_e/ersd201101_e.pdf.

[11] R. Leal-Arcas, *Climate Change and International Trade* (Edward Elgar Publishing, 2013), p. 93.

[12] S. Barrett, 'Climate Change and International Trade: Lessons on their Linkage from International Environmental Agreements', Centre for Trade and Economic Integration, The Graduate Institute, Geneva (Switzerland), 2010, p. 14.

[13] A. Cosbey, 'Green Industrial Policy and the World Trading System', ENTWINED Issue Brief 17, 2013, available at: http://www.iisd.org/pdf/2013/entwined_brief_green_industrial.pdf.

> renewable electricity-generating equipment, biofuels); directly address environmental problems (e.g. environmental remediation technologies); are produced in a way that is environmentally preferable to their competitors (e.g. organic agriculture).[14]

Thus trade, the traditional foe of environmental protection, has manifold ways by which to redeem itself. This chapter proposes several ways in which trade can promote climate change mitigation.

Following this introduction, section 2 of the chapter examines the TTIP in the context of sustainable development and energy, looking at the main sustainability goals and the role of the TTIP in addressing issues such as raw materials, energy efficiency and renewable energy generation. Section 3 introduces the TPP as a twenty-first century trade agreement, with a discussion of how particular provisions of its Environment chapter have affected the parties to the TPP. The section considers enforcement of the Environment chapter as well as the dimension relating to sustainable development in the leaked version of the chapter. Section 4 compares the TPP with the TTIP, followed by a conclusion in Section 5.

2. THE TRANSATLANTIC TRADE AND INVESTMENT PARTNERSHIP

2.1 An Introduction

The TTIP is a proposed RTA between the United States and the European Union and its Member States. The TTIP was first conceived in November 2011, following a US-EU Summit and the sixth meeting of the Transatlantic Economic Council.[15] Leaders asked the US-EU High Level Working Group on Jobs and Growth to identify 'policies and measures to increase US-EU trade and investment to support mutually beneficial job creation, economic growth, and international competitiveness'.[16] The

---

14 Ibid., p. 3.

15 Office of the United States Trade Representative, 'Fact Sheet: United States to Negotiate Transatlantic Trade and Investment Partnership with the European Union', 13 February 2013, available at: http://www.ustr.gov/about-us/press-office/fact-sheets/2013/february/US-EU-TTIP.

16 US-EU High Level Working Group on Jobs and Growth, 'Final Report: High Level Working Group on Jobs and Growth', 11 February 2013, p. 1, available at: http://www.ustr.gov/sites/default/files/02132013%20FINAL%20HLWG%20REPORT.pdf (citations omitted) (hereinafter Final Report: High Level Working Group on Jobs and Growth).

High Level Working Group concluded that the development of a comprehensive bilateral trade and investment agreement would provide the most benefits for the parties.[17]

Following the global recession and the financial and Eurozone crises, it was felt that an increase in the exchange of investment, goods and services would strengthen economies and create jobs.[18] Development of the TTIP is under way: the first round of negotiations took place in July 2013; the seventh finished in October 2014.[19] Talks have progressed cautiously. The parties initially aimed to conclude the TTIP by the end of 2014; however, a final deal before the 2016 US presidential election may be more likely, if at all.

The TTIP aims to further economic growth, investment and trade between the EU and US by reducing or eliminating tariffs and by removing 'behind-the-border' technical barriers to export.[20] These barriers include national regulations, standards and approval procedures that are not yet aligned and can hamper trade.[21] Strong implementation, monitoring and enforcement structures will also be needed to ensure effective implementation. The European Commission expects a €119 billion annual benefit from the TTIP, a benefit for the US of more than €95 billion annually, and a benefit for the rest of the world of almost €100 billion. The TTIP could also create hundreds of thousands of jobs.[22]

The TTIP has the potential to be a broad-ranging agreement that covers most, if not all, issues and policy goals; or contentious negotiations could lead to a moderate and weakened agreement, or even no agreement at all.[23] The outcome will depend on the dedication, focus and interests of the governments and negotiators.[24]

---

[17] Ibid.

[18] T. Barker and G. Workman, 'The Transatlantic Trade and Investment Partnership: Ambitious but Achievable,' Atlantic Council and Bertelsmann Foundation, April 2013.

[19] European Commission, 'In Focus: Transatlantic Trade and Investment Partnership Documents and Events, Negotiation Rounds – Press Material', 9 January 2015, available at: http://ec.europa.eu/trade/policy/in-focus/ttip/documents-and-events/index_en.htm#negotiation-rounds.

[20] European Commission, 'About TTIP', available at: http://ec.europa.eu/trade/policy/in-focus/ttip/about-ttip.

[21] Ibid.

[22] European Commission, 'Independent Study Outlines Benefits of EU-US Trade Agreement', available at: http://europa.eu/rapid/press-release_MEMO-13-211_en.htm.

[23] Barker and Workman, n. 18 above.

[24] Ibid, pp. 6–7.

2.2 European Union Trade Policy and Next Generation Agreements

A number of elements of EU institutional and trade policy on the environment, energy and natural resources are likely to determine its terms and goals in negotiating and developing the TTIP. Sustainable development is an explicitly stated goal of the EU within the Treaty of Lisbon,[25] and has been a part of EU policy since 2001.[26] The EU currently has its own Sustainable Development Strategy, which aims to identify and help to develop actions that allow the EU to attain its sustainable development goals through efficient resource use, realizing ecological and social innovation potential, environmental protection and, in the end, achieving prosperity.[27] The Strategy emphasizes that global solidarity will be needed to meet the challenges of sustainable development and that it is important for the EU to work in partnership with other nations of the world.[28] One operational objective within the Strategy is to '[i]nclude sustainable development concerns in all EU external policies … by making it an objective of multilateral and bilateral development cooperation'.[29]

These new challenges and objectives have reformed EU trade policy. The European Commission's Communication, 'Global Europe: Competing in the World', outlines new priorities and approaches for EU trade policy that address those concerns, including access to energy resources, protection of the environment, and sustainability.[30] The EU has also stated that its practice is to include a chapter on Trade and Sustainable Development in the RTAs that it concludes.[31] One example of such a

---

[25] Treaty of Lisbon amending the Treaty on European Union and the Treaty establishing the European Community [2007] OJ C 306/1, paras 4, 24.

[26] See Bartels (Chapter 4, this volume).

[27] European Commission, 'Renewed Sustainable Development Strategy', 15–16 June 2006, available at: http://register.consilium.europa.eu/doc/srv?l=EN&t=PDF&gc=true&sc=false&f=ST%2010917%202006%20INIT.

[28] Ibid., p. 3.

[29] Ibid., p. 21.

[30] European Commission, 'Global Europe: Competing in the World: A Contribution to the EU's Growth and Jobs Strategy', (Communication) COM(2006) 567 final.

[31] European Commission, 'EU-US Transatlantic Trade and Investment Partnership – Trade and Sustainable Development: Initial EU Position Paper', available at: http://trade.ec.europa.eu/doclib/docs/2013/july/tradoc_151626.pdf (hereinafter Trade and Sustainable Development Position Paper).

'next generation' RTA, which includes a chapter on Trade and Sustainable Development, is that between the EU and the Republic of Korea.[32] It provides an excellent point of comparison for determining what the EU may aim to include in the TTIP with the US.

With respect to TTIP negotiations, the EU has released Initial Position Papers on a number of topic areas, which include trade and sustainable development, and raw materials and energy.[33] These Position Papers state that any Trade and Sustainable Development chapter in the TTIP should cover: (i) trading in sustainable and climate friendly goods, services and technologies; (ii) sustainability assurance schemes; and (iii) corporate social responsibility standards.[34] They also state that general trade provisions, such as those on non-discrimination and the elimination of import and export duties, should apply to raw materials and energy, and any additional specific concerns related to this sector should be developed and included in the TTIP.[35] The EU is likely to offer a Trade and Sustainable Development chapter that addresses these areas; if such a chapter is not explicitly included, the EU will ensure that the same principles and protections are included elsewhere in the TTIP.[36]

Some have suggested that the Trade and Sustainable Development chapters of next generation RTAs are not as effective as they appear to be.[37] The principle of sustainable development has not been made a concrete and violable obligation.[38] In addition, the EU is not as internally coherent[39] with regard to its labour and environmental standards, and the integration of these EU standards by the Member States is what makes its RTA commitments effective.[40]

---

32 [2011] OJ L 127/6. See Croquet (Chapter 6, this volume) for an in-depth analysis of sustainable development provisions in the EU-Korea FTA.

33 European Commission, 'EU-US Transatlantic Trade and Investment Partnership – Raw Materials and Energy: Initial EU Position Paper', available at: http://trade.ec.europa.eu/doclib/docs/2013/july/tradoc_151624.pdf (hereinafter Raw Materials and Energy Position Paper).

34 Trade and Sustainable Development Position Paper, n. 31 above, pp. 2–3.

35 Raw Materials and Energy Position Paper, n. 33 above, p. 2.

36 See Bartels (Chapter 4, this volume).

37 Ibid.

38 Ibid.

39 See Damro (Chapter 2, this volume).

40 See Bartels (Chapter 4, this volume).

2.3 The TTIP and Sustainable Development

The EU and the US have each set out a number of sustainable development goals in statements regarding the TTIP, and as general trade goals.[41] Additionally, as members of the World Trade Organization (WTO), the EU, its 28 Member States and the US are committed to sustainable development, as stated in the preamble to the Agreement establishing the World Trade Organization.[42] The United Nations 2005 World Summit Outcome document introduces three pillars of sustainable development: (i) environmental protection; (ii) economic development; and (iii) social development.[43] This definition of sustainable development provides a useful framework through which to analyse the potential for the topic within the TTIP.

2.3.1 Environmental protection

In recent trade agreements concluded by the EU and the US, both entities have taken a number of steps to support environmental standards and sustainable development concerns. In the Environment chapter of its free trade agreement (RTA) with South Korea, the US encouraged high levels of protection for the environment and the application and enforcement of environmental laws; it outlined procedures to investigate alleged violations; it developed mechanisms and institutional arrangements to enhance environmental performance; and it created opportunities for cooperation and public participation.[44] The EU covered many of the same issues in its (RTA) with Korea, and stated that trade should promote

---

[41] Office of the United States Trade Representative, 'Trade and Sustainable Management of Natural Resources', Trade and Sustainable Development Position Paper, available at: http://www.ustr.gov/trade-topics/environment/trade-and-sustainable-management-natural-resources; Office of the United States Trade Representative, 'U.S. Objectives, U.S. Benefits in the Transatlantic Trade and Investment Partnership', available at: http://www.ustr.gov/about-us/press-office/press-releases/2014/March/US-Objectives-US-Benefits-In-the-TTIP-a-Detailed-View.

[42] Agreement establishing the World Trade Organization, 15 April 1994, available at: http://www.wto.org/english/docs_e/legal_e/04-wto.pdf.

[43] United Nations General Assembly, '2005 World Summit Outcome', 25 October 2005, para 48, available at: http://www.un.org/womenwatch/ods/A-RES-60-1-E.pdf.

[44] Free Trade Agreement between the United States and the Republic of Korea, Chapter 20, http://www.ustr.gov/trade-agreements/free-trade-agreements/korus-RTA/final-text (hereinafter US-Korea RTA).

sustainable development.[45] It is likely that the TTIP will contain provisions similar to those in previous Environment and Trade and Sustainable Development chapters.

Multilateral environmental agreements (MEAs) that have already been concluded by the EU and the US would be a good source of developed assessments and agreed-upon standards that could be used to unify environmental standards between the two regions. For example, an Annex to the US-Korea RTA specifically lists MEAs to which both signatories are a party.[46] The US named some MEAs in its '2014 Trade Policy Agenda and 2013 Annual Report', which cover areas that include trade in endangered species, maritime and fishery issues, ozone-depleting substances, biological diversity, hazardous wastes, biosafety and organic pollutants.[47] The EU has specified many of the same international agreements as having particular importance for trade negotiations.[48] The content, protection and guidelines in these MEAs should be integrated into the TTIP, and should be made enforceable by the parties.

The EU has specified the United Nations Framework Convention on Climate Change (UNFCCC) as one of the central MEAs that should underlie the environmental protection element of the TTIP,[49] and the US has remained involved in UNFCCC negotiations. The EU and the US should consider inclusion of the UNFCCC into any listing of MEAs, as it would help to address the growing issue of climate change mitigation and adaptation.[50]

2.3.2 Economic sustainability

Economic sustainability and development encompass the idea that business, practices and operations occur in such a way that they efficiently

---

[45] Free Trade Agreement between the European Union and its Member States, of the one part, and the Republic of Korea, of the other part [2011] OJ L127/6, Chapter 13 (hereinafter EU-Korea RTA).

[46] US-Korea RTA, n. 44 above, Annex 20-A.

[47] Office of the United States Trade Representative, '2014 Trade Policy Agenda and 2013 Annual Report of the President of the United States on the Trade Agreement Program', March 2014, p. 157, available at: http://www.ustr.gov/sites/default/files/2014%20Trade%20Policy%20Agenda%20and%202013%20Annual%20Report.pdf (hereinafter 2014 Trade Policy Agenda and 2013 Annual Report).

[48] Trade and Sustainable Development Position Paper, n. 31 above, p. 2.

[49] Ibid., p. 2.

[50] For further discussion on the link between trade and climate change, see R. Leal-Arcas, *Climate Change and International Trade* (Edward Elgar Publishing, 2013).

and responsibly use resources, while avoiding the creation of environmental concerns, but still continuing to make a profit. Facilitating trade in sustainable and green goods, technologies, information and services is an important part of creating an economically sustainable business climate in the EU and the US. It is likely that measures to encourage economic sustainability measures[51] will be included in the TTIP as both the EU and the US have mentioned it as a goal.

In the EU-Korea RTA, the EU specifically highlights the economic side of sustainable development: 'The Parties shall strive to facilitate and promote trade and foreign direct investment in environmental goods and services, including environmental technologies, sustainable renewable energy, energy efficient products and services and eco-labelled goods, including through addressing related non-tariff barriers.'[52] The Agreement also includes a term on sustainability structures and schemes that further economic sustainability: 'The Parties shall strive to facilitate and promote trade in goods that contribute to sustainable development, including goods that are the subject of schemes such as fair and ethical trade and those involving corporate social responsibility and accountability.'[53] The Environmental chapters in recent US RTAs have no parallel language, although these concepts do align with stated US trade priorities.[54]

The TTIP is likely to include an economic development term similar to that discussed above in order to promote sustainable operations and development for businesses in both regions. Sustainability assurance schemes, fair and ethical trade initiatives, corporate social responsibility concepts, and other voluntary tools could encourage these important goals, while making them a desirable element in transatlantic business practices; they should be included in the TTIP.

2.3.3 Social sustainability

Lastly, social sustainability is a core part of sustainable development. This is the idea that policies, processes and systems that support sustainable development also improve social goals such as equality, diversity and quality of life. Although a number of areas could be considered, including human rights agreements, labour standards are

---

51 That is, measures that encourage economic sustainability, such as unified standards that allow cross-border technology transfer or programmes to share research and development efforts and information.

52 EU-Korea RTA, n. 45 above, Article 13.6.2.

53 Ibid.

54 See 2014 Trade Policy Agenda and 2013 Annual Report, n. 47 above, I.8.

particularly relevant. Both parties have identified the protection of labour standards as being of importance in trade talks; this area is therefore likely to be covered in the TTIP.

The Trade and Sustainable Development chapters of recent EU RTAs highlight the value of multilateral agreements on labour standards and the goal of increasing employment.[55] It also outlines four major principles concerning fundamental rights: (i) freedom of association and collective bargaining; (ii) elimination of forced or compulsory labour; (iii) abolition of child labour; and (iv) elimination of discrimination.[56] These concepts are also tied within the agreement to the standards of the International Labour Organization (ILO).[57] Recent US RTAs also include a chapter on labour recognizing the same principles of fundamental rights and the applicability of the ILO and its policies; encouraging enforcement and public awareness of labour laws; and creating mechanisms for cooperation and consultation.[58]

The TTIP is likely to include a term similar to those in earlier EU and US RTAs, recognizing the importance of labour standards and principles of fundamental rights. It will probably refer to the ILO, of which the US and all EU countries are members. The ILO has issued non-binding resolutions, guidelines and codes of practice on a number of topics, as well as standards ratified by some Member States.[59] Publications and other documents produced by the ILO could form the basis for labour standards encouraged and enforced by the TTIP.[60]

2.4 The TTIP and Energy

2.4.1 Raw materials and natural resources

In its Final Report, the US-EU High Level Working Group on Jobs and Growth identified the raw materials and energy sector as a trade area that deserves particular attention in developing rules and modes of cooperation.[61] Energy has become a pressing issue: the increase in the

---

[55] EU-Korea RTA, n. 45 above, Article 13.4.

[56] Ibid.

[57] Ibid.

[58] US-Korea RTA, n. 44 above, Chapter 19.

[59] International Labour Organization, available at: http://www.ilo.org/global/lang–en/index.htm (accessed 26 May 2014).

[60] Beke and Hachez (Chapter 8, this volume), and Marx and Soares (Chapter 7, this volume).

[61] Final Report: High Level Working Group on Jobs and Growth, n. 16 above, p. 6.

world's population and the improvement in living standards have contributed to an increase in energy demand.[62] Governments are thinking more strategically about energy control: how to secure a supply of raw materials and energy resources, and how to emphasize green and secure generation methods.[63]

However, the trade in raw materials and energy has not been fully covered by current international trade and investment rules.[64] The EU has argued that the rules in various WTO agreements do not adequately address international trade in energy and raw materials. The WTO has strong rules regarding import barriers, but weaker rules addressing export barriers, which tend to be the complicating factor in energy trading.[65] Additionally, there is no definition of 'energy services' in the General Agreement on Trade in Services, and an absence of rules governing international trade in energy goods.[66] Finally, other complications include trade and distribution monopolies in some countries, local content requirements, and lack of transparency in licences for exploitation or trade.[67] The TTIP could address some of these gaps and issues regarding trade between the EU and the US to facilitate the movement of energy goods and services and potentially provide a model for energy trade liberalization by other international actors.[68]

One of the anticipated benefits of the TTIP is increased exports by the US of liquefied natural gas (LNG) to the EU, which would greatly benefit the region's energy strategy. Trade in LNG would reduce the EU's

---

[62] Raw Materials and Energy Position Paper, n. 33 above, p. 1. See also R. Leal-Arcas and A. Filis, 'The Fragmented Governance of the Global Energy Economy: A Legal-Institutional Analysis' (2013) 6(4) *Journal of World Energy Law and Business* 1–58; R. Leal-Arcas and A. Filis, 'Conceptualizing EU Energy Security through an EU Constitutional Law Perspective' (2013) *Fordham International Law Journal* 36(5) 1225–301; R. Leal-Arcas and A. Filis, 'The Energy Community and the Energy Charter Treaty: Special Legal Regimes, their Systemic Relationship to the EU, and their Dispute Settlement Arrangements' (2014) *Oil, Gas & Energy Law Journal* 12(2) 1–42.

[63] See generally E. Abu-Gosh and R. Leal-Arcas, 'The Conservation of Exhaustible Natural Resources in the GATT and WTO: Implications for the Conservation of Oil Resources' (2013) *The Journal of World Investment and Trade* 14(3) 480–531.

[64] Raw Materials and Energy Position Paper, n. 33 above, p. 1.

[65] Ibid.

[66] Ibid.

[67] Ibid.

[68] On the difficulties posed by the fragmented global energy governance system, see R. Leal-Arcas et al., *International Energy Governance: Selected Legal Issues* (Edward Elgar Publishing, 2014).

dependence on Russian gas,[69] thereby diversifying its portfolio of external raw materials sources. Currently, the US Department of Energy must approve each export of LNG abroad, although the process is nearly automatic when the LNG is being shipped to a country with which the US has concluded an RTA.[70] This approval process is an example of a 'behind-the-border' barrier. Becoming a preferential partner with an RTA may satisfy the EU, and no change may be needed in the US regulatory scheme to open trade. Alternatively, negotiations may encourage the US to reduce or eliminate this permitting scheme or other existing tariffs or licensing programmes, along with other barriers to export, so that energy products and raw materials may cross borders more freely.[71]

Market conditions may mean that the benefits of LNG trade that the EU expects may not materialize. Because energy prices are higher in Asia, it is possible that substantial exports to the EU will occur only when Asian demand is weak.[72] Additionally, the American Henry Hub pricing system for LNG differs markedly from the current method of pricing natural gas in the EU, which is on a local market basis.[73] European suppliers may be less interested in contracting for LNG, especially if the Henry Hub price rises above the European market price.[74] However, it would allow European suppliers to leverage the US LNG prices in negotiations with other suppliers, and some may be willing to pay a premium for the LNG if it means a preferable security of supply.[75] The TTIP has great potential to open trade in energy and raw

---

69 R. Leal-Arcas, 'The EU and Russia as Energy Trading Partners: Friends or Foes?' (2009) *European Foreign Affairs Review* 14(3) 337–66.

70 A. Walstad, 'Transatlantic Trade Negotiations Reach Second Stage', (2013) 3 (221) *Natural Gas Daily* E1.

71 On this point, see the pertinent remarks made by Mark Kantor to the OGEMID/Transnational Dispute Management community on 26 March 2014 (on file with the authors): 'Under current U.S. law there is blanket approval for the export of U.S. natural gas to countries with which the US has a RTA. Otherwise, [...] U.S. export licenses for natural gas must be granted on a case-by-case basis. Currently, the U.S. does not have a full-fledged RTA with any EU Member State. One consequence of the TTIP [...] would be to eliminate the existing US requirement of case-by-case natural gas export approvals for the 28 EU Member States.' In this sense, the TTIP would be greatly beneficial for EU energy security enhancement by minimizing the EU's dependency on Russian energy.

72 Walstad, n. 70 above.

73 Ibid.

74 Ibid.

75 Ibid.

materials, particularly LNG, but the resulting economic benefits are not guaranteed.

The EU would like to see the inclusion in the TTIP of elements of the Extractive Industries Transparency Initiative (EITI), arguing that it reflects the domestic legislation of the EU and the US.[76] The EITI is an international standard of transparency for oil, gas and mineral resources, and is developed and overseen by a coalition of actors, including governments.[77] The EITI has two tiers of participation: (i) countries that are EITI-compliant and have met all the requirements, and (ii) countries that are EITI candidates and are implementing EITI, but have not yet met all of its requirements.[78] The US is an EITI candidate country, while European countries are much less active and only a few are showing an interest in the EITI.[79] It is possible that the EITI may be integrated into the TTIP, but with the current lack of commitment from the parties it may not be an easy point for negotiators to agree upon.

2.4.2 Energy efficiency and renewable energy generation

Energy efficiency and the promotion of renewable energy are central energy policy goals for both the EU and the US. Because these technologies and product standards are closely related to the trade in green technologies, goods and services discussed above as a form of economic sustainable development,[80] the analysis and conclusions drawn in that subsection are relevant to the goal of supporting energy efficiency and renewable energy.

One way in which the TTIP could support these goals is to build upon the work of the Asia-Pacific Environmental Cooperation (APEC) Forum's List of Environmental Goods. The purpose of this list is to compile categories of products that should receive reduced tariffs because they are

---

[76] Raw Materials and Energy Position Paper, n. 33 above, p. 2.

[77] Extractive Industries Transparency Initiative, 'What is the EITI?', available at: http://eiti.org/eiti.

[78] Extractive Industries Transparency Initiative, 'EITI Countries', available at: http://eiti.org/countries.

[79] Extractive Industries Transparency Initiative, 'Other Countries', available at: http://eiti.org/countries/other.

[80] See, for instance, R. Leal-Arcas and A. Filis, 'Certain Legal Aspects of the Multilateral Trade System and the Promotion of Renewable Energy', in C.L. Lim and B. Mercurio (eds), *International Economic Law after the Crisis: A Tale of Fragmented Disciplines* (Cambridge University Press, 2014).

environmentally responsible.[81] One example is renewable energy technology, such as solar panels and wind turbines; the list also includes pollution control and environmental monitoring technologies.[82] Including a term in the TTIP that specifically sets a goal to eliminate or reduce tariffs and behind-the-border barriers covering a list of renewable energy and other green technologies inspired by the APEC's list would greatly further the goal of promoting energy efficiency and renewable energy generation.

3. THE TRANS-PACIFIC PARTNERSHIP

3.1 An Introduction

3.1.1 A twenty-first century agreement

The Trans-Pacific Partnership is a free trade agreement which is being currently negotiated amongst 12 Asia-Pacific nations – namely, the United States, Japan, Mexico, Canada, Australia, Malaysia, Chile, Singapore, Peru, Vietnam, New Zealand and Brunei Darussalam. The parties to the treaty account for 40 per cent of global GDP.[83] The TPP has been described as a 'comprehensive and high standard' free trade agreement which aims to liberalize trade in virtually all goods and services and includes commitments beyond those established in the WTO.[84] The first formal round of TPP negotiations was held in Melbourne in March 2010

---

[81] Office of the United States Trade Representative, 'APEC List of Environmental Goods: Promoting Exports, Creating Jobs, and Advancing Green Growth and Sustainable Development', available at: http://www.ustr.gov/about-us/press-office/fact-sheets/2012/september/apec-environmental-goods.

[82] Ibid.

[83] Office of the United States Trade Representative, 'Trans-Pacific Partnership Ministers Chart Path Forward on Key Issues and Confirm Next Steps on Japan's Entry', Joint Statement of TPP Ministers, 30 April 2013, available at: http://www.ustr.gov/about-us/press-office/press-releases/2013/april/joint-statement-tpp-ministers.

[84] I. Fergusson, M. McMinimy and B. Williams, 'The Trans-Pacific Partnership (TPP): Negotiations and Issues for Congress', Congressional Research Service, 20 March 2015, Summary, available at: https://www.fas.org/sgp/crs/row/R42694.pdf.

with 200 officials from Australia, the US, New Zealand, Chile, Singapore, Brunei, Peru and Vietnam.[85] Since then, several rounds of secretive negotiations have taken place, the TPP's proposed Environment chapter was leaked and there has been little public involvement. The US entered into TPP negotiations in March 2008.[86]

The TPP is the successor of the Trans-Pacific Strategic Economic Partnership Agreement, also known as the P4 Agreement, which was being negotiated by Brunei Darussalam, Chile, New Zealand and Singapore.[87] The P4 Agreement negotiations essentially matured into the TPP to accommodate the US interest of bringing in like-minded countries. The P4 is the first multiparty RTA connecting countries in Asia, Latin America and North America which aim to create a high-standard template for an ultimate free trade agreement.[88] It also pursued total liberalization in trade in goods and services.[89] While the TPP is a separate agreement, it essentially builds upon the P4 Agreement.

The TPP is touted as providing 'a new standard of global trade and incorporating next-generation issues',[90] making it a landmark '21st-century trade agreement'.[91] To validate this, the TPP seeks to not exclude sensitive sectors such as agriculture, unlike other trade agreements, and aims for zero tariffs.[92] It also has a docketing provision to progressively

---

[85] Organization of American States, Foreign Trade Information System, available at: http://www.sice.oas.org/TPD/TPP/Negotiations/Reports/Round_I_update_e.pdf.

[86] http://tppinfo.org.

[87] Ching-Wen Hsueh, 'A Greener Trade Agreement: Approaches to Environmental Issues in the TPP Negotiations' (2013) 8(2) *Asian Journal of WTO & International Health Law & Policy* 521–42, at 522.

[88] M.K. Lewis, 'The Trans-Pacific Partnership: New Paradigm or Wolf in Sheep's Clothing?' (2011) 34(27) *Boston College International & Comparative Law Review* 32–4.

[89] Ibid, pp. 32–3.

[90] United States Trade Representative (USTR), 'Outlines of the Trans-Pacific Partnership Agreement', November 2011, available at: http://www.ustr.gov/about-us/press-office/fact-sheets/2011/november/outlines-trans-pacific-partnership-agreement.

[91] The USTR explains a twenty-first century trade agreement as one which 'addresses new and emerging issues, incorporates new elements reflecting our values and priorities, and responds to the 21st century challenges our citizens face'. Among these challenges, a sustainable and healthy environment is a principal concern of the present century: see USTR, 'Trans-Pacific Partnership: Frequently Asked Questions', p. 1, available at: http://www.ustr.gov/sites/default/files/TPPFAQ.pdf.

[92] Ching-Wen Hsueh, n. 87 above, at p. 523.

include like-minded members who, however, will not take part in the negotiating process.[93] It also promotes next generation reforms in areas such as the environment and labour standards.[94] The TPP represents an example of a mega RTA, dwarfed only by the WTO.

However, the TPP negotiations are being conducted with a level of secrecy not witnessed with any previous trade agreement:[95] even US Congress has been critical about the opaqueness surrounding it.[96] Concerns exist on how a '21st-century agreement' shapes up on issues such as biodiversity, environment, labour standards and, broadly, sustainable development. Moreover, approximately only 600 'cleared advisors' representing corporations and trade blocs are privy to the negotiating process at the expense of the general public and civil society.[97]

3.1.2 The need for the Trans-Pacific Partnership

The goal of the TPP negotiation process is to create a platform for economic integration across the Asia-Pacific region. The aim is to design a high-quality agreement to establish a foundation for economic growth for the development and creation of employment in the member countries.[98] However, the agreement has been criticized deeply by the public for various reasons, especially for lack of transparency. The leaked text of the TPP's Environment chapter deals with what the 12 parties to the TPP propose in negotiations with regard to fisheries, biodiversity and climate change, as well as trade and investment in environmental goods and

---

93 M. Nash-Hoff, 'The Trans-Pacific Partnership Would Destroy our National Sovereignty', *Huffingtonpost Business, The Blog*, 3 January 2013, available at: http://www.huffingtonpost.com/michele-nashhoff/the-transpacific-partners_b_2766729.html.

94 See remarks by M. Sapiro, 'U.S. Trade Policy: Levelling the Playing Field', Remarks at the National Association of Business Economists, 25 February 2014, available at: http://iipdigital.usembassy.gov/st/english/texttrans/2014/02/20140226294123.html#axzz2wrsJHNKa.

95 WikiLeaks, 'Secret Trans-Pacific Partnership Agreement (TPP) – IP Chapter', available at: https://wikileaks.org/tpp/pressrelease.html.

96 Public Citizen, 'Congressional Democrats Escalate Criticism of Substance, Process of Obama's First Trade Pact – the Trans-Pacific Partnership', 27 June 2012, available at: http://www.citizen.org/documents/release-congressional-democrats-escalate-criticism-6-27-12.pdf.

97 W. Mauldin, 'U.S. Says Not "Rushing" Asia-Pacific Trade Deal', *The Wall Street Journal*, 26 September 2013, available at: http://online.wsj.com/news/articles/SB10001424052702303796404579099632713091994.

98 Organization of American States, Foreign Trade Information System, available at: http://www.sice.oas.org/TPD/TPP/TPP_e.ASP.

services. In the next section, we analyse whether the Environment chapter of the TPP manages to introduce sustainable twenty-first century environmental standards.

3.2 The Environment Chapter

The importance of conserving the environment for well-being on Earth has been universally recognized and various agreements have been concluded to curb environmental harm. These agreements are created also with a view to limit damage caused to future generations. In this context, the TPP includes an Environment chapter, of which WikiLeaks released a draft version. Article SS.1 of the leaked draft chapter reads as follows:

> Article SS.1: Definitions
>
> For purposes of this Chapter:
>
> **environmental law** means any statute or regulation of a Party, or provision thereof, including any that implement its obligations under a multilateral environmental agreement, the primary purpose of which is the protection of the environment, or the prevention of a danger to human life or health, through:
>
> (a) the prevention, abatement, or control of the release, discharge, or emission of pollutants or environmental contaminants;
> (b) the control of environmentally hazardous or toxic chemicals, substances, materials, and wastes, and the dissemination of information related thereto; or
> (c) the protection or conservation of wild flora or fauna, including endangered species, their habitat, and specially protected natural areas[99,100]
>
> but does not include any statute or regulation, or provision thereof, directly related to worker safety or health, nor any statute or regulation, or provision thereof, the primary purpose of which is managing the subsistence or aboriginal harvesting of natural resources.[101]

---

[99] 'Specially protected natural areas' – as defined by the party in its legislation.

[100] The parties recognize that such protection or conservation may include the protection or conservation of biological diversity.

[101] WikiLeaks, 'Environment Chapter of the TPP', Consolidated Text, 24 November 2013, available at: https://wikileaks.org/tpp2/static/pdf/tpp-treaty-environment-chapter.pdf (hereinafter Draft TPP).

The definition notably excludes sensible management of existing natural resources and aboriginal management of resources, including traditional knowledge, culture and genetic resources.

'Environmental law' is a vast term and the above definition does not do it justice. The United Nations Environment Programme provides a brief summary of issues which could be covered within the ambit of environmental law.[102] It states that it is 'a system of complex and interlocking statutes, common law, treaties, conventions, regulations and policies which seek to protect the natural environment which may be affected, impacted or endangered by human activities'.[103] It also states that environmental law as a distinct system arose in the 1960s in major industrial economies and that it has been 'seen as a critical means of promoting sustainable development'.[104] Moreover, environmental policy principles such as the polluter-pays principle, the precautionary principle and environmental justice have played a major role in environmental law reforms.

While trade is important and inevitable, it cannot come at the cost of sustainable development, which touches upon all aspects of human well-being, including the social, economic and environmental aspects.

3.2.1 The need for an Environment chapter

The leaked Environment chapter of the TPP consists of 18 articles which deal with various issues such as multilateral environmental agreements, corporate social responsibility, mechanisms to enhance environmental performance, cooperation frameworks, trade and climate change, and trade and biodiversity, among others. Various articles deal with the environment, trade and sustainable development. According to the first paragraph of Article SS.2 of the draft chapter, the objectives of the Environment chapter are to promote mutually supportive trade and environment policies, implement a high level of environmental protection, enforce environmental laws, and enhance the capacities of the parties to address trade-related environmental issues through cooperation. The second paragraph states that cooperation among the parties to the TPP to protect the environment and manage their natural resources in a sustainable manner strengthens their environmental governance. The third

---

102 See http://www.unep.org/training/programmes/Instructor%20Version/Part_2/Activities/Interest_Groups/Decision-Making/Core/Environmental_Law_Definitions_rev2.pdf.

103 Ibid.

104 Ibid.

paragraph expressly mentions that it is inappropriate to use environmental legislation to restrict trade or investment between the parties to the TPP. This seems to suggest that environmental protection should not come at the cost of economic growth.

Article SS.3 refers to general commitments and emphasizes the importance of the protection of the environment in a way that it mutually supports both trade and the environment in the context of sustainable development. According to Article SS.3.4, all parties to the TPP must enforce their environmental laws in a manner so as to not affect trade or investment between the parties. On a careful reading of this paragraph, it can be seen that the drafters of the agreement have emphasized trade and investment over the environment and the effect that trade can have on the environment.

The Montreal Protocol is mentioned in Article SS.4 of the draft text. The depletion of the ozone layer has been an alarming cause of concern since the first hole in the ozone layer was found in 1985 in Antarctica.[105] This discovery startled the world and triggered the enforcement of many international treaties and national laws upholding the need for sustainable development.

3.2.2 Enforcement of the Environment chapter

The TPP provides certain procedural measures to enforce the protection of the environment.[106] It also talks about the establishment of arbitral tribunals to decide matters of dispute that may arise.[107] Furthermore, the TPP dictates that each party shall make use of or establish consultative mechanisms, such as national advisory committees, in order to regulate the proper implementation of the TTP's Environment chapter.[108] Article SS.10 deals with the importance of cooperation in striking a balance between sustainable development, on the one hand, and trade and investment, on the other. Yet, this provision, though useful, does not mention the ways and means in which this balance can be reached. The agreement is also not strong enough on the enforcement mechanism. For parties to take this agreement seriously, there should be certain stringent provisions. The TPP draft text does not mention the consequences that parties may suffer if they breach any article in the Environment chapter.

105 C. Andre and M. Velasquez, 'Ozone Debate: Environmentalists and Business Collide – Again', available at: https://www.scu.edu/ethics/publications/iie/v3n1/ozone.html.

106 Draft TPP, n. 101 above, Article SS.5.

107 Ibid., Article SS.12.4.

108 Ibid., Article SS.6.

Domestic regulations Article SS.9 of the draft TPP refers to various voluntary mechanisms to enhance environmental performance, which should be designed in a way that maximizes the environmental benefits of the parties and avoids unnecessary technical barriers to trade. However, terms such as 'voluntary' and 'avoidance of unnecessary barriers to trade' dilute the entire process. 'Voluntary' mechanisms would lead to a regulatory race to the bottom. The voluntary mechanisms include auditing, reporting and the sharing of information and expertise.[109] These mechanisms help to educate and ensure transparency and help in capacity building, essential for any new-age trade agreement. Furthermore, none of the 12 countries negotiating the agreement can be classified as a least developed country; they would therefore be in a position to introduce such measures over a progressive time-bound period. These mechanisms could also be helpful for potential investors, a constant fear among whom is arbitrary penalization in the garb of public policy legislation, including environmental. Audit reports from independent and reliable organizations could be a real asset for future dispute settlements.

Article SS.11 states that each party is to designate senior government representatives as a national contact point responsible for the implementation of the TPP's Environment chapter. Article SS.12 deals with consultation and dispute resolution in the event of conflict between the parties. These obligations on the parties to formulate committees and enforce either direct or indirect laws may bring slight changes in the domestic regulation of the parties to the agreement. However, if the domestic regulations are framed in such a way as to pursue trade and investment while keeping the environment and sustainability in mind, this particular chapter will prove to be beneficial to society as a whole, in spite of it placing a burden on the parties to introduce new domestic laws and regulations.

Corporations and sustainability Sustainability is an important consideration for corporations in dealing with trade and investment. Corporations play an important role in economic and social development: they should use natural resources with the utmost care and generate less waste so as to provide for present and future generations. In the TPP's Environment chapter, trade and investment are mentioned several times as is the notion of corporate social responsibility (in Article SS.8). According to this article, parties to the TPP should encourage enterprises operating within their territory or jurisdiction to adopt voluntarily their

---

[109] Ibid., Article SS.9(1).

policies and principles of corporate social responsibility related to the environment, in accordance with internationally recognized standards and guidelines.[110] The wording of Article SS.8 is important for achieving sustainable development. Moreover, Articles SS.2 and SS.3, regarding the objectives and general commitments of the TPP, emphasize the importance of mutually supportive trade and environment policies in promoting sustainable development.

However, there is no mention of any particular stringent actions in the event of failing to implement these provisions. Moreover, Article SS.4(1) and (2), on multilateral environmental agreements, emphasizes the importance of 'mutual supportiveness between trade and environment laws and policies' between the parties to the TPP on trade and environment issues, whereas the third paragraph offers any TPP party whose trade or investment is affected as a result of another TPP party failing to comply with its treaty obligations under an MEA the ability to request the establishment of a committee to consider the matter.

3.3 The TPP and Sustainable Development

3.3.1 Trade and biodiversity

While the role of conservation and sustainable use of biological diversity in achieving sustainable development is recognized,[111] the Environment chapter is committed only to promoting and encouraging such sustainable use, including the fair and equitable sharing of benefits, without making binding commitments. A major weakness of the provision is the fact of not requiring the consent of, and including in the benefit-sharing mechanisms, local communities who are engaged in the preservation of biodiversity and genetic resources. At present, only the parties' consent is required.[112] This seems to be against the United Nations Declaration on the Rights of Indigenous People (UNDRIP).[113] Moreover, any cooperation in the preservation of biodiversity is not absolute, but only in areas of mutual interest of the parties.[114] This cherry-picking, however, does not seem to be a sustainable model.

---

[110] Ibid., Article SS.8.

[111] Ibid., Article SS.13(1).

[112] Ibid., Article SS.13(5).

[113] UN General Assembly, United Nations Declaration on the Rights of Indigenous Peoples (UNDRIP), adopted by the General Assembly, 2 October 2007, UN Doc. No. A/RES/61/295, Article 31.

[114] Draft TPP, n. 101 above, Article 13(7).

These provisions are weak when compared with rules in other chapters of the TPP, including Intellectual Property, which would enable the commercial exploitation of biodiversity.[115] Reports suggest that four countries (Malaysia, Peru, Vietnam and Brunei) wish to extend the gains from using derivatives of genetic materials to the local communities.[116] This, however, faces opposition from the US and New Zealand.[117] Another concern is that, while parties to the TPP have the sovereign right to determine access to their genetic resources[118] and to share the gains from their utilization,[119] a US counter-proposal seeks to remove these provisions.[120] Furthermore, the US proposal also attacks the rights of indigenous and local communities to maintain their traditional knowledge and practices by substituting 'commitment', as it appears in Article SS.13(3) of the draft TPP, with 'recognize the importance'.[121] However, on a positive note, the US proposal makes conservation and sustainable biological diversity use mandatory.[122]

3.3.2 Trade and climate change

Considering the presence of the US (which is the only country that has not ratified the Kyoto Protocol), it is significant that the leaked draft text recognizes climate change as a global concern and the importance of implementing commitments under the UNFCCC/Kyoto Protocol.[123] However, the various mitigation and adaptation measures identified under Article SS.15(3) would only be in the form of 'cooperation on the

---

115 Jane Kelsey, 'TPPA Environment Chapter & Chair's Commentary Posted by WikiLeaks: Issues for NZ', 16 January 2014, available at: https://wikileaks.org/tppa-environment-chapter.html.

116 This request is consistent with Article 5 of the Nagoya Protocol.

117 Kelsey, n. 115 above.

118 Draft TPP, n. 101 above, Article SS.13(4).

119 Ibid., Article SS.13(2).

120 C. Taverner, 'A Low Standard of Ambition at TPP Talks: Corporations Oust Environmentalists from the Negotiating Table', *Georgetown International Environmental Law Review Blog*, 6 March 2014, available at: http://gielr.wordpress.com/2014/03/06/a-low-standard-of-ambition-at-tpp-talks-corporations-oust-environmentalists-from-the-negotiating-table.

121 Article SS.X(4) of the draft text of the TPP Environment Chapter of 14 February 2014, not to be confused with the 24 November 2013 Environment Chapter consolidated text of the TPP. The text of 14 February 2014 is available at: http://www.redge.org.pe/sites/default/files/20140218%20biodiversity%20climate%20change%20TPP.pdf.

122 Ibid., Article SS.X(2).

123 On the position of the US regarding the Kyoto Protocol, see generally Leal-Arcas, n. 11 above, Chapter 5.

complementary, trade-related, aspects of these efforts in areas of mutual interest', subject to domestic capabilities.[124] Strikingly, the locution 'areas of mutual interest' curtails cooperation significantly, and no clarification or interpretation of its ambit exists. Furthermore, while it is agreed that multiple economic and environmental policy measures exist in dealing with climate change, the draft text limits the discussion to only 'relevant and appropriate' occasions, instead of making it a continuous process.[125] Significantly, under Article SS.15(6), the parties agree to take cooperative and capacity building measures to implement their Asia-Pacific Economic Cooperation commitments, including crucial discussions on reducing fossil fuel subsidies. It is to be noted that the US counter-proposal has attempted to even forgo the term 'climate change' by substituting it with 'low-emissions economy'[126] and, moreover, it has removed any reference to the UNFCCC. Furthermore, the term 'adaptation' is no longer to be found in the US draft, which means that anticipation and acting upon future climate change effects would not be within the purview of the TPP were the US draft to be accepted.

3.3.3 Marine fisheries

Provisions in the TPP to regulate fishing are littered with half-hearted measures, such as the requirement that parties 'shall seek' the setting up of a fishing management system[127] and affirm commitment towards preventing maritime pollution.[128] This is in spite of the recognition that parties are the major consumers, producers and traders of fisheries[129] and that overfishing is a global problem. Depletion of fishing stocks will also have an immediate impact on their livelihood and on the economies of these countries; non-binding obligations are therefore futile.

Furthermore, fishing subsidies are prohibited only in respect 'over-fished'[130] stocks and vessels listed for illegal, unreported or unregulated (IUU) fishing,[131] instead of for *all* stocks, where parties shall make 'best efforts' – a legally vague and unenforceable term. Such a prohibition may

---

[124] Draft TPP, n. 101 above, Article SS.13(3).

[125] Ibid., Article SS.15(4).

[126] See US Counter-proposal to the TPP Environment Chapter, 14 February, 2014, available at: http://www.redge.org.pe/sites/default/files/20140218%20bio diversity%20climate%20change%20TPP.pdf.

[127] Draft TPP, n. 101 above, Article SS.16(3).

[128] Ibid., Article SS.16(5).

[129] Ibid., Article SS.16(1).

[130] Ibid., Article SS.16(6)(a).

[131] Ibid., Article SS.16(6)(b).

not be effective, as most subsidies will most likely not be specifically targeted to overfished species.[132] The US has proposed that the subsidies that target the fishing of overfished stocks (Article SS.16(6)(a)) be framed in such a way that *all* overfished stocks are targeted.[133] Furthermore, subsidies are allowed also for capacity-building of non-overfished stocks. While developmental considerations influence this, a better solution would be to restrict such subsidies only to small-scale industries.[134]

It is surprising that, in relation to IUU fishing, TPP parties are merely required to 'endeavor to improve cooperation'.[135] In the absence of binding dispute resolution mechanisms, no remedy exists where fish stocks are sourced using IUU methods.

3.3.4 Trade and conservation

Article SS.17 deals with international trade in forest, wildlife and living marine resources. The text in Article SS.17(2) states that each party to the TPP 'affirms its commitment' to ensure that international trade in flora and fauna does not harm other species by implementing its obligations under the Convention on International Trade in Endangered Species of Wild Fauna and Flora[136] but, with the exception of the US, no other country agrees to any enforceable dispute resolution system on this issue;[137] nor is trade carried out in violation of laws designed to protect flora, fauna and lumber obligatorily curtailed.[138]

---

[132] Sierra Club, World Wildlife Fund and Natural Resources Defense Council, 'Analysis of Leaked Environment Chapter Consolidated Text', 15 January 2014, p. 3, 15 January 2014, available at: http://action.sierraclub.org/site/DocServer/TPP_Enviro_Analysis.pdf?docID=14842.

[133] Ibid.

[134] A.G. Mulgan, 'Why Japan is Lagging on the TPP', *East Asia Forum*, 30 May 2012, available at: http://www.eastasiaforum.org/2012/05/30/why-japan-is-lagging-on-the-tpp.

[135] Draft TPP, n. 101 above, Article SS.16(14).

[136] 12 ILM 1085 (1973).

[137] Sierra Club et al., n. 132 above, p. 4.

[138] Draft TPP, n. 101 above, Article SS.17(5).

4. COMPARING THE TPP WITH THE TTIP ON SUSTAINABLE DEVELOPMENT

4.1 Scope

On the basis of the leaked draft, one can conclude that the TPP is fundamentally a trade agreement with a mollifying Environment chapter. Article SS.2(1) states that the objective of the Environment chapter is to 'promote mutually supportive trade and environment policies; promote high levels of environmental protection and effective enforcement of environmental laws; and enhance the capacities of the Parties to address trade-related environmental issues [...]'.[139] The draft chapter also recognizes the perils of encouraging trade and investments at the expense of weak environmental provisions.[140]

However, in practice this enlightenment remains merely aspirational. Article SS.2(3) proscribes using environmental legislation as a disguised restriction on trade and investment. The provision appears to be vague and broad in the absence of determining tests for 'disguised restrictions'. Further, in order to have a healthy co-existence of trade and environmental provisions, a sound enforcement mechanism is essential, which is completely absent across the agreement. For example, under Article SS.4(3), any non-compliance by parties who are signatories of any MEA will be scrutinized only where such non-compliance affects their trade and investments. Various other provisions of the Environment chapter also reiterate trade promotion as the ultimate objective of the TPP, in spite of the recognition of urgent environmental challenges that the parties face.[141]

Consider this in comparison with the United States-Peru Trade Promotion Agreement (PTPA), under which parties have an obligation to enforce MEAs listed in the agreement[142] and to ensure no violation of obligations provided under that treaty.[143] Equally, as of May 2014, the

---

139 Draft TPP, n. 101 above.

140 Draft TPP, n. 101 above, Article SS.3(6). Accordingly, no retrospective dilution of environmental laws is encouraged in order to strengthen trade and investments.

141 Ibid., Article SS.15.3.

142 United States-Peru Trade Promotion Agreement (PTPA), adopted 12 April 2006, in force 1 February 2009, Article 18.2.

143 Ibid., Articles 18.3.2 and 18.3.3.

insertion of a chapter on energy trade in the TTIP was under consideration, given that energy security, in the context of sustainable development, is not simply a transatlantic issue, but one of global concern.

4.2 Enforcement

In the context of the TTIP, but also more broadly, the EU makes it clear that it 'wants its trade policy to support economic growth, social development, and environmental protection. Coherence and mutual supportiveness [...] are the basis for achieving sustainable development'.[144] On a close look at the draft TPP Environment chapter, there seem to be no provisions regarding enforcement, while in the case of the TTIP both economies have shown a clear interest in having provisions aimed at the enforcement of laws and regulations in a coherent manner.

On 26 June 2006, the Council of the European Union launched its Renewed Sustainable Development Strategy.[145] This strategy sets out the regulations with regard to sustainable development that is to govern all EU policies and activities. The strategy further states that the main challenge is to gradually change the 'current unsustainable consumption and production patterns and the non-integrated approach to policy-making'.[146] On a close inspection of the TPP, it can be seen that sustainable development has been given little importance in comparison, in spite of its inextricable link with the environment.

The EU report further emphasizes the reduction of environmental pollution and promotes sustainable development so as to break the link between economic growth and environmental degradation.[147] It further sets out policy guidelines to make better laws and regulations with regard to sustainable development, including the involvement of individuals and businesses in formulating laws, ways to make the polluter pay, and the need to adopt the precautionary principle.[148] It also talks about the Lisbon Strategy,[149] the aim of which is to make Europe 'the most competitive and dynamic knowledge-based economy in the world, capable of sustainable economic growth with more and better jobs and

---

[144] European Commission, 'Sustainable Development', available at: http://ec.europa.eu/trade/policy/policy-making/sustainable-development.

[145] Council of the European Union, 'Review of the EU Sustainable Development Strategy', 10917/06, 26 June 2006.

[146] Ibid., p. 2.

[147] Ibid., p. 3.

[148] Ibid., p. 6.

[149] Ibid.

greater social cohesion'.[150] In contrast, the TPP has not included many provisions in its Environment chapter.

4.3 Dispute Resolution

The TPP was touted as a twenty-first century trade agreement. A major requirement under such an agreement is the inclusion of strong, enforceable environmental provisions.[151] In fact, this has been a recognized position under earlier bilateral agreements between some TPP members, especially those involving the US. Resulting from a bipartisan consensus between US Congress and President G.W. Bush signed in 2007, all US trade agreements were intended to have an enforceable environmental chapter. Therefore, the US-Korea RTA and the PTPA include binding obligations to meet commitments under MEAs, where disputes would be settled through arbitration if such obligations fail.[152]

Under the TPP, however, parties have no obligation to enforce any environmental commitment under the Environment chapter. While the dispute resolution process is multi-layered,[153] and includes an arbitral tribunal,[154] the arbitration report is merely recommendatory in value, as is the case in commercial arbitration.[155] In fact, parties 'shall endeavor' to agree on a 'mutually satisfactory action plan' following the report.[156] Therefore, even if recourse is agreed to, a requesting party may have to agree to a compromise in the event of a serious environmental violation. If indeed a 'satisfactory' solution is all that is to be gained from the dispute settlement, spending time and money on arbitration is utterly unnecessary. In any case, where such recourse is refused, there are no other avenues available.

In the context of the TTIP, the EU Commission is very keen to have a strong investor-state dispute settlement (ISDS) system, as it considers the protection of EU investors in the US to be a crucial element of the TTIP.

---

150 Lisbon European Council, Presidency Conclusions, 23–24 March 2000.

151 Natural Resource Defence Council, 'Green Groups: Leaked Trans-Pacific Partnership Environment Chapter Unacceptable', Press Release, available at: http://www.nrdc.org/media/2014/140115.asp.

152 US-Korea RTA, n. 44 above, Article 20.9.3(a)–(b) and 20.9.6(a)–(c). See also Articles 21(2) and (4) of the PTPA, n. 142 above.

153 Draft TPP, n. 101 above, Article SS.12(1) (Environment consultations); Article SS.12(2) (Senior Representative consultations); Article SS.12(3) (Ministerial consultation).

154 Ibid., Article SS.12(4).

155 Ibid., Article SS.12(5).

156 Ibid., Article SS.12(12).

This notion comes from the fact that if EU investors may not have the right to appear before local US courts or local US courts cannot deal with an EU claim because of differences in judicial culture, they would have no forum before which to bring a legal action for compensation. It is in this sense that the EU Commission wishes to include an ISDS provision in the TTIP.[157] In the specific case of sustainable development, if the parties disagree it would be necessary to find a dispute settlement mechanism such as government consultations and impartial third-party assessments.[158]

4.4 Implementation

While Article SS.4(1) of the draft TPP considers the implementation of MEAs to be critical, it does not insist on a binding dispute resolution system for non-compliance;[159] it merely notes that each party 'affirms its commitment to implement' the MEAs to which it is a party.[160] Furthermore, a major challenge under the TPP is the absence of a list of MEAs to which parties affirm commitment. This is a conscious omission, considering the divergent interests across the board in respect of signed MEAs. For example, it is well known that the US opposes the current commitments under the Kyoto Protocol to reduce greenhouse gas emissions as they stand; the Americans are also not party to the Convention on Biological Diversity, which grants indigenous people rights over their genetic resources and biodiversity; nor have they – along with Australia, New Zealand, and Canada – signed the United Nations Declaration on the Rights of Indigenous Peoples.[161] These positions are in tune with the political and economic compromises that such MEAs represent.

In the TTIP context, both economies are committed to the effective domestic implementation of labour and environmental standards.[162] For that to happen, the EU's view is that 'an effective mechanism should be based on transparency, regular dialogue, and close cooperation between the Parties' on any matter related to sustainable development.[163]

---

157 See EU Commission, 'Why is the EU Including Investor to State Dispute Settlement in the TTIP?', TTIP, Questions and Answers, available at http://ec.europa.eu/trade/policy/in-focus/ttip/questions-and-answers.

158 Trade and Sustainable Development Position Paper, n. 31 above, p. 4.

159 Draft TPP, n. 101 above, Article SS.4(3), footnote 4.

160 Ibid., Article SS.4.1.

161 UNDRIP, n. 113 above.

162 Trade and Sustainable Development Position Paper, n. 31 above, p. 2.

163 Ibid., p. 4.

4.5 Sovereign Determination in Legislation

A further challenge of a twenty-first century agreement is the leeway given to sovereign determination while enacting environmental laws.[164] It is essential to understand that the rhetoric of developed/developing countries has not progressed. At the same time, in the absence of any such limitations in the Investment chapter of the TPP, any environmental legislation that confers a higher standard of protection compared with existing international standards may be deemed to be too restrictive with respect to a twenty-first century agreement. This situation may invite the attention of the dreaded investor-state dispute settlement process under the Investment chapter. Some clarification would be required with respect to interpretation of the Environment and Investment chapters.

In the context of the TTIP, the EU and the US are committed to high levels of environmental protection in order to reach 'a comprehensive and ambitious approach to trade and sustainable development issues'.[165] Moreover, in the chapters on trade and sustainable development in its earlier RTAs, the EU has tried to ensure that 'increased trade is mutually supporting environmental protection'.[166] As in the case of the TPP, the EU would like the TTIP to provide each party with the 'right to regulate in order to reflect its own sustainable development priorities'[167] – in other words, recognizing each party's right to define and regulate its own domestic levels of environmental protection as they deem necessary.[168]

5. CONCLUSION

With regard to the TTIP, one of the complaints as negotiation talks have progressed is that the process is not sufficiently transparent, and does not satisfactorily include public comment. Various elements have been built into the development of the TTIP to assuage these grievances, including: (i) the publication of negotiating objectives prior to each round; (ii) on the US side, the creation of a Public Interest Trade Advisory Committee to provide expert input; and (iii) on the EU side, public comment periods. The TTIP, however, has the potential to become a highly successful and influential RTA, with its terms possibly becoming a model structure for

---

164 Draft TPP, n. 101 above, Article SS.3(2).

165 Trade and Sustainable Development Position Paper, n. 31 above, p. 1.

166 Ibid., p. 2.

167 Ibid.

168 Ibid.

future trade negotiations. The EU and the US have a great opportunity to encourage and facilitate sustainable development, green technologies, renewable energy, and increased trade in raw materials and energy; this chapter has discussed ways in which the TTIP can achieve this. It has yet to be seen whether the parties will prioritize these environmental and energy goals, whether such terms could be successful, or whether the TTIP can be successfully concluded at all. TTIP talks have continued to progress through several rounds, and leaders from the EU and US are reaffirming an aim to conclude negotiations by the end of 2015. However, concluding the TTIP by such a date seems unlikely.

As for the TPP, upon a close inspection of the above mentioned articles of its Environment chapter, the emphasis seems to have been given to trade and investment over environmental considerations. Article SS.3(1)–(3) deals with general commitments and places importance on mutually supportive trade and environmental policies, as well as on the protection of the environment with a view to sustainable development. Further, the article states that the parties' domestic laws will be for the betterment of the environment. However, upon an examination of paragraphs (4) and (6), it becomes apparent that there is a contradiction, as at first paragraph (4) mentions that environmental law must not be drafted in such a way as to hamper trade and investment, while paragraph (6) states the opposite.

The insertion of the Montreal Protocol in Article SS.4.4 is important with respect to sustainability. Article SS.6 deals with setting up national advisory committees for the implementation of the Environment chapter. To establish a committee, certain changes have to be made in the domestic laws of the respective countries. Setting up a committee also requires funds and resources, which would certainly affect developing countries, since they are economically less healthy than developed economies. Even Article SS.11 talks about establishing an 'Environment Committee', comprising senior government representatives, or their designees, of the relevant trade and environmental authorities of each party to the TPP responsible for the implementation of the chapter. This again places an additional burden on the parties.

The TPP's Environment chapter demonstrates a lack of clarity with regard to the environment and sustainability. Even though the TPP's main purpose is trade liberalization and investment protection, there is less focus on the environment and sustainability in the chapter that was specifically drafted to protect the environment. While the Environment chapter touches upon crucial areas of environmental protection that can pave the way for future talks, it does not inspire. Furthermore, the TPP seems to be facing obstacles, and parties still seem to be indecisive on crucial matters.

Finally, can the TTIP learn any lessons from the TPP? There are currently no textual proposals available for either the sustainable development or energy and raw materials provisions in the TTIP; therefore, it is hard to determine whether TTIP negotiators are managing to avoid the weaknesses in and obstacles seen with the TPP. Fact sheets on the subject issued by the European Commission indicate a continued dedication towards the principles of environment and sustainability. The development of unified standards for goods and trade is central to making the TTIP an effective trade agreement, given the already comparatively low barriers to trade between the US and EU. These standards will help to ensure that environmental and sustainability provisions in the TTIP are not mere aspirational statements, but are effective and enforceable provisions that advance these goals. It therefore seems that RTAs, while conducive to greater trade liberalization, face the same concerns as multilateral trade agreements when it comes to the environment and sustainable development. It is hoped that the human race as a whole will eventually learn to move beyond short-term gains.

6. The climate change norms under the EU-Korea Free Trade Agreement: between soft and hard law

Nicolas A.J. Croquet*

1. INTRODUCTION

The European Union (EU or Union), 27 of its Member States and the Republic of Korea (the Contracting Parties) signed a Free Trade Agreement (FTA) on 6 October 2010 (the EU-Korea FTA or the Agreement), which was intended to have unlimited duration.[1] This regional trade agreement (RTA) provisionally entered into force on 1 July 2011 pending the Member States' ratification thereof.[2] The signing of the EU-Korea FTA was preceded by the adoption of the Framework Agreement for Trade and Cooperation between the EU, its Member States and South Korea of 10 May 2010 (the 2010 Cooperation Agreement).[3]

* The author wishes to thank Dr Rebecca Brubaker, Mr Giles Chappell, Dr Axel Marx and Professor Jan Wouters as well as the editors of Edward Elgar Publishing and the KU Leuven Centre for Global Governance Studies for their editorial assistance and substantive suggestions.

[1] Free Trade Agreement between the European Union and its Member States, of the one part, and the Republic of Korea, of the other part [2011] OJ L 127/6, art 15.11. Croatia, although not an original signee of the EU-Korea FTA, acceded to the Agreement on 1 July 2013. See <http://ec.europa.eu/trade/policy/countries-and-regions/countries/south-korea/> accessed 6 August 2015.

[2] Commission, 'Report from the Commission to the European Parliament and the Council: Annual Report on the Implementation of the EU-Korea Free Trade Agreement', COM(2013) 100 final 2.

[3] Framework Agreement between the European Union and its Member States, of the one part, and the Republic of Korea (entry into force 1 June 2014) [2013] OJ L20/2.

Despite the EU-Korea FTA being presented as embodying a novel type of RTA because of its comprehensive nature,[4] its direct climate change provisions (in Chapter 13) still enjoy a low degree of hard law normativity as a result of their generality, looseness, and policy-oriented and conditional language. This low degree of hard law normativity is confirmed by the provision of a non-adjudicatory dispute settlement mechanism limited to consultations and an institutionalized form of mediation.

The high level of soft law or the low level of hard law normativity that characterizes the EU-Korea FTA's direct climate change provisions stands in contrast with and is counterbalanced by the higher level of hard law normativity attached to its indirect climate change provisions: (i) trade-furthering provisions with respect to environmental goods and energy services; (ii) trade-restricting provisions in the name of listed environmental protection grounds or of a legitimate objective; and (iii) good administration principles, defence rights and transparency standards broadly understood.

This difference in the soft law/hard law continuum between the two series of climate change provisions, however, should not and does not prevent normative interactions between them. Chapter 13 of the EU-Korea FTA produces various spillover effects on the FTA's indirect climate change provisions by informing the interpretation of those provisions on environmental goods and energy services that enjoy specific tariff concessions and market access commitments, by shedding light on the meaning attached to the general exceptions to the liberalization of trade in goods or services or to freedom of establishment, by informing the notion of 'legitimate objective' under the Technical Barriers to Trade (TBT) chapter, and by triggering good administration principles, transparency standards and defence rights in the administration of climate change legislation.

---

[4] Commission, 'Proposal for a Council Decision Authorising the Signature and Provisional Application of the Free Trade Agreement between the European Union and its Member States and the Republic of Korea', COM(2010) 136 final 3; Commission's DG Trade, 'The EU-Korea Free Trade Agreement in Practice', Brussels 2011, 3; Der-Chin Horng, 'Reshaping the EU's FTA Policy in a Globalizing Economy: The Case of the EU-Korea FTA' (2012) 46(2) *Journal of World Trade* 301, 304.

2. CONTEXT FOR THE INTEGRATION OF CLIMATE CHANGE CONSIDERATIONS WITHIN THE EU-KOREA FTA

In its 2006 Renewed EU Sustainable Development Strategy, the Council of the EU insisted on the need for the European Commission (the Commission) and the EU Member States to increase efforts to use international trade as a means towards pursuing 'genuine global sustainable development'.[5] The Council encouraged the EU to make environmental standards more ambitious when concluding regional and bilateral trade or cooperation agreements with non-EU countries.[6] In its Communication entitled 'Global Europe: Competing in the World' ('Global Europe' Communication), the Commission, while confirming its commitment to multilateral trade negotiations, conveyed its interest in furthering international trade rules by addressing policy issues that are not yet conducive to negotiations at the multilateral level (such as investment, public procurement and competition).[7] The Commission insisted that, in order to be successful, FTAs had to be comprehensive in their scope and to govern trade-related disciplines beyond or to a higher extent than those already regulated by the World Trade Organization (WTO) agreements.[8] For the Commission, 'new competitiveness-driven FTAs would need to be comprehensive and ambitious in coverage, aiming at the highest possible degree of trade liberalisation including far-reaching liberalisation of services and investment'.[9] The Commission announced that, at the same time, bilateral trade relationships had to better reflect concerns for sustainable development, for instance, through the incorporation of 'new co-operative provisions in areas relating to labour standards and environmental protection'.[10] In an Annex to the 'Global Europe' Communication, the Commission argued that '[t]rade in environmentally friendly

---

[5] Council of the EU, 'Review of the EU Sustainable Development Strategy – Renewed Strategy', Document 10117/06, 21.

[6] Ibid 21.

[7] Commission, Communication from the Commission to the Council, the European Parliament, the European Economic and Social Committee and the Committee of the Regions, 'Global Europe: Competing in the World: A Contribution to the EU's Growth and Jobs Strategy', COM(2006) 567 final 8.

[8] Ibid 8.

[9] Ibid 9.

[10] Ibid 9.

products should be encouraged and the EU should promote the use of best available technologies both in bilateral and multilateral trade agreements'.[11]

The EU political institutions, in designing their 'new approach' to external trade policy, may have been influenced by the Organisation for Economic Co-operation and Development's 2007 Report on Environment and Regional Trade Agreements (OECD Report).[12] This report indicates that those RTAs by which OECD Members are bound regulate environmental measures in three main ways: (i) as mere exceptions to the substantive trade provisions; (ii) as part of a separate chapter from the substantive trade provisions or of a side agreement; or (iii) in a way that reconciles or combines aspects of the above two methods (a mixed method).[13] The EU and the Republic of Korea have reflected all three methods of regulation referred to by the OECD in the elaboration and drafting of the EU-Korea FTA (through its climate change policy framework and its trade-furthering and trade-restricting provisions)[14] and of the 2010 Cooperation Agreement (through its generic provisions on respectively energy, transport, environment and natural resources, and climate change viewed as a block).[15]

The EU-Korea FTA is not novel as regards the consideration of climate change and environmental concerns. Before the conclusion of the EU-Korea FTA, the EU had already signed several RTAs covering climate change, many of which have expressly included climate change topics such as those related to renewable energy, energy efficiency or the implementation of the Kyoto Protocol.[16] They have addressed these

---

[11] Commission, Commission Staff Working Document, Annex to the Communication from the Commission to the Council, the European Parliament, the European Economic and Social Committee and the Committee of the Regions, 'Global Europe: Competing in the World – A Contribution to the EU's Growth and Jobs Strategy', SEC(2006) 1230, 25.

[12] Rok Zvelc, 'Environmental Integration in EU Trade Policy', in Elisa Morgera (ed.), *The External Environmental Policy of the European Union* (Cambridge University Press 2012) 174, 194.

[13] OECD, Environment and Regional Trade Agreements, 15 June 2007, summary available at: <http://www.oecd.org/env/environmentandregionaltrade agreements.htm> (accessed 30 December 2013).

[14] EU-Korea FTA (n 1) arts 2.6, 2.15(1), 4.1, 7.5–7.8, 7.11–7.14, 13.5(3), 13(6)(2).

[15] 2010 Cooperation Agreement (n 3) arts 17, 18, 23, 24.

[16] Kyoto Protocol to the United Nations Framework Convention on Climate Change; UN Doc FCCC/CP/1997/7/Add.1, 10 December 1997, 37 ILM 22 (1998), art 2.

topics via their environmental protection and/or energy cooperation clause(s), the enforcement of which is ensured through dispute settlement mechanisms consisting of direct consultations, the intervention of a cooperation council and/or arbitration proceedings.[17]

3. HARD LAW VERSUS SOFT LAW

It is worth briefly outlining the main doctrinal definitions of soft and hard law put forward in the legal literature with a view to unfolding the different levels of normativity that characterize the climate change framework under the EU-Korea FTA. Jan Klabbers argues that soft law refers to acts that are intended to 'influence behavior, but without creating law'.[18] Christine Chinkin views soft law as covering three categories of norms: (i) non-binding resolutions endorsed by international organizations (referred to as 'non-legal soft law'); (ii) international treaties composed of soft obligations (referred to as 'legal soft law'); and (iii) statements laying down international law principles and issued by individuals acting in a private capacity.[19] From this perspective, the softness of the norm can derive from the form of its instrument, its core content and/or the nature of its author.[20] Chinkin also takes the position that, if an international treaty merely referred to the 'gradual acquiring of standards' or to 'general goals and programmed action', it would have to

---

[17] Euro-Mediterranean Agreement establishing an Association between the European Communities and their Member States, of the one part, and the Hashemite Kingdom of Jordan, of the other part [2002] OJ L 129/3, art 74; Euro-Mediterranean Agreement establishing an Association between the European Communities and their Member States, of the one part, and the State of Israel, of the other part [2000] OJ L 147/3, art 51(1); Economic Partnership Agreement between the CARIFORUM States, of the one part, and the European Community and its Member States, of the other part [2008] OJ L 289/3, art 138 and 183(5); Stabilisation and Association Agreement between the European Communities and their Member States, of the one part, and Bosnia and Herzegovina, of the other part: <http://ec.europa.eu/world/agreements/prepareCreateTreatiesWorkspace/treatiesGeneralData.do?step=0&redirect=true&treatyId=7201> (accessed 30 December 2013), art 108.

[18] Jan Klabbers, *An Introduction to International Institutional Law* (2nd edn, Cambridge University Press 2009) 182.

[19] Christine Chinkin, 'The Challenge of Soft Law: Development and Change in International Law' (1989) 38 *International and Comparative Law Quarterly* 850, 851.

[20] Ibid 851.

be seen as embodying soft law norms.[21] Chinkin concludes that soft law norms are not naturally conducive to an adjudicatory dispute settlement: they lend themselves better to non-judicial forms of dispute settlement and to 'self-regulation between interested participants'.[22] Francis Snyder defines soft law as 'rules of conduct which, in principle, have no legally binding force but which nevertheless may have practical effects'.[23]

Kenneth Abbott and Duncan Snidal distinguish between hard and soft law norms not as part of a binary opposition but rather as part of a continuum.[24] The degree of softness and of hardness of a particular norm would hinge on three yardsticks: (i) the level of legal obligation (that is, the formally binding or non-binding nature of the obligation); (ii) the level of precision of the obligation (that is, looseness versus specificity); and (iii) the level of delegation to a third party (that is, an entity detached from and unrelated to the parties to the dispute) in its enforcement or dispute settlement mechanism.[25] Both authors see in 'hortatory rules' a typical illustration of norms enjoying a low degree of precision and of delegation while, at the same time, embodying general standards that may be used as benchmarks for assessing behavioural practices.[26] They associate a high degree of delegation with rules whose dispute settlement mechanism involves judicial and arbitral institutions, and a low degree of delegation with rules whose dispute settlement mechanism involves political institutions.[27] Similarly, Alan Boyle refers to three meanings of soft law that gravitate towards the form of a legal instrument, its substantive content and its dispute settlement framework.[28]

The Court of Justice of the European Union (CJEU) has put forward some judicial benchmarks that may also inform the normative force attached to the FTA's climate change provisions and thus their characterization in the soft law/hard law continuum.[29] The CJEU has recognized

---

21 Ibid 851.

22 Ibid 862.

23 Francis Snyder, 'The Effectiveness of European Community Law: Institutions, Processes, Tools and Techniques' (1993) 56 *The Modern Law Review* 19, 32.

24 Kenneth Abbott and Duncan Snidal, 'Hard and Soft Law in International Governance' (2000) 54(3) *International Organization* 421, 422, 424.

25 Ibid 424.

26 Ibid 443.

27 Ibid 432.

28 Alan Boyle, 'Some Reflections on the Relationship of Treaties and Soft Law' (1999) 48 *International and Comparative Law Quarterly* 901, 902.

29 Nicolas Croquet, 'The Import of International Customary Law into the EU Legal Order: The Adequacy of the Theory of Direct Effect', in Catherine

itself as competent to ascertain whether an international treaty concluded by the EU with a third country is directly effective, absent any express determination by its drafters regarding its internal legal effects.[30] It has ruled that for an EU secondary act (such as a regulation, directive or decision) to be subject to its validity review (for example, through an annulment action or a request for a preliminary invalidity ruling) in the event of direct conflict with an international treaty, the nature and broad logic of the treaty must not preclude such a review, and the content of the treaty provision invoked must be sufficiently clear, precise and unconditional.[31] The CJEU has interpreted the unconditionality criterion as precluding the presence of further implementing powers in the enforcement of a treaty norm unless the exercise of such powers is automatic and does not entail or call for the use of discretion by the implementing authority.[32] The case law of the EU Courts on the status of the General Agreement on Tariffs and Trade 1947 (GATT 1947) and of WTO law in the EU legal order suggests that the nature of the international treaty's dispute settlement mechanism may impinge on the CJEU's direct effect analysis,[33] even though in the *Air Transport Association of America* case the (European) Court of Justice was prepared to relax the importance of this factor when the dispute settlement mechanism relies on both a consultation/negotiation phase and an arbitration procedure.[34] In relation to mixed agreements falling under the shared competence of the Union and of its Member States – which is the case of RTAs that regulate

---

Barnard and others (eds), *Cambridge Yearbook of European Legal Studies 2012–2013* (Hart 2014) 47, 52–6.

[30] Case C-149/96 *Portugal* v *Council* [1999] ECR I-8395 [34]. For a similar ruling, see also Case C-104/81 *Hauptzollamt Mainz v Kupferberg & Cie* [1982] ECR 3641 [17]; Case C-240/09 *Lesoochranárske zoskupenie VLK*, Judgment of 8 March 2011 [17].

[31] Case T-338/08 *Stichting Natuur en Milieu v Commission*, Judgment of 14 June 2012 [53]; Case T-396/09 *Vereniging Milieudefensie and Others v Commission*, Judgment of 14 June 2012 [53]; Case C-366/10 *Air Transport Association of America and Others v Secretary of State for Energy and Climate Change*, Judgment of 21 December 2011 [49]–[56]; Case C-18/90 *Office National de l'Emploi v Kziber* [1987] ECR 3719 [15].

[32] Case C-162/96 *Racke v Hauptzollamt Mainz* [1998] ECR I-3655 [40]; *Air Transport Association of America*, ibid [75]–[76].

[33] Joined Cases 21/72 to 24/72 *International Fruit Company and Others* [1972] ECR 1219 [21]–[26]; *Portugal* v *Council* (n 30) [36]–[39].

[34] *Air Transport Association of America* (n 31) [83].

environmental matters[35] – the CJEU has attributed to itself the power to determine whether these agreements enjoy direct effect in the Member States' legal systems (that is, whether they may be directly invoked by individuals and private legal entities before domestic courts), including those provisions that fall within the competence of Member States provided that the latter provisions concern a subject-matter that is otherwise significantly regulated by EU legislation.[36] The focus of the CJEU's direct effect analysis with regard to mixed agreements has been on whether their provisions are sufficiently clear, precise and unconditional given their wording, purpose and nature.[37]

The following sections are premised on the understanding of soft law and hard law conveyed by Abbott, Snidal and Boyle and on the judicial benchmarks put forward by the EU Courts in their direct effect analysis. However, given that the EU-Korea FTA constitutes hard law vis-à-vis the Contracting Parties by virtue of its form, only two of the three yardsticks endorsed by these authors are relied upon in order to underline the different levels of softness and hardness of the Agreement's climate change provisions at a substantive and institutional level: (i) their degree of precision; and (ii) the degree of delegation to a third party reflected in their enforcement/dispute settlement mechanism. The first benchmark may be said to be three-dimensional. It is informed by three essential substantive criteria concerned with the inherent quality of the norm: (i) clarity, (ii) detailed nature, and (iii) self-sufficiency. The second benchmark points to the extent to which the dispute settlement body enjoys independence in addressing a dispute over the interpretation and/or application of a norm and thus to its adjudicatory (as opposed to political) inclination. The above benchmarks and substantive criteria, which impinge upon the soft law versus hard law debate, have been reflected in the EU Courts' direct effect analysis, as it has been shown above.

---

[35] See art 4(2) of the Treaty on the Functioning of the European Union (TFEU), which confirms that environmental protection and energy as a whole constitute areas of shared competence between the Union and its Member States: Consolidated Version of the Treaty on the Functioning of the European Union [2012] OJ C 326/47.

[36] *VLK* (n 30) [36], [40].

[37] Case 12/86 *Demirel* [1987] ECR 3719 [14]; *Kupferberg* (n 30) [22]–[27]; *Kziber* (n 31) [17].

4. DIRECT CLIMATE CHANGE PROVISIONS OF THE EU-KOREA FTA

Direct climate change provisions require the Contracting Parties to further substantiate national and international environmental laws as autonomous disciplines of law. Chapter 13 focuses on the improvement of environmental and climate change standards that best reconcile the need for increased trade in goods and services and sustainable development. The EU-Korea FTA's direct climate change provisions are composed of *renvoi*, *rendez-vous*, standstill, 'horizontal coherence'[38] and transparency clauses. These clauses are fairly general, loose and conditional as a result of their policy-oriented nature, their reliance on pre-existing international environmental law instruments and the need for further cooperative arrangements. Although it contains modest references to corporate social responsibility (CSR) and to the need for public participation in the elaboration and adoption of environmental law measures that affect trade between the Contracting Parties, the language of Chapter 13 directs no injunction to and confers no enforceable right directly upon individuals or private entities; this confirms its lack of self-sufficiency and its reliance on further implementation measures. Furthermore, the dispute settlement mechanism contained in Chapter 13, which is not open to private parties, is political in nature. It devolves few dispute-resolving powers upon the actors intervening in its consultation and mediation procedures, and is not concerned primarily with applying rules of law. Chapter 13, contrary to Chapter 14, calls for a 'dejudicialization' of the dispute settlement process.

4.1 *Renvoi* Clauses

Renvoi clauses in the EU-Korea FTA context are confirmatory clauses that urge the Contracting Parties to live up to their pre-existing climate change treaty commitments. They have the effect of regionalizing international environmental legal obligations that bind the Union, the EU Member States and the Republic of Korea at the multilateral level. While these clauses do not have any substantive added value, their institutional merit lies in the fact that these pre-existing treaty commitments now fall

[38] Expression borrowed from Fabienne Bossuyt, 'The Social Dimension of the New Generation of EU FTAs with Asia and Latin America: Ambitious Continuation for the Sake of Policy Coherence' (2009) 14(5) *European Foreign Affairs Review* 703, 720.

under the Chapter 13 dispute settlement mechanism in the event of a dispute over their interpretation and/or application. The EU and the Republic of Korea delegations to the WTO have emphasized that the reference to these international environmental law instruments was intended to reassert their importance and to ensure that the Contracting Parties 'effectively implement' them.[39]

Article 13.5(2) of the EU-Korea FTA stipulates that the Contracting Parties 'reaffirm their commitments to the effective implementation in their laws and practices of the multilateral environmental agreements to which they are party'. The Contracting Parties also 'reaffirm their commitment to reaching the ultimate objective of the United Nations Framework Convention on Climate Change [(UNFCCC)] and its Kyoto Protocol'.[40] This 'ultimate objective', enshrined in Article 2 of the UNFCCC and reproduced in the preamble to the Kyoto Protocol, consists of the 'stabilization of greenhouse gas [(GHG)] concentrations in the atmosphere at a level that would prevent dangerous anthropogenic interference with the climate system'.[41] This objective should be reached 'within a time-frame sufficient to allow ecosystems to adapt naturally to climate change, to ensure that food production is not threatened and to enable economic development to proceed in a sustainable manner'.[42] The allusion in Chapter 13 to the Kyoto Protocol, however, does not imply that the Republic of Korea, although a non-Annex I Party to the UNFCCC, would accordingly become regionally bound by those general obligations that Article 2 of the Kyoto Protocol places upon Annex I Parties to the UNFCCC and that are designed to promote sustainable development (such as the reinforcement of energy efficiency in critical areas of the Contracting Parties' national economy; the promotion of 'sustainable forms of agriculture'; the reduction of methane emissions; the progressive diminution or elimination of market imperfections, subsidies and tax incentives in GHG-emitting sectors that would be detrimental to the UNFCCC's ultimate objective). The preamble to the Kyoto Protocol indeed refers to Article 2 of the UNFCCC as the 'ultimate objective' to be achieved by all Parties to the UNFCCC and the Kyoto Protocol, including therefore those Parties that are not listed as Annex I

---

[39] WTO Committee on Regional Trade Agreements, 'Free Trade Agreement between the European Union and the Republic of Korea, Goods and Services – Questions and Replies', 14 June 2012, WT/REG296/2 [53].

[40] EU-Korea FTA (n 1) art 13.5(3).

[41] United Nations Framework Convention on Climate Change, New York, 9 May 1992, 1771 UNTS 107, 31 ILM 849 (1992), art 2.

[42] Ibid art 2.

Parties under the UNFCCC. Accordingly, Article 13.5(3) of the EU-Korea FTA has a declaratory effect, but in no way is it constitutive of new environmental obligations premised on the Kyoto Protocol.

4.2 *Rendez-vous* Clauses

Rendez-vous clauses refer to those provisions of the EU-Korea FTA which call for more cooperation between the Contracting Parties and ultimately for further climate change commitments at the bilateral, regional and/or multilateral levels.

Pursuant to Article 13.5(3) of the EU-Korea FTA, the Contracting Parties have agreed to cooperate 'on the development of the future international climate change framework in accordance with the Bali Action Plan'.[43] Article 13.5(3) is thus organizational in nature by requiring the Contracting Parties to negotiate and ultimately to bilaterally, regionally or multilaterally adopt more climate change legal obligations while building upon this international environmental policy document. Moreover, Annex 13 of the EU-Korea FTA, to which Article 13.11 of the EU-Korea FTA refers, states that climate change cooperation should cover 'issues relating to global carbon markets, ways to address adverse effects of trade on climate, as well as means to promote low-carbon technologies and energy efficiency'.[44] Finally, Article 13.5(1) of the EU-Korea FTA, while acknowledging the merits of international environmental governance, requires the Contracting Parties to consult with each other and to cooperate on those 'trade-related environmental issues of mutual interest'. Chapter 13 may, in this respect, have the effect of 'creating expectations concerning matters which must be taken into account in good faith in the negotiation of further instruments'.[45]

It is not surprising, therefore, that the Trade and Sustainable Development Committee issued a Joint Statement on 27 June 2012 in which it announced that it would 'discuss at the next Trade and Sustainable Development Committee specific aspects of the FTA's contribution to green growth, including initiatives in the area of eco-labelling' and

---

[43] EU-Korea FTA (n 1) art 13.5(3).

[44] Annex 13 'Cooperation on Trade and Sustainable Development' [2011] OJ L 127/1335, art 1(f).

[45] Boyle (n 28) 908. Alan Boyle arrived at this conclusion in the context of Article 3 of the UNFCCC.

'continue to regularly exchange views in order to define other relevant topics for future discussion'.[46]

4.3 Standstill Clauses

An environmental standstill clause prohibits the parties to an RTA from adopting less demanding environmental protection standards than those prevailing at the time of the entry into force of the treaty. Such a clause may be said to characterize Article 13.3 of the EU-Korea FTA, which stipulates:

> Recognising the right of each Party to establish its own levels of environmental and labour protection, and to adopt or modify accordingly its relevant laws and policies, each Party shall seek to ensure that those laws and policies provide for and encourage high levels of environmental and labour protection, consistent with the internationally recognised standards or agreements referred to in Articles 13.4 and 13.5, and shall strive to continue to improve those laws and policies.

However, the impact of this standstill obligation is limited by Article 13.1(3) of the EU-Korea FTA, which clarifies that the Agreement places no obligation on the Contracting Parties to harmonize their environmental standards. This is a clear sign that the EU-Korea FTA does not purport to approximate the Contracting Parties' environmental laws but instead to achieve convergence between them, especially when they have an impact on the Contracting Parties' trade relationship.

4.4 'Horizontal Coherence' Clauses

A 'horizontal coherence' clause is a provision in an RTA which creates bridges between the various objectives underpinning the treaty and enables its various chapters to be interpreted consistently with each other. With respect to the EU-Korea FTA, the 'horizontal coherence' clauses purport to relate Chapter 13's environmental governance framework to the Agreement's specific trade-furthering and trade-restricting provisions.

The contribution to sustainable development in the course of international trade has been presented as a core objective of the EU-Korea

[46] Trade and Sustainable Development Committee under the Korea-EU Free Trade Agreement, 'Joint Statement to the Civil Society Forum on the Outcomes of the 1st Trade and Sustainable Development Committee', 27 June 2012, Brussels.

FTA.[47] Article 1(1) of the Agreement stipulates that the Contracting Parties shall 'strive to ensure that this objective is integrated and reflected at every level of the Parties' trade relationship'. The Contracting Parties acknowledge the interdependency of economic development, social development and environmental protection.[48] They are also required to 'strengthen their trade relations and cooperation in ways that promote sustainable development'.[49] While each Contracting Party may set its own level of environmental protection, the adoption of environmental standards may, in no way, serve any protectionist trade purpose.[50] Put differently, the invocation by any Contracting Party of environmental standards in the face of trade commitments must be genuine. Conversely, the Contracting Parties must seek to 'facilitate and promote trade and foreign direct investment in environmental goods and services, including environmental technologies, sustainable renewable energy, energy efficient products and services and eco-labelled goods, including through addressing related non-tariff barriers'.[51] This provision suggests that the Contracting Parties should liberalize trade in environmental goods and services as much as possible within the bounds set by the Agreement's substantive trade provisions.

The presence of these 'horizontal coherence' clauses should not overshadow the fact that the EU-Korea FTA, through its Chapter 13, is not only concerned with those environmental matters and measures that affect the Contracting Parties' trade relationship but also with those that have no such impact, even though the latter are more adequately addressed in the 2010 Cooperation Agreement.[52] This is supported by the

[47] EU-Korea FTA (n 1) art 1.1(2).

[48] Ibid art 13.1(2).

[49] Ibid art 13.1(3).

[50] Ibid art 13.2(2).

[51] Ibid art 13.6(2).

[52] Under its autonomous 'Climate Change' provision, the Contracting Parties are required to 'intensify dialogue and cooperation at political, policy and technical levels'. This climate change provision is without prejudice to developments taking place in such avenues as the UNFCCC and to the Contracting Parties' respective competences in this area of law. The Contracting Parties' cooperative relationship must be aimed at fighting climate change, promoting the efficient use of resources, exchanging know-how on trading scheme frameworks, improving public and private sector financing instruments which may support action against climate change, increasing collaboration on low-carbon technology research and supporting developing countries' mitigation and adaptation action via the Kyoto Protocol Flexible Mechanisms. See 2010 Cooperation Agreement (n 3) art 24.

definition of 'scope' found in Article 13.2 of the EU-Korea FTA, according to which Chapter 13 governs the Contracting Parties' measures that affect not only 'trade-related aspects of labour' but also environmental issues in the context of the Contracting Parties' objective of integrating sustainable development concerns into their trade relationship '[e]xcept as otherwise provided in this Chapter'. The latter caveat conveys the possibility of treaty clauses calling for convergence between the Contracting Parties' environmental and climate laws regardless of their impact on trade.

In addition, while most of the provisions of Chapter 13 focus on the need for a balanced relationship between trade and sustainable development, a few of them are concerned with environmental governance as an independent public policy concern. This is the case with Article 13.5 of the EU-Korea FTA whereby the Contracting Parties 'reaffirm their commitments to the effective implementation in their laws and practices of the multilateral environmental agreements to which they are party'. This is also the case with Annex 13 of the EU-Korea FTA – to which Article 13.11 of the Agreement refers – which indicates an open-ended and subsidiary area of cooperation, namely 'other forms of environmental cooperation as the Parties may deem appropriate'.[53] Chapter 13 thus encourages the adoption of additional national and international environmental and climate change legal initiatives that are founded on pre-existing multilateral environmental law commitments regardless of their impact on trade.

4.5 Corporate Social Responsibility

Fabienne Bossuyt, in her 2009 article entitled 'The Social Dimension of the New Generation of EU FTAs with Asia and Latin America: Ambitious Continuation for the Sake of Policy Coherence', observed that the EU did not intend to insert any CSR provision in the 'new generation of FTAs'.[54] While the EU-Korea FTA contains no general CSR clause in its Chapter 13, it does allude to it from specific sustainable development angles in a way that confirms the lack of centrality of the individual and of corporations in the Agreement's environmental governance framework. Article 13.6 of the EU-Korea FTA requires the Contracting Parties to ease trade in those goods that make a contribution to sustainable

---

53 Annex 13 (n 44) art 1(m).

54 Bossuyt (n 38) 704.

development, in particular those goods that entail CSR and accountability. In other words, the Contracting Parties should facilitate the international trade of goods where the producers of those goods commit to abide by the principal CSR principles recognized and called for by representative international inter-governmental organizations (such as the United Nations, the OECD and the EU), and thus to voluntarily implement non-binding labour, environmental and human rights standards in the production, marketing and transportation of their goods. Furthermore, Annex 13 lists among its priority areas of cooperation the exchange of information on CSR and accountability – an area of cooperation that would allow for discussions 'on the effective implementation and follow-up of internationally agreed guidelines, fair and ethical trade, private and public certification and labelling schemes including eco-labelling and green public procurement'. The Commission's 2001 Green Paper 'Promoting a European Framework for Corporate Social Responsibility' – by which the EU may have been influenced when providing for limited CSR clauses in the EU-Korea FTA – defined CSR as 'a concept whereby companies decide voluntarily to contribute to a better society and a cleaner environment'.[55] In its 2001 Green Paper, the Commission insisted that, through CSR, 'companies integrate social and environmental concerns in their business operations and in their interaction with their stakeholders on a voluntary basis'.[56] The Green Paper, in particular, invited transnational corporations to 'encourage better environmental performance throughout their supply chain' in Europe and internationally.[57]

4.6 Transparency Clause

Chapter 13 requires transparency in the way in which the Contracting Parties develop, adopt and implement any environmental measure that

---

[55] Commission, Green Paper, 'Promoting a European Framework for Corporate Social Responsibility', Brussels, COM(2001) 366 final 4. This document was later revisited in the Communication from the Commission to the European Parliament, the Council, the European Economic and Social Committee and the Committee of the Regions, 'A Renewed EU strategy 2011–2014 for Corporate Social Responsibility', COM(2011) 681 final, Brussels, 25 October 2011.

[56] Commission's 2001 Green Paper (n 55) 6.

[57] Ibid 15.

affects trade between them.[58] Transparency entails, in particular, communication to and consultation with non-state actors.[59] Article 13.9 of the EU-Korea FTA, very modestly and in broad terms, attempts to make procedural the environmental and climate change governance framework prevailing in the Contracting Parties' trade relationship by calling for a limited form of public participation in decision-making and public access to information in environmental matters. Such a call for transparency is merely exhortatory and drafted in the form of a good efforts obligation rather than a result-based obligation. This provision is the closest that Chapter 13 gets to relating environmental governance to the individual in the language of broadly defined principles of good administration.

4.7 Dispute Settlement and Enforcement Clauses

The EU-Korea FTA calls for the creation of a specialized Committee on Trade and Sustainable Development composed of senior officials of the Contracting Parties' respective administrations.[60] This body is designed to oversee the implementation of Chapter 13 at the inter-governmental level.[61] In addition, the Contracting Parties are each required to establish a Domestic Advisory Group on Sustainable Development composed of independent representatives of civil society to represent, in particular, environmental, labour and business organizations. These bodies are to advise on the implementation of Chapter 13 at the national level.[62]

Chapter 14, including its arbitration procedure, is not applicable to Chapter 13, the dispute settlement under which is instead regulated by a *sui generis* three-fold procedure.[63] In the first stage, in the event of a dispute over the implementation of Chapter 13, the complaining Contracting Party is required to seek government consultations with the other Contracting Party. The Contracting Parties are to endeavour to promptly reach a mutually satisfactory resolution of the dispute in line with the activities of multilateral international organizations whose opinion they

---

58 EU-Korea FTA (n 1) art 13.9.

59 Ibid art 13.9.

60 Ibid art 13.12.

61 Ibid art 13.12(3). The Committee on Trade and Sustainable Development organized its first meeting on 26 June 2012: Commission, 'Report from the Commission to the European Parliament and the Council: Annual Report on the Implementation of the EU-Korea Free Trade Agreement' COM(2013) 100 final 2.

62 EU-Korea FTA (n 1) art 13.12(4)–(5).

63 Ibid art 13.16.

may request if they deem it to be appropriate. In the second stage, the Committee on Trade and Sustainable Development may intervene at the Contracting Parties' request if the latter consider the dispute to require further discussion; the Committee may attempt to resolve the dispute itself with the advice of the Domestic Advisory Group(s).[64] If the first two stages (the second being optional and contingent upon the Parties' consent) fail to produce a mutually satisfactory resolution of the dispute, and provided that the disputants have not decided otherwise, any complaining Contracting Party may request the establishment of a panel of experts. The experts on the panel must be independent of the Contracting Parties and of the organizations represented in the Domestic Advisory Groups, and be selected by each Contracting Party from a list of 15 persons enjoying expertise in trade and sustainable development. The panel receives submissions from the Contracting Parties in dispute and may request additional advice and information from them, the Domestic Advisory Groups and/or international organizations. The panel has 90 days from the date of selection of the last expert in which to present a report to the Contracting Parties. The absence of any formal requirement to comply with the panel's report is noteworthy: the Contracting Parties must simply endeavour to 'accommodate' the panel's advice or recommendations. The Committee on Trade and Sustainable Development is tasked with monitoring the implementation of the panel's recommendation(s).[65]

The dispute settlement mechanism in Chapter 13 thus consists of a negotiation phase (dialogue and consultation between the Contracting Parties in dispute), an ordinary mediation phase under the leadership of the Committee on Trade and Sustainable Development and an institutionalized mediation phase through the panel of experts proceedings. A mediation procedure typically enables a third party (the mediator) to put new proposals to the disputants with the intention of achieving a compromise solution after relying on the disputants' respective factual assessments, and thus without conducting an independent investigation.[66]

---

[64] Ibid art 13.14.

[65] Ibid art 13.15.

[66] Mediation and conciliation traditionally allow a third party to actively facilitate or restore the negotiation process, to provide an additional communication channel, to propose a solution to the parties to the dispute, and, in the case of conciliation, to conduct an investigation or a detailed fact-finding mission independently of the disputants' submissions: John Merrills, *International Dispute Settlement* (5th edn, Cambridge University Press 2011) 26, 58; Lori Damrosch and Others, *International Law: Cases and Materials* (Thomson

Mediation in the second phase is conditional on the first phase not being successful and is left to the discretion of all Contracting Parties involved in the dispute: it is not an automatic step in the Chapter 13 dispute settlement procedure. However, the panel of experts proceedings in the third phase go further than a classic form of mediation in that the Contracting Parties to the EU-Korea FTA must give due consideration to the panel's proposals and may not dismiss them right at the outset; the proceedings are, after all, subject to the scrutiny of the Committee on Trade and Sustainable Development as far as the Contracting Parties' 'accommodation' of the panel of experts' report is concerned.

The dispute settlement procedure is highly inter-governmental and has no direct private party involvement, even though civil society may indirectly influence the outcome of any Chapter 13 dispute through consultation with the Domestic Advisory Group(s) by either the Committee on Trade and Sustainable Development or the panel of experts in their respective mediation proceedings. No individual or private party may directly file a complaint against a Contracting Party for breach of its Chapter 13 climate change and environmental law commitments through the initiation of the consultation and/or the mediation phase(s). Although the majority of the Union's RTAs that are equipped with specific climate change provisions confer upon any Contracting Party thereto the unilateral power to launch arbitration proceedings against the other Contracting Party (or Contracting Parties) – whether at first instance or after exhausting an intermediary political dispute settlement procedure (as a result of the cooperation council's failure to resolve the dispute or unsuccessful direct consultations) – these arbitration proceedings are not open to private parties.[67]

4.8 Overall Normativity

Chapter 13's climate change framework enjoys a low level of hard law normativity or a high level of soft law normativity with regard to its substantive and procedural (transparency) provisions and to its dispute settlement mechanism.

Reuters 2009) 563–4; John Collier and Vaughan Lowe, *The Settlement of Disputes in International Law* (Oxford University Press 1999) 27; Malcolm Shaw, *International Law* (6th edn, Cambridge University Press 2013) 1022–4.

[67] Euro-Mediterranean Agreement establishing an Association with the State of Israel (n 17) art 75; Euro-Mediterranean Agreement establishing an Association with Jordan (n 17) art 97; Economic Partnership Agreement between the CARIFORUM States (n 17) arts 202–223.

Its substantive and procedural climate change provisions are fairly imprecise. These provisions enjoy a low degree of clarity and detail based on their exhortatory and aspirational language: they are tainted by the open-ended and loose nature of the objectives they set out (whether directly or through *renvoi*) and the absence of concrete climate change agenda.

The low level of precision attributed to Chapter 13's substantive and procedural climate change provisions may also be inferred from their lack of self-sufficiency based on the following three observations. First, Chapter 13 calls for more cooperation at the bilateral and the multilateral levels and thus for further implementation measures that presuppose the use of political discretion. The (European) Court of Justice, in *Air Transport Association of America*, was disinclined to attach any direct effect to the Kyoto Protocol on account of the degree of flexibility which certain Parties to the Protocol enjoy in implementing their GHG commitments and of the role of the Conference of the Parties in adopting relevant procedures and mechanisms to deal with situations of non-compliance.[68] Second, Chapter 13 requires the adoption of further organizational measures in order to achieve some transparency (in the form of consultation and access to information) in the elaboration, adoption and implementation of environmental measures affecting the Contracting Parties' trade relationship. Third, given the very modest references to CSR and the absence of overall rights-oriented language in Chapter 13, the latter's climate change and environmental governance framework does not accord a central role to individuals and corporations as subjects of the Agreement's direct climate change commitments; this, in turn, implies the need for further legal initiatives aimed at placing legal obligations and conferring individual rights upon non-state actors. This lack of precision was already reflected in the Union's earlier RTAs, which also lacked detail, clarity and self-sufficiency in the formulation of their renewable energy and energy efficiency objectives.[69] The low level of hard law normativity attached to the Chapter 13 dispute settlement mechanism exacerbates the soft law nature of its substantive and procedural climate change provisions and confirms Chinkin's suggested correlation between norms that qualify as soft law based on their very content and the lack of adjudicatory features in their dispute settlement process.[70]

68 *Air Transport Association of America* (n 31) [75]–[76].

69 See Section 2 above.

70 Chinkin (n 19) 850, 851.

The dispute settlement mechanism in Chapter 13 embodies a low level of delegation to a third party, a conclusion which transpires from three institutional observations. First, any dispute over the implementation of Chapter 13 is subject to a consultation and ultimately to an institutionalized form of mediation procedure. Second, the panel of experts may issue reports which the disputing Contracting Parties must consider but which they are free to depart from. Third, nothing is said about the applicable law in the dispute settlement process. Whereas the constitutive instruments of most international adjudicatory bodies do not require their members to be trained lawyers, they do at least make reference to the applicable law in one way or another. Reports of panels of experts are therefore more likely to be policy-oriented than rule-oriented. The dispute settlement mechanism in Chapter 13 may be said to reflect what Klabbers describes as 'an overtly political mode of dealing with conflicts',[71] albeit constrained by some formal procedures.

The EU-Korea FTA does not make environmental protection a less worthy objective than the liberalization of goods, services and economic activities. In fact, both objectives are treated as equal from a value-based perspective; there is thus no principled hierarchy between the two. However, Chapter 13 is normatively weaker than the Agreement's core trade and general transparency chapters in that it does not spell out any detailed provision on how to effectively implement the various sustainable development obligations placed upon the Contracting Parties, and on how to achieve transparency in the development, adoption and implementation of environmental measures affecting trade between the Contracting Parties. Chapter 13 thus resembles a constitutional framework not in terms of sanctioning any individual human right (which it fails to do overall subject to its embryonic transparency provision) but in terms of setting out collective goals the implementation of which requires further inter-governmental negotiation. Most of the provisions falling within this constitutional framework may be said to constitute 'WTO-plus provisions' – in other words, norms that 'extend beyond the WTO disciplines'.[72]

---

71 Klabbers (n 18) 182.
72 Horng (n 4) 315.

5. INDIRECT CLIMATE CHANGE PROVISIONS OF THE EU-KOREA FTA

The EU-Korea FTA's indirect climate change provisions, while not specifically concerned with climate change, govern the topic incidentally as an object of international trade, as a restriction on international trade or on market access, or through the provision of good administration principles and defence rights. Contrary to its direct climate change provisions that fall under Chapter 13's politicized dispute settlement mechanism, the Agreement's indirect climate change provisions are subject to Chapter 14 adjudicatory dispute settlement procedure.

5.1 Trade-Furthering Provisions

Each Contracting Party is required to reduce or remove customs duties on goods originating from the other Contracting Party within the limits set in their respective 'tariff schedules'.[73] These tariff schedules cover a certain number of environmental goods that integrate or apply renewable energy technologies (such as solar collectors and photovoltaic cells) or that may be used as materials for generating renewable energy (such as tallow, residues and/or waste).[74] No Contracting Party may increase an existing customs duty or impose a new duty on an originating good of the other Contracting Party unless otherwise stipulated in a Contracting Party's tariff schedule.[75]

Annex 7-A-1 and Annex 7-A-2 – which contain the EU's Lists of Commitments on respectively the Cross-Border Supply of Services and Establishment in pursuance of Articles 7.7 and 7.13 of the EU-Korea FTA – cover the '[p]roduction of electricity, transmission and distribution of electricity on own account', the 'wholesale trade services of electricity, steam and hot water' and '[s]ervices incidental to energy distribution'.[76] In these sectors and subsectors, the Union and its Member States are bound by specific market access commitments, by the principle of national treatment (subject to cross-sectoral qualifications defined in Annex 7-A-1 and Annex 7-A-2) and by the overarching most-favoured

---

[73] EU-Korea FTA (n 1) art 2.5(1).

[74] Annex 2-A 'Elimination of Customs Duties' [2011] OJ L 127/83.

[75] EU-Korea FTA (n 1) art 2.6.

[76] Annex 7-A-1 'EU's List of Commitments on Cross-Border Supply of Services in Conformity with Article 7.7' [2011] OJ L 127/1165; Annex 7-A-2 'EU's List of Commitments on Cross-Border Supply of Services in Conformity with Article 7.13' [2011] OJ L 127/1198.

nation (MFN) clause (subject to cross-sectoral qualifications defined in Annex 7-B's List of MFN Treatment Exemptions).[77] Annexes 7-A-1 and 7-A-2 clarify that the listed market access commitments are not to produce any 'self-executing' effect: they should not be understood as granting any right directly to individuals and legal entities.[78]

5.2 Trade-Restricting Provisions

Chapter 2 of the EU-Korea FTA incorporates Article XX of the General Agreement on Tariffs and Trade 1994 (GATT 1994) through *renvoi* in recognizing the Contracting Parties' power to provide certain exceptions to the liberalization of trade in goods.[79] Article XX(b) GATT 1994 authorizes WTO Members to adopt and enforce measures that are 'necessary to protect human, animal or plant life or health' whereas Article XX(g) GATT 1994 authorizes the adoption and enforcement of measures that relate to 'the conservation of exhaustible natural resources', provided that the latter are 'made effective in conjunction with restrictions on domestic production or consumption'. A measure falling under an Article XX(b) or an Article XX(g) general exception, in addition, must not be applied in a way that would constitute 'a means of arbitrary or unjustifiable discrimination between countries where the same conditions prevail, or a disguised restriction on international trade' (Article XX chapeau).[80]

Chapter 7 of the EU-Korea FTA empowers the Contracting Parties to adopt measures derogating from its rules on 'trade in services, establishment and electronic commerce'. Such derogation measures must be 'necessary' to protect human, animal and/or plant life or health, or must 'relate to' the conservation of exhaustible natural resources, provided in the latter case that they are 'made effective in conjunction with restrictions on domestic production or consumption'. As with the general exceptions in Chapter 2, derogation measures adopted pursuant to Chapter 7 may not be applied in a way that would constitute 'a means of arbitrary or unjustifiable discrimination between countries where like conditions prevail, or a disguised restriction on establishment or cross-border supply of services'.[81] Chapter 7 reproduces all the general

---

[77] EU-Korea FTA (n 1) arts 7.5–7.8 and 7.11–7.14.

[78] Annex 7-A-1 (n 76) art 6; Annex 7-A-2 (n 76) art 6.

[79] EU-Korea FTA (n 1) art 2.15(1).

[80] General Agreement on Tariffs and Trade (15 April 1994, entered into force 1 January 1995) 1867 UNTS 187.

[81] EU-Korea FTA (n 1) art 7.50(b)(c).

exceptions provided for in Article XIV of the General Agreement on Trade in Services (GATS) while adding the derogation ground based on the conservation of exhaustible natural resources.[82]

Chapter 4 of the EU-Korea FTA incorporates the TBT Agreement[83] through *renvoi*. Article 2.2 of the TBT Agreement provides that technical regulations (that is, documents that set out requirements relating to a product's characteristics or its related processes and production methods, and compliance with which is mandatory under the law of a WTO Member) may not be prepared, adopted or applied 'with a view to or with the effect of creating unnecessary obstacles to international trade'.[84] Article 2.2 of the TBT Agreement requires any technical regulation to be 'no more trade-restrictive than necessary' in order to 'fulfil' a legitimate objective, in particular the protection of human health and safety, of animal or plant life or of the environment.

5.3 General Transparency Standards

Although not addressing climate change expressly, Chapter 12 of the EU-Korea FTA will have some indirect repercussions on the administration by the Contracting Parties of their climate change and environmental legislation by conferring upon individuals and private operators certain procedural guarantees and remedies, and by ensuring the application of good governance principles in all matters covered by the EU-Korea FTA. Compared with all the RTAs concluded by the EU before the signature of the EU-Korea FTA, the latter contains the most detailed transparency framework. For instance, the Agreement establishing an Association between the European Community and the Republic of Chile simply refers to the need for the Contracting Parties to provide for contact points and the exchange of information, to the need for further bilateral and multilateral cooperation in the area of transparency in trade matters, and to the requirement to publish trade measures of general application.[85] Chapter 12 introduces the following guarantees and principles:

---

[82] General Agreement on Trade in Services (adopted 15 April 1994, entered into force 1 January 1995), 1869 UNTS 183.

[83] EU-Korea FTA (n 1) art 4.1.

[84] Agreement on Technical Barriers to Trade, 15 April 1994, Marrakesh Agreement establishing the World Trade Organization, Annex IA, Legal Instruments – Results of the Uruguay Round, 1868 UNTS 120 (1994), art 2.2.

[85] Agreement establishing an Association between the European Community and its Member States, of the one part, and the Republic of Chile, of the other part [2002] OJ L 352/3, arts 190–192.

- the right of review and of appeal before judicial or administrative courts/bodies;
- requirements concerned with the 'regulatory quality' of the Contracting Parties' internal laws and the need for them to cooperate in this subject area;
- provisions on enquiries and entry points through 'appropriate mechanisms';
- recognition of the principle of non-discrimination in the application of transparency standards between the citizens of the Contracting Parties ('non-discrimination clause');
- the requirement to make measures of general application accessible to interested persons via an 'officially designated medium';
- the requirement to use best efforts to publish in advance proposed measures of general application;
- the requirement to provide reasons for measures of general application vis-à-vis their objective and rationale ('statement of reasons clause');
- the requirement to provide interested persons with 'reasonable opportunities' to comment on proposed measures of general application and to use best efforts to account for such comments in the decision-making process ('public participation clause'); and
- defence rights in administrative proceedings (such as the opportunity for any interested party to present his or her views before the closure of the administrative action).[86]

Chapter 12 injects a procedural dimension into the EU-Korea FTA and makes the Agreement more individual-oriented by ensuring that any climate change and environmental law measure adopted pursuant to the EU-Korea FTA or falling within its scope complies with principles of good administration, transparency standards, defence rights and judicial/administrative review requirements. In that respect Chapter 12 mirrors some of the guarantees provided for in the UN Economic Commission for Europe Convention on Access to Information, Public Participation in Decision-making and Access to Justice in Environmental Matters (Aarhus Convention).[87] For Marco Macchia, the Aarhus Convention belongs to the category of international arrangements which, unlike the Kyoto Protocol, confer procedural rights directly upon private actors and are not

[86] EU-Korea FTA (n 1) art 12.3–12.8.

[87] UN Economic Commission for Europe (UN/ECE), Convention on Access to Information, Public Participation in Decision-making and Access to Justice in Environmental Matters, 2161 UNTS 447, 38 ILM 517 (1999).

addressed only to states: the Convention, therefore, 'is intended for civil society'.[88] Although the Aarhus Convention does call for further organizational measures and may thus not satisfy the self-sufficiency dimension, several of its provisions are nonetheless tainted by hard law characteristics arising from their high degree of clarity and detail. One area of transparency in which the Aarhus Convention goes further than Chapter 12 concerns public access to environmental information relating to individual measures. Chapter 12 of the EU-Korea FTA limits the scope of its 'publication' provision to measures of general application whereas Article 4 of the Aarhus Convention requires public authorities to allow for public access to environmental information, whether relating to a measure of general application or to an individual measure, following the filing of a request to that effect and subject to a series of public interest exceptions.

5.4 Common Dispute Settlement Mechanism

All of the indirect climate change provisions in the EU-Korea FTA are subject to the default dispute settlement procedure in Chapter 14. Under this general dispute settlement procedure, the Contracting Parties may seek to resolve a dispute over the interpretation and/or application of the indirect climate change provisions through consultations in good faith.[89] If the dispute is not resolved within specific time frames, the complaining Contracting Party may unilaterally request the establishment of an arbitration panel,[90] and must then notify the Contracting Party complained against of this request.[91] The parties to the dispute must adopt measures to enable them to comply in good faith with the arbitration panel's ruling within a 'reasonable period of time' to be agreed upon by the parties.[92] The arbitral award is binding upon the parties to the dispute, and may not confer any individual right(s) or obligation(s) upon natural or legal persons.[93]

---

88 Marco Macchia, 'Global Administrative Law Compliance: The Aarhus Convention Compliance Review System' (2008) 20(4) *European Review of Public Law/Revue européenne de droit public* 1317, 1321.

89 EU-Korea FTA (n 1) art 14.3.

90 Ibid art 14.4.

91 Ibid art 14.4.

92 Ibid art 14.8–9.

93 Ibid art 14.17.

Chapter 14 dispute settlement procedure overall is depoliticized even though political arrangements may always be agreed upon at the consultation stage. As is apparent from the above, neither the consultation phase nor the arbitration proceedings are open to private entities. In addition, Chapter 14 makes it clear that the final arbitral award may not be relied upon by individuals and private entities in order to assert rights against other private actors or a public body of a Contracting Party in subsequent proceedings before the Contracting Parties' own courts. The absence of consideration of private parties in the Chapter 14 dispute settlement mechanism is no surprise since, unlike most investment treaties, trade agreements have rarely been subject to a hybrid form of dispute settlement under which private parties may bring a complaint against a Contracting Party directly before a transnational adjudicatory body.[94] Chapter 14 arbitral awards could presumably still produce interpretative effects in private law or public law actions launched by non-state actors before the Contracting Parties' courts when questions are raised relating to the interpretation and/or validity of an implementation measure adopted pursuant to the EU-Korea FTA.

5.5 Overall Normativity

The indirect climate change provisions of the EU-Korea FTA enjoy a higher degree of hard law normativity than does Chapter 13. A medium level of precision may be assigned to the tariff schedules and the specific services market access commitments. Whereas they are regulated in a fair amount of detail and clarity given the definition of the terms used and the adoption of the UN Central Product Classification system, they suffer objectively from their inherent lack of self-sufficiency: as trade-furthering provisions, they are all subject to general exceptions the use of which is left to the political discretion of the Contracting Parties.

Nevertheless, the EU Courts have assessed the self-sufficiency requirement differently depending on whether the trade-furthering provisions fall under an RTA or under the GATT/WTO law. In *SAMI*, the (former) European Court of Justice (ECJ) held that the Tariff Protocols concluded

---

[94] Surya Subedi, *International Investment Law: Reconciling Policy and Principle* (Hart 2012) 202–4; Michael Reisman, 'The Future of International Investment Law and Arbitration', in Antonio Cassese (ed.), *Realizing Utopia: The Future of International Law* (Oxford University Press 2012) 275–86.

in pursuance of the GATT 1947[95] could not be directly effective given that they required adoption by the Parties of their own customs tariffs and thus were not unconditional.[96] In *Germany v Council*, the ECJ attributed the lack of unconditionality of the GATT 1947 in part to the possibility of derogations from its provisions and to the great flexibility in its clauses.[97] However, in *Opel Austria*, the (former) Court of First Instance (CFI) was less stringent in its assessment of the unconditionality requirement. It held that Article 10 of the European Economic Area (EEA) Agreement – which prohibits the imposition of customs duties on imports and exports as well as any charges having equivalent effect on the goods originating from the Contracting Parties – contained 'an unconditional and precise rule, subject to a single exception which is itself unconditional and precise'.[98] The Court deemed Article 10 to be directly effective in the context of an annulment action targeted at Council Regulation 3697/93 of 20 December 1993 withdrawing tariff concessions.[99] The EU Courts have thus attached higher normative force to the trade-furthering provisions of RTAs than to their equivalent provisions under the GATT 1947 or WTO law, notwithstanding that the former provisions call equally for possible derogation measures.

In light of this case law, the self-sufficiency feature of the trade-furthering provisions in the EU-Korea FTA should not be affected by the presence of derogation clauses when the latter are clearly defined. Having said that, the fact that the list of specific market access commitments states that such services commitments do not produce any self-executing effect may be a sign that the drafters of the EU-Korea FTA did not treat commitments to liberalize trade in services as self-sufficient: they will require further implementation measures before they can be invoked and relied upon directly by private operators before the Contracting Parties' domestic courts. In other words, the level of precision of the Contracting Parties' tariff schedules for the liberalization of trade in goods is higher than that characterizing their specific services market access commitments from the perspective of the EU Courts.

---

[95] The text of the General Agreement on Tariffs and Trade before the entry into force of the WTO Agreement: see General Agreement on Tariffs and Trade (30 October 1947) 55 UNTS 194.

[96] Joined Cases 267-269/81 *Amministrazione delle finanze dello Stato v SPI and SAMI* [1983] ECR 801 [24], [26].

[97] Case C-280/93 *Germany v Council* [1994] ECR I-4973 [106].

[98] Case T-115/94 *Opel Austria v Council* [1997] ECR II-39 [102].

[99] Ibid [102].

The provisions of the EU-Korea FTA that regulate exceptions to the international trade in goods or services and internal restrictions on market access also enjoy a medium level of precision. They lack detail and clarity when not read in light of WTO law and its corresponding case law. The terms 'necessary' and 'relate' used as criteria for scrutinizing derogations from the EU-Korea FTA's core provisions on the liberalization of international trade in goods and services are defined neither in the Agreement itself nor in the GATT 1994, even though their definition may be borrowed implicitly from case law of the WTO Dispute Settlement Body (DSB).[100]

With respect to Chapter 4 of the EU-Korea FTA, which regulates internal restrictions on market access through TBTs, its lack of detail stems from two observations. First, the TBT Agreement, which is incorporated through *renvoi* in Article 4.1 of the EU-Korea FTA, does not define the notion of legitimate objective and lists only a few examples thereof. Second, the term 'necessary' is not defined in the EU-Korea FTA even though its definition may be implicitly borrowed from the TBT Agreement as interpreted by the WTO DSB.[101] The use of these general exceptions and of TBTs is by definition left to the political discretion of the Contracting Parties.

The provisions of Chapter 12 overall are more precise than the Chapter 13 rudimentary transparency provision, although the degree of clarity, detail and self-sufficiency in Chapter 12 varies according to the provision in question. The non-discrimination clause, the statement of reasons clause and the provision concerned with defence rights in administrative proceedings are tainted by a high level of clarity and self-sufficiency even though they are not particularly detailed. Several Chapter 12 provisions

---

[100] Appellate Body, *United States – Import Prohibition of Certain Shrimp and Shrimp Products*, WT/DS58/AB/R, adopted 12 October 1998 [159]; Appellate Body, *European Communities – Measures Affecting Asbestos and Asbestos-Containing Products*, WT/DS/135/AB/R, adopted 12 March 2001 [170]; Appellate Body, *Korea – Measures Affecting Imports of Fresh, Chilled and Frozen Beef*, WT/DS/161/AB/R, adopted 11 December 2000 [163], [164], [166]; Appellate Body, *China – Measures Related to the Exportation of Various Raw Materials*, WT/DS398/AB/R, adopted 30 January 2012 [355]; Appellate Body, *United States – Measures Affecting the Cross-Border Supply of Gambling and Betting Services*, WT/DS285/AB/R, adopted 7 April 2005 [292].

[101] Appellate Body, *United States – Measures Concerning the Importation, Marketing and Sale of Tuna and Tuna Products*, WT/DS381/AB/R, adopted 16 May 2012 [311]–[323]; Appellate Body, *United States – Certain Country of Origin Labelling (COOL) Requirements*, WT/DS384/AB/R and WT/DS386/AB/R, adopted 29 June 2012 [368]–[379].

are, however, not self-sufficient even though they might be relatively clear and detailed. The rights of review and appeal before judicial and administrative courts/bodies indeed presuppose the establishment of judicial and administrative appeals and bodies. The same can be said about the 'regulatory quality and performance' requirements, which call for cooperation between the Contracting Parties in different ways, including through exchanges of information. Moreover, the requirement to publish measures of general application requires the adoption of a suitable 'electronic medium', and the provision concerned with enquiries and entry points requires the setting up of 'appropriate mechanisms', the modalities of which are left to the Contracting Parties' discretion.

A particular Chapter 12 provision which lacks clarity concerns the Contracting Parties' obligations to 'endeavour' – in other words, to use their best efforts – to publish in advance measures of general application and to account for comments made by interested persons on contemplated measures of general application. The language of these obligations reflects the Contracting Parties' focus on the means and the diligence to be used in striving for an objective rather than on the achievement of the results themselves. Such obligations enjoy a low degree of clarity in the absence of any guidance on how to exercise these best efforts or this diligence. A parallel can be drawn with Article 8 of the Aarhus Convention, which requires the Parties thereto to 'strive to promote effective public participation at an appropriate stage' in the elaboration of 'executive regulations' and/or of 'generally applicable legally binding normative instruments'.[102] In the Implementation Guide to the Aarhus Convention, the soft law nature of Article 8 was inferred from its 'indicative' wording and its emphasis on the Parties' best efforts (rather than on a set end-result) in performing their treaty obligations.[103]

Chapter 14's dispute settlement mechanism hardens the normative force attached to the above indirect climate change provisions: it entails a significant level of delegation to an independent organ tasked with resolving disputes between the Contracting Parties over the interpretation and/or application of the EU-Korea FTA's indirect climate change provisions through binding decisions. Although the dispute settlement mechanism is self-contained in the relationship between the Contracting Parties, it leaves on the face of it no room for any procedural involvement

---

[102] Aarhus Convention (n 87) art 8.

[103] Stephen Stec and Susan Casey-Lefkowitz, *The Aarhus Convention: An Implementation Guide* (UN/ECE 2000) 119, <http://www.unece.org/fileadmin/DAM/env/pp/acig.pdf> (accessed 30 December 2013) (Aarhus Implementation Guide).

on the part of private parties, and its awards are not directly enforceable by individuals and private operators vis-à-vis other non-state actors or a Contracting Party's public body.

6. NORMATIVE INTERACTIONS BETWEEN THE AGREEMENT'S DIRECT AND INDIRECT CLIMATE CHANGE PROVISIONS

Chapter 13 may have spillover effects over the rest of the EU-Korea FTA by amounting to a form of environmental constitutional framework. This framework informs those specific treaty provisions aimed at furthering the liberalization of trade in goods and services and of freedom of establishment and at regulating restrictions on international trade and on market access. It also triggers those procedural provisions of the Agreement designed to ameliorate the regulatory quality, accessibility, transparency and good administration of measures of general application falling within the purview of the EU-Korea FTA. The production of these spillover effects is confirmed by the presence in Chapter 13 of 'horizontal coherence' clauses[104] and of a rudimentary transparency provision, which call for inter-chapter consistency. From an enforcement perspective, Chapter 13 dispute settlement mechanism does not rule out the simultaneous activation of Chapter 14 default dispute settlement as a result of the inevitable presence of overlapping issues between sustainable development questions, trade-furthering and trade-restricting matters, and finally transparency concerns.

With regard to the Contracting Parties' tariff schedules, Chapter 13 may have the effect of supporting the widest possible interpretation of these tariff concessions when they involve environmental goods. A wide interpretation of the tariff schedules could have the effect of including within generic classifications new forms of renewable energy technology not yet reflected in the UN Central Product Classification. Chapter 13 may also call for an interpretation of energy services market access commitments to cover renewable energy services and not merely conventional energy sources.

As a result of Chapter 13's normative influence over Articles 2.15(1) and 7.50(b)(c) of the EU-Korea FTA, any climate change measure is presumed to pursue relevant legitimate objectives listed therein (the protection of human, animal and plant life or health, or the conservation

---

[104] Expression borrowed from Bossuyt (n 38) 704.

of exhaustible natural resources). The impact of Chapter 13 on Chapter 4 of the EU-Korea FTA could be that any climate change measure may implicitly be presumed to pursue a legitimate objective understood autonomously if it materializes in a mandatory document affecting a product's characteristics, related process or method of production.

Any internal environmental legal instrument adopted in furtherance of Chapter 13 would also need to comply with Chapter 12 procedural guarantees and good administration principles, which in turn should contribute to clarifying and making the climate change legislation of Korea, the EU and its Member States more accessible and susceptible to administrative and judicial review. Chapter 12 thus supplements the embryonic transparency provision in Chapter 13 by laying down substantial principles and guarantees that are more easily individualized.

Divergences of views on sustainable development issues may have to be discussed and resolved within both a mediation and an arbitral framework given the interdependency between the chapters of the EU-Korea FTA. This institutional interdependency results from the fact that Chapter 13 may call for the Contracting Parties to adopt environmental and climate change measures that either further pre-existing international environmental law commitments (with or without any impact on trade) or specifically affect trade between the Contracting Parties. This institutional interdependency also arises from the Agreement's transparency and good administration provisions. Any climate change legislation and implementing measure adopted pursuant to Chapter 13 must comply with the Chapter 12 'transparency' requirements broadly understood and with the Chapter 13 rudimentary transparency provision, assuming that the former are designed to supplement the latter. The EU and the Republic of Korea delegations to the WTO have conceded the possibility of 'cross-cutting issues' governed by both Chapter 13 and another chapter of the EU-Korea FTA with the consequence that any dispute over their interpretation and/or application would either be subject to 'the most appropriate procedure' or have to be reviewed through the dispute settlement procedures of both Chapters 13 and 14 in a piecemeal fashion.[105]

[105] WTO Committee on Regional Trade Agreements, 'Free Trade Agreement between the European Union and the Republic of Korea, Goods and Services – Questions and Replies', 14 June 2012, WT/REG296/2 [55].

7. CONCLUSION

Chapter 13 of the EU-Korea FTA, when read in isolation from the other chapters of the Agreement, enjoys a high level of soft law normativity, and conversely a low level of hard law normativity, without prejudice to its legally binding character arising from its treaty nature. Its *rendez-vous*, *renvoi*, standstill and transparency clauses, as well as its modest CSR references, testify to a low degree of clarity, detail and self-sufficiency. These clauses, unaccompanied by any concrete climate change agenda, reflect in essence best efforts legal obligations rather than result-based obligations. In addition, Chapter 13 climate change and generic environmental provisions are subject to an institutionalized form of mediation that leaves little power to the independent members of the panel of experts and no room for any procedural involvement of private parties. Having said that, this low level of hard law normativity is counterbalanced by the higher level of hard law normativity that characterizes the core trade provisions and 'transparency' standards of the EU-Korea FTA. These provisions are more precise from a clarity, detail and/or self-sufficiency angle, and the dispute settlement mechanism tailored to them entails a higher degree of delegation to a third party given the provision of an arbitration procedure that may be activated unilaterally by any Contracting Party in the event of a stalemate in the consultation phase. Chapter 14 arbitral dispute settlement mechanism, while being self-contained in the relationship between the Contracting Parties, is also not open to private parties. Based on the Contracting Parties' express intention, individuals and legal persons may not rely directly on the arbitral awards in order to assert any right against private or public bodies before the Contracting Parties' domestic courts.

The merit of Chapter 13 lies in its normative interactions with the indirect climate change provisions of the EU-Korea FTA by urging the Contracting Parties to interpret the Agreement's trade-furthering and trade-restricting provisions in the most environmental law-friendly way, and by triggering good administration principles and defence rights that supplement the embryonic transparency provision in Chapter 13.

Chapter 13 acts as a superstructure within the EU-Korea FTA; in other words, it constitutes an environmental governance constitutional framework, which instils policy directions in three spheres of decision-making: (i) decision-making designed to liberalize trade in environmental goods and services within the bounds set by the Contracting Parties' tariff schedules and specific market access commitments; (ii) decision-making designed to restrict trade in goods and services, freedom of establishment, or market access in the name of environmental protection or of climate change policies (for instance, the increase in the production, transmission, distribution and consumption of renewable energy, the increase in energy efficiency and the reduction of GHG emissions); and (iii) the elaboration of environmental legislation with no impact on trade with a view to achieving further convergence on climate change matters by expanding the Contracting Parties' prior multilateral environmental law commitments.

The hard law normativity of the climate change constitutional framework of an RTA, such as Chapter 13 of the EU-Korea FTA, may increase through the transfer of dispute settlement powers to a transnational adjudicatory body empowered to impose a final resolution of a dispute on the Contracting Parties. However, arbitral panels may be ill-equipped to adjudicate upon policy-oriented disputes in the absence of precise environmental legal rules to be applied. In the face of abstract and ill-defined environmental governance norms, the arbitrators' adjudicatory tasks, if provided for in an RTA, may end up focusing more on shaping rather than applying regional climate change law, with the risk that the arbitrators turn into climate change lawmakers. An example of a recent RTA concluded by the EU and equipped with a strong international dispute settlement mechanism is the Trade Agreement between the EU and its Member States and Colombia and Peru (EU-Colombia/Peru FTA).[106] The direct climate change provisions of this RTA are substantively imprecise given the Parties' mere obligation to promote climate change and renewable energy measures in such a way as to limit TBTs.[107] This low level of precision is, however, outweighed by a dispute settlement mechanism entailing a high level of delegation to a third party since this RTA subjects its overarching climate change framework to an arbitral procedure.[108]

---

[106] Trade Agreement between the EU and its Member States and Colombia and Peru, 26 June 2012, <http://trade.ec.europa.eu/doclib/press/index.cfm?id=691> (accessed 30 December 2013). See also Commission, 'The EU's Bilateral Trade and Investment Agreements – Where are We?', MEMO/13/915, 18 October 2013. This RTA has been provisionally applied since 1 March 2013 pending completion of its ratification process: 'Notice concerning the Provisional Application between the European Union and Peru, of the Trade Agreement between the European Union and its Member States, of the one part, and Colombia and Peru, of the other part' [2013] OJ L 56/1.

[107] Ibid art 275.

[108] Ibid arts 301–302.

The overarching climate change framework of RTAs would enjoy a higher level of precision at the substantive level if they were to regulate the main poles of climate change (that is, energy efficiency, renewable energy and GHG reductions) more directly and less through *renvoi* or by reference to the need for further cooperation. Clear qualitative and quantitative targets, as well as a concrete implementation time schedule, should be outlined in such framework provisions. The latter should not only contain collective policy goals but also confer individual rights upon relevant stakeholders. Transparency provisions labelled in the language of human rights are to supplement any climate change, environmental or sustainable development constitutional framework.

The Aarhus Convention may serve as a model for the conclusion of future comprehensive RTAs. Their overarching climate change frameworks would, as a result, include specific provisions on public access to climate change information relating to individual or general measures, on public participation in domestic climate change decision-making (in the form of consultation rights), and on access to justice in climate change matters (in the form of a reconsideration right and/or a right to administrative/judicial review). Such provisions could be turned into directly enforceable guarantees, at least for most of their modalities, through the insertion of an express self-executing clause. The Aarhus Convention, while not entirely self-sufficient in its treaty language, was nevertheless presented (politically at least) as a source of public rights and human rights intended to directly regulate the relationship between individuals and private entities, on the one hand, and governments on the other hand.[109] In other words, '[w]hereas most multilateral environmental agreements cover obligations that Parties have to each other, the Aarhus Convention covers obligations that Parties have to the public'.[110]

---

[109] Aarhus Implementation Guide (n 103) 1.

[110] Ibid 1. The term 'public' for the purposes of the Aarhus Convention refers to natural or legal persons without consideration of nationality or to associations/groups of persons as understood under the Contracting Parties' respective national laws: see Aarhus Convention (n 87) art 2.4.

7. Does integrating labour provisions in free trade agreements make a difference? An exploratory analysis of freedom of association and collective bargaining rights in 13 EU trade partners

Axel Marx and Jadir Soares*

1. INTRODUCTION

The chapters in this section discuss how the protection of environmental and human rights issues are increasingly integrated into trade agreements concluded by the European Union (EU). Many of these measures are of a more recent nature and the question of whether they are effective is still unresolved. Campling et al. (forthcoming) recently argued that there is currently very little research available on the effectiveness of the existing provisions and have proposed a research agenda to fill this gap.

One barrier to a systematic assessment of the impact is data availability (ILO, 2013). Relatively little data is available to assess to what degree human rights and, more specifically, labour standards have been protected. Several general human rights indicators and indexes exist, such as Freedom House and the Cingranelli-Richards (CIRI) Human Rights indicators, but these indicators and indexes are not always suitable to assess the impact on the protection of labour rights (Kucera, 2001, 2002; Mosley, 2011; Marx, Soares and Van Acker, 2015). As a result, additional

* The authors thank Bregt Natens and Dylan Geraets for comments on an earlier draft of this chapter and Dominique De Brabanter, Wouter Van Acker and Lucy Strang for help in data gathering and fact finding. They acknowledge support by the European Commission under the FP7 programme (grant agreement €320,000).

data needs to be gathered to make an assessment of the impact of trade agreements on the protection of labour rights.

This chapter aims to contribute to this effort by focusing specifically on the protection of freedom of association and collective bargaining (FACB) rights in a selected number of countries with which the EU has signed a free trade agreement which includes provisions on the protection of labour rights. Building on the work by David Kucera (2001; 2002) and Layna Mosley (2011), this research presents the empirical results of a data collection effort that aims to capture the degree to which FACB rights are protected. The chapter extends the initial time series of 1985–2002 developed by Mosley with an additional ten years, thus providing a time series covering almost 30 years for 73 countries, including most countries which have concluded a trade agreement with the EU (Marx, Soares and Van Acker, 2015). From this sample of 73 countries we select 13 countries with whom the EU has signed a trade agreement which contains specific language on the protection of labour rights. Our analysis shows an overall deterioration in the protection of FACB rights in these countries.

The chapter proceeds as follows. First, we introduce FACB rights and substantiate the focus on these rights for research into the effectiveness of including labour rights provisions in trade agreements. This section will also provide the selection of cases which will be further analysed. The selection of cases includes those countries/cases with which the EU has signed a trade agreement which includes substantial provisions on the protection of FACB rights. Next, we present the construction of the FACB rights index, including a differentiation between rights protection in law and in practice. In a third step, we present the main findings and provide a brief discussion. The chapter ends with a conclusion.

2. FREEDOM OF ASSOCIATION AND COLLECTIVE BARGAINING RIGHTS

In order to analyse the impact on labour rights we decided to focus on two specific rights: namely, freedom of association and the effective recognition of the right of collective bargaining. FACB rights are key components in the international treaties and declarations referred to in the trade agreements, including the International Labour Organization (ILO) Declaration on Fundamental Principles and Rights at Work adopted in

1998 (ILO Declaration),[1] the Universal Declaration of Human Rights, and the 2008 Declaration on Social Justice for a Fair Globalisation, which identified freedom of association and the right of collective bargaining as key pre-conditions for the attainment of inclusive economic growth and decent work. In addition, several policy documents of international organizations point to the importance of these two rights for inclusive and sustained economic growth (see, for example, the World Commission on the Social Dimension of Globalization, 2004). The ILO Declaration covers the core rights and standards laid down in four principles and eight conventions. These principles are: (i) freedom of association and the effective recognition of the right of collective bargaining; (ii) the elimination of all forms of forced or compulsory labour; (iii) the effective abolition of child labour; and (iv) the elimination of discrimination and respect for employment and occupation. As stated by the ILO, the 'Declaration makes it clear that these rights are universal, and that they apply to all people in all States – regardless of the level of economic development'.[2]

The principle of freedom of association and the effective recognition of the right of collective bargaining is laid down in two conventions. The Freedom of Association and Protection of the Right to Organize Convention (ILO Convention No. 87) came into force on 4 July 1950 and by 2014 had been ratified by 153 states.[3] It refers to the right of workers to create collective organizations without interference (International Labour Conference, 2008). The right of freedom of association is also recognized as a basic human right in the Universal Declaration of Human Rights (Article 20). Linked to the right of freedom of association is the right of collective bargaining. The convention concerning the application of the principles of the right to organise and collective bargaining (ILO Convention No. 98) came into force on 18 July 1951 and has been ratified by 164 states.[4] This right allows workers to freely negotiate their working

---

[1] See http://www.ilo.org/declaration/thedeclaration/textdeclaration/lang–en/index.htm.

[2] See http://www.ilo.org/declaration/thedeclaration/lang–en/index.htm.

[3] ILO, Convention concerning Freedom of Association and Protection of the Right to Organise, C87, adopted 9 July 1948, in force 4 July 1950, available at: http://www.ilo.org/dyn/normlex/en/f?p=NORMLEXPUB:12100:0::NO::P12100_INSTRUMENT_ID:312232.

[4] ILO, Convention concerning the Application of the Principles of the Right to Organise and to Bargain Collectively, C98, adopted 1 July 1949, in force 18 July 1951, available at: http://www.ilo.org/dyn/normlex/en/f?p=1000:12100:0::NO::P12100_ILO_CODE:C098.

conditions. These rights were chosen for further analysis for two distinct reasons: substantial and methodological.

2.1 The Substantive Importance of FACB

In the context of trade policy, these rights are of specific importance. First, they are considered basic rights in that they allow workers to organize themselves and increase their capacity to negotiate other labour standards. Second, the importance of the protection of these rights is illustrated by the fact that a violation of FACB rights was invoked to suspend the EU's GSP+ trade preferences for Belarus (EU Regulation 1933/2006;[5] see also Yap, Chapter 9, this volume). This suspension of GSP+ has been applied in three cases only (Myanmar, Sri Lanka and Belarus). Third, in a proliferating number of bilateral, trilateral or multilateral (economic and trade) agreements, social clauses which directly refer to the relevant ILO conventions have been taken on board. This is the key interest of this chapter.

Some of those agreements have very weak or general provisions that refer only in general terms to human rights. For example, the Euro-Mediterranean Agreement between the EU and Kingdom of Morocco in Article 2 states: 'Respect for the democratic principles and fundamental human rights established by the Universal Declaration of Human Rights shall inspire the domestic and external policies of the Community and of Morocco and shall constitute an essential element of this Agreement.' Equally weak provisions, or even none at all, can be found in agreements with Algeria, Egypt, Jordan, Mexico, the Palestinian Territories, South Africa, Tunisia and Turkey. The agreement with Chile contains some stronger commitments in Article 44 on social cooperation. This provision states:

> The Parties recognise the importance of social development, which must go hand in hand with economic development. They will give priority to the creation of employment and respect for fundamental social rights, notably by promoting the relevant conventions of the International Labour Organisation covering such topics as the freedom of association, the right to collective bargaining and non-discrimination, the abolition of forced and child labour, and equal treatment between men and women.

---

[5] Council Regulation (EC) No.1933/2006 of 21 December temporarily withdrawing access to the generalised tariff preferences from the Republic of Belarus, [2006] OJ L 405.

Other trade agreements contain far more elaborated provisions on labour rights and even include monitoring instruments. Article 72 of the EU-Cariforum Agreement (which includes Antigua & Barbuda, Bahamas, Barbados, Belize, Dominica and the Dominican Republic) addresses the behaviour of investors, and stipulates:

> The EC Party and the Signatory CARIFORUM States shall cooperate and take, within their own respective territories, such measures as may be necessary, inter alia, through domestic legislation, to ensure that: [...] (b) Investors act in accordance with core labour standards as required by the International Labour Organization (ILO) Declaration on Fundamental Principles and Rights at Work, 1998, to which the EC Party and the Signatory CARIFORUM States are parties. (2) [...] These core labour standards are further elaborated, in accordance with the Declaration, in ILO Conventions concerning freedom of association, the elimination of forced labour, the abolition of child labour and the elimination of discrimination in the work place ... (c) Investors do not manage or operate their investments in a manner that circumvents international environmental or labour obligations arising from agreements to which the EC Party and the Signatory CARIFORUM States are parties.

Article 73 deals with the maintenance of standards and requires that '[t]he EC Party and the Signatory CARIFORUM States shall ensure that foreign direct investment is not encouraged by lowering domestic environmental, labour or occupational health and safety legislation and standards or by relaxing core labour standards or laws aimed at protecting and promoting cultural diversity'. Furthermore, the agreement includes specific provisions on objectives and multilateral commitments under Article 191 which refer to the ILO Declaration and the conventions included in the ILO Declaration. Article 191 includes:

> 1. The Parties reaffirm their commitment to the internationally recognised core labour standards, as defined by the relevant ILO Conventions, and in particular the freedom of association and the right to collective bargaining, the abolition of forced labour, the elimination of the worst forms of child labour and nondiscrimination in respect to employment. The Parties also reaffirm their obligations as members of the ILO and their commitments under the ILO Declaration on Fundamental Principles and Rights at Work and its Follow-Up (1998) [...] 3. The Parties recognise the beneficial role that core labour standards and decent work can have on economic efficiency, innovation and productivity, and they highlight the value of greater policy coherence between trade policies, on the one hand, and employment and social policies on the other.

Building on this provision, Articles 192 and 193 refer to the level of social protection and stipulate that parties cannot lower their level of protection to attract investment.

Provisions of similar detail to those in the EU-Cariforum agreement can be found in the EU-Colombia and Peru (and recently Ecuador) agreement. Article 269 of this agreement deals with multilateral labour standards and agreements and states *inter alia*: '3. Each Party commits to the promotion and effective implementation in its laws and practice and in its whole territory of internationally recognised core labour standards as contained in the fundamental Conventions of the International Labour Organisation.' Subsequent articles contain provisions on upholding standards (Article 277); monitoring mechanisms, which consist of reviews of sustainability impact (Article 279); institutional and monitoring mechanisms (Article 280); and domestic monitoring mechanisms (Article 281).

The agreement between the EU and Central-America (Costa Rica, El Salvador, Guatemala, Honduras, Nicaragua and Panama) also contains several provisions on the protection of labour rights. Article 2 ('Objectives') states that the parties agree that the objectives are *inter alia* to: '(g) at least maintain and preferably develop the level of good governance, social, labour and environmental standards achieved through the effective implementation of international conventions of which the Parties are part at the time of entry into force of this Agreement.' Article 42, on employment relations and social protection under paragraph (f), explicitly refers to the ILO's core conventions; Article 286 includes similar provisions to those referred to above on multilateral labour standards and agreements, again referring to the ILO core conventions. This article also includes a provision which reaffirms the commitment to effectively implement a series of ILO conventions, including Nos. 87 and 98. This is followed by Article 291 on upholding levels of social protection.

Finally, the agreement between the EU and South Korea also contains several provisions on labour standards including references to the ILO conventions. The EU-South Korea trade agreement also includes the objective (in Article 1.1) 'to promote foreign direct investment without lowering or reducing environmental, labour or occupational health and safety standards in the application and enforcement of environmental and labour laws of the Parties'. Article 13.4(3) ('Multilateral Labour Standards and Agreements') refers to the ILO Declaration. Institutional monitoring (Article 13.12) and transparency (Article 13.9) measures to spot possible violations of these rights also form part of the agreement.

The above overview shows that there is significant variation in how the trade agreements integrate the protection of labour rights, and that some agreements have substantial provisions on such rights. Those countries with whom the EU has signed a trade agreement with strong provisions are Chile; the EU-Cariforum agreement (with Antigua and Barbuda, Bahamas, Barbados, Belize, Dominica and the Dominican Republic); the EU-Colombia and Peru agreement; the EU-Central America agreement (with Costa Rica, El Salvador, Guatemala, Honduras, Nicaragua and Panama); and the EU-South Korea agreement. For 13 of these partner countries, we were able to collect data (see below, Section 3): these are Antigua and Barbuda, Bahamas, Barbados, Belize, Chile, Colombia, Costa Rica, Dominica, the Dominican Republic, Ecuador, Panama, Peru and South Korea (the Group of 13).

2.2 The Methodological Importance of FACB Rights

A focus on FACB rights is also based on methodological grounds. There are three distinct reasons to focus on FACB rights. First, as noted above, more aggregate composite human rights indicators, such as Freedom House and the Cingranelli-Richards (CIRI) Human Rights indicators, are not always suitable for assessing the impact on specific labour rights. They bring together a whole set of different human rights which are not related to labour rights, such as freedom of the press and religious freedom. The use of composite indicators covering a diverse set of rights makes them vulnerable to ecological fallacy-type errors (Robinson, 1950) – that is, drawing conclusions from observations at the level of the composite indicator which might not hold for its components separately. In other words, a composite indicator might show improvement in general while specific components might be deteriorating (further violations). In order to address these limitations, David Kucera (2001, 2002) developed a new indicator which specifically aimed to capture the degree to which two specific core labour conventions are protected – namely, ILO Convention 87 (Freedom of Association and the Protection of the Right to Organise Convention) and ILO Convention 98 (Right to Organise and Collective Bargaining Convention).

Layna Mosley used this indicator to develop a time series from 1985 to 2002 on the protection of freedom of association and collective bargaining. Her study showed that the protection of FACB rights was declining on a global scale, which raises doubts about the global protection of at least two core labour conventions for the period 1985 to 2002. These efforts already provide us with an interesting time series. This generates a second methodological advantage. A time series allows us to analyse an evolution over time. By expanding the time series developed by Mosley we can analyse the evolution of specific rights over an almost thirty-year period.

Third, the way in which Kucera and Mosley constructed their indexes allows for a separation of the evolution of the protection of FACB rights in law and in practice. The coding of the index consists of an assessment of 37 categories (see below, Annex 1 to this chapter) which can be divided into the protection of these rights in law and in practice. The categories that cover violations in law are based on the incorporation of labour rights (derived from ILO Conventions 87 and 98) into domestic law: for example, the absence of the legal right to strike, the absence of the right of collective bargaining, or a restriction on the foreign financial contributions a union is allowed to receive. The situation in practice is measured by categories which focus on the protection of these rights in practice, such as reports of trade union members who have been fired on the ground of union activities or reported interferences with union rights of assembly, demonstration and free opinion.[6]

3. FACB INDEX: DATA COLLECTION

David Kucera developed an index of freedom of association and collective bargaining based on 37 evaluation criteria, considering both *de jure* and *de facto* violations of these two labour rights. The author identified the 37 evaluation criteria based on ILO Conventions 87 (freedom of association) and 98 (right to collective bargaining). The assessment of the 37 evaluation criteria is based on a content analysis of three distinct sources per year per country: the International Confederation of Free Trade Unions' Annual Survey of Violations of Trade Union Rights,[7] the US State Department's Country Reports on Human Rights Practices,[8] and the ILO's Reports of the Committee on Freedom of Association.[9]

[6] With reference to Annex 1, if we found reported violations to categories 6, 8, 13, 14, 15, 16, 18, 19, 20, 21, 22, 24, 25, 26, 29, 30, 32, 33, 34, 35 and 37 we coded them as violations of the protection in law; if we found reported violations to categories 1, 2, 3, 4, 5, 7, 9, 10, 11, 12, 17, 23, 27, 28, 31 and 36 we reported them as violations in practice.

[7] The ITUC's sources were gathered with the help of the ITUC itself: 2003 and 2004 were available in a paper format only, 2006, 2007 and 2013 were available online, and the others were sent to us as pdf files.

[8] http://www.state.gov/j/drl/rls/hrrpt.

[9] http://www.ilo.org/dyn/normlex/en/f?p=1000:11000:0::NO:::

Within the above mentioned sources the coders[10] looked for any references to violations of the 37 items for each of the countries and years identified (see Annex 1 below). Violations in respect of each of the 37 items were measured as a dummy variable. When one of the sources reported a violation for a specific country a '1' was given to that country. If none of the three sources provided indications for a violation a '0' was given.

Each category also carried a weight as some violations are more serious than others. The weight depends on the severity of a violation, usually ranging from 1 to 2. Three severe types of violation have a special weight of 10: the ban on all unions (category 6), the absence of any union activity arising from social/economic breakdown (category 7), and the general prohibition of collective bargaining (category 24).[11] As a result, the score for a given country and year is the sum of all scores (0 or 1) for each of the 37 categories multiplied by the weight for the specific category. Theoretically, the highest score on this scale is 86.5. However, the highest score observed in the research population was 29.75, for Turkey in 2007. The theoretically lowest score (0) was observed several times.

In order to make the results more easily and visibly understandable we reversed the scores and rescaled them on a 0–10 scale. This means that a higher score (10, or close to 10) refers to better labour rights situations with fewer violations of FACB rights, and a lower score indicates more severe violations. In other words, an upward trend indicates an improvement in the protection of FACB; a downward trend indicates a deterioration.

In order to further refine the analysis, we made a distinction between two groups of categories: those covering violations in law, on the one hand, and violations in practice on the other.[12] The categories covering violations in law assume the incorporation of labour rights (derived from ILO Conventions 87 and 98) into domestic law. Examples are the absence of the legal right to strike (category 32), the absence of the right of collective bargaining (category 24), and a restriction on the foreign

---

[10] The authors coded the violations. In case of doubt, the authors decided on how to code a specific instance. A list of decision of doubts is included in the methodological note which is available from the authors.

[11] There is a small difference between Kucera and Mosley on using the weights. We follow the procedure followed by Mosley.

[12] The law categories are: 6, 8, 13, 14, 15, 16, 18, 19, 20, 21, 22, 24, 25, 26, 29, 30, 32, 33, 34, 35 and 37. The practice categories are: 1, 2, 3, 4, 5, 7, 9, 10, 11, 12, 17, 23, 27, 28, 31 and 36.

financial contributions a union is allowed to receive (category 23). The situation in practice is measured by the remaining practice categories, covering issues such as trade union members being fired for union activities (category 10) and an employer limiting the agenda in collective bargaining (category 28). This distinction between law and practice becomes relevant when we analyse the results. Some countries, for example, have a spotless record in law, but have a contrasting situation on the ground. Another potential important difference between the two categories concerns the dynamics. The score on violations in practice changes more profoundly under the influence of domestic disturbances or economic downturns. At the same time, changing existing law can take a long time, therefore resulting in a far more stable score for violations in law.

4. THE PROTECTION OF FACB RIGHTS WITH SELECTED TRADE PARTNERS

4.1 Results

Figure 7.1 shows, for the selected Group of 13, the overall trend in the protection of FACB rights (full line), the protection in law (dotted line) and the protection in practice (striped line). In addition, we include for each a linear trend line. These graphs reveal several interesting observations.

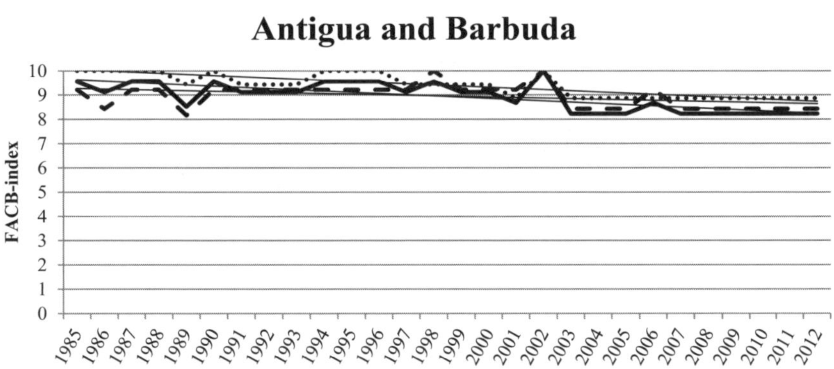

Bahamas

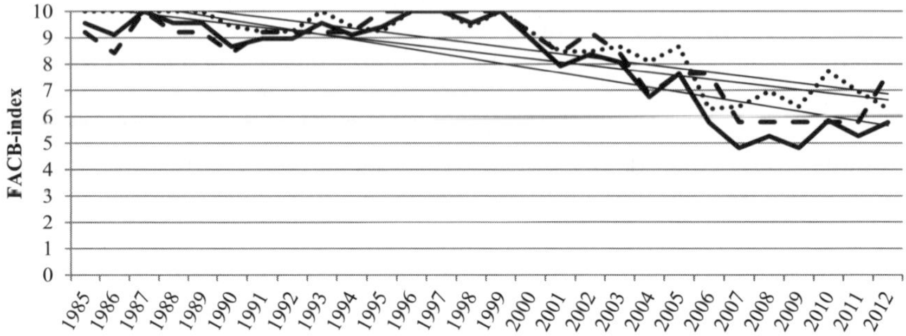

Barbados

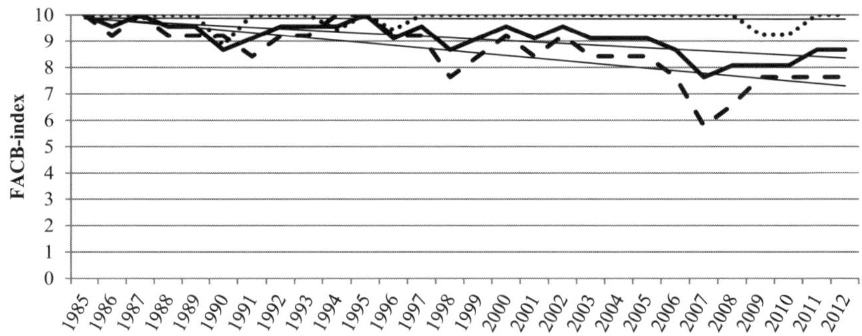

Belize

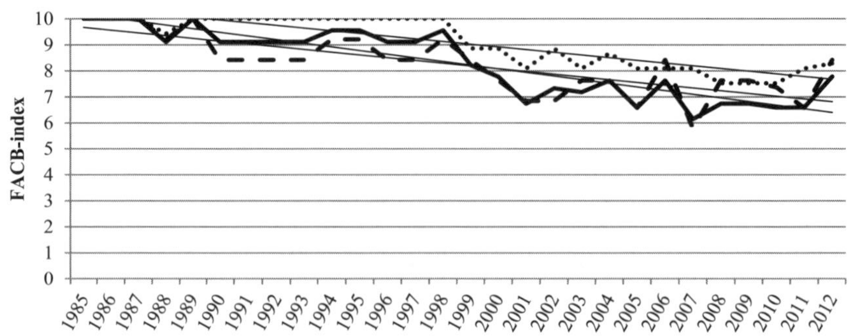

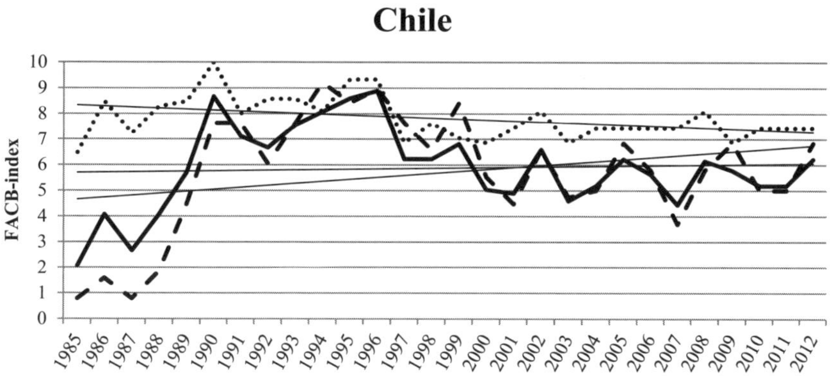
Chile
FACB-index
0
1
2
3
4
5
6
7
8
9
10
1985 1986 1987 1988 1989 1990 1991 1992 1993 1994 1995 1996 1997 1998 1999 2000 2001 2002 2003 2004 2005 2006 2007 2008 2009 2010 2011 2012

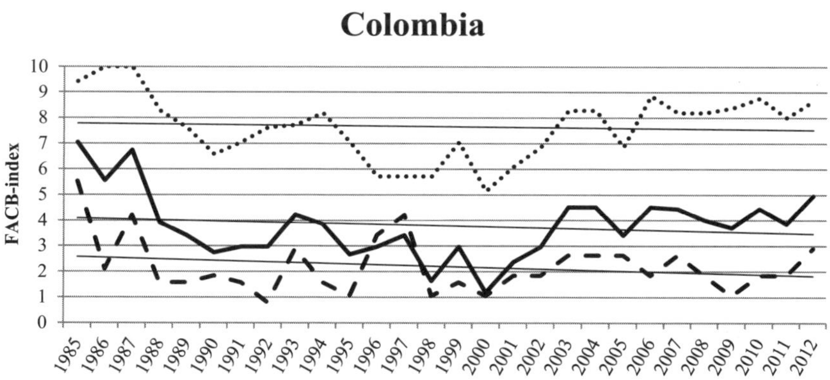
Colombia
FACB-index
0
1
2
3
4
5
6
7
8
9
10
1985 1986 1987 1988 1989 1990 1991 1992 1993 1994 1995 1996 1997 1998 1999 2000 2001 2002 2003 2004 2005 2006 2007 2008 2009 2010 2011 2012

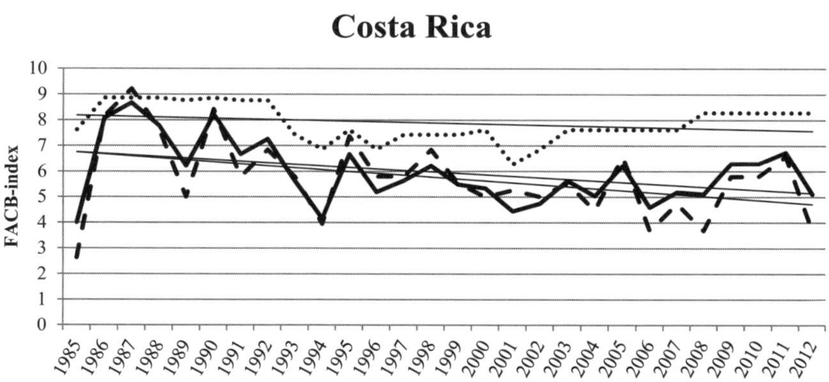
Costa Rica
FACB-index
0
1
2
3
4
5
6
7
8
9
10
1985 1986 1987 1988 1989 1990 1991 1992 1993 1994 1995 1996 1997 1998 1999 2000 2001 2002 2003 2004 2005 2006 2007 2008 2009 2010 2011 2012

Dominica

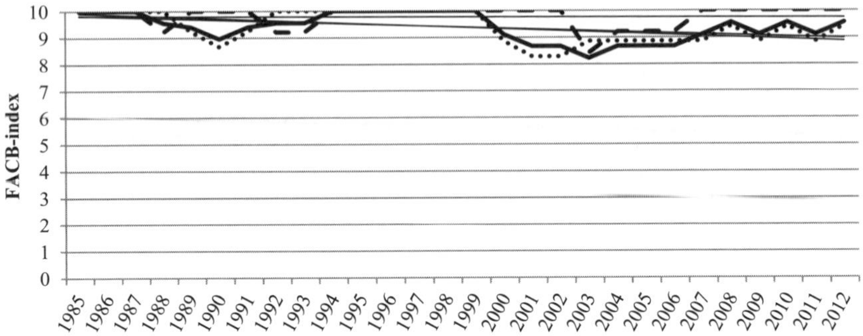

Dominican Republic

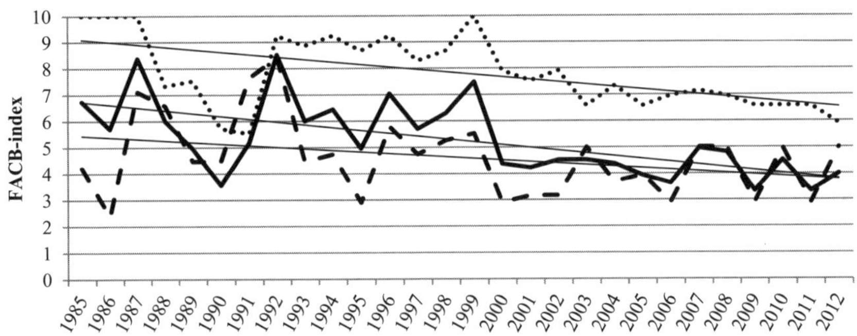

Ecuador

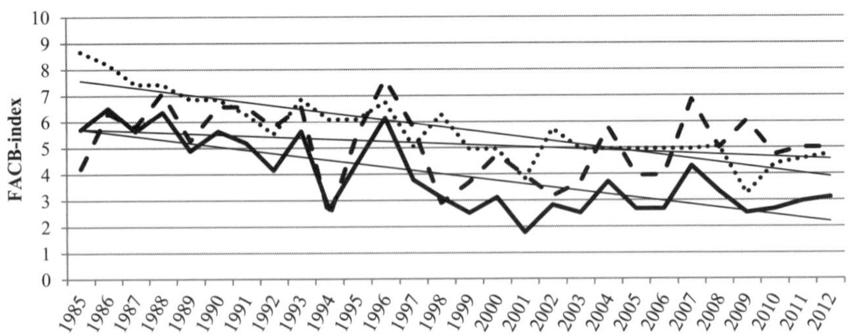

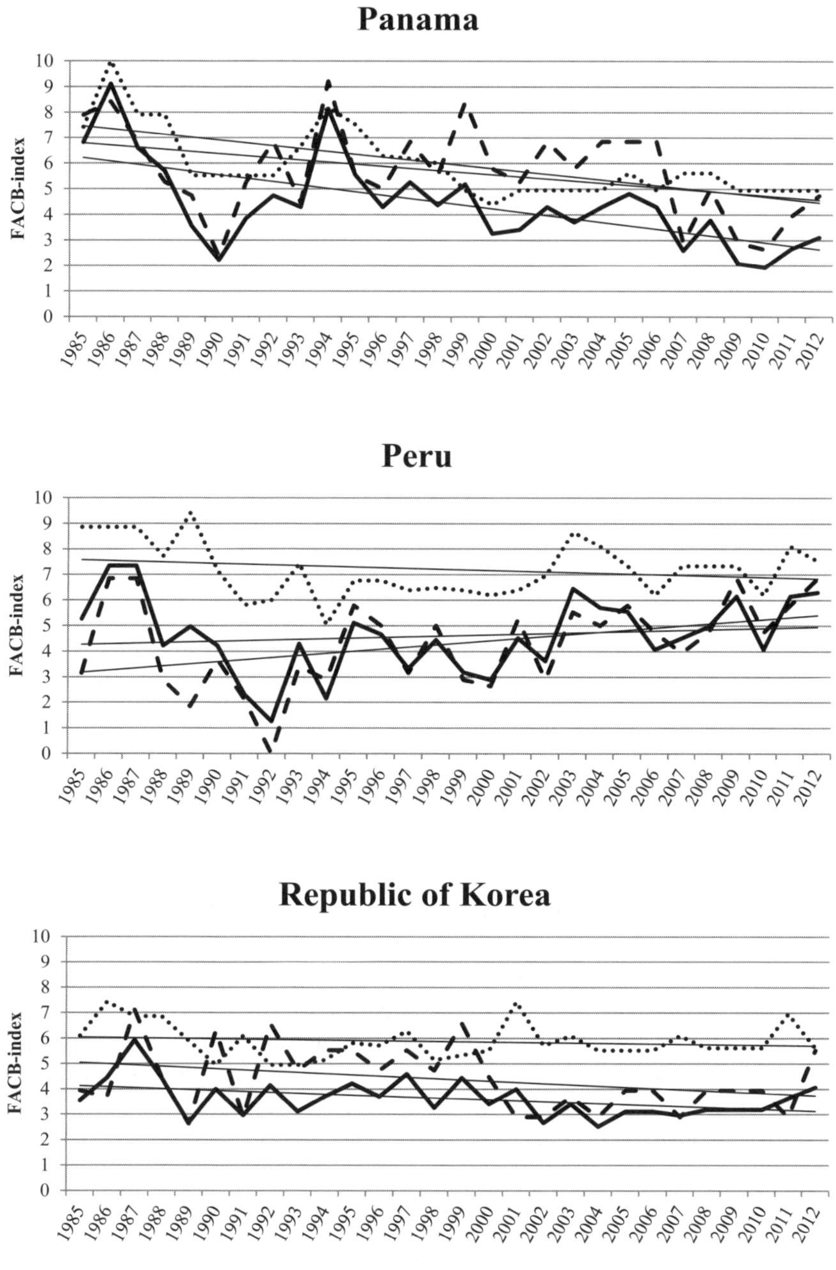

Figure 7.1 *Evolution of the protection of FACB in rights in total, in law and in practice for 13 countries*

First, for all countries included in the analysis, violations of FACB rights are present in all cases notwithstanding that all of them have ratified the relevant ILO conventions. Hence, the empirical data clearly shows a compliance gap with regard to the enforcement of international conventions. This finding corresponds with earlier research which shows the difference in ratifying international commitments and agreements, and effective compliance with obligations embedded in these international commitments and agreements (Simmons, 2009; Mosley, 2011; Hafner-Burton, 2013).

Second, there is very significant variation between countries in the overall protection of FACB rights. The scores range from approximately a perfect 10 score for some countries, mostly in the 1980s, to very low scores of 2 and 3 out of 10 for other countries throughout the overall period. By way of comparison, the average score for EU Member States over the same time period is approximately 8.5 (see Marx, Soares and Van Acker, 2015). Some countries, such as Barbados or Antigua and Barbuda, have a high overall score in the later years, while others, such as Ecuador, have a very low score. In the latter countries, there are not only many violations of FACB rights, they are also systematic over time. Although we include linear trend lines to capture the overall trend, we should note also that the time series do exhibit non-linear patterns and show strong variation between two, three or four consecutive years. The latter is especially the case for Chile (whole period), Costa Rica (before 2000), Dominican Republic (1990s), Ecuador (early 1990s), Panama (whole period) and Peru (whole period). How to further interpret these strong fluctuations will require further case-based research. Overall, given the ratification of the relevant ILO conventions by these countries, these scores reveal a very significant enforcement and compliance gap.

Third, most of the analysed countries show a clear decline in the protection of FACB rights over time. Aside from Chile and Peru, all other countries show a downward trend over the studied period. Admittedly this linear trend might hide non-linear fluctuations, but the overall trend is negative. In some cases, this downward trend is very drastic, such as in the cases of Ecuador and Belize. In other cases, the negative trend is less obvious. Considering that the trade agreements, including provisions relating to the protection of FACB rights, entered into force during the studied period, one may question their impact. Our results indicate that the protection of FACB rights does not increase with their inclusion in a trade agreement, although admittedly these stronger provisions on FACB rights are of a rather recent nature. We can further explore this by comparing different periods at the country level.

Table 7.1 presents an average score on the FACB index for the first five years of measurement and for the last five years, as well as the percentage change between the two periods. For our group of 13 countries (with strong provisions on FACB rights) we observe a decline in FACB rights protection of 27 per cent, compared with 16 per cent for the overall population of 73 countries for which we have data (see Marx, Soares and Van Acker, 2015). Hence, we observe a stronger decline in FACB rights protection. However, the group of 73 is biased as it includes all EU and other OECD countries. If we compare the trend against a control group selected from the 73 countries we observe a less marked decrease in our group of 13 compared to a control group for which the FACB index decreased by 35 per cent. This control group consists mainly of other countries with which the EU or US have signed trade agreements and includes the following countries: Algeria, Argentina, Bahrain, Brazil, Brunei Darussalam, China, Egypt, Jordan, Libyan Arab Jamahiriya, Mexico, Morocco, Oman, South Africa, Taiwan, Thailand, Tunisia, Turkey, Uruguay and Venezuela. The latter comparison suggests that the group of 13 are doing slightly better than other comparable cases. However, to make this analysis more robust, more data on other countries needs to be collected. These results might suggest that the inclusion of the FACB rights in trade agreements might have some (marginal) effect (slowing down the decline in the protection of these rights) but is not able to reverse a downward trend. To be sure, the downward trend can be explained by several factors, as discussed in Marx, Soares and Van Acker (2015), such as better reporting and monitoring. These effects, however, should hold for all countries and will influence our group of 13 to the same extent as the control group. The point being made here is that we do not observe an immediate effect of a trade agreement on the protection of FACB rights. It is, of course, possible that these FTAs with human rights clauses have contributed to the protection of FACB rights, and that the downward trends observed have been caused by another factor, not considered in this study. However, looking at these downward trends, it is clear that these agreements have not been effective enough (or not as good as expected).

We can zoom in even further on this by focusing more on the periods immediately before and after the date of the FTA. Table 7.2 provides an overview of when the negotiations were concluded, the agreements were signed and when they entered into force. The table also shows FACB scores before and after the trade agreement was negotiated. Since negotiations started some time before the agreement entered into force, one could expect some anticipatory behaviour, in both the economic as well as the political respect. Hence, as a cut-off point we take the date of

Table 7.1 Comparison of FACB Index scores of the Group of 13 with other groups

	1985–1990		2008–2012
Average score 13 countries	7.132764		5.585185
Percentage change		–27.7086%	
Average score all countries	7.804972		6.714764
Percentage change		–16.236%	
Average control group	6.734503		4.97232
Percentage change		–35.4399%	

the conclusion of negotiations and compare the average FACB scores before and after that date. We take equivalent periods. Hence if the negotiations were concluded in 2007, we calculated the average on the basis of the following six years (2007 included) and the preceding six years; if they were concluded in 2009 (Korea), we calculated the average of four years before and after; for the 2010 agreements we calculated the average over three years, and for Chile we calculated the averages on the basis of 11 years. For Ecuador we do not have data to compare.

Table 7.2 shows that there is no clear evidence that the protection of FACB rights increases after finalizing a trade agreement. Some countries show a rather stable pattern with overall quite low scores on the protection of FACB rights and some small improvements (Colombia, Costa Rica, Peru and South Korea) or decline (Antigua and Barbuda, Panama) in the protection of such rights. Some other countries (such as Bahamas, Barbados and Chile) show a marked decline. Overall, the conclusion of a trade agreement does not seem to create a watershed moment in which we observe a marked increase in better protection of specific rights.

Finally, as could be expected, the cases show a difference in the protection of FACB rights in law (dotted line) and in practice (striped line). In all cases,[13] the protection in law is stronger than the protection in practice. This indicates an implementation or enforcement gap. These differences can be very obvious, as illustrated by Colombia. In this case, there is a marked difference between the two lines. In general, the trend lines for the protection in law and the protection in practice follow a similar pattern, both in direction (upward/downward) and strength. In

[13] Except for some specific and short periods.

Table 7.2 Comparing FACB rights protection: before and after the conclusion of a trade agreement

	Trade Agreements			FACB Index	
	Negotiations concluded	Signed	Entered into force	Before	After
Antigua & Barbuda	2007	2008	2008	8.66	8.22
Bahamas	2007	2008	2008	7.41	5.29
Barbados	2007	2008	2008	9.11	8.19
Belize	2007	2008	2008	7.18	6.76
Chile	2002	2002	2003 (2005 for services)	6.91	5.56
Colombia	2010	2012	2013	4.04	4.41
Costa Rica	2010	2012	2013	5.53	6.04
Dominica	2007	2008	2008	8.59	9.33
Dominican Republic	.007	2008	2008	4.19	4.16
Ecuador	2014	–	–	–	–
Panama	2010	2012	2013	2.81	2.56
Peru	2010	2012	2013	5.20	5.50
South Korea	2009	2010	2011	3.09	3.51

some cases we can observe a divergence in which the protection in law (dotted line) remains stable, while the protection in practice (striped line) decreases significantly. One explanation for these differences could be, as discussed by Levi et al. (2012), the lack of state administrative and regulatory capacity to enforce contracts and protect rights. Another possible reason is that governments in countries with low regulatory quality and weak rule of law can create regulations that they do not intend to respect as a short-term response to international or domestic pressure (Levi et al., 2012; see also the discussion in Simmons (2009)). This distinction between the protection in law and in practice is also interesting from the perspective of the inclusion of labour rights provisions in trade agreements. One could expect that countries that are bound by trade agreements with strong FACB rights provisions exhibit an increase in the protection of FACB rights in law, not necessarily followed by an increase in divergence. These are the so-called 'false positives' (Simmons, 2009) – countries that signal compliance with international regulation by translating it into domestic law without following it up with actual enforcement. In other words, one could hypothesize a divergence between protection in law and protection in practice after a trade agreement has been negotiated. We do not observe this divergence, which indicates that the institutional (in law) changes also remain limited following the entry into force of a trade agreement.

5. CONCLUSION

These exploratory results show no clear evidence that trade agreements with labour provisions result in increased protection of the two core labour rights of freedom of association and collective bargaining. On the contrary, we find a steady decline in the protection of these two rights. This is not to argue that these provisions have no effect. Indeed, we have no information on what would have happened without the inclusion of labour provisions in these agreements. In addition, the protection of these rights is influenced by several factors, and in another contribution (Marx, Soares and Van Acker, 2015) we identify and discuss the determinants of FACB rights protection. This overview shows that the protection of these rights is determined by a set of international and domestic factors. These factors not only include the ratification of treaties and conventions or the inclusion of these rights in specific agreements, but also include government composition, the nature of the political system, trade openness, foreign investment, and a range of other factors. Changes in these factors might also contribute to the decline in the protection of these rights.

In this context special attention could turn to trade openness. Several studies have analysed the impact on labour standards protection of trade openness, measured by the ratio of the sum of imports and exports to GDP. The results of these studies are mixed, pointing mostly to a negative relationship between trade openness and the protection of labour standards. Busse (2004) analysed 71 developing countries and found a robust negative effect (reducing compliance) in a panel data analysis for data from 1970 to 2000. Neumayer and De Soysa (2006), on the other hand, found a positive effect of trade openness on labour standards in their cross-sectional analysis using Kucera's measure of FACB rights; this result is robust across various specifications, including different control variables and samples (only developing countries versus all countries). However, the studies published by Mosley (2011) present evidence of an opposite (negative) effect of trade openness. Mosley argues that the effect of trade openness is different from foreign direct investment, the latter contributing to better practices. However, trade openness, especially through subcontracting, produces more violations of labour rights as governments are tempted to reduce the provision or enforcement of such rights as a result of cost competition (Mosley and Uno, 2007; Mosley, 2011; see also Levi et al., 2012). Given the exponential growth of international trade over the last five decades (Hoekman, 2014), it might well be hypothesized that trade openness generates downward pressures on the protection of FACB rights which are not offset by international conventions or the inclusion of the protection of these rights in trade agreements. This chapter suggests that the overall pattern of FACB protection over the last 30 years is downward. This coincides with an ever increasing volume of trade. Further case-based research is needed to investigate the specific interaction between trade openness and the protection of FACB rights at the country level to further explain what the effect is, how they interact and how trade agreements can counter possible negative effects.

REFERENCES

Busse, Matthias (2004), 'On the Determinants of Core Labour Standards: the Case of Developing Countries', *Economics Letters* **83** (2), 211–17.

Campling, Liam et al. (forthcoming), 'Working Beyond the Border? A New Research Agenda for the Evaluation of Labour Standards in EU Trade Agreements', *International Labour Review*.

Cingranelli, David L. and David L. Richards (1999), 'Respect for Human Rights after the End of the Cold War', *Journal of Peace Research*, **36** (5), 511–34.

Cingranelli, David L. and David L. Richards (2008), *The Cingranelli-Richards (CIRI) Human Rights Data Project Coding Manual Version 2008.3.13*, available at: http://ciri.binghamton.edu/documentation/ciri_coding_guide.pdf (accessed 10 January 2014).

Freedom House (2013), 'Freedom in the World 2013: Democratic Breakthroughs in the Balance', available at: http://www.freedomhouse.org (accessed 9 January 2014).

Hafner-Burton, Emilie M. (2005), 'Trading Human Rights: How Preferential Trade Agreements Influence Government Repression', *International Organization*, **59** (3), 593–629.

Hafner-Burton, Emilie M. (2013), *Making Human Rights a Reality*, Princeton, NJ: Princeton University Press.

Hoekman, Bernard (2014), *Supply Chains, Mega-Regionals and Multilateralism. A Road Map for the WTO*, London: CEPR Press.

International Labour Conference (2008), *Freedom of Association in Practice: Lessons Learned*, Report of the Director-General, Global Report under the follow-up to the ILO Declaration on Fundamental Principles and Rights at Work, 97th Session, 2008, Report I, Geneva: International Labour Office, available at: http://www.

ilo.org/wcmsp5/groups/public/–dgreports/–dcomm/documents/publication/wcms_096122.pdf.

International Labour Organization (2013), *Social Dimensions of Free Trade Agreements / International Labour Organization; International Institute for Labour Studies*, Geneva: ILO.

Kucera, David (2001), 'Measuring Fundamental Rights at Work', *Statistical Journal of the United Nations*, **18**, 175–86.

Kucera, David (2002), 'Core Labour Standards and Foreign Direct Investment', *International Labour Review*, **141** (1–2), 31–69.

Kucera, David (2004), 'Measuring Trade Union Rights: A Country-Level Indicator Constructed from Coding Violations Recorded in Textual Sources', Working Paper No. 50, Geneva: International Labour Office, Statistical Development and Analysis Unit.

Levi, Margaret et al. (2012), 'Aligning Rights and Interests: Why, When and How to Uphold Labor Standards', Background Paper for the World Development Report 2013.

Marx, Axel, Jadir Soares and Wouter Van Acker (2015), 'The Protection of International Labour Rights. A Longitudinal Analysis of the Protection of the Rights of Freedom of Association and Collective Bargaining over 30 years in 73 Countries', in Axel Marx, Jan Wouters, Laura Beke and Glenn Rayp (eds), *Global Governance of Labour Rights*, Cheltenham, UK and Northampton, MA, USA: Edward Elgar Publishing.

Mosley, Layna (2011), *Labor Rights and Multinational Production*, New York: Cambridge University Press.

Mosley, Layna and Saika Uno (2007), 'Racing to the Bottom or Climbing to the Top? Economic Globalization and Collective Labor Rights', *Comparative Political Studies*, **40** (8), 923–48.

Neumayer, Eric and Indra De Soysa (2006), 'Globalization and the Right to Free Association and Collective Bargaining: An Empirical Analysis', *World Development*, **34** (1), 31–49.

Robinson, William S. (1950), 'Ecological Correlations and the Behavior of Individuals', *American Sociological Review*, **15** (3), 351–7.

Simmons, Beth A. (2009), *Mobilizing Human Rights: International Law in Domestic Politics*, Cambridge: Cambridge University Press.

World Commission on the Social Dimension of Globalization (2004), *A Fair Globalization: Creating Opportunities For All*, Geneva: International Labour Organization.

ANNEX 1

Table 7A.1 *Kucera's template for measuring FACB rights violations*

Category	Description	Weight
	Freedom of association/collective bargaining related liberties	
1	Murder or disappearance of union members or organizers	2
2	Other violence against union members or organizers	2
3	Arrest, detention, imprisonment or forced exile for union membership or activities	2
4	Interference with union rights of assembly, demonstration, free opinion, free expression	2
5	Seizure or destruction of union premises or property	2
	Right to establish and join union and worker organizations	
6	General prohibitions	10
7	General absence resulting from socio-economic breakdown	10
8	Previous authorization requirements (*does not include requirements that unions register with governments, unless these requirements are deemed onerous by the ILO*)	1.5
9	Employment conditional on non-membership in union	1.5
10	Dismissal or suspension for union membership or activities (*includes dismissal for strike activities*)	1.5
11	Interference of employers (attempts to dominate unions)	1.5
12	Dissolution or suspension of union by administrative authority	2
13	Only workers' committees and labour councils permitted	2
14	Only state-sponsored or other single unions permitted (*includes allowing only one union per industry or sector*)	1.5
15	Exclusion of tradable/industrial sectors from union membership	2
16	Exclusion of other sectors or workers from union membership (*includes exclusion of public sector workers from union membership; excluding 'essential services' is acceptable, provided the definition of 'essential services' is not excessively broad (i.e. following ILO guidelines, limitations on armed forces' union membership are acceptable)*)	2
17	Other specific *de facto* problems or acts of prohibition	1.5
18	(No) right to establish and join federations or confederations of unions	1.5
19	Previous authorization requirements regarding above row	1

Table 7A.1 (continued)

Category	Description	Weight
	Other union activities	
20	(No) right to elect representatives in full freedom (*includes requirement that union leaders must work full time in a given industry*)	1.5
21	(No) right to establish constitutions and rules	1.5
22	General prohibition of union/federation participation in political activities (*includes limits on union contributions to political parties*)	1.5
23	(No) union control of finances (*includes situations in which unions receive a substantial portion of financing from government sources, or rules that unions may not receive financial contributions from abroad or from certain groups*)	1.5
	Right to collectively bargain	
24	General prohibitions	10
25	Prior approval by authorities of collective agreements	1.5
26	Compulsory binding arbitration (*includes systems in which compulsory binding arbitration is necessary before a (legal) strike may be called*)	1.5
27	Intervention of authorities (*includes unilateral setting of wages by authorities*)	1.5
28	Scope of collective bargaining restricted by non-state employers	1.5
29	Exclusion of tradable/industrial sectors from right to collectively bargain	1.75
30	Exclusion of other sectors or workers from right to collectively bargain (*includes the exclusion of civil servants or all public sector workers; excluding 'essential services' is acceptable, provided the definition of 'essential services' is not excessively broad*)	1.75
31	Other specific *de facto* problems or acts of prohibition (*includes 'no legal right' to bargain collectively (but no legal prohibition on doing so)*)	1.5
	Right to strike	
32	General prohibitions	2
33	Previous authorization required by authorities (*includes requirement for official approval prior to strike; a requirement to notify officials prior to a strike is not coded as a violation*)	1.5
34	Exclusion of tradable/industrial sectors from right to strike	1.5

Category	Description	Weight
35	Exclusion of other sectors or workers from right to strike (*includes the exclusion of civil servants or all public sector workers; excluding 'essential services' is acceptable, provided the definition of 'essential services' is not excessively broad*)	1.5
36	Other specific *de facto* problems or acts of prohibition	1.5
	Export processing zones	
37	Restricted rights in EPZs (*includes export processing zones, free trade zones, and/or special economic zones*)	2

Source: Kucera (2002); weights according to Mosley (2011).

PART III

'Exporting' social and environmental compliance through unilateral conditional market access

8. The EU GSP: a preference for human rights and good governance? The case of Myanmar

Laura Beke and Nicolas Hachez

1. INTRODUCTION

The entry into force of the Lisbon Treaty has firmly anchored the principles of democracy, the rule of law and human rights in the European Union (EU)'s external relations (see, for example, Article 21 of the Treaty on European Union (TEU)). The EU has therefore set out to use its well-established Common Commercial Policy (CCP) (Article 207 of the Treaty on the Functioning of the European Union (TFEU)) to 'make trade work in a way that helps human rights' (Council of the EU, 2012) through a 'sticks and carrots' approach (Vandenberghe, 2008), by which commercial incentives are made conditional upon compliance with the EU's normative agenda. The CCP can in this light be understood as a 'trump card that the EU uses to reward (or sanction) countries when they pursue (or refuse) structural reforms' (Keukeleire, Thiers and Justaert, 2009: 156). Throughout its CCP, the EU is thus seeking to advance a 'deep trade agenda' (Postnikov and Bastiaens, 2014) and to realize a much discussed 'trade-development-human rights nexus'. This is done by granting preferential market access to developing countries in exchange for the promotion and enforcement of human rights standards under its unilateral Generalised System of Preferences (GSP), and by including human rights clauses in its bilateral trade agreements (Fierro, 2001).

In order to better understand why, how, and to what effect the EU uses its CCP as an instrument of governance, this chapter seeks to shed light on the conditionality of the GSP aimed at inducing structural reforms regarding human rights, sustainable development and good governance in third (developing) countries. An interesting feature of the GSP for the purpose of studying trade policies in this light stems from the observation that, as opposed to multilateral and bilateral agreements, it takes the form of a unilateral regulation, does not allow third (developing) countries to negotiate its terms (Portela, 2010), and thus theoretically provides the EU with more clout to simultaneously pursue both its commercial and normative agenda abroad (Damro, Chapter 2, this volume). By contrast, the EU's human rights leverage is bound to decrease in its bilateral agreements, as the relevant human rights conditionality clauses are subject to negotiations between two or more parties. At a time when the EU's trade and development policies have not only become more integrated into a cross-cutting 'nexus' (Orbie and Kerremans, 2013; Carbone and Orbie, 2014) but furthermore have become more politicized (Young and Peterson, 2013), the recent reform of the GSP has thus been described as the 'centerpiece' of the EU's trade and development strategy (Siles-Brugge, 2014: 49). Indeed, in its 2012 Communication on 'Trade, Growth and Development', the Commission itself hailed it as 'the flagship EU trade policy instrument supporting sustainable development and good governance in developing countries' (European Commission, 2012: 13).

In practice, as will be seen below, the GSP's human rights conditionality has been enforced on only three occasions. Myanmar's[1] trade preferences were suspended following allegations of forced labour practices. In 2007, Belarus was declared to be in violation of International Labour Organization (ILO) Conventions 87 (freedom of association) and 98 (collective bargaining). In 2010, the Commission found that Sri Lanka had been violating the UN International Covenant on Civil and Political Rights, the Convention against Torture and the Convention on the Rights of the Child. In addition, three official investigations have been launched by the EU to evaluate allegations of human rights violations: Pakistan in 1997, following allegations of child labour practices; El Salvador in 2008, with regard to the effective implementation of ILO Convention 87; and Bolivia in 2012 on the grounds of insufficiently implementing the UN Single Convention on Narcotic Drugs.

In July 2013, the EU decided to reinstate GSP preferences for Myanmar – a landmark move which had hitherto never been undertaken in the history of the GSP – and proclaimed that 'a new chapter in bilateral relations' had emerged (Council of the EU, 2013), following the process of political and economic reform since 2011 and the decision of the ILO to suspend its restrictive resolution on Myanmar in June 2011.

---

[1] Without any prejudice to political connotations, the designation 'Myanmar' will be used over 'Burma' throughout this chapter, except when 'Burma' appears in a quote.

Many, however, were left unconvinced as to whether the country was by then sufficiently complying with the GSP's human rights conditions, and the question therefore arises whether ulterior motives existed, and whether there generally is an increased tendency for the EU to use its CCP as an instrument of other policy objectives pursued by the EU under external action, most notably structural diplomacy, in the aftermath of the 'normative trade era' brought in by the Lisbon Treaty (Damro, Chapter 2, this volume; Larik, Chapter 3, this volume). After briefly presenting the GSP as a governance instrument at the service of human rights, sustainable development and good governance, and after presenting the debate that it has risen to its suitability for the task, the chapter will scrutinize the stated reasons why the EU decided to withdraw Myanmar's GSP preferences in 1997 and subsequently reinstate them in 2013, and what that might indicate about the delicate balance between the EU's commercial and normative agenda on the global scene (Yap, Chapter 9, this volume).

2. THE GSP AND ITS RECENT REFORM: MAKING TRADE WORK IN A WAY THAT HELPS HUMAN RIGHTS?

2.1 The GSP as a Governance through Trade Instrument: How Does it Work?

The GSP is an autonomous trade arrangement through which the EU provides non-reciprocal preferential market access to developing countries and territories. The primary objective of the GSP is to contribute to the reduction of poverty and the promotion of sustainable development and good governance by generating additional revenue from trade (GSP Regulation 2012: Recitals 4 and 7).

The principle of a GSP as an innovative governance scheme linking trade to development was adopted in 1968 at the UNCTAD II Conference in New Delhi. According to Resolution 21(ii),

> the objectives of the generalized, non-reciprocal, non-discriminatory system of preferences in favour of the developing countries, including special measures in favour of the least advanced among the developing countries, should be: (a) to increase their export earnings; (b) to promote their industrialization; and (c) to accelerate their rates of economic growth.[2]

[2] See http://unctad.org/en/Pages/DITC/GSP/About-GSP.aspx.

The GSP was made compatible with the most-favoured nation (MFN) treatment prevalent in international trade law in 1979 when the 'enabling clause' was adopted as an exception to Article I of the General Agreement on Tariffs and Trade (GATT) (the MFN principle) during the Tokyo Round.[3] This clause enabled and gave legal basis to the GSP in the international trade legal regime, thereby permitting the extension of the system beyond the original 10 years for which it had been adopted. The GSP since then exists on a permanent basis.

More than 40 years have passed since the EU introduced its version of the GSP in 1971, the first of its kind, under which it has been granting preferential market access to developing countries in the form of tariff reductions, and which has since then evolved considerably.

Currently there are 13 national GSP schemes in place.[4] Incidentally, the EU and the United States (US) have been the only international trade actors to grant their GSP programmes, respectively since 1991 and 1984, on conditions pertaining to human rights, environmental protection, good governance, and the like (Portela, 2010; Kryvoi, 2008).

In the EU, such 'conditionality' is applied on two bases:

- *Negative*, which means that preferences may be withdrawn if the beneficiary country fails to comply with the stated conditions. This type of conditionality came into effect in 1995, as the new GSP Regulation then provided that benefits could be withdrawn in a case of violation of ILO Conventions 29 and 105 on forced labour.
- *Positive*, which means that eligible countries may gain additional preferences by complying with stated conditions pertaining notably to human rights. This type of conditionality was introduced by the EU in 1991 to provide incentives to some Latin-American countries to comply with their commitments to combat drug trafficking (Wouters et al, 2014: 45).

The inclusion of conditionality in the GSP thereby augmented its profile as a trade instrument at the service of public interest goals such as development, as well as for broader public policy objectives such as human/labour rights, climate change and the fight against corruption or, as the EU has put it, 'the integral concept of sustainable development'

---

[3] See 'Differential and More Favourable Treatment Reciprocity and Fuller Participation of Developing Countries', Decision of 28 November 1979 (L/4903), https://www.wto.org/english/docs_e/legal_e/tokyo_enabling_e.pdf.

[4] See http://unctad.org/en/Pages/DITC/GSP/About-GSP.aspx.

(GSP Regulation 2012: Recital 11). The human rights and good governance conditionality element initially focused on abiding by selected labour standards and ILO Conventions, and has since then been progressively enhanced and extended to include a larger number of international conventions which beneficiary countries are to adopt and effectively implement (see 2.3.1 below).

Conditionality, however well-intentioned, has proved to be quite difficult to implement. Principles of international trade law have come in the way, which led India to file a complaint before the World Trade Organization (WTO) Dispute Settlement Body – in the famous *EC – Tariff Preferences* case – which ruled that the 'drug arrangement' under the EU GSP Regulation, which was granted to certain countries with particular drug issues, was contrary to WTO law, notably as it did not comply with the non-discriminatory character of GSP schemes mandated by the enabling clause (Bartels, 2007).[5]

In 2005, the system was therefore profoundly reformed (Bartels, 2007; Orbie and Tortell, 2009), and discrimination concerns were addressed through the establishment of a three-tier system, making the granting and withdrawal of conditional benefits more objective.

2.1.1 Differentiated arrangements

Three separate preferential regimes – providing progressively increased trade benefits – thus now operate under the EU GSP scheme:

- a 'general arrangement': this provides reductions or suspensions of tariff duties on a number of products listed in Annex V of the GSP Regulation for all beneficiary countries and territories listed in Annex II of the GSP regulation;
- a 'special incentive arrangement for sustainable development and good governance' (the 'GSP+'): this provides additional benefits for 'vulnerable' beneficiaries of the general arrangement (see 2.1.2.1 below) that have ratified and are effectively implementing 27 international conventions on human rights and sustainable development, as listed in Annex VIII to the GSP Regulation; and
- a 'special arrangement for the least-developed countries' (LDCs) – also known as the 'Everything But Arms' (EBA) initiative[6] – which provides duty-free and quota-free access to the EU market for all

[5] *EC – Conditions for the Granting of Tariff Preferences to Developing Countries* (WT/DS246), 20 September 2004.

[6] http://trade.ec.europa.eu/doclib/docs/2014/october/tradoc_152839.pdf.

countries marked as LDCs on the United Nations Development Programme's Human Development Index (HDI), for all products except arms and armaments.

Preferences are differentiated on several bases. First, reductions of tariffs are less generous for so-called 'sensitive' products (as 'determined by the situation of the sector manufacturing the same products in the Union': see European Commission, 2004: 5, and GSP Regulation 2012: Article 7). Second, some countries do not receive preferences on certain products when their industry for those products is considered to be competitive on international markets without such preferences. This is the so-called 'product graduation' (see 2.3.1 below and GSP Regulation 2012: Article 8).

According to the EU Commission, '[i]n 2013, almost €93 billion of imports received GSP preferences – more than €74 billion of imports from countries under the general arrangement, around €4.5 billion of imports from GSP+ beneficiaries and more than €14 billion of imports from EBA countries' (European Commission, 2014a: 5). By comparison, in 2013 global EU imports of goods were worth €11,457.5 billion.[7] Therefore, GSP-covered imports represented less than 1 per cent of all EU imports in goods, which might put into question the self-declared 'generosity' (European Commission, 2014a: 11) of the GSP, or suggest that the EU is 'buying' its trade-development-human rights nexus at a cheap price (see Ramdoo, de Roquefeuil and Bilal, 2011: 4).

2.1.2 GSP+ as a special instrument for human rights, sustainable development and good governance

Although all three arrangements are to some extent conditional on respect for certain human rights, the GSP+ arrangement is the most explicit governance instrument for human rights, sustainable development and good governance. Below we outline briefly how this instrument works.

2.1.2.1 Eligibility First, there are a number of eligibility criteria to the GSP+. The most important is to be a beneficiary of the general scheme, and to be 'vulnerable', which means that imports into the EU must be low and concentrated on a few products, making that country's trading industries insufficiently integrated within the international trading system

---

[7] Commission trade statistics: http://ec.europa.eu/trade/policy/countries-and-regions/statistics.

and vulnerable to variations in the market (GSP Regulation 2012: Article 9(1)(a) and Annex VII).

2.1.2.2 Conditionality In addition to these 'eligibility' criteria, a GSP+ beneficiaries must take a number of active steps to meet the following conditions (Article 9(1)(b)–(f)). First, they must have ratified 27 'core' international conventions pertaining to human/labour rights, sustainable development and good governance, listed in Annex VIII of the GSP Regulation. Second, the 'relevant monitoring bodies' of such conditions must not have identified 'a serious failure to effectively implement any of those conventions'. Finally, the GSP+ beneficiary must provide several binding commitments for the future:

- to maintain ratification of all 27 conventions;
- to accept without reservation the reporting requirements imposed by those conventions; and
- to cooperate with the Commission in the monitoring of the continued fulfilment of these conditions.

2.1.2.3 Granting process In terms of process, GSP+ beneficiary status is granted on the basis of individual applications showing that the requesting party fulfils the above conditions (GSP Regulation 2012: Article 10(1)). The application is reviewed by the Commission after notification to the Council and Parliament. The Commission then decides by delegated act (see 2.2.3 below) whether or not to include the country in question in the list of GSP+ beneficiaries (GSP Regulation 2012: Annex III).

The Commission has adopted Delegated Regulation (EU) No. 155/2013 of 18 December 2012 establishing rules related to the procedure for granting the special incentive arrangement for sustainable development and good governance under Regulation (EU) No. 978/2012 of the European Parliament and of the Council applying a scheme of generalised tariff preferences, which substantiates the application and granting process.

2.1.2.4 Monitoring and withdrawal In a number of cases, preferences may be 'temporarily withdrawn' (see also Yap, Chapter 9, this volume).

With regard to temporary withdrawal from the whole GSP scheme, Article 19 of the GSP Regulation 2012 provides that – notably in a case of serious and systematic violations of the core conventions mentioned in Part A of Annex VIII, and also when a country is guilty of exporting goods made by prison labour or of unfair trading practices – temporary withdrawal may be decided upon by the Commission.

With regard to the GSP+ conditions, the Commission must 'keep under review' the status of ratification of the 27 conventions, and 'monitor' their effective implementation and the beneficiaries' cooperation with the conventions' monitoring bodies. Moreover, each GSP+ beneficiary must cooperate in the monitoring process, notably by providing information on the fulfilment of the conditions (GSP Regulation 2012: Article 13). Every two years, the Commission reports to the Parliament and the Council on the fulfilment status of those conditions (GSP Regulation 2012: Article14(1)).

If the Commission has a 'reasonable doubt' that the GSP+ conditions are no longer being fulfilled by a beneficiary, it may 'initiate the procedure for the temporary withdrawal' (GSP Regulation: Article 15(3)), which may result in a withdrawal of the GSP+ preferences.

2.2 Criticism of the GSP: Illegitimate, Unfair and Ineffective?

Since its inception, the GSP – particularly in respect of its conditionality provisions – has been subject to criticism, along different lines.

2.2.1 Effective implementation of conditionality?

First, some have remarked that conditionality was very seldom enforced. As indicated above, benefits have been withdrawn on only three occasions to date: against Myanmar, Belarus (withdrawal from the whole scheme) and Sri Lanka (withdrawal from GSP+). A few other countries have been investigated by the Commission for various alleged violations, but have escaped sanctions: Pakistan (1997), El Salvador (2008) and Bolivia (2012). This quite sporadic enforcement of conditionality provisions, despite the many opportunities to do so, has led observers and EU institutions, such as the European Parliament, to express dissatisfaction over a perceived imbalance between positive conditionality, which readily affords benefits to a large number of countries willing to commit to certain objectives and values, and negative conditionality, which hardly seems to sanction those beneficiaries which do not live up to their commitments. The question is therefore asked whether such provisions are really making a difference in that strings are not really attached to the preferences (although see Yap, Chapter 9, this volume, in respect of the particular context of the Rana Plaza collapse in Bangladesh).

Some have warned, however, in view of this situation – and drawing a parallel with the non-existent enforcement of the so-called 'essential elements clauses' in EU free trade agreements (FTAs) (Beke et al., 2014:

68–71) – that negative conditionality and collateral sanctions should be wielded with particular caution, and in any event as a solution of last resort, lest it hurts populations more than it does the governments that violate human rights (Bartels, 2008: 13; Vandenberghe, 2008: 577). Bartels, for example, argues for impact assessment before inflicting (trade) sanctions upon a country (2012: 31).

Yet, it must be noted that the incentive provided by GSP+ to at least *ratify* certain human rights instruments in exchange for trade benefits seems to have been effective (Bartels, 2008: 13) – '[t]he prospect of additional market access under GSP+ appears to have positively affected ratification of ILO core labour conventions in […] Bolivia, Colombia, Venezuela, Mongolia and El Salvador' (Orbie and Tortell, 2009: 672).

However, this progress in ratification does not seem to be matched with progress in implementation on the ground. Illustratively, the 2010 mid-term review of the GSP concluded that 'GSP+ conditionality is believed to have had very limited impact in encouraging increased implementation and compliance with convention mandates' (Gasiorek et al., 2010: 161). The actual effectiveness of GSP+ to enhance respect for human rights has been further put in doubt by academics (Wardhaugh, 2013), and the unequal impact on ratification and implementation, for that matter, has been admitted to by the Commission itself (European Commission, 2014a: 7). Therefore, one could conclude that, in most cases, GSP+ beneficiaries have been quite diligent in providing the commitments outlined above, but as a result lack of enforcement those commitments have not all been lived up to.

2.2.2 Double standards

Perhaps the most often voiced criticism against GSP+ is that of 'double standards' – namely, that similar situations receive different treatments. In practice, some countries would be sanctioned, whereas others would get away with the same violations (Fierro, 2003: 378). Not surprisingly, a 'dichotomy between norms and interests' has been diagnosed (Carbone and Orbie, 2014: 5), whereby the EU decides on norm enforcement only after calculating whether or not it is in its interest to do so (Vandenberghe, 2008; Orbie and Tortell, 2009; Portela, 2010).

Indeed, if we look at the politics of conducting FTAs, it has been noted that 'the vast majority of free trade agreements that the EU is pursuing or has pursued have been with more affluent countries whose markets matter to EU exporters […]. Thus development considerations have *not* been the driver for the EU's bilateral trade strategy' (Young and Peterson, 2013: 516). Moreover, the human rights clause in FTAs has never been triggered against powerful partners (Beke et al., 2014: 69). One is thus left to wonder whether this selectivity in applying conditionality also holds, *mutatis mutandis*, for the EU's non-reciprocal trade strategy like the GSP and its alleged human rights considerations. We will examine this question further in the case study below.[8]

Another line of criticism linked to double standards has to do with the rights surveyed. Although the list of conventions potentially covers the whole spectrum of human rights, some have wondered whether labour rights violations were more prone to lead to sanctions under the GSP than violations of civil and political rights. In the history of GSP sanctions and investigations, Belarus and Myanmar were suspended on the basis of labour rights violations, whereas Sri Lanka was on the basis of civil and political rights violations. Among the countries which have undergone investigation, Pakistan and El Salvador were suspected of violating labour standards, whereas Bolivia was suspected of not complying with the UN Single Convention on Narcotic Drugs. Even if labour rights violations have accounted for four out of six withdrawal procedures, the 2010 independent mid-term review of the GSP, however, indicates that failure to effectively implement core labour standards conventions does not necessarily lead to withdrawal, or even to an investigation.[9] The review conducted case studies on the effective *de jure* implementation of the 27 Conventions[10] in Georgia, Nicaragua and Peru, and found not only that not all conventions were effectively implemented, but also that '[i]n all three countries, effective implementation was strongest for the conventions covering the environment and governance and weakest for the core labour conventions' (Gasiorek et al., 2010: 159).

Finally, a certain degree of arbitrariness seems to surround the list of conventions upon which GSP conditionality is based. This criticism was more forceful before 2005 when only eight ILO conventions formed the hard basis for conditionality under the special incentive arrangements.[11] Since then, the list of GSP+ conventions has been expanded and now virtually covers the whole spectrum of human rights, but oddities still remain. For instance, the Apartheid Convention was included in the GSP Regulation until the last reform, although it had not been ratified by all

---

8 See Bartels (Chapter 4, this volume).

9 See Marx and Soares (Chapter 7, this volume).

10 Meaning whether the convention was ratified and transposed into domestic law, and whether the procedural reporting requirements of the convention had formally been met.

11 Other 'special incentive schemes' also existed for 'the protection of the environment' or 'combating drug trafficking', but were not benchmarked against specific international conventions.

EU Member States themselves (Schneider, 2012). Also, the UN Migration Convention has not been included, although it is considered to be a core human rights convention. Considering that the EU and its Member States are the target of intense criticism over their migration policy, one is thus left to wonder whether, when it comes to promoting and enforcing human rights, the EU and its Member States hold themselves to the same standards as their trading partners.

2.2.3 Lack of transparency and legal certainty in the suspension process

The criticism concerning alleged double standards has certainly been fuelled by a widespread feeling that the negative conditionality process was marred by opacity, lack of objectivity and legal certainty. Many elements were listed in support of such criticism.

With regard to the criteria for an investigation to be triggered, whereas the GSP Regulation mentions 'serious and systematic violations' of human rights conventions for all three arrangements in general or 'reasonable doubts' that conditions are breached for GSP+, and whereas the party under investigation is associated with the process, the Commission retains considerable discretion in deciding whether to launch an investigation and withdraw preferences, as both criteria above are amenable to a wide margin of appreciation.

Moreover, the standard of review and the actual reasons that might warrant temporary withdrawal in the eyes of the Commission remain largely unknown. All seems to indicate that the threshold to opt for temporary withdrawal is fairly high (Orbie and Tortell, 2009: 676), as trade preferences were withdrawn, in the case of Belarus and Myanmar, based on the establishment by the ILO of a Commission of Inquiry, which is considered to be the worst condemnation in terms of human rights implementation (Orbie and Tortell, 2009: 679). Based on this, Portela and Orbie (2014) argue that an authoritative condemnation by the ILO facilitates the imposition of trade sanctions by the EU. Langan (2014), in turn, argues that 'by aligning with the policy discourse of the ILO, the European Commission presents its economic agenda as conforming to modern economic thought' (Carbone and Orbie, 2014: 4). Again, these considerations do not help to present the GSP withdrawal process in the most objective and transparent light. Moreover, with regard to violations other than those relating to labour rights, the obligation to base withdrawal notably on the reports and recommendations of monitoring bodies may not reassure those searching for objectivity, as some of the listed conventions (such as the Genocide or the Apartheid

Conventions) do not have monitoring mechanisms in place (Schneider, 2012: 305).

In order to instil a dose of (democratic) legitimacy to this process, some authors have called for the European Parliament, as a natural defender of human rights, to be more closely associated with this process (Bartels 2008: 20). Their concerns might have been heard. The '2012 GSP regulation has granted the European Parliament a role in the decision-making process: decisions on withdrawal are adopted by delegated [acts of the Commission], which can be revoked by the Parliament or Council anytime' (Portela and Orbie, 2014: 66–7). Moreover, the Commission must notify the Parliament and the Council when it decides to launch an investigation (for GSP+, GSP Regulation 2012: Article 15(3); for the general arrangement, Article 19(3)), and reports every two years to the same bodies on the general functioning of GSP+ (GSP Regulation 2012: Article 14). As confirmed by one EU official at the time of writing, both the Commission and the European External Action Service (EEAS) have been in the process of preparing such 'GSP reports' by January 2016. Following this increased accountability mechanism, more inter-institutional suggestions for reform are bound to be suggested in order to enhance the transparency of the GSP monitoring process in the years to come.

2.3 The Reform of the GSP: Towards Better Governance through Trade?

As indicated above, the EU GSP has been through many reform processes. The most recent reform was adopted in 2012 (GSP Regulation 2012) and entered into force on 1 January 2014. The reason for this reform was to adapt not only to the changes brought about by the Lisbon Treaty (and notably to take stock of the new prerogatives of the Parliament), but also to the changing international trading landscape, characterized by increasingly widespread liberalization, and by the emergence of new trading giants such as the BRICS (European Commission, 2014a: 6). The new regulation was also designed to respond to the criticism above, notably in respect of the lack of transparency and certainty in the granting and withdrawal procedure.

In the following paragraphs, we examine the main tenets of the reform and whether they are likely, in theory, to make the GSP a better instrument of governance.

2.3.1 Refocusing the scheme on the 'most needy'

According to the 2012 GSP Regulation, a number of developing countries which have historically been eligible for GSP have now entered a new stage of development – one in which they are successful in trading and no longer really need preferences in order to enter global markets and thrive in them. Those countries have reached a point where development should rather be effected through domestic reform, which the EU is encouraging through other means (GSP Regulation 2012: Recital 9).

For the following reasons, such countries are no longer eligible for preferences. First, if too many countries, including the more advanced, receive preferences, the less advanced have to compete on the same playing field with much better equipped traders, and therefore they do not obtain the head start they need to make their industry take off, most notably their 'infant industry' which is not well established and arguably needs some help to emerge in the international arena. Second, given that tariffs are generally falling worldwide, the preferences granted through GSP are less significant for the less advanced (a phenomenon referred to as 'preference erosion'), and therefore they need this head start even more now than they used to (European Commission, 2014a: 8).

The GSP was therefore overhauled, as announced in the 2011 Agenda for Change, in order to focus on 'those most in need' (Carbone and Orbie, 2014: 2). The number of 176 countries and overseas territories which qualified under the former GSP scheme has been drastically reduced, along the following lines:

(a) A number of countries were no longer granted GSP beneficiary status, as they 'graduated' from the scheme based on their level of income. Countries listed as high/upper middle income countries by the World Bank during the most recent three years, based on GNI per capita, no longer need preferences to trade effectively. Therefore, they no longer qualify and can only reintegrate into the scheme if their classification changes (which is why they remain, theoretically, 'eligible'). This affects seven high-income countries, one territory, and fourteen upper-middle-income countries.

(b) 'Product graduation' has been tweaked to ensure it does not negatively affect the remaining beneficiaries. Product graduation is applied when imports of particular groups of products originating in a particular GSP beneficiary are very competitive and do not need preferences to enter the EU market (European Commission, 2014a: 10). In such a case, imports of those products do not receive preferences, whereas imports of other products originating in the same country retain their preferences. Product graduation does not apply to GSP+ and EBA.

(c) The 'vulnerability' eligibility criteria for GSP+ (see 2.1.2.1 above) were also relaxed, so that more countries may now apply.[12]
(d) Applications for GSP+ are now accepted on a continuous basis and no longer every 1.5 years.
(e) With regard to human rights, sustainable development and good governance conditionality, the number of core conventions (27) remains equal, but the Apartheid Convention – which is no longer considered relevant for the purposes of the scheme – has been replaced by the UN Framework Convention on Climate Change. The commitments of the beneficiaries with regard to the conventions were also made more precise, as they now expressly include a *binding* commitment to ratify and effectively implement the conventions, to accept without reservation the conventions' reporting requirements, and to cooperate fully with international monitoring bodies (GSP Regulation 2012: Article 9).
(f) Twenty-six partner countries which benefit from preferences through other means, which are equally or more preferential (such as trade agreements), were removed from the scheme (GSP Regulation 2012: Article 4(1)(b)), but may be reintegrated if those other preferences cease to apply (which is why they remain, theoretically, 'eligible').
(g) Thirty-three overseas countries and territories are no longer eligible for GSP because they have their own development scheme with the EU or with another developed country such as the US, Australia and New Zealand (European Commission, 2014a: 7).

As a result of these recent reforms, 96 countries remain in the scheme, arguably those which need preferences the most. This group consists of 47 low-income/lower-middle-income countries which may benefit from GSP only (34) or GSP and GSP+ (13), and 49 least developed countries which qualify under the EBA initiative.

Some authors, however, doubt that the bottom line of the GSP reforms concerning income and product graduation will actually 'refocus' the scheme on the most needy. It is argued that the rationale is rather to force out key emerging trading actors and their most successful industries from the preferences of the GSP in order to increase the EU's leverage in the negotiation of 'flagship' free trade agreements, such as those with India

---

12 Pakistan, Philippines and Ukraine became eligible.

or countries in the Association of Southeast Asian Nations (ASEAN) (Siles-Brugge 2014: 54–5).

2.3.2 Increasing stability and legal certainty, and strengthening monitoring

Other modifications were introduced to enhance legal certainty and stability in the scheme, and ensure better reactivity to market development, as well as more overall transparency and predictability through procedural simplification and strengthened monitoring.

First, the duration of the GSP schemes was extended to 10 years instead of the previous three. The EBA does not have an expiry date.

Second, as mentioned above, the Commission was granted the right to adopt delegated acts to adapt the Annexes of the GSP Regulation to integrate or remove beneficiaries, to apply graduation, to decide on temporary withdrawal or reintegration of a beneficiary, as well as to decide on procedural rules for applying the scheme, for granting beneficiary status, and deciding on temporary withdrawal. All those decisions can therefore now be made without using the much longer ordinary legislative procedure and, as a result, a quicker response can be given to new developments, thereby making it easier for the scheme to benefit those who need (and deserve) it the most. Accordingly, the status and commitments of beneficiaries will be monitored continuously, with a view to applying any needed change in a timely fashion. However, all changes in beneficiary status (income, product graduation or temporary withdrawal) will only take place after a transitional period to allow the interested beneficiary to prepare for the change and not be unduly prejudiced by it (even though some of those changes will be the result of 'sanctions').

With regard to temporary withdrawal (either in the general scheme or in GSP+), the reform also sought to objectivize rules and reasons, in order to provide better stability and predictability to the scheme, but also to carve out a number of 'antechambers'– intermediate steps which represent opportunities for the country under fire to mend its ways and avoid withdrawal (Portela, 2010: 158).

The temporary withdrawal procedures from GSP or GSP+ are now as follows (see GSP Regulation 2012: Articles 15 and 19):

(a) 'Where the Commission considers that there are sufficient grounds justifying temporary withdrawal' from the whole scheme (such as 'serious and systematic violations' of core human and labour rights listed in Annex VIII); or '[w]here [...] the Commission has a reasonable doubt that a particular GSP+ beneficiary country does not respect its binding undertakings', the Commission may 'initiate the procedure' for temporary withdrawal from either the whole scheme or from GSP+. A complaint in this regard may be filed by any interested person.

(b) The country in question is notified, as well as the Council and the Parliament, and a notice is published in the Official Journal of the EU, stating the reasons which warrant the initiation of the withdrawal procedure.

(c) A period, not exceeding six months, is specified during which the Commission will:

- 'monitor and evaluate' the situation of the country concerned by withdrawal from the GSP scheme as a whole; and
- give the opportunity to the GSP+ beneficiary under review to submit observations.

(d) Under both procedures, the beneficiary in question is provided 'with every opportunity to cooperate'. However, once a breach of the GSP+ conditions is alleged, the burden of proof is reversed to the country concerned, which must demonstrate the contrary.

(e) The Commission will seek information to form its final decision, notably but not only information stemming from the relevant monitoring bodies. 'Without prejudice to other sources, this could [also] include information from civil society, social partners, the European Parliament and the Council' (GSP Regulation 2012: Recital 15).

(f) In the procedure for withdrawal from the GSP as a whole, the Commission drafts a report within three months of the expiry of the period specified above, to which the country in question may respond.

(g) The Commission decides within three months of the period specified above for GSP+ and six months for GSP.

(h) Temporary withdrawal takes effect six months after the adoption of the decision, giving a further opportunity to the beneficiary to redress its situation.

(i) The Commission may then, if it considers that withdrawal is no longer justified under Article 15 or 19, decide to reinstate preferences.

The procedure for temporary withdrawal was further substantiated by the Commission in Delegated Regulation (EU) No. 1083/2013 of 28 August 2013 establishing rules related to the procedure for temporary withdrawal of tariff preferences and adoption of general safeguard measures under

Regulation (EU) No. 978/2012 of the European Parliament and the Council applying a scheme of generalised tariff preferences.

As indicated above, although the procedure is quite detailed and provides ample opportunity for the beneficiary under review to defend or redeem itself, the Commission retains considerable discretion as to whether to launch a withdrawal procedure and assess whether withdrawal is warranted. Indeed, in spite of the progress made under the most recent GSP reform, a lack of comprehension still exists as to which countries have been subject to withdrawal and which have not (Vandenberghe, 2008: 573). However, it seems that the EU procedure is judged to be 'transparent and fair' compared with its US counterpart (Hepple, 2008: 164).

3. THE CASE OF MYANMAR

As a counterpoint to the above theoretical overview of the GSP in its latest form – which is hailed as being more effective for both the economic and human development of beneficiary states – the remainder of this chapter will look at how the GSP as a governance instrument for human rights has worked in practice in the emblematic case of Myanmar, which was withdrawn from GSP as a result of labour rights violations, and then reintegrated following reform.

3.1 Introduction

Myanmar achieved independence from the United Kingdom (UK) in 1948 and from that point became a regular member of the international community – becoming a party to, among others, the UN, the GATT, the International Monetary Fund, the World Bank, the International Finance Corporation, the International Development Association, the Asian Development Bank, and later the WTO and ASEAN. In 1962, Myanmar collapsed into a military regime (the Burmese Socialist Programme Party, or BSPP) which persisted until 2011; it was frequently listed as one of the most repressive regimes in the world (Freedom House, 2007: 17), characterized by widespread violations of civil and political rights as well as of economic, social and cultural rights, most notably labour rights.

This did not prevent Myanmar from being treated on an equal footing with other developing countries, and from being included in generous development cooperation funds, projects and programmes, such as the GSPs of the EU and the US. It was not until the 1980s, when the government violently repressed sporadic protests sparked by a catastrophic economic situation, that Western donors, multilateral lending institutions and multinational corporations started to react. Remarkably, the UN Security Council never adopted a resolution imposing sanctions on Myanmar, because of vetoes by Russia and China, which led to the situation that sanctions against Myanmar generally remained somewhat ad hoc and uncoordinated (Beaucillon, 2012: 23). Moreover, certain high-profile corporations (such as oil companies Unocal and Total) remained in the country (see generally Burma Independence Advocates, 2011: 1–14).

The US withdrew Myanmar from its GSP scheme in 1989, while the EU followed in 1997. The EU reintegrated Myanmar in 2013; the US has not yet done so.

3.2 EU Exercise of its Normative Power through Trade and Diplomacy

In 1995 a complaint was filed before the European Commission jointly by the International Confederation of Free Trade Unions and the European Trade Union Confederation against violations of labour rights in Myanmar (Kryvoi, 2008; Orbie and Tortell, 2009; Portela, 2010). In January 1996 the European Commission accordingly started an investigation into the alleged use of forced labour by the military regime.

The investigation established that forced labour was practised in Myanmar, which constitutes a breach of ILO Convention No. 29. This conclusion was not supported by a fact-finding mission as the regime did not allow the EU to send one, but experts and NGOs were heard (Portela and Orbie 2014: 67). Moreover, this decision was rooted in a largely convergent international context. As indicated above, the US suspended its GSP benefits to Myanmar long before the EU did. Additionally, the ILO had launched in 1996 a Commission of Inquiry against Myanmar, and in 2000 it even adopted, for the very first time, a resolution under Article 33 of its Constitution to call on Myanmar to comply with Convention No. 29 (Howse and Genser, 2008: 171–2). The decision to withdraw preferences against Myanmar was later confirmed in the GSP Regulations of 2001, 2005, 2008 and 2012 (with ‘the political situation’ cited as the reason rather than labour rights violations).

Finally, although the Security Council never acted against Myanmar, the EU, along with other countries, had taken a very large number of sanctions against Myanmar under the Common Foreign and Security Policy (CFSP) (Kryvoi, 2008; Gebert, 2013; Alamgir, 2008; Beaucillon,

2012; Portela, 2010; Giumelli, 2013; Giumelli and Ivan, 2013), 'including an arms embargo and wielded visa bans for individuals associated with the ruling junta' (Portela and Orbie, 2014: 67–8). Therefore, suspension of GSP preferences seemed to be logical.

In 2008, a wind of reform started to blow on Myanmar, and President Thein Sein relinquished power to a civil government. Elections were authorized and long-time opponent, Nobel Prize and Sakharov Prize laureate, Aung San Suu Kyi was released from house arrest and entered the Parliament in 2012. Although Myanmar cannot yet exactly be described as a land of freedom, as a result of this positive evolution the EU started to ease the pressure on Myanmar by phasing out sanctions and lifted them all in April 2013, with the exception of the arms embargo (Council Decision 2013/184/CFSP). Reinstatement of GSP preferences therefore appeared to be the logical follow up. It was approved by the Council and the Parliament in 2013, with retroactive effect from 12 June 2012 as the Commission stated that its decision came '[f]ollowing the decision by the Conference of the International Labour Organisation (ILO) to lift its negative opinion on Myanmar on 13 June 2012' (European Commission, 2014b: 2).

Therefore, 'GSP withdrawal followed CFSP sanctions, while reinstatement of GSP preferences followed the lifting of CFSP sanctions' (Portela and Orbie, 2014: 67–8). In the following section we will seek to uncover some of the stated and unstated reasons which might have motivated the decision by the EU to lift GSP sanctions on Myanmar.

3.2.1 Reasons

The decision to withdraw preferences from Myanmar met with little opposition, given the egregious nature of the violations and the isolation of the regime on the international scene and within the EU (Tsogas, 2000: 365). Yet, is it possible to make sense of this decision, both in terms of the EU's stated GSP objectives and in terms of the its sanctioning practices so far?

Again, there is little question that Myanmar fell within the conditions for withdrawing GSP preferences (the GSP Regulation at the time specifically referred to forced labour and violations of ILO Convention No. 29 as grounds for withdrawal), but so might arguably many other beneficiary countries which have never been sanctioned. If we compare the suspensions of benefits against Myanmar and against Belarus (2007), we have already noted that these were the only two countries that have had a Commission of Inquiry launched against them by the ILO. Yet, many authors have also remarked that the actual magnitude of violations in the two countries did not exist at the same scale:

> In Burma thousands of people were tortured and forced to work on exhausting projects. Belarus does not look very impressive in this context, because the reported violations did not amount to torture, physical injuries or systematic use of force against trade union leaders. The main problem in Belarus is that independent trade unions have hard times registering their organizations, their leaders are often squeezed out of jobs. (Kryvoi, 2008: 238)

One explanation of why Belarus was sanctioned along with Myanmar despite this imbalance in the seriousness of the violations has to do with the fact that, from one revision to the next, the GSP Regulation has progressively widened the scope of offences that could warrant withdrawal (Portela, 2010: 160). However, at this rate, it is quite surprising that Myanmar, Belarus and, more recently, Sri Lanka are the only suspended states. Notably, the case of Pakistan, which escaped sanctions, is puzzling when one knows that at the time in that country 'thousands of people were forced to work, beaten and tortured; millions of people suffered from contemporary forms of slavery' (Kryvoi, 2008: 238).

In this regard, some have explained this difference in treatment by the fact that in both Myanmar and Belarus the government was severely anti-democratic and conducted policies which directly hurt its own people, whereas in Pakistan political participation was not entirely absent, and the labour rights violations were rather the act of the private sector than of the government itself (Kryvoi, 2008: 238). Moreover, the Pakistani government had taken action to remedy some of the worst violations and kept the Commission regularly informed about the situation (Hepple 2008: 164), in addition to being a key partner in the West's combat against terrorism (Kryvoi, 2008: 240).

Therefore, although the limited number of cases does not allow the drawing of any definitive finding as to the reasons that might trigger temporary withdrawal, it seems that the fact that a country is internationally isolated because of its anti-democratic, freedom-killing and oppressive policies towards its own people, coupled with the pre-existence of CFSP sanctions, are key factors in explaining withdrawal.

Portela and Orbie (2014, 71–3) cite the following criteria for supplementing CFSP sanctions with GSP withdrawal:

- authoritative condemnation by the ILO;
- a connection between the violation(s) in question and government action is manifest; and
- condemnations of the CFSP have not led to GSP sanctions when considerable commercial or strategic EU interests were at stake in the target countries as a result of resistance by a 'blocking

> minority' in the Council [referring specifically to China and Russia in the Pakistani case].

As expected, we can therefore sense that the conditions for temporary withdrawal enumerated in the GSP Regulation are never applied without a good dose of geostrategic or economic calculation, drawing on the CFSP or on self-interest rather than on the desire to realize the trade-development-human rights nexus. The fact that GSP Regulations from 2005 to 2012 have confirmed the Myanmar withdrawal by reference to 'the political situation' and no longer to labour rights violations seems to indicate that, in order to see its preferences reinstated, Myanmar needed to show political change and satisfy the requirement of the CFSP common position (Council Common Position 2003/297/CFSP) along with improvements on the labour rights front (Portela and Orbie, 2014: 71, Bartels 2008: 9). History seems to have proved that to be correct, as it is only after a political transition happened in Myanmar and CFSP sanctions were lifted that GSP was reinstated (admittedly the EU waited for the ILO to remove its Article 33 measures to take its decision: see Regulation (EU) No. 607/2013: Recital 6).

3.2.2 Effects

In the case of Myanmar, EU sanctions, including the withdrawal of GSP preferences, were followed by improvement on the ground, which subsequently led to the reinstatement of GSP benefits. This sequence of events might signal that the EU's sanctions policy was a success, and that trade policies are an effective governance tool for, among others, human rights and democracy. But is it really so?

First, from a numbers perspective, one must observe that the EU (and US) trade sanctions did not prevent the Myanmar industry and its trade volumes from growing significantly in the last two decades. Analysing Myanmar's trade volume and growth rates in the period 1990–2005, Alamgir (2008: 980) demonstrates how 'impressively positive' they have been in spite of the sanctions imposed:

> In 1990, exports and imports amounted to $472 million and $880 million, respectively. By 2005, they stood at $3.5 billion and $1.9 billion, respectively. By 2002 the country had reversed a chronic trade deficit and begun running a trade surplus, which in 2005 amounted to almost $1.6 billion. The primary driver of this reversal of fortune has been energy exports (mainly gas) [...]. The most significant shift in Myanmar's exports is the spectacular rise of mineral fuels since 2000 as the largest export-earning sector.

The main reason for this growth of the Myanmar economy lies in the fact that non-Western economic actors have not bought into the trading sanctions imposed by the West – in fact, quite the contrary (Alamgir, 2008: 987). Nevertheless, Myanmar was also able to increase its commercial dealings with the EU itself: its exports to the EU more or less doubled between 1990 and 2012, whereas admittedly imports from the EU dropped sharply. However, this might have been caused by Myanmar's diversification of sources from which to import (Giumelli and Ivan, 2013: 29). Similarly, despite the fact that certain EU multinationals decided to leave the country, some EU corporations did not follow suit. In fact,

> Europe was the largest investor in Burma between 1995 and 2005 with cumulative FDI worth $1.8 billion; in comparison, the total FDI from ASEAN member countries was about half this. The UK and France were the major investors in Burma for the same ten-year period of 1995–2005, while the US was top investor from North America (Gebert, 2013: 4).

The oil sector flourished particularly as it was not the target of sanctions, and EU oil giants such as Total were eager to cash in on their investments there (Alamgir, 2008: 994, Gebert, 2013: 7). Therefore, trade sanctions imposed by the EU are unlikely to have put the kind of pressure on the BSPP regime necessary for it to relinquish power. On the contrary, some argue that it might have had the reverse effect: since the country was already very isolated at the time when GSP was withdrawn, reducing trade further perhaps meant a missed opportunity for the country to open up, and for those opposed to the regime to have any interaction with the outside world. Therefore, trade sanctions may have counter-productively reinforced the junta by depriving their opponents of a chance to disseminate their struggle (Portela, 2014: 12). Furthermore,

> the case of GSP suspension in Burma underlines an inherent contradiction in the idea of withdrawing trade preferences from countries where undesirable labour practices exist. By reverting to less favourable terms of trade, the general economic situation of the country worsens, which is in turn likely to translate into an increase in child and forced labour (Portela, 2010: 155).

3.3 Epilogue

Myanmar has now reintegrated into the circle of respectable nations, and is officially again worthy of receiving trade benefits from the EU.

This landmark move – which had hitherto never been undertaken in the history of the GSP – opened 'a new chapter in bilateral relations' between the EU and Myanmar (Council of the EU, 2013). Much to the dismay of civil society organizations, however, it was noted that 'European governments, in their eagerness to wrest Myanmar from China's influence have been tempted to embrace the new government before genuine reforms are adopted' (Human Rights Watch, 2013: 13). Admittedly, much progress remains to be achieved on the human rights front:

> The improved relationship between main-stream opposition leaders and the semi-civilian government does not mean that the country has achieved a significant political development. In addition to simmering communal tensions across the country, the fighting in Kachin and Shan states continues. Between 300 and 400 political prisoners remain incarcerated, and arbitrary arrests of student activists and labour right[s] activists continue. [And the] continuing arms embargo alone will not make any difference to the military strength of Burma as the semi-civilian government will effectively use the revenues it gains from Western investments to buy weapons from other countries solely to persecute its own people (Burma Independence Advocates, 2013: 1).

These concerns also resonated with the European Parliament, which, in spite of its earlier endorsement of reinstating GSP preferences for Myanmar, moved swiftly to adopt a resolution on the country's treatment of its minorities, in which it 'recalls that the European Union has recently reinstalled its [GSP] vis-à-vis Burma/Myanmar; reiterates the conditionality of these preferences as regards respect for fundamental freedoms and human rights; [and] urges the Commission to monitor closely the progress made by the Burmese authorities in respecting these conditions' (European Parliament, 2013a).

Meanwhile, across the Atlantic, the US Congress held a public hearing on 4 June 2013 in order to address the same human rights-related question of re-admitting Myanmar to its list of GSP beneficiaries. It concluded that 'although [the country] has recently instituted new labor laws, it has not sufficiently demonstrated its willingness to address forced labor and worst forms of child labor issues, or to grant freedom of assembly or collective bargaining' (Jones, 2014: 12).

Economically, however, Myanmar is opening fairly quickly and investors are gathering at its doors. It seems that Chinese investors have taken the lead, and that EU investors might miss out on the opportunity if they do not act soon. Therefore, the EU launched, in March 2014, the negotiations for a bilateral investment treaty (BIT) with Myanmar, while the Council urged EU investors to 'promot[e] the practice of the highest standards of integrity and corporate social responsibility', referring specifically to the OECD Guidelines for Multinational Enterprises, the

UN Guiding Principles on Business and Human Rights and the EU's corporate social responsibility strategy for 2011–14. Some, however, worry that if a BIT is concluded under standard BIT terms, this might restrict the Myanmar government's policy space to the point of impeding the transition towards more democracy and human rights (Seattle to Brussels Network, 2014). This is, however, a different debate.

4. CONCLUDING REMARKS AND IMPLICATIONS

This chapter has analysed conditionality policies enshrined in the EU GSP as a way to assess the way in which trade policies were put at the service of other objectives such as development, human rights, sustainable development and good governance.

On paper, the GSP looks like a continually improving piece of policy, which the 'neediest' developing countries crucially need in order to compete in international trading markets (Beretta, 2013). In that sense, whatever its underlying motives (see above), it seems that the recent reform might well benefit the less advanced developing countries (Ahmed, 2014). However, when it comes to human rights, sustainable development and good governance conditionality, the picture looks less favourable.

On the question of whether GSP conditionality is likely to induce change in beneficiary countries, without ruling that out altogether (notably with regard to the pre-benefit ratification of conventions), the case study on Myanmar shows that (the threat of) withdrawal is not a very powerful lever to induce beneficiaries to 'effectively implement' the best standards and to adopt the best practices. Two main reasons for this situation emerged from the case study. First, cases of actual withdrawal, or even investigation, have been low compared with reported violations. Second, the effect of the withdrawal of trade preferences will be minimal if it is not accompanied by:

- other economic or political sanctions;
- trade measures from other key trading partners;[13] and
- active support from the private sector.

[13] 'Empirical studies suggest that economic sanctions seem to be more effective when aimed against erstwhile friends and close trading partners. This is not the case with Belarus and Myanmar, which are not allies of the West. Both Belarus and Myanmar have a powerful non-Western "big brother", who turns a blind eye to violations of labor rights and human rights violations in general and provides economic support. Russia traditionally backed the current political

If those conditions are not met, it is likely that the regime in question will be able to continue to operate as usual and divert its trade flows towards other regions and other actors, potentially allowing it to thrive economically despite the sanctions. Admittedly, the combination of all these conditions is very difficult, if not impossible, to achieve, which is why one author has claimed (although this was before the reinstatement of preferences to Myanmar) that 'GSP withdrawals have the worst record of success of all EU sanctions' (Portela, 2010: 160).

From the point of view of the coherence and transparency of the conditionality process, although the various versions of the GSP Regulation have all sought to objectivize withdrawals, it must still be recognized that the Commission retains a wide margin of appreciation to decide to effect a withdrawal or even to undertake an investigation. Moreover, to date decisions on sanctions seem to have been dictated by reasons of geostrategic or economic expediency rather than by the resolve to foster the trade-development-human rights nexus. As one author quipped:

> If outcomes of trade conditionality of labour standards are in agreement with other policy objectives (as in the cases of Burma for the EU and Nicaragua for the USA), so much the better; if not (as with Pakistan for the EU and El Salvador for the USA) then labour standards are simply ignored. (Tsogas, 2000: 366)

In this last regard, the fact that, since 2012, withdrawal decisions may be taken by the Commission alone by way of delegated act might reduce the amount of political horse trading associated with contemplated GSP withdrawals, since all 28 Council members will no longer have to argue the case from their own self-interested point of view (though, of course, the Council and the Parliament may object to any Commission delegated act: see Article 290(2)(b) TFEU).

The above overview tends to give substance to Crawford's concern (1997: 70–71) that the EU, like most international actors, is adopting a realistic stance by subordinating its normative objectives to its direct political or economic interests, some even going so far as to fear that 'the increased competition with international actors means that the EU may have given up on its self-proclaimed normative distinctiveness to enter a contemporary version of power politics' (Carbone and Orbie, 2014: 5). Moreover, in recent years, developing and emerging countries – in an

---

regime in Belarus. China is the key trade, investment, and political partner of Myanmar' (Kryvoi, 2008: 242–3).

increasingly outspoken manner – have shown some annoyance with such a 'normative' vision of trade and international relations in a post-colonial context (Wetzel, 2012: 12), making it increasingly difficult to pursue a principled trade-development-human rights nexus.

A glimmer of hope may be found, however, in the fact that the EU now not only has a principled incentive to uphold human rights throughout its policies, but also has a legal obligation to do so; this could force it to adapt the way in which it applies its conditionality policies.

BIBLIOGRAPHY

Legislation

Regulation (EU) No. 978/2012 of the European Parliament and of the Council of 25 October 2012 applying a scheme of generalised tariff preferences and repealing Council Regulation (EC) No. 732/2008 (GSP Regulation 2012), [2012] OJ L 303/1.

Regulation (EU) No. 607/2013 of the European Parliament and of the Council of 12 June 2013 repealing Council Regulation (EC) No. 552/97 temporarily withdrawing access to generalised tariff preferences from Myanmar/Burma, [2013] OJ L 181/13.

Council Common Position 2003/297/CFSP of 28 April 2003 on Burma/Myanmar, [2003] OJ L 106/36.

Council Decision 2013/184/CFSP of 22 April 2013 concerning restrictive measures against Myanmar/Burma and repealing Decision 2010/232/CFSP, [2013] OJ L 111/75.

Delegated Regulation (EU) No. 1083/2013 of 28 August 2013 establishing rules related to the procedure for temporary withdrawal of tariff preferences and adoption of general safeguard measures under Regulation (EU) No. 978/2012 of the European Parliament and the Council applying a scheme of generalised tariff preferences, [2013] OJ L 293/16.

Literature

Ahmed, R. (2014), 'How Does the Revision of EU's GSP Scheme Influence the Exports of Bangladesh?', *Journal of Textile and Apparel, Technology and Management*, **8** (4), 1–18.

Alamgir, J. (2008), 'Myanmar's Foreign Trade and its Political Consequences', *Asian Survey*, **48** (6), 977–96.

Bartels, L. (2007), 'The WTO Legality of the EU's GSP+ Arrangement', *Journal of International Economic Law*, **10**, 869–86.

Bartels, L. (2008), 'The Application of Human Rights Conditionality in the EU's Bilateral Trade Agreements and Other Trade Arrangements with Third Countries', *Study for the European Parliament*, available at http://www.europarl.europa.eu/RegData/etudes/etudes/join/2008/406991/EXPO-INTA_ET%282008%29406991_EN.pdf.

Bartels, L. (2012), 'A Model Human Rights Clause for the EU's International Trade Agreements', German Institute for Human Rights and Misereor, available at http://www.institut-fuer-menschenrechte.de/uploads/tx_commerce/Studie_A_Model_Human_Rights_Clause.pdf.

Beaucillon, C. (2012), 'Comment choisir ses mesures restrictives? Guide pratique des sanctions de l'UE', European Union Institute for Security Studies, Occasional Paper No. 100, available at https://www.academia.edu/2566028/Comment_choisir_ses_mesures_restrictives_Guide_pratique_des_sanctions_de_lUE.

Beke, L., D. D'Hollander, N. Hachez and B. Pérez de las Heras (2014), 'Report on the Integration of Human Rights in EU Development and Trade Policies', available at http://www.fp7-frame.eu/wp-content/materiale/reports/07-Deliverable-9.1.pdf.

Beretta, L.C. (2013), 'Reforming the EU GSP in Europe: Defining the New Map of Tariff Preferences and Supply Options', *Global Trade and Customs Journal*, **7** (8), 217–23.

Burma Independence Advocates (2011), 'Burma Sanctions Regime: The Half-Full Glass and a Humanitarian Myth – A Preliminary Assessment of Political and Humanitarian Conditions under Sanctions', available at http://www.burmaadvocates.org/Burma%20Sanctions%20Assessment.pdf.

Burma Independence Advocates (2013), 'EU is Ready for Blood Money in a Sham Democracy', available at http://burmaadvocates.org/onewebmedia/Statement_EU_Sanctions.pdf.

Carbone, M. and J. Orbie (2014), 'Beyond Economic Partnership Agreements: the European Union and the Trade-Development Nexus', *Contemporary Politics*, **20** (1), 1–9.

Council of the European Union (2012), 'Catherine Ashton Visits Burma/Myanmar to Open a New Chapter in the Relationship', A 197/12, available at http://www.consilium.europa.eu/uedocs/cms_Data/docs/pressdata/EN/foraff/129861.pdf.

Council of the European Union (2013), 'Factsheet: The EU and Myanmar/Burma – A New Chapter in Bilateral Relations', EU13-475EN, available at http://eu-un.europa.eu/articles/en/article_14125_en.htm.

Crawford, G. (1997), 'Foreign Aid and Political Conditionality: Issues of Effectiveness and Consistency', *Democratization*, **4** (3), 69–108.

European Commission (2004), 'The European Union's Generalised System of Preferences – GSP', available at http://trade.ec.europa.eu/doclib/docs/2004/march/tradoc_116448.pdf.

European Commission (2012), 'Trade, Growth and Development – Tailoring Trade and Investment Policy for those Countries Most in Need', Communication from the Commission to the European Parliament, the Council and the European Economic and Social Committee, 27 January 2012, COM(2012) 22 final, available at http://trade.ec.europa.eu/doclib/docs/2012/january/tradoc_148992.pdf.

European Commission (2014a), 'The EU's Generalised Scheme of Preferences (GSP)', available at http://trade.ec.europa.eu/doclib/docs/2014/november/tradoc_152865.pdf.

European Commission (2014b), 'EBA, Who Benefits?', available at http://trade.ec.europa.eu/doclib/docs/2014/october/tradoc_152839.pdf.

European Parliament (2013a), Resolution of 13 June 2013 on the situation of Rohingya Muslims (2013/2669(RSP)).

European Parliament (2013b), Resolution of 23 May 2013 on the reinstatement of Myanmar/Burma's access to generalised tariff preferences (2012/0251(COD)).

Fierro, E. (2001), 'Legal Basis and Scope of the Human Rights Clauses in EC Bilateral Agreements: Any Room for Positive Interpretation?', *European Law Journal*, **7** (1), 41–68.

Fierro, E. (2003), *The EU's Approach to Human Rights Conditionality in Practice*, The Hague: Martinus Nijhoff.

Freedom House (2007), 'The Worst of the Worst – The World's Most Repressive Societies', available at https://freedomhouse.org/sites/default/files/WotW2007.pdf.

Gasiorek, M. et al. (2010), 'Mid-term Evaluation of the EU's Generalised System of Preferences', Centre for the Evaluation of Regional Integration at Sussex, available at http://trade.ec.europa.eu/doclib/docs/2010/may/tradoc_146196.pdf.

Gebert, K. (2013), 'Shooting in the Dark? EU Sanctions Policies', European Council on Foreign Relations Policy Brief, available at http://www.ecfr.eu/page/-/ECFR71_SANCTIONS_BRIEF_AW.pdf.

Giumelli, F. (2013), 'How EU Sanctions Work: A New Narrative', European Union Institute for Security Studies, Chaillot Paper No. 129, available at http://www.iss.europa.eu/uploads/media/Chaillot_129.pdf.

Giumelli, F. and P. Ivan (2013), 'The Effectiveness of EU Sanctions – An Analysis of Iran, Belarus, Syria and Myanmar (Burma)', European Policy Centre Issue Paper No. 76, available at http://www.epc.eu/documents/uploads/pub_3928_epc_issue_paper_76_-_the_effectiveness_of_eu_sanctions.pdf.

Hepple, B. (2008), 'The WTO as a Mechanism for Labour Regulation', in B. Bercusson and C. Estlund (eds), *Regulating Labour in the Wake of Globalisation: New Challenges, New Institutions*, Oxford and Portland: Hart.

Howse, R. and J. Genser (2008) 'Are EU Trade Sanctions on Burma Compatible with WTO Law?', *Michigan Journal of International Law*, **29** (2) 165–96.

Human Rights Watch (2013), 'World Report 2013 – Events of 2012', available at http://www.hrw.org/sites/default/files/wr2013_web.pdf.

Jones, V. (2014), 'Generalized System of Preferences: Background and Renewal Debate', Congressional Research Service Report, available at https://www.fas.org/sgp/crs/misc/RL33663.pdf.

Kerremans, B. and J. Orbie (2013), 'Theorizing European Union Trade Politics: Contending or Complementary Paradigms?', *Journal of Contemporary European Research*, **9** (4), 493–500.

Keukeleire, S., R. Thiers and A. Justaert (2009), 'Reappraising Diplomacy: Structural Diplomacy and the Case of the European Union', *The Hague Journal of Diplomacy*, **4** (2), 143–65.

Kryvoi, Y. (2008) 'Why European Union Trade Sanctions Do Not Work', *Minnesota Journal of International Law*, **17**, 209–46.

Langan, M. (2014), 'Decent Work and Indecent Trade Agendas: the European Union and ACP Countries', *Contemporary Politics*, **20** (1), 23–35.

Orbie, J. and B. Kerremans (2013), 'Toward Engaged Pluralism in the Study of European Trade Politics', *Journal of Contemporary European Research*, **9** (4), 660–74.

Orbie, J. and L. Tortell (2009), 'The New GSP+ Beneficiaries: Ticking the Box or Truly Consistent with ILO Findings?', *European Foreign Affairs Review*, **14**, 663–81.

Portela, C. (2010), *European Union Sanctions and Foreign Policy: When and Why Do They Work?*, London: Routledge.

Portela, C. (2014), 'The EU's Use of "Targeted" Sanctions: Evaluating Effectiveness', CEPS Working Document 391, available at http://www.ceps.eu/system/files/WD391%20Portela%20EU%20Targeted%20Sanctions.pdf.

Portela, C. and J. Orbie (2014) 'Sanctions under the EU Generalised System of Preferences and Foreign Policy: Coherence by Accident?', *Contemporary Politics*, **20** (1) 63–76.

Postnikov, E. and I. Bastiaens (2014), 'Does Dialogue Work? The Effectiveness of Labor Standards in EU Preferential Trade Agreements', *Journal of European Public Policy*, **21** (6), 923–40.

Ramdoo, I., Q. de Roquefeuil and S. Bilal (2011), 'GSP Reform: Principles, Values and Coherence', European Centre for Development Policy Management (ECDPM), Briefing Note No. 24, available at http://ecdpm.org/wp-content/uploads/2013/11/BN-24-GSP-Reform-Principles-Values-Coherence-2011.pdf.

Schneider, F.B. (2012), 'Human Rights Conditionality in the EU's Generalised System of Preferences: Legitimacy, Legality and Reform', *Zeitschrift für europarechtliche Studien*, **3**, 301–28.

Seattle to Brussels Network (2014), 'S2B Statement on EU-Myanmar Investment Treaty – An Investment Treaty will Block Democratic Transition', available at http://www.tni.org/sites/www.tni.org/files/s2b_statement_on_eu-myanmar.pdf.

Siles-Brugge, G. (2014), 'EU Trade and Development Policy beyond the ACP: Subordinating Developmental to Commercial Imperatives in the Reform of GSP', *Contemporary Politics*, **20** (1), 49–62.

Tsogas, G. (2000), 'Labour Standards in the Generalized Systems of Preferences of the European Union and the United States', *European Journal of Industrial Relations*, **6** (3), 349–70.

Vandenberghe, J. (2008), 'On *Carrots* and *Sticks*: the Social Dimension of EC Trade Policy', *European Foreign Affairs Review* **13** (4), 561–81.

Wardhaugh, B. (2013), 'GSP+ and Human Rights: Is the EU's Approach the Right One?', *Journal of International Economic Law*, **16**, 827–46.

Wetzel, J. (2012), 'Introduction', in J. Wetzel (ed.), *The EU as a 'Global Player' in the Field of Human Rights*, London: Routledge.

Wouters, J., L. Beke, A.-L. Chané, D. D'Hollander and K. Raube (2014), 'A Comparative Approach to EU and US Approaches to Human Rights in External Relations', European Parliament Directorate for External Policies of the Union, EXPO/B/DROI/2014/27, available at http://www.europarl.europa.eu/RegData/etudes/STUD/2014/534981/EXPO_STU%282014%29534981_EN.pdf.

Young, A. and J. Peterson (2013), '"We Care about You, but … .:" The Politics of EU Trade Policy and Development', *Cambridge Review of International Affairs*, **26** (2), 497–518.

9. One step forward: the European Union Generalised System of Preferences and labour rights in the garment industry in Bangladesh

James Yap

1. INTRODUCTION

On 24 April 2013, Rana Plaza – an eight-storey building housing several garment factories on the outskirts of Dhaka in Bangladesh – collapsed, taking with it the lives of 1,129 people working inside. The day before, the building had been evacuated after workers spotted building damage on the second floor, but workers were reassured that it was safe to enter the next day.

The disaster led to intensified international scrutiny of labour conditions in Bangladesh, as it highlighted the occupational hazards for garment workers there. The Rana Plaza tragedy came close on the heels of a November 2012 fire at the Tazreen Fashions factory near Dhaka in which 112 perished, while a subsequent factory fire in October 2013 at the Aswad Knit Composite Mills complex near Dhaka claimed a further seven lives. In total, over 1,800 Bangladeshi garment workers have perished as a result of unsafe working conditions since 2005.

The tragedy at Rana Plaza – the world's worst industrial accident in 30 years – highlighted the connection between international trade and labour rights: the garment factories at Rana Plaza had supplied many prominent international brands such as Walmart, Mango, Benetton, Joe Fresh, and El Corte Ingles. This connection was lost on no one, as these and other international companies came under intense public pressure in the aftermath of the tragedy to ensure better working conditions for the labourers who make their clothes. In one response, a group of international apparel retailers from different countries around the globe has – in partnership with governments, NGOs, and trade unions – established the Accord on Fire and Building Safety in Bangladesh. The Accord is a legally binding five-year agreement that imposes obligations on signatory companies to fund measures such as safety inspections, remediation, training and a worker complaint process, all the while maintaining order levels in Bangladesh comparable with or greater than current levels for the duration of the programme. A second group – composed of North American companies such as Gap and Walmart who were leery of the Accord's legally binding commitments[1] – have established the Alliance for Bangladesh Worker Safety. The Alliance, also structured as a five-year agreement, calls for factory inspections in the first year as well as various other measures such as establishing elected workers' committees and offering financing to factories identified as in need of repairs.

Thus, a local crisis in working conditions in the apparel industry in Bangladesh has provoked a global response from a variety of sources. Of all the international actors that are stakeholders in this situation, however, arguably the biggest is the European Union (EU), to which the majority of Bangladesh's apparel exports are ultimately destined.[2] Moreover, Bangladesh is also one of the countries that benefits from the EU's Generalised System of Preferences (GSP) scheme of preferential tariffs. As such, Bangladesh in the aftermath of Rana Plaza is a fitting subject for a case study on the impact of the GSP on labour rights. More specifically, the EU's efforts to use the labour rights conditionality scheme embedded in the GSP programme to promote the reform of labour rights in Bangladesh present an opportunity to investigate the actual impact that the GSP's labour rights conditionality mechanisms can have. Unlike previous instances when the GSP's labour rights conditionality mechanism has been invoked, there has been some measured success in Bangladesh in inducing the government to implement measures for reform. It is therefore clear that labour rights conditionality in the GSP is capable of having at least some impact on labour rights in certain cases. However, the impact that the EU GSP's labour rights conditionality mechanism, as currently constituted, has is still very small in relation to the broad impact that international trade has on labour overall.

This study begins with some general background on the GSP in Section 2, followed by a review of the broader context of the GSP and labour rights in Section 3. This sets up Section 4, the heart of the study,

---

1 Steven Greenhouse, 'U.S. Retailers See Big Risk in Safety Plan for Factories in Bangladesh', *The New York Times,* 22 May 2013.

2 Bangladesh Garment Manufacturers and Exporters Association (BGMEA), 'Trade Information', available at http://bgmea.com.bd/home/pages/Trade Information#.VE0Vihavdin.

which examines the EU's efforts to leverage the GSP to induce labour rights reform in Bangladesh in the aftermath of Rana Plaza. Section 5 discusses the implications, before Section 6 closes with some concluding remarks and suggestions for reform.

2. GENERAL BACKGROUND TO THE GSP

The preferential tariff treatment granted to certain developing and least developed countries (LDCs) in the context of the Generalised System of Preferences is an exception to the World Trade Organization (WTO)'s 'most favoured nation' (MFN) principle. The MFN principle is the rule, enshrined *inter alia* in Article I of the General Agreement on Tariffs and Trade 1994 (GATT 1994), that requires every WTO Member to accord to all other Members any trade privilege it also accords to any other state. In other words, a WTO Member must treat another WTO Member at least as favourably in all matters of trade as it treats any other state in the world.

The MFN principle is a cornerstone of international trade law. However, it is by no means absolute and allows several significant exceptions. For one, Article XXIV GATT 1994 permits WTO Members to establish customs unions or free-trade areas, which is what enables regional trading blocs such as the North American Free Trade Agreement (NAFTA) to exist. Another important exception to the MFN principle is the GSP, which allows developed countries to accord non-reciprocal trade benefits to developing countries, an act which runs contrary to the MFN principle.

Historically, the GSP exception evolved from a series of existing preferential trade concessions that former colonial powers had bestowed upon their former colonies, with whom they enjoyed a pre-existing special trading relationship and, moreover, where many of their own nationals retained strong business interests. These arrangements were grandfathered into the GATT in 1947 as specific exceptions to the MFN principle.[3] Eventually, these individual ad hoc exceptions were consolidated into a generalized (hence the name) system allowing developed countries to accord such preferences to lesser developed countries generally.

---

[3] Michael J. Trebilcock and Robert Howse, *The Regulation of International Trade*, 3rd edn (Routledge, 2005), p. 477.

In 1971, the parties to GATT implemented what is known as the 'enabling clause', which permits member countries to offer trade concessions that derogate from the MFN principle in favour of developing countries, so long as the concessions are 'generalized, non-reciprocal and non-discriminatory preferences beneficial to the developing countries'.

There are thus four principal attributes required of a GSP programme. It must be generalized, which means that it must be made available to a class of countries with common attributes rather than specific individual countries. It must be non-reciprocal in that the granting country must not derive any benefit, trade-related or otherwise, in return. Further, it must be of demonstrable benefit to the targeted class of countries.

The requirement of non-discrimination was considered by the Appellate Body of the WTO in the *EC – Tariff Preferences* case. India had challenged the legality of the EU's 'drugs arrangement', a GSP programme that granted certain additional trade preferences to countries deemed to be facing a particular problem with the production and trafficking of narcotics within their borders. The Appellate Body, addressing the issue of non-discrimination, rejected India's argument that it entailed no differential treatment between all developing countries. Rather, it could allow special trade preferences granted to classes of developing countries sharing the same 'development, financial or trade need'. As long as these preferences were accorded equally to all countries sharing the same 'development, financial or trade need', then the requirement of non-discrimination was met. The Appellate Body further specified that the question of whether a country qualifies as having this need must be assessed according to a sufficiently objective standard, that there must be a nexus between that need and the preferences granted, and that the need must be one that can effectively be addressed through trade preferences.[4]

In 1971, the EU (then the European Economic Community) established the very first GSP programme to be introduced under the enabling clause. The programme has undergone various incarnations since that time, the most recent of which entered into effect on 1 January 2014. Among other things, the latest round of revisions has sharply reduced the number of eligible beneficiary countries from 177 to 90, in order to better focus on countries in need. Such countries were affected by competition from other, wealthier beneficiary countries that had emerged over the

---

[4] Appellate Body Report, *EC – Conditions for the Granting of Tariff Preferences to Developing Countries*, WTO Doc. WT/DS246/AB/R, 7 April 2004.

past two decades as advanced developing economies, but were still the largest users of the GSP scheme.

The EU GSP programme is a multi-tiered arrangement with each tier offering different degrees of benefits. At the highest tier of benefits is the Everything But Arms (EBA) scheme. Beneficiary countries designated under this scheme – of which Bangladesh is one – receive duty-free, quota-free access to the European market for absolutely all products other than arms and ammunition. This arrangement, being the most privileged level of trade incentives, is accordingly only granted to the group of LDCs as defined by the United Nations. At present, 49 countries are designated EBA beneficiaries, just over half of all GSP beneficiary countries. Of these, 34 are located in Africa and nine in Asia. Haiti and five countries in the South Pacific complete the list.

The rest of the beneficiary countries, whose development needs are not considered as great as those of the EBA countries, receive more limited trade privileges under the 'standard' GSP scheme (which actually covers fewer countries than the EBA scheme). Products originating in these countries receive either partial or total tariff reductions in roughly two-thirds of all product classes. Falling into this category are more advanced developing countries such as China, India, Nigeria and the Philippines.

Between these two levels of benefits there is a third tier which operates slightly differently from the others in that it is incentivized – that is, the trade privileges are contingent upon continued adherence to a set of conditions. This is the EU's 'special incentive arrangement for sustainable development and good governance', otherwise known as 'GSP+'. A GSP+ beneficiary country receives preferences in addition to those available under standard GSP, provided it remains in compliance with a list of 27 key international conventions.[5] These include conventions relating to:

- human rights (for example, International Covenant on Civil and Political Rights[6] and International Convention on Economic and Social Rights[7]);

[5] Annex VIII of Regulation (EU) No. 978/2012 of the European Parliament and of the Council of 25 October 2012 applying a scheme of generalised tariff preferences and repealing Council Regulation (EC) No. 732/2008 (GSP Regulation 2012), [2012] OJ L 303/1.

[6] 999 UNTS 171.

[7] 993 UNTS 3.

- labour rights (for example, Convention concerning Forced or Compulsory Labour[8] and Convention concerning Freedom of Association and Protection of the Right to Organise[9]);
- the environment (for example, United Nations Framework Convention on Climate Change[10] and Kyoto Protocol[11]); and
- governance (for example, United Nations Single Convention on Narcotic Drugs[12] and United Nations Convention against Corruption[13]).

The declared purpose of GSP+ is to promote sustainable development in vulnerable countries by helping to ease the special burdens and responsibilities resulting from ratifying and implementing the core international conventions on human and labour rights, environmental protection and good governance.

To qualify for GSP+ preferences, a country must be considered 'vulnerable', which for these purposes is measured in terms of its lack of diversification and insufficient integration into the international trading system. More specifically, a country qualifies for GSP+ preferences if any seven GSP categories represent more than 75 per cent of the total value of its imports into the EU, and if its imports into the EU of the GSP+ product categories represent less than 2 per cent of the value of total imports into the EU in those product categories. If a country meets these criteria, it may apply to the European Commission for access to this scheme. However, the Commission may also temporarily withdraw the preferences from any country that has already been granted access to them if it finds that that country has failed to meet its obligations under the various international instruments that it has undertaken to comply with as part of the GSP+ arrangement.[14] As part of the most recent round of revisions to the GSP programme, in order to encourage beneficiary countries to show genuine commitment to their obligations concerning human and labour rights, environmental protection and good governance, the EU implemented strengthened monitoring mechanisms to ensure that those countries are making good on their commitments.

---

8 39 UNTS 55.

9 68 UNTS 17.

10 1771 UNTS 107.

11 UN Doc. FCCC/CP/1997/7/Add.1, 10 December 1997.

12 976 UNTS 3.

13 2349 UNTS 41.

14 Article 15, Regulation 978/2012, n. 5 above.

For as long as they are meeting their obligations, however, GSP+ beneficiaries enjoy full removal of tariffs on essentially the same product categories as those covered under the general arrangement. As of February 2014, the Commission has approved the applications of 13 countries to become GSP+ beneficiaries, of a list of some three dozen whose economic development status makes them eligible to apply.

3. GSP AND LABOUR RIGHTS

Developed countries are under no obligation to offer any preferential trade access at all, and are thus perfectly entitled to – and commonly do – attach whatever conditions to these trade advantages they see fit to suit their own political or other objectives. For instance, the US GSP programme still contains vestigial Cold War-era statutory prohibitions on the designation of communist countries as beneficiary countries.[15] The inconsistent application of this prohibition in the past[16] suggests that politics plays an important role in the US GSP programme.[17]

Given the close connection between labour rights and international trade, labour rights conditionalities fit far more organically into a programme of trade preferences such as the GSP. The stated purpose of the EU GSP programme is specifically 'to foster the sustainable economic, social and environmental development of developing countries, with the *primary aim* of eradicating poverty'.[18] The EU conceives of its trade policy 'not only as an end in itself, but as a means to promote sustainable development more broadly'.[19] It is antithetical to such lofty objectives to allow goods originating in certain countries to gain competitive advantages resulting from the suppression of the rights of the workers involved in producing those goods. Some may certainly question whether international trade instruments are an appropriate platform through which to pursue these kinds of social objectives. They may argue

---

[15] 19 USC s. 2462(2)(a).

[16] Emily Blanchard and Shushanik Hakobyan, 'The U.S. Generalized System of Preferences: In Principle and Practice', (2015) 38(3) *The World Economy* 399–424.

[17] Ibid.; see also Daniel Lederman and Çaglar Özden, 'Geopolitical Interests and Preferential Access to U.S. Markets', (2007) *Economics & Politics* **19** (2), 235.

[18] Recital 3, Regulation 978/2012, n. 5 above (emphasis added).

[19] World Trade Organization, 'Trade Policy Review', report by the European Communities, WT/TPR/G/136.

that these objectives should be pursued through alternative means,[20] or even not at all.[21] Still others have argued that competitive advantages gained through non-adherence to international labour standards are minimal, suggesting that international trade bears little connection with labour rights.[22] Nevertheless, it is a widely held view that labour standards and other basic human rights are a fundamental component of genuine development, and this is the approach that the EU has adopted in formulating its GSP programme, the 'primary aim' of which is the eradication of poverty.

While the US implemented a comprehensive labour rights conditionality scheme in its GSP in 1984, the EU did not do so until the first round of major revisions to the original 1970s-era GSP scheme was completed in 1995.[23] EC Regulation 3281/94, which came into effect on 1 January 1995, introduced a mechanism providing for the temporary withdrawal of GSP benefits for the practice of forced labour, as well as a special incentive arrangement offering additional preferences for countries that have adopted more comprehensive labour rights legislation implementing

---

[20] See e.g. Jagdish Bhagwati, 'Trade Liberalisation and "Fair Trade" Demands: Addressing the Environmental and Labour Standards Issues', (1995) 18 *The World Economy* 745, 757; T.N. Srinivasan, 'International Labor Standards Once Again!', in *International Labor Standards and Global Economic Integration: Proceedings of a Symposium* (Washington, DC: US Department of Labor, Bureau of International Labor Affairs, 1994); Archon Fung, Dara O'Rourke and Charles Sabel, 'Realizing Labor Standards', in *Can We Put an End to Sweatshops?* (Boston, MA: Beacon Press, 2001) pp. 4–6; Kimberly Ann Elliott and Richard B. Freeman, *Can Labor Standards Improve Under Globalization?* (Washington, DC: Institute for International Economics, 2003).

[21] See e.g. Keith E. Maskus, 'Should Core Labor Standards Be Imposed Through International Trade Policy?', World Bank Working Paper No. 1817 (Washington, DC: World Bank, 1997); Lyn Squire and Sethaput Suthiwart-Narueput, 'The Impact of Labour Market Regulations', Policy Research Working Paper No. 1418 (Washington DC: World Bank, 1995); Pranab Bardhan, 'Some Up, Some Down', *Boston Review* 26.

[22] See e.g. Michael J. Trebilcock and Robert Howse, 'Trade Policy and Labor Standards', (2004) 14 *Minnesota Journal of Global Trade* 261, at 267.

[23] See George Tsogas, 'Labour Standards in the Generalized Systems of Preferences of the European Union and the United States', (2000) 6 *European Journal of Industrial Relations* 349.

three International Labour Organization (ILO) conventions.[24] Later, in 2001, in a further round of modifications, five more labour rights conventions were added to this last arrangement.[25] The same regulation added that regular GSP benefits could be temporarily withdrawn not just for forced labour but for any 'serious and systematic violation' of the standards set out in the ILO Declaration on Fundamental Principles and Rights at Work.

The *EC – Tariff Preferences* decision, however, precipitated further revisions to the system which brought it closer to what it is today. Currently, the EU GSP scheme for addressing labour rights concerns consists of two mechanisms. The first – the GSP+ system of incentivized trade preferences contingent upon a beneficiary country's continued adherence to international agreements on labour rights and other public goods – has already been described. The second is embodied in Article 19 of the GSP Regulation, which authorizes the Commission to temporarily withdraw any of the GSP arrangements from a beneficiary country for any 'serious and systematic violation of principles laid down' in the same 27 international treaties upon which access to the GSP+ is predicated, or for a number of other enumerated reasons, including the export of goods made by prison labour.[26]

The withdrawal procedures in both cases are nearly identical. Where it considers there are sufficient reasons to do so, the Commission may at any time officially initiate a temporary withdrawal procedure. This opens a monitoring and investigation period in which the beneficiary country is given the opportunity to give input. The Commission then has the discretion to withdraw benefits if the findings of the investigation justify

---

[24] Convention concerning Freedom of Association and Protection of the Right to Organise Convention (ILO Convention No. 87), 68 UNTS 17; Convention concerning the Right to Organise and Collective Bargaining (ILO Convention No. 98), 96 UNTS 257; Convention concerning Minimum Age for Admission to Employment (ILO Convention No. 138), 26 June 1973.

[25] Convention concerning Forced or Compulsory Labour (ILO Convention No. 29), 39 UNTS 55; Convention concerning the Abolition of Forced Labour (ILO Convention No. 105), 320 UNTS 291; Convention concerning Equal Remuneration (ILO Convention No. 100), 165 UNTS 303; Convention concerning Discrimination (Employment and Occupation) (ILO Convention No. 111), 362 UNTS 31; Convention concerning the Prohibition and Immediate Action for the Elimination of the Worst Forms of Child Labor (ILO Convention No. 182), 2133 UNTS161.

[26] The others are serious shortcomings in customs controls on drug trafficking, failure to comply with international conventions on anti-terrorism and money laundering, and serious and systematic unfair trading practices.

doing so. Perhaps the most important difference between the two procedures is that to initiate an Article 19 withdrawal procedure, the Commission must believe there to be 'sufficient grounds' to justify temporary withdrawal, whereas to initiate a GSP+ withdrawal procedure, the Commission need only have a reasonable doubt.

Thus, the Commission has two tools at its disposal to promote labour rights in beneficiary countries. It may withdraw GSP benefits from any beneficiary country for 'serious and systematic violation' of labour rights, and it may grant additional trade preferences contingent upon ratification and effective implementation of core labour rights treaties.

This has been referred to as a 'carrot and stick' approach.[27] However, this characterization is a little misleading. Both GSP+ and standard GSP preferences are benefits that can be withdrawn; it is not clear that one is a carrot and the other is a stick. The only difference is that an eligible country must apply to receive GSP+ benefits, whereas standard GSP benefits are granted automatically. As such, it is perhaps better to think of the GSP's scheme of labour rights conditionality as a layered scheme of incentives – standard GSP trade benefits contingent on not committing 'serious and systematic violation' of labour rights, and additional GSP+ benefits contingent on ratification and effective implementation of international labour rights (and other) instruments.

Moreover, this layered scheme applies only to the roughly three dozen countries that are eligible for GSP+ benefits, of which only 13 have applied and gained access to the scheme. It does not apply, for instance, to the 49 LDCs – arguably the countries that are most in need of help in effectively implementing these core international treaties – because they already have access to the EBA scheme of trade privileges, which is more advantageous than GSP+. For the majority of GSP beneficiary countries, therefore, there is no 'carrot and stick' – there is only 'carrot' or only 'stick', depending on how one chooses to frame it. In other words, the Commission has only one tool at its disposal to promote labour rights in those countries, and that is the temporary suspension of the GSP benefits – either under standard GSP or the EBA scheme – to which those countries are normally entitled. It is into this last category that Bangladesh, being an EBA beneficiary, falls.

---

[27] See e.g. Clara Portela and Jan Orbie, 'Sanctions under the EU Generalised System of Preferences and Foreign Policy: Coherence by Accident?', (2014) 20 *Contemporary Politics* 63; Jan Vandenberghe, 'On Carrots and Sticks: The Social Dimension of EU Trade Policy', (2008) 13 *European Foreign Affairs Review* 561; Jan Orbie, Hendrik Vos and Liesbeth Taverniers, 'EU Trade Policy and a Social Clause: A Question of Competences?', (2005) 3 *Politique européenne* 204.

This temporary withdrawal power has been invoked twice before in the labour rights context – the first time in relation to Burma and once more in relation to Belarus. It is useful to briefly review these cases before proceeding to examine what effect, if any, labour rights conditionality (as well as the GSP generally) has had in advancing labour rights in Bangladesh in the aftermath of the Rana Plaza disaster.

Burma

Soon after the EU first introduced labour rights conditionality into its GSP program, the new scheme was tested. On 7 June 1995, the European Trade Union Confederation (ETUC) and the International Confederation of Free Trade Unions (ICFTU) filed a joint complaint calling for the withdrawal of GSP benefits from Burma for its use of forced labour.

The widespread and systematic human rights abuses of Burma's military regime at the time were notorious and are well documented. In fact, Burma had been the subject of trade sanctions imposed by the EU since 1990, for forced labour as well as other widespread practices such as extrajudicial killings, arbitrary detentions and forced displacement. In terms of forced labour, substantial evidence indicated that civilians were regularly conscripted to work on roads and other construction projects or, most horrifically, even used as human minesweepers in counter-insurgency operations.[28] After a series of consultations and investigations, which met resistance from the Burmese military government, the Council authorized the temporary withdrawal of GSP benefits from Burma in March 1997.[29] The withdrawal appeared to have little negative impact on trade with the EU,[30] however, and forced labour practices and other human rights violations continued apace for many years until the government of Thein Sein, who took office as President in 2011, implemented a series of political reforms and moves towards democratization. These moves led to substantial gains in the field of international relations for Burma, long an international pariah state, and its GSP access

---

28 See e.g. Robert Howse and Jared Genser, 'Are EU Trade Sanctions on Burma Compatible with WTO Law?', (2008) 29 *Michigan Journal of International Law*, 165–96.

29 Council Regulation (EC) No. 552/97 of 24 March 1997 temporarily withdrawing access to generalized tariff preferences from the Union of Myanmar, [1997] OJ L 85/8.

30 Weifeng Zhou and Ludo Cuyvers, 'Linking International Trade and Labour Standards: The Effectiveness of Sanctions under the European Union's GSP', (2011) 45 *Journal of World Trade* 63.

was subsequently restored in July 2013, three months after the tragic events at Rana Plaza. However, reports of widespread labour rights violations, including forced labour, still persist, although the latter problem appears to be improving.[31]

Belarus

It took a decade after Burma's withdrawal of GSP benefits in 1997 for the mechanism to be invoked again. The process began in 2001, when the EU expanded the reasons for temporary withdrawal to include any 'serious and systematic violation' of the labour rights standards embodied in the ILO Declaration on Fundamental Principles and Rights at Work. Subsequently, in January 2003, the ETUC and ICFTU filed another complaint, this time in conjunction with the World Confederation of Labour. The complaint alleged serious violations of freedom of association and the right to collective bargaining in Belarus. The Commission initiated an investigation in December of that year. Belarussian authorities attempted repeatedly at several points throughout the process to demonstrate compliance, but the initial investigation found evidence to corroborate the allegations of serious and systematic violations and urged Belarus to remedy the situation by implementing a list of 12 specific recommendations issued by the ILO in its own Commission of Inquiry report into the matter in July 2004. Following Belarus' failure to implement these recommendations by the established deadline of 1 June 2005, and following the lapse of a further six-month period of monitoring and evaluation established by the Commission in August 2005 without any significant improvement in the situation, the EU suspended Belarus' GSP benefits with effect from June 2007.[32]

Both withdrawal processes appear to have had little, if any, impact on labour rights in the target countries. They certainly failed to induce changes sufficient to bring the target countries into satisfactory compliance with the applicable GSP labour rights conditionalities.

However, these are only the cases where the temporary withdrawal mechanism was actually engaged. The EU's strategy has consistently been to engage in dialogue and seek a diplomatic resolution first, using

---

[31] See e.g. United States Department of State, '2013 Country Reports on Human Rights Practices – Burma', 27 February 2014.

[32] Council Regulation (EC) No. 1933/2006 of 21 December 2006 temporarily withdrawing access to the generalised tariff preferences from the Republic of Belarus, [2006] OJ L 405/35.

the withdrawal mechanism as leverage, and a subsequent temporary withdrawal of benefits is a last-resort measure that actually signals a failure of the engagement process.[33]

In one case, a looming GSP withdrawal was actually averted through a successful process of engagement. In 1995, ETUC and ICFTU also filed a complaint against Pakistan concerning the practice of forced child labour, but this one had a different result from their complaint against Burma. This time, the EU decided not to take any action after Pakistan – which subsequently became a GSP+ beneficiary – adopted measures to address the situation.[34]

Further, in the cases of Burma and Belarus, a failure to bring about change does not necessarily mean a failure of the system. Particularly given the temporal proximity of each episode to the introduction of a new system of labour rights conditionality, the withdrawals may have served the strategic purpose of signalling to other potential target countries that the EU is perfectly willing to invoke the GSP withdrawal mechanisms where warranted. Of course, the punitive effect of these withdrawals on Burma and Belarus themselves was ultimately limited, particularly as each enjoyed far closer bilateral trade relations with another world power – China and Russia, respectively – that helped to offset any negative impact of the withdrawals, and in any event even trade with the EU did not appear to have been adversely affected in either case.[35] In this context, it is perhaps a positive sign that Belarus even engaged in the process to begin with. However, each country's situation is different, and any GSP beneficiary that is more dependent on close bilateral trade relations with the EU – as Bangladesh is, as will be seen below – would have good reason to think twice about whether it can afford to take a cavalier attitude towards the GSP benefits it enjoys. Such countries might do well to look to the case of former GSP+ beneficiary Sri Lanka as a cautionary tale.

One of the original beneficiaries when GSP+ was introduced in 2005 was Sri Lanka, which at the time had just seen the Indian Ocean tsunami of December 2004 kill 35,000 people and displace half a million others in the eastern part of the island nation. This inflicted further human tragedy upon a country that had, since 1983, been in the grip of a bloody

---

33 See e.g. Franziska Humbert, *The Challenge of Child Labour in International Law* (Cambridge, UK: Cambridge University Press, 2009), p. 310.

34 Ibid.; see also Barbara Brandtner and Allan Rosas, 'Trade Preferences and Human Rights', in Philip Alston, Mara Bustelo and James Heenan (eds), *The EU and Human Rights* (Oxford University Press, 1999), at pp. 699, 716–18.

35 Zhou and Cuyvers, n. 30 above.

and brutal civil war that had erupted out of historical ethnic tensions between the majority Sinhalese population and the minority Tamil population dominant in the northern and eastern parts of the island.

In 2009, with the Sri Lankan Army nearing victory, the European Commission decided to launch an investigation into allegations of grave human rights abuses by government forces. The investigation found evidence of widespread violations of the International Convention on Civil and Political Rights, the Convention against Torture, and the Convention on the Rights of the Child, all in contravention of Sri Lanka's obligations under the GSP+ programme. As a result, in February 2010, the EU Council adopted a regulation temporarily withdrawing GSP+ benefits from Sri Lanka. However, the Council also left a six-month window before entry into force of the withdrawal, hoping that this might prompt Sri Lanka to engage in constructive dialogue in an effort to retain their GSP+ benefits.

Sri Lankan government officials, however, instead chose defiance over diplomacy. Calling the move outrageous and politically motivated, they accused the EU of punishing innocent textile workers for human rights violations that never happened. Confidently predicting that the loss of GSP+ benefits would have little effect, the government allowed the six-month deadline to pass without making any effort to remediate the ongoing human rights crisis in the country.[36]

By 2013, however, the government was forced to admit that the loss of GSP+ had actually resulted in the loss of 10,000 jobs and the closure of 25 garment factories.[37] The government did not divulge how it had arrived at its calculations, and there is no way of independently verifying these numbers. It may very well be that the government was merely seeking to deflect blame for poor economic performance, and at the same time maintain its propaganda strategy of framing the GSP+ withdrawal as having punished vulnerable workers.[38] Nevertheless, it is an indication that a GSP withdrawal could entail substantial economic consequences for at least some countries.

---

[36] See e.g. James Yap, 'Beyond "Don't Be Evil": The European Union GSP+ Trade Preference Scheme and the Incentivisation of the Sri Lankan Garment Industry to Foster Human Rights', (2013) 19 *European Law Journal* 283.

[37] Ashwin Hemmathagama, 'Major Losses in Apparel Sector from Loss of GSP Plus: Sri Lanka Government', *Daily Financial Times*, 24 October 2013.

[38] For instance, the EU's own figures show that Sri Lanka's apparel exports actually increased by 6.7 per cent in euro value in 2012, a year in which its total worldwide exports decreased by 3.6 per cent in euro value.

4. THE EUROPEAN UNION GSP AND LABOUR RIGHTS IN BANGLADESH

Not long after the Rana Plaza disaster cast a global spotlight on labour conditions in Bangladesh, speculation began about the country's status as a GSP beneficiary of the EU. A mere six days after the factory collapsed, amid intense media attention on the tragedy, the EU released a statement hinting that Bangladesh's GSP benefits could be in jeopardy. This statement declared the EU 'willing and ready to assist the Bangladeshi authorities in any way it can to meet the required international standards' – but further warned that the EU was considering 'appropriate action', specifically raising the prospect of a temporary withdrawal under the GSP programme.[39]

This announcement was enough to prompt them to engage in discussions with EU representatives on ways to avoid any outcome that would put Bangladesh's GSP benefits in jeopardy. On 28 May 2013, Bangladesh Foreign Minister, Dipu Moni, met with EU Trade Commissioner, Karel De Gucht, and the two issued a statement expressing sorrow over the Rana Plaza tragedy and affirming their shared commitment to 'safeguard [Bangladesh's] Everything but Arms benefits through determined action to improve health and occupational safety standards in the export-oriented ready-made garment factories in Bangladesh'.[40]

The pressure increased when the US announced on 27 June 2013 that it had decided to cancel the preferences Bangladesh had previously enjoyed under its own GSP programme, citing concerns over labour rights. Although the US programme was of limited importance to Bangladesh, as it excluded most apparel items – in contrast to the EU programme, under which apparel items entering the EU from Bangladesh do qualify for preferential tariffs, and have a 78 per cent utilization rate[41] – the move magnified fears that the EU might follow suit.[42] However, on

---

[39] European Commission, 'Joint Statement by HR/VP Catherine Ashton and EU Trade Commissioner Karel De Gucht following the recent building collapse in Bangladesh', Brussels, 30 April 2013.

[40] European Commission, 'Joint Statement by EU Trade Commissioner Karel De Gucht and Bangladesh Foreign Minister Dr Dipu Moni following recent disasters in the Bangladeshi garment manufacturing industry', Brussels, 28 May 2013.

[41] Mustafizur Rahman, 'Trade Benefits for Least Developed Countries: the Bangladesh Case', United Nations Development and Social Affairs, July 2014.

[42] See e.g. Shafin Fattah, 'Suspension of US GSP: What Does This Mean for Bangladesh?', *The Daily Star*, 29 June 2013.

8 July 2013, representatives from Bangladesh, the EU and the ILO met in Geneva – with representatives from industry, employers, trade unions and other key stakeholders present – and agreed to a 'sustainability compact' to improve labour rights, working conditions and factory safety in the ready-made garment and knitwear industry in Bangladesh.[43]

The Compact is built on time-bound commitments undertaken by all three of Bangladesh, the EU and the ILO. It revolves around three target areas for improvement: (i) respect for labour rights, in particular freedom of association and the right of collective bargaining; (ii) structural integrity of buildings and occupational safety and health; and (iii) responsible business conduct. Only the first two, however, involve any commitments to concrete, verifiable outcomes.[44]

In terms of respect for labour rights, the Compact obliges Bangladesh to introduce and effectively implement a series of reforms designed to strengthen collective bargaining rights and compliance with international labour standards. Building on commitments made previously, Bangladesh pledged to introduce an amended Labour Law by the end of 2013, to include provisions on improving protection of the fundamental rights of freedom of association and collective bargaining, and establish Joint Committees for the improvement of occupational safety and health. Effective implementation of this law is to be monitored through regular reports to the ILO Committee of Experts, which will also review observations from social partners. Bangladesh also committed to strengthening the exercise of freedom of association and collective bargaining rights in the Export Processing Zones (EPZs). Finally, it made several commitments with respect to promoting awareness of labour rights, ensuring they are being exercised, and monitoring and enforcing them through various inspection and public reporting mechanisms.

With respect to structural integrity of buildings and occupational safety and health, Bangladesh pledged under the Compact to assess the structural building safety and fire safety of all active export-oriented ready-made garment and knitwear factories in the country by June 2014 – with the most populated factories assessed by the end of 2013 – and initiate remedial actions, including relocation of unsafe factories. At the same time, it has also committed to developing a publicly accessible database

---

43 See 'Joint Statement: Staying engaged: A Sustainability Compact for continuous improvements in labour rights and factory safety in the Ready-Made Garment and Knitwear Industry in Bangladesh', available at: http://trade.ec.europa.eu/doclib/docs/2013/july/tradoc_151601.pdf.

44 The last category only involves commitments in the nature of welcoming, recognizing, encouraging or taking note of.

containing information on inspections, violations, closures and remediations. The EU pledged development assistance support.

Meanwhile, in a statement announcing the deal, Commissioner De Gucht explicitly made note of the role of the GSP. Noting that ready-made garment exports represent 90 per cent of Bangladesh's exports to the EU and account for about 2.5 million jobs – mostly for women – he warned that 'Bangladesh – or for that matter any other Least Developed Country – cannot take for granted the trade preferences it currently enjoys'.[45]

It is often difficult to gauge with certainty the exact importance of any specific factor in a complex political negotiation process involving so many actors and stakeholders. However, it is telling to see here that, through multiple rounds of discussions, the EU remains committed to the strategy of leveraging GSP preferences as an incentive to keep Bangladesh engaged in the process. Moreover, after underscoring the importance of the GSP to Bangladesh specifically, Commissioner De Gucht goes on to direct the same warning at all LDCs that are beneficiaries of the EBA scheme.

Also telling is that Bangladesh, for its part, has to date remained engaged in the process. For instance, the government has participated in quarterly monitoring meetings with the EU, the US, and the ILO to follow the progress of the Compact implementation. The Bangladesh Secretaries of Labour, Commerce, and Foreign Affairs have also collaborated with representatives from the EU, US, Canada, the Netherlands and the United Kingdom towards monitoring implementation of the Compact.

The process is ongoing, and it remains to be seen whether it will result in concrete change for labour rights in Bangladesh, or whether it will ultimately prove to be unproductive, as in the case of Belarus. Early indications suggest that, so far, real progress is being made, although significant challenges still remain.

One year after the establishment of the Compact, the EU conducted an assessment of progress made so far on the commitments given therein. The ensuing progress report found that concrete improvements in the labour rights situation in Bangladesh could be observed so far. Most significantly, two weeks after the establishment of the Compact, Bangladesh enacted into law amendments to its 2006 Labour Act to bring it more into line with international labour standards, particularly with

---

[45] European Commission, 'Remarks by EU Trade Commissioner Karel De Gucht on the Launch of a Global Sustainability Compact in response to Bangladesh tragedies', Geneva, 8 July 2013.

respect to trade union registration and occupational health and safety conditions. For instance, one important amendment removes a provision requiring the Registrar of Trade Unions to provide names of union leaders to employers at the time of registration of a trade union, a provision which had resulted in mass terminations of employees just before registration.[46]

So far, there are some encouraging early signs that the recent amendments to the Labour Law are having concrete effects, particularly in the area of trade union registrations. The EU report noted that 2013 and the first half of 2014 saw the registration of 187 new trade unions, bringing the total number of trade unions in the country from 136 to 323.[47] This has been accompanied by an increase in reporting and investigation of unfair labour practices and cases filed in the labour courts, all of which suggests that workers are beginning to feel more empowered to assert their rights without fear of retribution.[48]

The government of Bangladesh also initiated the process of significantly upgrading its workplace inspection capacity, and introduced measures to improve the fire safety and structural integrity of buildings.[49]

Further, through the newly established National Tripartite Committee (NTC) – a body composed of representatives of government, workers' organizations and employers' organizations, with the advisory support of the ILO[50] – the government of Bangladesh has worked with the Accord and the Alliance on implementing a programme aimed at carrying out fire and building safety inspections of all export-oriented ready-made garment and knitwear factories in the country. According to the programme's schedule, the Accord will inspect 1,400 factories; the Alliance will take care of 608; and the government, through the NTC, will inspect 1,500 factories – all according to a set of harmonized standards agreed to in November 2013.

---

[46] European Commission, 'Technical Progress Report: Staying Engaged – A Sustainability Compact for continuous improvements in labour rights and factory safety in the Ready-Made Garment and Knitwear Industry in Bangladesh', 8 July 2014 (EC One-Year Progress Report).

[47] By October 2014, the number of new trade unions had risen to 236, bringing the total number to 372: see 'Bangladesh Sustainability Compact – Follow-up Meeting: Implementation review and progress stocktaking', 20 October 2014.

[48] EC One-Year Progress Report, n. 46 above.

[49] Ibid.

[50] International Labour Organisation, 'First Meeting of High Level Committee on Building and Fire Safety in RMG Factories', 7 June 2013.

Of the planned inspections, by the time of the EU progress report, the Accord had completed 834, the Alliance 604, and the NTC 282. The inspections already completed have resulted in the closures of 17 factories (two of which were inspected by the NTC) while 15 others were allowed to continue operations only after remedial actions were taken (none of which were inspected by the NTC).[51]

Meanwhile, the Directorate of Inspection of Factories and Establishments (DFE) launched a website in March 2014, which includes a publicly accessible database of ready-made garment factories.[52]

In releasing its report, the EU lauded all these achievements, noting that on the whole, trade union registrations are up, workers seem more aware and assertive of their rights, and that inspections are ongoing, with the results being made public and more inspectors set to be recruited. However, it also stressed that more is 'urgently required' to meet Bangladesh's commitments under the Compact.[53]

For instance, the report expressed concern over labour rights in Bangladesh's Export Processing Zones (EPZs), a series of eight designated areas that specialize in producing goods for export. EPZs are a key contributor to the Bangladeshi economy, consistently generating 16–18 per cent of its exports.[54] Approximately 382,000 workers are employed in these zones, of which 300,000 are employed in garment factories.

The purpose-built factories and uninterrupted supply of power and gas in the EPZs provide significant benefits in terms of factory safety. The buildings in the EPZ are designed for industrial use and must meet the more stringent safety requirements of the EPZ building code. In fact, since the establishment of the EPZs in 1980, there has been no fatal fire accident and no building has collapsed in an EPZ.

However, rights in the EPZs with respect to collective bargaining and freedom of association are a source of greater concern. The EPZs are exempt from the Labour Act, and labour rights in the EPZs are regulated under a separate regime. Protections afforded there are generally weaker than is the case in the rest of the country. For instance, workers in an EPZ do not have the right to form trade unions; nor does the system of labour inspections under the Labour Act apply to EPZs.

---

[51] EC One-Year Progress Report, n. 46 above.

[52] Ibid.

[53] European Commission, 'Staying Engaged: Bangladesh Sustainability Compact – One Year On', press release, Brussels, 8 July 2014.

[54] A.N.M. Asaduzzaman Fakir, Mohammad Shahin Miah and Mohammed Shakawat Hossain, 'Export Diversification and Role of Export Processing Zones (EPZ) in Bangladesh', (2013) 7 *ASA University Review* 96.

This has become a focal point of criticism for the Bangladesh government's record on labour rights. As noted above, the Compact calls for Bangladesh to strengthen freedom of association and collective bargaining rights in the EPZs. The US also included bringing labour rights in the EPZs in line with those enjoyed by workers elsewhere in the country as one of the conditions necessary to reinstate Bangladesh's preferences under its own GSP programme.[55]

The government of Bangladesh has made some small strides towards improving labour rights and working conditions in the EPZs. In December 2013, the government raised the minimum wage for workers in the EPZs, complete with food, medical, transport and attendance bonuses, as well as a yearly increment of 10 per cent on the base salary.[56] Further, in July 2014 Bangladesh's cabinet approved in principle a draft law that it claims will harmonize freedom of association and collective bargaining rights in the EPZs with the rest of the country. However, many have voiced concerns over whether the law, if eventually passed, will truly deliver on these commitments. For instance, the law's eschewal of the term 'trade union' in favour of 'workers' welfare association' has generated some scepticism – particularly as actual registration of the association remains at the discretion of the EPZs' regulating agency.[57]

Among the sceptics is the International Trade Union Confederation (ITUC), the successor to the ICFTU which filed the complaints against Burma, Pakistan and Belarus under the GSP programme. Together with fellow trade union confederations IndustriALL and UNI Global Union, ITUC has released its own one-year progress evaluation report of the Bangladesh Sustainability Compact.[58]

The union report acknowledges the 'real progress' made in the area of trade union registration. However, it asserts that many applications have yet to be acted upon, and others have been rejected even though they meet all requirements. It notes further that the surge in trade union registrations has not yet successfully translated into meaningful collective bargaining rights for workers – employers have been unresponsive to

---

[55] Office of the United States Trade Representative, Department of Labor, and State Department, 'Statement by the U.S. Government on Labor Rights and Factory Safety in Bangladesh', 19 July 2013.

[56] Tilka Binte Mehtab, 'EPZ RMG Workers' Minimum Wage Tk5,600', *Dhaka Tribune*, 25 December 2013.

[57] Mohosinul Karim, 'Cabinet Approves EPZ Labour Act', *Dhaka Tribune*, 8 July 2014.

[58] International Trade Union Confederation, IndustriALL and UNI Global Union, 'An Evaluation of the Bangladesh Sustainability Compact', 8 July 2013.

demands from unions to bargain collectively, and the government has taken little action to enforce the law when employers refuse to negotiate.

More disturbingly, union leaders have been subjected to unlawful intimidation, including dismissals and assaults. For instance, employees at one factory registered a trade union in January 2014 and made a request to management for collective bargaining in March. Since then, more than 60 workers have been fired, at least one union leader has been physically assaulted, and false criminal charges have been filed against the union's general secretary. As of the date of the union report, the government had yet to respond to the union's complaints. Reports of anti-union retaliation – sometimes violent – at other factories have been widespread,[59] prompting the US to call on the government 'to develop a credible and effective mechanism for responding to and addressing allegations of unfair labor practices'.[60]

Part of the problem, according to the union report, is that labour inspectors cannot impose penalties for violations themselves, but can only report them to the courts. Even these penalties are weak and do not serve as effective deterrents. Further, the government has been slow to implement its commitment to recruit more labour inspectors, and has been giving the inspectors already in place too few resources with which to complete their task.

Needless to say, the authors of the union report are sceptical of the government's commitment to fulfilling its obligations under the Compact. They cite 'lack of political will, failure of intra-governmental coordination, high levels of corruption, and the extraordinary dominance of the garment sector in government' as the fundamental barriers to meaningful progress.

Corruption, political resistance and other incidents of the garment industry's informal influence over public governance institutions in Bangladesh present serious obstacles to hopes for meaningful labour rights reform in the country. Legislative advances mean little in the face of rampant corruption and weak rule of law. For instance, legislative reforms have meant that the Registrar of Trade Unions is no longer supposed to provide employers with names of trade union leaders, but the EU notes that reports persist of authorities sharing this information informally anyway.

---

[59] See e.g. Human Rights Watch, 'Bangladesh: Protect Garment Workers' Rights', 6 February 2014.

[60] Office of the United States Trade Representative, 'GSP Action Plan Review Finds More Needs to be Done to Improve Worker Rights and Worker Safety in Bangladesh', 3 July 2014.

Similarly, when a building is inspected by government inspectors, observers charge that they 'do little or nothing to stop [labour rights and building safety code violations] because more often than not they are taking bribes to look the other way'.[61] Corruption among public officials is rampant: Transparency International has estimated that factory owners can pay up to $25,000 in bribes for various permits just to get a factory up and running.[62] Rana Plaza itself was built and run in violation of several regulations with the collusion of corrupt officials;[63] seven labour inspectors (of a total complement of 50) were suspended in June 2013 after a Ministry of Labour investigation found that they had renewed operating licences without even inspecting the premises.[64]

Weak rule of law is hardly a problem limited to the regulatory regime concerning workers' rights and safety in Bangladesh; rather, it is endemic to the governance institutions of the entire country. Transparency International's Corruption Perception Index, which measures the perceived levels of public sector corruption in countries worldwide, ranks Bangladesh in the bottom quartile of the 177 countries in its rankings, at 136th.[65] In one notable recent scandal, for instance, the World Bank pulled $1.2 billion in financing from the Padma Multipurpose Bridge project aimed at linking Dhaka with the southwest of the country, after credible evidence emerged that a high-level corruption conspiracy had colluded to have the project illicitly awarded to Canadian construction firm SNC-Lavalin.[66] Corruption in Bangladesh is a serious problem that extends far beyond workers' rights and safety in garment factories.

Moreover, the garment industry enjoys a particularly cosy relationship with government, or, perhaps more accurately, is inextricably integrated into it: it has been estimated that garment industry bosses account for fully 10 per cent of the country's parliamentarians, and countless other owners have strong political connections.[67] It is little surprise that so

---

[61] Joseph Allchin, 'One Year on from Rana Plaza, Little has Changed in Bangladesh's Factories', *Financial Times*, 17 July 2014. See also Steven Greenhouse and Julfikar Ali Manik, 'Stalemate Over Garment Factory Safety in Bangladesh', *The New York Times*, 25 June 2014.

[62] Iftekar Zaman, 'Corruption Rampant a Year after Bangladesh Factory Collapse', *Financial Times*, 24 April 2014.

[63] Ibid.

[64] Associated Press, 'Bangladesh Factory Inspectors Suspended in Deadly Collapse', *CBC News*, 13 June 2013.

[65] Transparency International, 'Corruption Perception Index 2013'.

[66] World Bank, 'World Bank Statement on Padma Bridge', 29 June 2012.

[67] John Chalmers, 'Special Report: How Textile Kings Weave a Hold on Bangladesh', *Reuters*, 3 May 2013.

many reports persist of garment factories blithely ignoring laws and regulations pertaining to workers' rights and safety, prompting one Bangladeshi civil society observer to remark that workers' rights reforms in Bangladesh are 'limited to superstructure',[68] because their intended effects are never observed on the ground. Transparency International Bangladesh – which, six months after Rana Plaza, published a report comprehensively cataloguing the nature, causes, extent and consequences of corruption in the garment industry – identifies establishing good governance as the 'first priority' in resolving the workers' rights and safety crisis in the Bangladesh garment industry.[69]

Another report, issued by the Stern Center for Business and Human Rights at New York University, identifies and examines another key aspect of the problem.[70] In what the Washington Post has called an 'open secret',[71] it is common practice for the larger, registered factories to subcontract work to a vast number of unofficial operations that run under-the-table garment factories from apartments, basements and rooftops. These unregistered underground set-ups operate unseen on the margins of the law, indifferent to government regulations pertaining to workers' rights and safety. Their sole preoccupation is to produce garments as quickly and as cheaply as possible – often when one of the established, above-ground operations is under pressure to meet a deadline – and workers' rights and safety are a secondary consideration.

This practice of subcontracting is deeply entrenched in the fabric of the Bangladeshi ready-made garment industry. The front-line exporting factories serve as the industry's interface with foreign buyers. Their operation requires significant investment of capital, maintaining sophisticated relationships with international buyers, and high production capacity. These factories accept orders from overseas and assume the first-line responsibility for meeting them. However, when orders outpace production capacity, the front-line factories turn to subcontractors. Factories – as

---

[68] 'The Reforms in Apparels Sector are Limited to Superstructure', *New Age*, 18 July 2014.

[69] Transparency International Bangladesh, 'Readymade Garments Sector: Problems of Good Governance and Way Forward', 31 October 2013. New Age, 'The Reforms in Apparels Sector are Limited to Superstructure', 18 July 2014.

[70] Sarah Labowitz and Dorothee Baumann-Pauly, 'Business as Usual is Not an Option: Supply Chains and Sourcing after Rana Plaza', Center for Business and Human Rights at NYU Leonard N. Stern School of Business, April 2014 (NYU Report).

[71] See e.g. Jason Motlagh, 'A Year after Rana Plaza: What Hasn't Changed since the Bangladesh Factory Collapse', *The Washington Post*, 18 April 2014.

well as profit margins – grow smaller and smaller as work is subcontracted and re-subcontracted down the chain, putting downward pressure on workers' rights and safety standards.

It is in these operations, many suggest, where the bulk of the workers' rights and safety problems in the country's garment industry are to be found. At the same time, however, because of their size and relative obscurity, they are also the most poorly regulated under the country's various workers' rights and safety standards. Some of these operations are so small and informal that they are not themselves aware that such standards exist.[72] Further, the inspections and other programmes of the Accord and the Alliance are concerned only with the 1,894 factories (of an estimated 5,000 to 6,000 in the country) that maintain direct relationships with their members; neither addresses their indirect suppliers. As one unregistered factory owner noted, '[w]e're hiding. Those customers won't like my factory because it's a tin shed.'[73] In this way, the bulk of both public and private regulatory oversight ends up targeting only the factories on the surface layer of the industry, overlooking the more deeply embedded operations where oversight is perhaps most needed.

The NYU Report describes how the entire system operates in a way that fosters the practice of subcontracting. Suppliers that generate the highest order and export volume receive the greatest access to capital, as financing and export credits are made available on the basis of actual production volume, rather than production capacity. This incentivizes suppliers to take orders beyond their actual capacity. Further, while many international brands outwardly express disapproval of unauthorized subcontracting, their behaviour fosters it. For instance, the exigencies of the fast fashion industry lead buyers to insist on strict adherence to deadlines. If a front-line supplier misses a shipping deadline, it may be compelled to rush the shipment by air at its own expense, or absorb a 5 per cent penalty, in an industry where profit margins can be as low as 3–4 per cent. However, in a country as underdeveloped as Bangladesh, occasional production delays as a result of power outages or other disruptions are inevitable, and in such cases subcontracting becomes necessary in order to avoid a damaging financial loss. So instrumental is the practice of subcontracting in supporting and stabilizing the garment industry that many insiders believe that the industry could not operate under current conditions without it.

---

72 Tripti Lahiri and Christina Passariello, 'Why Retailers Don't Know Who Sews Their Clothing', *Wall Street Journal*, 24 July 2013.

73 NYU Report, n. 70 above, at p. 24.

To address this problem, the government has proposed measures to try to extend regulatory oversight to subcontractor factories. Specifically, it has introduced a draft guideline that it says will establish transparency and accountability in the subcontracting system. The guideline would require all third-party manufacturers to be a member of an industry association. Compliance with all the relevant labour laws would be monitored by a committee consisting of government officials and apparel makers and exporters.[74] However, given the difficulties the government has had in effectively regulating the front-line factories – which are ostensibly the larger, more sophisticated operations – there are serious questions as to whether additional regulation alone can be an effective solution to workers' rights and safety issues in the smaller, unregistered factories.

5. IMPLICATIONS

It is still too early to definitively assess whether the international coordinated effort to exert pressure on Bangladesh to improve workers' rights and safety in its garment industry in the wake of the Rana Plaza tragedy will lead to meaningful positive change. What is clear is that the project faces significant challenges. Issues such as the garment industry's informal influence in government and the prevalence of subcontracting are deeply rooted and systemic problems, which will require fundamental institutional reform to overcome.

It is also clear, however, that there has so far been modest but clear movement in the right direction. Further, the threatened withdrawal of the GSP has been a 'key motivator' in prompting the Bangladeshi government to take what action it has.[75] In particular, the combined effect of this threat with the actual cancellation of the US preferences has played an important role. The US preferences themselves are of very limited significance to Bangladesh because they exclude most items of apparel and therefore do not really benefit the garment industry. Nevertheless, their cancellation serves to add an air of reality to the danger of losing the far more important EU preferences.

Of course, a measured success in Bangladesh, put together with failures to effect meaningful change in Burma and Belarus, hardly add up to a successful track record for the GSP's ability to incentivize labour

[74] 'Sub-contracting Guideline for Apparel Industry Drafted', *Dhaka Herald*, 6 November 2013.

[75] NYU Report, n. 70 above, at p. 9.

rights policy change in a beneficiary country. However, there are reasons to hope that the experiences in Burma and Belarus do not suggest that the GSP cannot be a reasonably productive mechanism for promoting labour rights elsewhere.

First, the experience in Burma must be viewed with caution, given the unique, pariah nature of that government, and the fiercely stubborn intransigence with which it resisted all international pressure of any kind.

As for Belarus, other factors may explain the ineffectiveness of GSP withdrawals in promoting change there. The prospect of losing trade preferences under the EU GSP has varying degrees of significance for different beneficiary countries. On the one hand, in Belarus, it was estimated at the time that the decision to withdraw GSP preferences would mean a difference of 3 per cent of the standard tariff, affecting some 10 per cent of its exports[76] – the effect of the GSP removal was therefore somewhat limited. In Bangladesh, however, the situation is vastly different. The EU is Bangladesh's largest trade partner, receiving 57 per cent of its exports in 2012, a total of €9.9 billion. Despite the controversy over the Rana Plaza tragedy, that figure grew by 10 per cent to €10.9 billion in 2013, and a further 13 per cent to €12.3 billion in 2014. Of this figure, textiles and textile articles accounted for €10.2 billion, or 94 per cent in 2013, and €11.4 billion, or 93 per cent in 2014.[77] As noted in the statement by Commissioner De Gucht quoted above,[78] thanks to the EBA scheme of the GSP, these ready-made garments qualify for duty-free and quota-free entry into the EU market, and account for 2.5 million jobs, mostly for women.

Yet these statistics alone do not fully convey the breadth of the special significance the garment industry has for the country. In 1971, Bangladesh emerged from its brutal liberation struggle with an economic and social structure in tatters, and no significant domestic industry to speak of. In the mid-1970s, however, South Korean companies began to establish garment businesses in the country. At the time, the US and European governments had quotas in place on garment imports from various developing countries under the Multi-Fibre Arrangement, a multinational system that governed the global garment industry at the

---

76 Giselle Bosse and Elena Korosteleva-Polglase, 'Changing Belarus? The Limits of EU Governance in Eastern Europe and the Promise of Partnership', (2009) 44 *Cooperation and Conflict* 143, 153.

77 European Commission, Directorate-General for Trade, see http://trade.ec.europa.eu/doclib/docs/2006/september/tradoc_113349.pdf.

78 European Commission, 'Remarks by EU Trade Commissioner', n. 45 above.

time. When the South Koreans reached their quota, they noticed that Bangladesh offered relative proximity and political stability (compared with war-ravaged Vietnam and Cambodia), as well as low wages and a favourable quota situation. Local entrepreneurs pounced on these new opportunities, setting off a rapid economic revival in the 1980s. The garment industry has powered Bangladesh's economic growth ever since – garment exports reached 53 per cent of total exports in 1995, growing to 75 per cent in 2000 and 79 per cent in 2011.[79] As the World Bank notes, the country has seen 15 million people rise out of poverty since 1992. In the last decade alone, Bangladesh has enjoyed rapid economic and human development, with sustained economic growth of nearly 6 per cent annually accompanied by increases in life expectancy, literacy and per capita food intake.[80]

Many also argue that the garment industry has achieved tremendous progress for the Bangladeshi women who dominate its workforce. In a largely rural and conservative Muslim society, it has eroded the traditional paradigm which would typically see women grow up without being allowed in public unescorted, before getting married and becoming economically dependent on their husbands before the age of 16. Instead, it has enabled women to move to the city and enjoy some independence while forming the backbone of the country's economy and wielding much of its personal economic clout.[81] The garment industry has thus been an integral part of the country's development since its inception, socially as well as economically.

The far greater importance of GSP benefits to Bangladesh than to Belarus could therefore account for the discrepancy in the effect that their threatened withdrawal has had, so far, in each country. Similarly, in Pakistan, the government's more cooperative attitude might be connected with the fact that, in 1995, the EU was Pakistan's largest trade partner and apparel was its leading export.[82] The limited data available thus far therefore suggest that a threatened withdrawal of GSP benefits is more likely to induce a cooperative response the more important those benefits are to the target country. If the EU GSP were comparable with the US

---

79 World Bank, 'Consolidating and Accelerating Exports in Bangladesh', June 2012, at p. 3.

80 World Bank, 'Bangladesh Overview', available at http://www.worldbank.org/en/country/bangladesh/overview.

81 Kenneth R. Weiss, 'Bangladesh Women Find Liberty in Hard Labor', *Los Angeles Times*, 13 March 2014.

82 World Trade Organisation, 'Pakistan: February 1995', 8 February 1995.

GSP in significance to Bangladesh, for instance, it is doubtful whether the government would be as motivated to cooperate.

6. CONCLUSIONS AND SUGGESTIONS FOR REFORM

The EU's attempt to leverage the GSP programme's labour rights conditionalities in Bangladesh has succeeded in producing some limited change there, unlike in Burma and Belarus. However, little more than that can be said at this juncture. The threatened withdrawal of the EU GSP – combined with intense international pressure from a host of other sources – has so far only resulted in modest gains for workers in Bangladesh.

If the public good under consideration here were one that is less intrinsically connected with international trade – such as, for example, freedom of expression – it might nevertheless suffice to say that any progress, no matter how small, is still progress, and the GSP's labour rights conditionality scheme therefore has a positive impact.

However, a proper analysis must be contextual – one step forward is not progress when accompanied by two giant leaps backward. The fact is that the GSP already has a strong impact on labour rights regardless of any built-in conditionalities. After all, there is a reason why labour rights was the first conditionality introduced in the EU's GSP system. That is, the GSP has a particularly strong connection with labour rights because it helps to generate the economic activity necessary to sustain labour, and in turn violations of labour rights. There is even evidence to suggest that the growth of the garment industry in Bangladesh has actually been driven in part by the weakness in workers' rights – the World Bank identifies low labour costs as Bangladesh's primary competitive advantage over rival garment-producing countries.[83] This advantage is enhanced by the GSP benefits, which the World Bank identifies as Bangladesh's second most significant competitive advantage.[84] Thus, in the case of Bangladesh, the GSP's effect may have been to tip the balance of competitive advantages further in favour of a country whose success is driven by low labour costs. It means little, in an environment of severe labour rights repression that is in part enabled by the GSP, to then say that the GSP's labour rights conditionality scheme has achieved modest gains in improving this situation.

---

83 World Bank, 'Consolidating and Accelerating Exports', n. 79 above, at p. 4.

84 Ibid., at p. 5.

The question at hand is whether GSP conditionality mechanisms can be an effective tool to promote labour rights. Given the close natural links between international trade and labour rights, the answer to this question cannot be limited to whether the GSP labour rights conditionality scheme can have a minimal net positive impact on labour rights. Rather, the answer must also assess whether the conditionality scheme enables the GSP as a whole to foster economic development that does not leave labour rights behind (remember the EU GSP's stated objective of promoting 'sustainable' development). Under this more rigorous metric, it is difficult to conclude that the labour rights conditionality mechanisms in the EU GSP have had very much success in promoting workers' rights and safety in Bangladesh.

In a way, this result is not surprising. The EU GSP system is designed to afford the Commission only a very crude and unsophisticated mechanism to promote labour rights. This mechanism only provides the Commission with the ability to take the most drastic measure possibly available under the GSP system, and only where the labour rights situation has deteriorated to the point where violations have become 'serious and systematic'. Further, it is a very blunt instrument in that it inflicts damage on not just its intended target – the beneficiary state's government – but also potentially on a host of other actors, including vulnerable low-wage workers. This may help to explain why the Commission has used this mechanism only very sparingly in the past, and seems anxious to avoid having to do so in Bangladesh.

It may be useful for the Commission to have more flexibility with respect to both remedial measures available as well as possible stages of intervention. Of course, flexibility will always be limited by the imperative of conformity to the rules of international trade law. However, the GSP needs a mechanism to monitor and address labour rights violations before they become 'serious and systematic'. The Bangladesh experience shows that once labour rights violations have reached this level, they can be very difficult to uproot, because the practices at the heart of the problem may have become very deeply entrenched in the system.

Of course, given the number of countries that are GSP beneficiaries, the cost required to actively monitor and engage all of them on their labour rights situation to the extent necessary may not be practical. However, given the evidence that suggests that GSP benefits may only be an effective motivational factor above a threshold level of importance to a country's economy, the monitoring could perhaps be focused on countries that make particularly high use of the GSP. For instance, each country could have a quota on exports that qualify for GSP benefits in the EU. This quota would vary from country to country, but in order to ensure compliance with international trade law, it would be defined in an objectively determinable way according to some metric that measures importance to the country's economy – for instance, as a particular percentage value of the country's GDP or total exports.

Above this quota, GSP benefits would be contingent on enrolment in and adherence to a special programme that would be designed to monitor the labour rights situation in a country and provide whatever support or direction is needed to continually ensure that it does not reach an unacceptable level. Such a programme might contain a mandatory factory/workplace audit and inspection system, trade union membership targets, annual evaluations and other mechanisms to ensure that adequate workers' rights and safety regulations are in place and enforced. It could be administered by the EU directly, or in partnership with an outside organization such as the ILO.

It might also benefit from adjudicative mechanisms of the same nature as those found in many bilateral investment treaties or free trade agreements, allowing individuals (or agents acting on their behalf) to file claims and have them adjudicated before a tribunal. The United States' recent decision to proceed with a labour enforcement case against Guatemala under the Dominican Republic-Central America-United States Free Trade Agreement (CAFTA-DR) illustrates how international trade instruments can become a forum for labour rights dispute settlement.[85] Barry and Reddy have presented one possible example of what a multilateral labour rights monitoring agency linked to international trade might look like, complete with investigation and adjudication mechanisms.[86]

Meanwhile, the GSP as currently constituted is still capable of having an effect on labour rights, albeit one that is very minimal. More specifically, once labour rights violations in a country have become 'serious and systematic', it can be used to provide that country's government with an incentive to improve the situation, proportional in magnitude to the GSP's importance to that country. In order to have a greater impact, however, the GSP scheme needs a mechanism to address labour rights violations before they become 'serious and systematic', because the experience in Bangladesh shows that once they reach that

---

[85] See Office of the United States Trade Representative, 'United States Proceeds with Labor Enforcement Case against Guatemala', 18 September 2014.

[86] Christian Barry and Sanjay G. Reddy, *International Trade and Labor Standards: A Proposal for Linkage* (New York: Columbia University Press, 2008), at pp. 80–85.

point, they can become so deeply entrenched that they require fundamental, systemic change to fix. Nevertheless, although much more is needed, the results achieved by the GSP in Bangladesh in the aftermath of Rana Plaza have been a step in the right direction. Hopefully, in conjunction with the other international pressure being brought to bear on the government and the garment industry in Bangladesh, it will be enough to make a meaningful difference for the country's garment workers.

10. Extraterritorial regulation of natural resources: a functional approach

Cedric Ryngaert* and Marieke Koekkoek

1. INTRODUCTION

The European Union (EU) is currently profiling itself as an environmental frontrunner by actively pursuing the protection and adoption of environmental norms throughout all policy areas. This pursuit of environmental objectives also has an external dimension in that the EU uses trade measures to 'unilaterally' condition market access for products from third countries on compliance with EU environmental standards.[1] However understandable and perhaps commendable these actions are, by actively trying to export EU norm values through – at least partly – the 'extraterritorial' application of EU law, they may be in tension with international principles of jurisdiction that are geared towards delimiting international spheres of competence, and more generally with the right of foreign nations to freely make their own decisions regarding the balance to be struck between economic and environmental imperatives.

The most prominent and well-known example of EU externalization of its own environmental regulation is the much-discussed Directive 2008/101/EC (Aviation Directive).[2] To remind the reader, this Directive included in the EU's Emissions Trading System (EU ETS) emissions from airline companies, including foreign companies, flying to and from EU destinations. Such regulatory extension was a source of great

* Cedric Ryngaert's research for this contribution was funded by ERC Starting Grant 336230 and the NWO VIDI research scheme.

[1] For further background on the EU's governance through international trade and its effect on achieving non-trade objectives, see Larik (Chapter 3, this volume).

[2] Directive 2008/101/EC of the European Parliament and of the Council of 19 November 2008 amending Directive 2003/87/EC so as to include aviation activities in the scheme for greenhouse gas emission allowance trading within the Community, [2009] OJ L 8/3 (Aviation Directive).

controversy, as the scheme covered the entire commercial route of aircraft departing from or arriving in the EU, including the flight stretches outside European airspace.[3] In response to a preliminary question posed by a British court, however, the Court of Justice of the EU (CJEU) found that the measure was *not* extraterritorial in nature. Among other considerations, the Court motivated its decision by referring to the territorial link of the flights: since all either departed from or arrived at an airport in the EU, and the EU is free to impose conditions on the commercial activities carried out within its territory, there was no extraterritorial application of the measure.[4] After all, aviation operators had a choice to *not* enter the European – territorial – market and so could have avoided compliance with EU legislation.[5] In *ATAA*, the CJEU embraced a rather strict interpretation of 'extraterritoriality',[6] by apparently limiting the application of the concept to situations which have no link whatsoever with the regulating entity, and considering situations having *some* territorial link to fall squarely within the territoriality principle. Given the Court's opposition to the territorial effects doctrine in transnational competition law proceedings,[7] this may be surprising. Ultimately, the decision in *ATAA* might not so much have been based on international principles of jurisdiction, but rather on the desire to

---

[3] Article 3 read together with Annex 1 of the Aviation Directive, n. 2 above.

[4] C-366/10 *Air Transport Association of America and Others v Secretary of State for Energy and Climate Change*, Judgment, 21 December 2011 [2011] ECR I-13755 (*ATAA Case*), stating that 'certain matters contributing to the pollution of the air, sea or land territory of the Member States originate in an event which occurs partly outside that territory is not such as to call into question, in the light of the principles of customary international law capable of being relied upon in the main proceedings, the full applicability of European Union law in that territory': ibid., para. 129; see also ibid., para. 128.

[5] Ibid., para. 127.

[6] Uwe M. Erling, 'Introductory Note to the Court of Justice of the European Union: Air Transport Association of America (ATA) et al. v. Secretary of State for Energy & Climate Change' (2012) 51(3) *International Legal Materials* 535.

[7] See Joined Cases C-89/85, C-104/85, C-114/85, C-116/85, C-117/85 and C-125/85 to C-129/85, *A. Ahlström Osakeyhtiö and Others v Commission*, 27 September 1988, [1988] ECR 5193 (ECJ) (*Wood Pulp*), paras 16–18, in which the effects doctrine was rejected in favour of a territorial 'implementation' doctrine.

facilitate effective climate change policy.[8] The CJEU's somewhat artificial reliance on territoriality did little to placate the objections of the EU's trading partners against the Aviation Directive,[9] although it is of note that they did not explicitly state that the Directive was illegal under international law.[10] Eventually, in response to international pressure, the EU temporarily excluded aviation from its ETS while efforts were made to negotiate a multilateral solution.[11]

The vicissitudes of the Aviation Directive[12] are not unique. A respectable number of this type of trade measure are in existence, not only in the EU but also elsewhere.[13] This chapter reviews three EU legal instruments containing such measures:

(i) the Regulation laying down the obligations of operators who place timber and timber products on the market (Timber Regulation);[14]
(ii) the Directive on the promotion of the use of energy from renewable sources (RED);[15] and
(iii) the Regulation on trade in seal products (Seals Regulation).[16]

---

8 Geert De Baere and Cedric Ryngaert, 'Air Transport Association of America and the EU's Contribution to the Strict Observance and Development of International Law' (2013) 18(3) *European Foreign Affairs Review* 389, 400–403.

9 See Council of the International Civil Aviation Organization (19th Session), Inclusion of International Civil Aviation in the European Union Emissions Trading Scheme (EU ETS) and its Impact, C-W/13790, 17 October 2011.

10 De Baere and Ryngaert, n. 8 above, 409.

11 See European Commission, ICAO, COM 20/12, 15 November 2012.

12 For an understanding of the Aviation Directive's consistency with multilateral trade obligations, see Lorand Bartels, 'The WTO Legality of the Application of the EU's Emission Trading System' (2012) 23(2) *The European Journal of International Law* 429.

13 Belina Anderson, 'Unilateral Trade Measures and Environmental Protection Policy', (1993) 66 *Temple Law Review* 751.

14 Regulation (EU) No. 995/2010 of the European Parliament and of the Council of 20 October 2010 laying down the obligations of operators who place timber and timber products on the market, [2010] OJ L 295/23 (Timber Regulation).

15 Directive 2009/28 on the promotion of the use of energy from renewable sources and amending and subsequently repealing Directive 2001/77/EC and 2003/30/EC, [2009] OJ L 140 (RED).

16 Regulation No. 1007/2009 of the European Parliament and of the Council on trade in seal products, [2009] OJ L 286/36 (Seals Regulation).

These instruments have been selected because they all contain an extraterritorial component, and because they are all aimed at the protection of natural resources writ large: respectively forests, the atmosphere, and certain animals.

Given the commonality of their goals (the protection of global public goods), one can expect these instruments to follow a similar regulatory pattern and to be subject to the same standards of legal review. The aim of this contribution is to ascertain whether the measures contained in these instruments are indeed comparable, and – whether or not they are comparable – trade measures aimed at the protection of natural resources pass the test of international legality. When conducting this legality test we use public international law rules of jurisdiction as our normative framework.[17]

For each measure the existing international legal framework, the extraterritorial aspect and their potential trade implications will be examined in turn (Section 2). Following this, the unilateral character of the measures will be problematized (Section 3), after which the legality of the extraterritorial aspect of the measures will be ascertained (Section 4). Finally, some concluding observations will be made as to the jurisdictional challenges posed by such trade measures in pursuing environmental objectives.

2. EU MEASURES THAT PROTECT NATURAL RESOURCES

In this part, the three selected legal instruments – the Timber Regulation, the Renewable Energy Directive and the Seals Regulation – will be introduced and contextualized.

The presentation of each instrument follows a similar structure. In the first section, the content of the instrument is briefly presented, with an emphasis on its extraterritorial aspects. The second section sets out the

---

[17] The measures in question could also be reviewed in light of other legal norms, such as those laid down in the agreements concluded under the auspices of the World Trade Organization (WTO); after all, measures conditioning market access restrict international trade and may thus be in tension with WTO law. However, a review in light of international trade law is the subject of other chapters in this volume: see Mavroidis (Chapter 12, this volume) and Geraets and Natens (Chapter 11, this volume). That being said, in passing, reference is made to trade law, especially where the degree of contestation of the measure is discussed.

international framework protecting – or not – the same global public good and examines to what extent the EU instrument gives effect to, or at least relates to the international framework. Thirdly, the EU's reasons for unilaterally adopting the said instruments are scrutinized. Fourthly and finally, the international implications of the EU's measures – including international protest and legal challenges – are flagged.

The data and insights gathered in this part will feed into the legality analysis carried out in the next part (Section 3), where it is argued that the legality of a jurisdictional assertion is a function of the character of the substantive norm or value protected by the assertion. Indeed, the more a substantive norm furthered unilaterally has a basis in an international framework supported by states, or in a desire to protect recognized global public goods (and the weaker its impact on the economic or trade opportunities of foreign operators), the higher the chances that the unilateral jurisdictional assertion will survive legality challenges. In this next part (Section 4) the three measures will be tested against this principle.

2.1 The Timber Regulation

2.1.1 Content of the Regulation

The 'EU Regulation laying down the obligations of operators who place timber and timber products on the market' (Timber Regulation) prevents the placement on the market of the EU of illegally harvested timber and products derived therefrom and, in so doing, aims to combat illegal logging.[18] The extraterritorial aspect of the measure lies in the fact that it establishes due diligence requirements with which operators in the *country of origin* have to comply, so as to prevent the placing on the market of illegally harvested timber.[19]

2.1.2 International framework

The Timber Regulation is embedded in an international legal framework concerning forest governance. Ever since the end of the Second World War, the Food and Agricultural Organization (FAO) Forestry Department has had a specific focus on maintaining the supply of timber.[20] From the

---

18 Timber Regulation, Recital 3.

19 Timber Regulation, Articles 4 and 6.

20 Jeremy Rayner, Alexander Buck and Pia Katila (eds), 'Embracing Complexity: Meeting the Challenges of International Forest Governance. A Global Assessment Report', Global Forest Expert Panel on the International Forest

1970s onwards, forests acquired an environmental and sustainability value in their own right. Notably the 1972 Declaration of the United Nations Conference on the Human Environment (Stockholm Declaration)[21] and the 1992 Rio Declaration on Environment and Development (Rio Declaration),[22] have galvanized international efforts to manage the world's natural resources in a sustainable manner. In Rio, sustainable forestry was included specifically in the Forest Principles,[23] and further defined in the Convention on Biological Diversity (Biodiversity Convention)[24] as well as the United Nations Framework Convention on Climate Change (UNFCCC).[25]

The main impetus for the Timber Regulation was probably the 2001 Bali Declaration,[26] which acknowledged the importance of the elimination of the trade in illegally logged timber. Such trade, facilitated by corruption and poor governance, was recognized as a significant cause of forest degradation. Following up on the international consensus reached in Bali, several regional and national initiatives were developed to promote domestic good forest governance.[27] The Timber Regulation could be considered to be one of them.

Regardless of the merits of the Bali Declaration, there is, however, currently no binding international agreement on the combatting of illegal logging of timber.[28] Nonetheless, it is of note that, where possible, the Timber Regulation refers to an international mandate which the EU has

---

Regime, International Union of Forest Research Organizations, World Series Vol. 28 (2010), p. 76.

[21] Declaration of the United Nations Conference on the Human Environment, 1972, available at: http://www.unep.org/Documents.Multilingual/Default.asp?documentid=97&articleid=1503 (accessed 15 May 2014).

[22] UNGA Resolution A/CONF.151/26 (Vol. I), adopted by the General Assembly at the UNCED, Rio de Janeiro, 3–14 June 1992.

[23] Report of the United Nations on Environment and Development, Non-legally Binding Authoritative Statement of Principles for a Global Consensus on the Management, Conservation and Sustainable Development of all Types of Forests, A/CONF.151/26 (Vol. III), Annex III, 14 August 1992.

[24] The Convention on Biological Diversity, adopted at Rio de Janeiro 1992, 1760 UNTS 79; 31 ILM 818, Article 6(b), available at: http://www.cbd.int/convention/text/ (accessed 18 April 2014).

[25] United Nations Framework Convention on Climate Change (UNFCCC), 1771 UNTS 107; S. Treaty Doc No. 102-38; UN Doc. A/AC.237/18 (Part II)/Add.1; 31 ILM 849 (1992).

[26] Ministerial Declaration, Forest Law Enforcement and Governance East Asia Ministerial Conference, Bali, September 2001, p. 2.

[27] Rayner, Buck and Katila, n. 20 above, 117.

[28] As recognized in the Timber Regulation, Recital 14.

obtained, for example, in the context of the UNFCCC[29] and on the basis of the Convention on International Trade in Endangered Species (CITES).[30]

2.1.3 Explaining the adoption of the Regulation

The EU Timber Regulation responds not only to an international concern about illegal logging. It is also part of a detailed EU-wide policy related to forestry management, and could thus be seen as the external extension of its internal protective practices.

After the adoption of the Rio Declaration, in 1993, several general guidelines for sustainable forestry management in Europe were enacted emphasizing the importance of competitive ecological, economic and social sustainable forest management,[31] in which due account was given to existing international instruments to guide the general principles upon which the policy should be based.[32] The EU adopted a Forest Law Enforcement, Governance and Trade Action Plan (EU FLEGT Action Plan) in 2003,[33] which was to become the basis for the Timber Regulation. The EU FLEGT Action Plan promotes sustainable forest management in third countries where there is a higher risk of poor governance in forest sectors by emphasizing governance reforms and capacity building.[34] It does so by defining the illegal harvesting of timber on the basis of compliance with the national laws of the country of origin.[35] The Timber Regulation builds on and strengthens this EU

---

[29] Timber Regulation, Recital 3.

[30] Convention on International Trade in Endangered Species of Wild Fauna and Flora (CITES), 27 UST 1087, TIAS 8249, adopted Switzerland, 13 January 1976. For implementation in the EU: Council Regulation (EC) No. 338/97 of 9 December 1996 on the protection of species of wild fauna and flora by regulating trade therein, [1997] OJ L 61/1.

[31] Communication from the Commission to the Council, the European Parliament, the Economic and Social Committee and the Committee of the Regions on a Forest Strategy for the European Union, 18 November 1998, COM(1998) 649 final, p. 6.

[32] Reference is made to the commitments made by EU Member States under the Rio Declaration and the Helsinki resolutions: see Committee on Agriculture and Rural Development, PE 213.578/fin. A4-0414/96, Thomas Rapport, 18 December 1996, para. 3.

[33] Council Regulation (EC) No. 2173/2005 of 20 December 2005 on the establishment of a FLEGT licensing scheme for imports of timber into the European Community, [2005] OJ L 347 (FLEGT Regulation).

[34] FLEGT Regulation, Recital 2.

[35] FLEGT Regulation, Article 2(g).

FLEGT Action Plan: whereas the Action Plan applies only to voluntarily committed partner countries,[36] the Timber Regulation extends obligations to all importers of timber on the European market.[37]

The Timber Regulation was not established solely out of an altruistic concern for sustainable forestry, however. The Regulation is also an attempt at 'levelling the playing field', as discussed in the introduction to this chapter: the EU's subjection of EU producers to a stringent regime aimed at tackling illegal logging *within* the EU would be undermined, and EU producers would be put at a competitive disadvantage, if timber placed on the market by foreign operators were not subject to equally strict rules.[38] It is of note, however, that the rules applicable to foreign producers are not of the EU's making: the EU is only redeploying definitions of illegal logging contained in the national laws of the *country of origin*.[39] The Timber Regulation should thus be seen primarily as strengthening forestry law *enforcement* rather than setting new rules for forestry governance.

2.1.4 International implications

The Timber Regulation affects international trade in the sense that the unilaterally established due diligence system (DDS) increases the administrative burden for producers and makes them vulnerable to potential 'market power abuse' by the EU, thus raising the cost of international trade. Since the majority of these producers come from countries with a relatively weak regulatory framework in place, it might be expected that the Timber Regulation will substantially raise costs for foreign operators, thereby potentially restricting the international trade in timber. The transaction costs for producers are further increased because several countries have put in place legislation with a similar aim but establishing slightly different requirements.[40]

As it may be assumed that producers from poorer countries will have greater difficulty in fulfilling the DDS requirements, *de facto* they may be discriminated against when it comes to accessing the EU market, although it should be noted that the Timber Regulation offers several options to mitigate this risk.[41]

---

36 FLEGT Regulation, Article 3(1).

37 Timber Regulation, Article 1.

38 Timber Regulation, Article 2(c).

39 Timber Regulation, Recitals 7, 9, Article 4(1).

40 Rayner, Buck and Katila, n. 20 above, 117.

41 Where appropriate, technical and other assistance is offered to operators: see Timber Regulation, Articles 13, 3, 20(2).

2.2 The Renewable Energy Directive

2.2.1 Content of the Directive

The Directive on the promotion of the use of energy from renewable sources (RED) is the latest EU Directive to promote this objective.[42] The Directive establishes a 10 per cent mandatory renewable energy target for transport fuels to be reached by 2020,[43] of which at least 35 per cent should be derived from the use of biofuels or bioliquids.[44] The Directive further establishes that *imported* renewable energy will count in the calculation of a Member's emissions reduction target when it complies with the sustainability criteria set out by the Directive.[45] The observance of these sustainability criteria is enforced through a detailed outlining of acceptable mechanisms to ensure the sustainability of biofuels and bioliquids production.[46]

The extraterritorial aspect of the RED lies in the EU's unilateral establishment of the sustainability criteria. These criteria determine what qualifies as sustainable biofuels, and apply to the entire production process,[47] including processes in non-EU countries of origin. Admittedly, imports of biofuels into the European market which do not comply with the RED's sustainability criteria are not prohibited. However, as the use of such imported biofuels would not count towards the mandatory renewable energy targets of EU Member States, it is unlikely that 'unsustainable' biofuels would be competitive in the European market. Thus, the RED indirectly regulates the production process of biofuels in the country of origin and therefore – at least in part – applies extra-territorially.

2.2.2 International framework

While the sustainability requirements in RED are formally determined unilaterally by the EU, they do find their roots in internationally

---

[42] Directive 2009/28/EC of the European Parliament and of the Council of 23 April 2009 on the promotion of the use of energy from renewable sources and amending and subsequently repealing Directives 2001/77/EC and 2003/30/EC, [2009] OJ L 140/16 (RED).

[43] RED, Recital 8, Article 3(4).

[44] RED, Article 17(2).

[45] RED, Recital 65, Article 17(1).

[46] RED, Article 17(5).

[47] Communication from the Commission on voluntary schemes and default values in the EU biofuels and bioliquids sustainability scheme, [2010] OJ C 160/1, para. 2.2.3.

identified concerns related to the production of biofuels and bioliquids, concerns with respect to biodiversity, food security and indirect land use. These concerns have to a certain extent found their way into the final version of the RED. For one thing, the RED provides that biofuel production land should not be derived from areas designated for nature protection as appointed by relevant national law or competent authority, or the protection of rare and endangered species included in lists drawn up by intergovernmental organizations or the International Union for the Conservation of Nature (IUCN).[48] For another, the RED relies on the FAO's definition of 'primary forests', and provides that these cannot be used for the conversion of land to support the production of biofuels.[49] Furthermore, biofuels derived from biodiverse grasslands will not be considered as contributing to the mandatory renewable energy target.[50] Risks related to food security and social sustainability were addressed by reference to the Conventions of the International Labour Organization (ILO),[51] the Cartagena Protocol on Biosafety[52] and CITES. Limitations on the origin of land find their justification in the European commitment to combat climate change.[53] Finally, RED relies on several transnational voluntary certification schemes that already address the sustainability of biofuels.[54]

An overarching international framework of biofuels is lacking, however. In fact, one of the motivations for the use of EU-determined

---

48 RED, Recital 69, Articles 17(3)(b), 18(4). The IUCN is the oldest global environmental organization with a membership of both governmental and non-governmental organizations. It operates on the basis of knowledge provided by scientists and experts spread across 160 countries, see http://www.iucn.org/about/ (accessed 4 June 2014).

49 RED, Recital 69, Article 17(3)(a). 'Primary forests' are determined as 'naturally regenerated forest of native species, where there are no clearly visible indications of human activities and the ecological processes are not significantly disturbed': see Forestry Department, Food and Agriculture Organization, United Nations, 'Global Forest Resources Assessment 2010, Terms and Definitions', Forest Resource Assessment Programme, Working Paper 144/E (2010), p. 12.

50 Reference is made to the Biodiversity Convention, n. 24 above, Article 6(b): parties are obligated to integrate biodiversity in all relevant sectors.

51 See RED, Article 17.7.

52 Cartagena Protocol on Biosafety to the Convention on Biological Diversity (Cartagena Protocol), 2226 UNTS 208; 39 ILM 1027 (2000); UN Doc. UNEP/CBD/ExCOP/1/3 (2000), at 42.

53 RED, Recitals 1, 70, 71.

54 Stefano Ponte and Carsten Daugbjerg, 'Biofuel Sustainability and the Formation of Transnational Hybrid Governance', (2015) 24(1) *Environmental Politics* 96.

sustainability criteria was precisely to influence the international debate,[55] rather than vice versa. Arguably, consumer objections against conversion of highly biodiverse land or land designated for nature protection purposes for the production of biofuels is strongest in Europe, thus influencing the EU's progressive stance.[56] Ultimately, this makes the EU's unilateralism less strongly rooted in an international framework, although it is clearly geared towards protecting global public goods.

2.2.3 Explaining the adoption of the Directive

The EU should certainly be commended for requiring the production of biofuels to be sustainable. Still, other – less environmentally oriented motives – have also influenced the EU's increased focus on biofuels.[57] This is not surprising, as the EU is one of the world's main producers of biodiesel, and international trade in biodiesel has increased considerably.[58] In fact, RED pursues several objectives at the same time: next to combatting climate change, it aims to reduce the transport sector's reliance on oil, create job opportunities in rural areas, stimulate investment in the energy sector and create a competitive internal market.[59] Thus, by advocating specific standards rivalling those of its competitors, the EU aims to further the trade interests of its own producers instead of merely promoting the use of renewable energy.

2.2.4 International implications

Given the economic importance of biofuels, the RED has significant trade implications. In particular, the Directive increases production costs,

---

55 Kati Kulovesi, Elisa Morgera and Miquel Muñoz, 'Environmental Integration and Multifaceted International Dimensions of EU Law: Unpacking the EU's 2009 Climate and Energy Package' (2011) 48(3) *Common Market Law Review* 829, at 878–9.

56 RED, Recital 69.

57 Stavros Afionis and Lindsay C. Stringer, 'European Union Leadership in Biofuels Regulation: Europe as a Normative Power?' (2012) 32 *Journal of Cleaner Production* 114, at 115, 120.

58 Other major producers are Argentina, the United States, and Brazil: Kees Kwant and others, 'Overview of World Bioenergy Trade: IEA Task 40', IEA Bioenergy ExCo65, Nara (Japan), 12–14 May 2010, available at: http://www.ieabioenergy.com/wp-content/uploads/2013/10/ExCo65-P1-Overview-of-World-Bioenergy-Trade-Task-40-Ir-K.-Kwant.pdf (accessed 5 April 2014).

59 Green Paper, 'A European Strategy for Sustainable, Competitive and Secure Energy', COM(2006) 105 final, 8 March 2006, p. 3; Communication from the Commission, 'An EU Strategy for Biofuels', COM(2006) 34 def., 8 February 2006, p. 3.

as producers have to comply with divergent standards, depending on the country of importation – although the sustainability criteria in the RED to some extent overlap with those in established voluntary guidelines.[60] Furthermore, the RED's definition of highly biodiverse grassland is relatively vague,[61] leading to legal uncertainty in third countries where this type of land is abundant, such as Brazil.[62] These points of critique have caused other leading producing countries of biofuels to protest against the sustainability criteria contained in the RED,[63] and have led to the initiation of a dispute settlement procedure at the WTO.[64]

2.3 The Seals Regulation

2.3.1 Content of the Regulation

The Regulation on trade in seal products (Seals Regulation)[65] sets out conditions for the import of products derived from seals.[66] It aims to improve animal welfare and is grounded in the moral belief vested among citizens of the EU that the nature of seal hunting is cruel.[67] The extraterritorial aspect of the measure is that it unilaterally establishes conditions under which seal hunting conducted outside the EU is deemed

---

60 RED, Article 18(4). See Evgenia Pavlovskaia, 'Mechanisms to control the fulfillment of the EU sustainability criteria for transport biofuels in Directive 2009/28/EC' (2014) 2(1) *New Ground Research Journal of Legal Studies Research and Essays* 16, at 17, 28.

61 RED, Article 17(3)(c).

62 Wybe Th. Douma and Steffen van de Velde (eds), 'EU Environmental Norms and Third Countries: the EU as Global Role Model?', Centre for the Law of EU External Relations (CLEER), CLEER Working Paper 2013/5, p. 12.

63 WTO News, 'Concerns Raised over Trade Restrictions on Dairy Products, Biofuels, Cars and Seafood', 18 October 2013, available at: http://www.wto.org/english/news_e/news13_e/good_18oct13_e.htm (accessed 18 April 2014).

64 Request for the Establishment of a Panel by Argentina, *European Union – Anti-Dumping Measures on Biodiesel from Argentina*, WT/DS473/5, 13 March 2014; Request for Consultations, *European Union – Anti-Dumping Measures on Biodiesel from Indonesia*, WT/DS480/1, G/L/1071, G/ADP/D104/1, 17 June 2014.

65 Regulation No. 1007/2009 of the European Parliament and of the Council on trade in seal products, [2009] OJ L 286/36 (Seals Regulation).

66 Seals Regulation, Article 3.

67 Seals Regulation, Preamble, Recitals 1, 4, 11 relating to cruelty and humane treatment; Preamble, Recitals 5, 9, 10 relating to animal welfare.

'humane'; products that do not meet these conditions cannot be traded between third countries and the EU (nor within the EU for that matter).[68]

2.3.2 International framework

It is somewhat challenging to distinguish the appropriate international legal framework in which the Seals Regulation could be embedded, as the Regulation does not have one primary goal.[69] The Regulation mentions animal welfare in connection with the moral concerns that would exist among European consumers over the manner in which seals are hunted and killed.[70] This suggests that both the protection of animal welfare and the protection of 'public morals' are objectives of the Regulation.[71] Animal welfare as an objective of the Seals Regulation may find some support in international treaties concerned with maintaining biodiversity (Biodiversity Convention) and the protection of endangered species (CITES). However, since seals in general are not an endangered species and CITES is as such not aimed at improving the welfare of individual animals, CITES can hardly be seen as a basis for the Regulation.[72] In reality, the EU has very much been a first international mover when it comes to promoting animal welfare,[73] and the Seals Regulation fits this mould.

---

[68] Exceptions to the conditional trade ban are contained in Seals Regulation, Articles 3.1, 2(a), 2(b).

[69] Nikolas Sellheim, 'The Goals of the EU Seal Products Trade Regulation: from Effectiveness to Consequence', (2015) 51(3) *Polar Record* 274, 287.

[70] Seals Regulation, Preamble, Recital 10.

[71] Sellheim, n. 69 above, p. 276.

[72] Commission of the European Communities, Proposal for a Regulation of the European Parliament and of the Council concerning trade in seal products, COM/2008/0469 final, 23 July 2008, p. 7. See also Council Regulation (EC) No. 338/97 of 9 December 1996 on the protection of species of wild fauna and flora implements the Convention on International Trade in Endangered Species of Wild Fauna and Flora (CITES 1973) within the community, [1997] OJ L 61, Annex.

[73] Since 1974, the EU has a history of regulating the protection of animal welfare: Committee on Agriculture and Rural Development, Report on the Evaluation and Assessment of the Animal Welfare Action Plan, 2006–2010 A7-0053/2010, p. 6. It has to some extent been successful in promoting its Animal Welfare Strategy at the international level; DG SANCO, Evaluation of the EU Policy on Animal Welfare and the Possible Policy Options for the Future, J7296, 22 December 2010, p. 3.

2.3.3 Explaining the adoption of the Directive

During the legislative process towards concluding the Regulation, several scientific assessments were undertaken of the most important issues raised in relation to seal hunting.[74] Notably, a report by the European Food Safety Authority (EFSA) exerted influence on the Commission, a report which concluded that in principle humane killing was possible during a seal hunt, but practice had shown that, in general, insufficient caution was taken and accordingly seals suffered.[75] The report, however, could not comprehensively conclude how far-reaching this difference between theory and practice was.[76] Ultimately, the moral choice was made to ban seal products given their apparent impact on animal welfare.

2.3.4 International implications

Despite its relatively minor economic importance, the trade impact of the Seals Regulation was felt by the main producers of seal products, most of whom are located *outside the EU*. Under the Regulation, these producers may only import their products into the EU when their products fall within one of the narrow exceptions related to traditional hunting and marine resource management. Given these trade restrictions, Canada and Norway challenged the Seals Regulation before a WTO Panel and later before the Appellate Body.[77]

The Appellate Body (AB) in this case found the exceptions to the import ban on seal products violated Article I:1 and the requirements of the chapeau of Article XX of the General Agreement on Tariffs and Trade (GATT) 1994,[78] although in principle the conditional import ban fell within the scope of the public morals exception.[79] Of particular relevance to this chapter is the AB's discussion of the question of extraterritoriality. The AB held that the Seals Regulation did not impose extraterritorial obligations, as it was designed to address seal hunting activities occurring

---

[74] Ferdi de Ville, 'Explaining the Genesis of a Trade Dispute: the European Union's Seal Trade Ban' (2012) 34(1) *Journal of European Integration* 37, at 48.

[75] European Food and Safety Authority (EFSA), 'Animal Welfare Aspects of the Killing and Skinning of Seals – Scientific Opinion of the Panel on Animal Health and Welfare' (2007) *EFSA Journal*, at 3.

[76] Ibid.

[77] Panel Report, *European Communities – Measures Prohibiting the Importation and Marketing of Seal Products*, WT/DS400/R, WT/DS401/R, 25 November 2013.

[78] Appellate Body Report, *European Communities – Measures Prohibiting the Importation and Marketing of Seal Products*, WT/DS400/AB/R, WT/DS401/AB/R, 22 May 2014, paras 5.95, 5.290 (AB Report, *EC – Seal Products*).

[79] Ibid., para. 5.167.

'within and outside the Community' and the seal welfare concerns of European citizens.[80] As the parties had not addressed the systemic impact of an implied jurisdictional limitation of Article XX(a) GATT, the AB refrained from further commenting on the issue.[81] This reasoning is similar to that applied by the CJEU in the *ATAA* case referred to above: for both the CJEU and the AB, the existence of a territorial (EU) link between the legal instrument and its object of regulation suffices to dispel extraterritoriality concerns.

3. THE UNILATERAL CHARACTER OF THE MEASURES: A COMPARISON

The Timber Regulation, the RED and the Seals Regulation all condition the import of a natural resource into the European market on satisfying certain environmental requirements to be fulfilled by the producer in the country of origin. As these measures impact upon producers based elsewhere – at least if they wish to access the EU market – they could be considered to be partly extraterritorial, even if the trade measure itself is taken on EU territory.

As the measures emanate from one actor, without the latter's consent, they could all be characterized as *unilateral*.[82] Still, these instruments are less unilateral than may appear at first sight. First, some of them are partly based on legal norms developed within a multilateral context. This is the case, for example, in relation to the RED, the sustainability criteria of which find their origin in the Biodiversity Convention, the Cartagena Protocol, several ILO Conventions and CITES. Other measures rely in part on international voluntary certification schemes (such as, in relation to the Timber Regulation, the Forest Stewardship Council certification scheme).[83]

---

[80] Ibid., para. 5.173.

[81] Ibid.

[82] Although there is no international definition of the term 'unilateral', the measures are qualified here as 'the expression of will of only one state or group of states without the consent of affected states': see Pierre-Marie Dupuy, 'The Place and Role of Unilateralism in Contemporary International Law' (2000) 11(1) *European Journal of International Law* 19, at 20. Also Erich Vranes, *Trade and the Environment, Fundamental Issues in International Law, WTO Law and Legal Theory*, Oxford University Press (2009), p. 174.

[83] It should be noted that the use of voluntary certification schemes is a double-edged sword. On the one hand, it can diminish the administrative burden for producers and lower market barriers. On the other hand, such schemes can

Secondly, the Timber Regulation and the RED allow operators to rely on a variety of methods to show compliance with the conditions included in the measures, and offer the possibility of entering into a voluntary partnership agreement, appoint a European monitoring organization[84] and prevent overlap with existing certification schemes.[85] This demonstrates that the EU gives due consideration to the fact that producers in third countries might have difficulties in fulfilling all the requirements as a result of insufficient resources or poor infrastructure. The Seals Regulation stands out in this respect and may be said to be more 'unilateral' than the Timber Regulation and the RED.[86]

Thirdly, some of the measures reflect international developments with a similar objective. The Timber Regulation, for instance, is rather strongly situated in multilateral efforts underlining the significance of responsible forest management. Although no international agreement on illegal logging exists, an international consensus was, and is, crystallizing on the basis of which the EU seems to justify the move forward with its own regulation, as could also be gleaned from the new EU Forest Strategy 2013.[87]

The level of reflection of international developments is somewhat more diffuse with respect to the RED. As indicated earlier, the sustainability criteria in the RED can, to a certain extent, be traced back to multilateral conventions on the protection of biodiversity, climate change and labour

---

have an uneven impact on trade. This disproportionately divides the burden of costs shared by producers from different countries: see Axel Marx and Dieter Cuypers, 'Forest Certification as a Global Environmental Governance Tool: What is the Macro-effectiveness of the Forest Stewardship Council?' (2010) 4(4) *Regulation & Governance* 408, at 412.

84 Recital 7, Recital 9, Timber Regulation; see also Articles 3 and 20(2).

85 Communication from the Commission on voluntary schemes and default values in the EU biofuels and bioliquids sustainability scheme, [2010] OJ C 160/1, at p. 1.

86 This was also noted by the WTO Appellate Body (AB Report, *EC – Seal Products*, n. 78 above, paras 5.326, 5.337): as Article 6 of the Implementing Regulation left full discretion to the recognized body designated to assess compliance with the conditions of importation, the application of the conditional import ban did not pass the 'test' of the Chapeau of Article XX.

87 Commission Staff Working Document, 'The Legally Binding Agreement on Forests'; accompanying the document, Communication from the Commission to the European Parliament, the Council, the European Economic and Social Committee and the Committee of the Regions, 'A New EU Forest Strategy: for forests and the forest-based sector', COM(2013) 659 final/SWD(2013) 343 final, 20 September 2013, p. 4. The EU links this new Forest Strategy with international forestry discussions.

standards. However, the measure as a whole does not reflect an international consensus as to what constitutes *sustainable* production of biofuels. This has become especially apparent in the context of the WTO, where other main producers have challenged the sustainability criteria featuring in the RED. The main concern over the Directive appears to be grounded in the existing scientific uncertainty regarding the adequacy of the sustainability criteria used by the EU.[88] Ultimately, the Directive may appear as a convenient congregation of interests in, on the one hand, maintaining an environmentally friendly reputation and, on the other, promoting a more competitive, independent and sustainable energy sector in the EU. This congregation of interests may not be fully reflective of an international consensus.

The Seals Regulation, finally, is the least reflective of international developments. Admittedly, there is an embryonic international legal framework regarding the protection of animal welfare, but there is no international consensus regarding the welfare of seals. The EU does not hide that its efforts to regulate seal hunting are justified by animal welfare concerns that exist among citizens of the *European society*,[89] rather than of international society at large.[90]

---

[88] See the objection of Brazil, which requested the EU to remove trade barriers for its agriculture and agro-energy products: UNCTAD, 'The Emerging Biofuels Market: Regulatory, Trade and Development Implications', UNCTAD/DITC/TED/2006/4, New York and Geneva, 2006, p. 5.

[89] Commission Staff Document, Annex to the Communication from the Commission to the European Parliament and the Council on a Community Action Plan on the Protection and Welfare of Animals 2006–2010. See also Communication from the Commission to the European Parliament and the Council of 23 January 2006 on a Community Action Plan on the Protection and Welfare of Animals 2006–2010, COM(2006) 13; European Parliament, Committee on the Internal Market and Consumer Protection, 'Internal Market and Consumer Protection Committee Chair Announces Strong Committee Vote in Favour of a Ban on Seal Products in the EU', 2 March 2009, available at: http://www.europarl.europa.eu/document/activities/cont/200903/20090303ATT50685/20090303ATT50685EN.pdf (accessed 10 April 2014).

[90] Julinda Beqiraj, 'The Delicate Equilibrium of EU Trade Measures: The Seals case' (2013) 14(1) *German Law Review* 279, at 297. This focus on *European consumers* may also explain why transit of seal products through EU territory is not covered by the regulation: Robert Howse and Joanna Langille, 'Permitting Pluralism: The Seal Products Dispute and Why the WTO Should Accept Trade Restrictions Justified by Non-instrumental Moral Values' (2011) 37(2) *The Yale Journal of International Law* 368, at 384.

4. REVIEWING THE EXTRATERRITORIALITY OF EU UNILATERALISM REGARDING THE PROTECTION OF NATURAL RESOURCES

The three EU legal instruments discussed above all have an extraterritorial dimension insofar as they purport to regulate conditions in third countries, provided that operators based there intend to access the EU market. The exercise of such extraterritorial jurisdiction is controversial under rules of public international law. After all, the basic jurisdictional notion is that states will apply their laws primarily to conduct occurring within their own territory – in legal doctrine referred to as the 'territorial principle'.[91] The activities of economic operators are no longer confined to the territory of a single state, however, but straddle different states. Any state with which the operator or its transaction has a nexus may then feel inclined to apply its law.[92] Such regulation has an extraterritorial dimension in that it may apply to the foreign portions of the operator's activities, thus potentially encroaching on other nations' sovereignty and imposing multiple regulatory burdens on economic operators.

In the field of environmental regulation with respect to production processes, with which we are concerned here, international solutions in the form of common substantive standards and enforcement procedures have long been preferred, and the unilateral conditioning of imports via production process standards has been the exception rather than the rule.[93] Nonetheless, as the discussed EU measures demonstrate, the use of unilateral trade measures with extraterritorial effect may well become a more common instrument to protect certain environmental values and natural resources where multilateral negotiations have been slow to progress,[94] and where the effectiveness of domestic regulation aimed at environmental protection could be undermined by foreign operators.

---

[91] Harold G. Maier, 'Jurisdictional Rules in Customary International Law', in Karl M. Meessen (ed.), *Extraterritorial Jurisdiction in Theory and Practice*, The Hague: Kluwer Law International (1996) pp. 64–102, at 87 (arguing that any assertion of jurisdiction outside the territory of the regulating state is suspicious and should be deemed unjustifiable until proven otherwise).

[92] Compare Inge Kaul and others (eds), *Global Public Goods*, New York: Oxford University Press (1999), p. xxi (drawing attention to the growing gap between policy-making and the state's territory).

[93] Jennifer A. Zerk, 'Extraterritorial Jurisdiction: Lessons for the Business and Human Rights Sphere from Six Regulatory Areas', Working Paper No. 59 of the CSR Initiative, June 2010, p. 188.

[94] Douma and van de Velde, n. 62 above, p. 20.

While such unilateral measures are extraterritorial insofar as they impose standards on foreign production processes, technically speaking, the trade measures are aimed at conduct *within* the territory of the regulating state – namely territorial market access. Thus, unlike the case of classic extraterritoriality, the regulator applies its laws on the basis of a clear nexus with its own territory.[95] At first sight, it is difficult to contest that such action is justified by the territorial principle, even if the action is aimed at changing behaviour abroad.

International trade law has not yet fully come to grips with this jurisdictional challenge.[96] Also, this recent challenge has gone largely unheeded in jurisdictional theory, which has traditionally concerned itself with criminal and antitrust matters. In this part we tentatively attempt to fill this gap. The research question here is whether the unilateral pursuit of environmental protection through trade measures, with the attendant extraterritorial effects, is countenanced by the international law of jurisdiction.

As extraterritoriality often raises red flags in international relations, it is key to have a clear understanding of the concept in advance. When considering its ordinary meaning, an extraterritorial measure is one taken by a state with the aim of regulating conduct outside its borders. Accordingly, this state does not entertain a territorial link with this conduct. In classic jurisdictional theory, extraterritorial measures are frowned upon, as the right of a state to legislate, adjudicate and enforce norms is territorially bound.[97] This principle emanates from the fundamental structure of the international legal order as a system of sovereign states holding the right to exercise their competences over their designated territories and the population residing within them.[98] The law of jurisdiction, and in particular its cornerstone the territorial principle,[99] ensures that conflict is prevented between states as to which state is entitled to exercise its competences. As extraterritorial jurisdiction upsets this regulatory balance between states, such jurisdiction is allowed only

---

[95] Francesco Francioni, 'Extraterritorial Application of Environmental Law', in Meessen, n. 91 above, pp. 122–46, at 123.

[96] This challenge typically comes to the fore where international trade and non-trade objectives overlap. For a discussion of jurisdiction and non-trade objectives within the WTO, see Mavroidis (Chapter 12, this volume).

[97] Hannah L. Buxbaum, 'Territory, Territoriality, and the Resolution of Jurisdictional Conflict' (2009) 57(2) *American Journal of Comparative Law* 631, at 632.

[98] Maier, n. 91 above, pp. 76, 83.

[99] Ibid., p. 67.

on the basis of a number of limited permissive grounds – notably personality, security and universality (which were mainly developed in the criminal law).[100]

Applying this jurisdictional framework to the extent relevant to our referent object, the environment and natural resources, one may submit that a state is allowed to exercise jurisdiction in order to address environmental harm arising outside its territory where such harm has been caused by a state's own national (the nationality principle) or has caused effects within its own territory (objective territoriality).[101] It may appear that the latter principle may have some traction with respect to unilateral trade measures, insofar as it justifies jurisdictional claims over extraterritorial conduct that is causing immediate and substantial adverse effects on the environment within the territory of the regulating state.[102] However, in respect of unilateral measures that address threats to global public goods, the territoriality principle has less explanatory value, as such threats are not aimed at the territory of a particular state. After all, as traditionally conceived, the territoriality principle is, just like the other principles of jurisdiction, largely directed to facilitating *reactive* measures in situations where one state suffers direct environmental harm caused by another state. In contrast, unilateral measures that tackle challenges to environmental global public goods are *proactive* rather than *reactive*: they aim to benchmark global minimum standards for production processes taking place extraterritorially, without such processes causing direct harm to the regulating state.

It has been suggested that such measures should be considered as 'territorial extensions' of domestic or EU law rather than extraterritorial measures, in that, while being focused on circumstances abroad, the underlying policy decision and the trade impediments are based in the territory of the regulating state.[103] Following this line of argument,

---

[100] Cedric Ryngaert, *Jurisdiction in International Law*, Oxford: Oxford University Press (2008), p. 86. See also Malcolm N. Shaw, *International Law*, 6th edn, Cambridge: Cambridge University Press (2008), pp. 645–6.

[101] As far as the latter is concerned, logically it cannot be assumed a state would have consented to a prohibition to protect itself against harm solely because this harm originates outside its territory: see Maier, n. 91 above, p. 69.

[102] In a competition law context compare Case T-102/96 *Gencor* [1999] ECR II-753, para. 90.

[103] Joanne Scott, 'Extraterritoriality and Territorial Extension in EU Law' (2014) 62(1) *American Journal of Comparative Law*, 87–125, 89.

unilateral trade measures are not extraterritorial because they are instrumental to the promotion of internal policy objectives.[104] Moreover, they may be considered as being effectively multilateral as they protect global public goods, to which no single state can reasonably object. This more relaxed approach to territoriality may arguably be better suited to the transnational regulatory challenges currently posed to states and world public order.[105]

On the other hand, unilateral measures promoting environmental norms (potentially) provoke resentment from third countries, as testified to by the international outcry following the adoption of the EU Aviation Directive. Third states seem to take the view that the regulating state, or the EU, fails to adequately take account of their interests, and unfairly and illegitimately forces such measures upon them to advance national interests. This foreign protest, if couched in legal terms, may affect the international legality of unilateral trade measures.[106] Indeed, such protest could be seen to signal a (perceived) conflict of the measure with state sovereignty in violation of the doctrine of jurisdiction, as previously outlined.

Can a middle way be found between these different approaches – the one emphasizing *territoriality* and the other denouncing *extraterritoriality*? Let us first observe that it need not be fatal to a jurisdictional assertion that it *also* protects national interests. After all, states will normally only adopt regulation when it is also in their interest. Typically, they act unilaterally to protect the integrity of *internal* regulation, the effectiveness of which would be frustrated if it is not 'extraterritorialized'.[107] This means that for the objective of a measure to be fulfilled, it is necessary to regulate certain conduct outside the territory of the regulating state, thereby indirectly affecting foreigners.[108] At the same time, this 'extraterritorialization' also safeguards the competitiveness of

---

104 Ibid., pp. 106–7.

105 Maier, n. 91 above, p. 100 (arguing that, as certain contemporary concerns are no longer exclusively domestic issues, the question of jurisdictional competence should evolve and should no longer be looked at primarily in terms of connections with a state's territory).

106 Buxbaum, n. 97 above, p. 674.

107 See in general, Scott, n. 103 above.

108 A distinction can be made between measures that have direct and indirect extraterritorial effect: see Vranes, n. 82 above, p. 165 (referring to H.J. Schlochauer, *Die Extraterritoriale Wirking von Hoheitsakten nach dem Öffentliche Recht der Bundesrepublik Deutschland und nach Internationalem Recht*, Frankfurt am Main: Vittoriao Klostermann (1962)).

domestic operators, who may be put at a disadvantage by the lax domestic regulation to which their foreign competitors are subject.

It is argued here that where the protection of domestic trade interests may only be incidental to the protection of *global interests*, such as the protection of natural resources,[109] 'extraterritorial' levelling of the regulatory playing field may be considered to be legitimate, even in the face of international protest, especially where the global interests to be furthered have a normative basis in international legal or political instruments.[110] After all, such measures do not just promote parochial interests, but international interests to which the entire international community may already have subscribed, or *would* subscribe to were it not for collective action failures. When the asserting state can make a prima facie case that the measure is aimed at the protection of global public goods such as the atmosphere or marine resources,[111] the burden of proof may shift to the opposing state to show that the measure is not so aimed, but instead essentially furthers national interests.

Different types of extraterritoriality could thus be distinguished, based on the 'function' fulfilled by the extraterritorial aspect of the measure. This function could then serve as an indication of the measure's legality under international law.

In a graphic form, the distinction would appear as shown in Figure 10.1.

An 'interest' in this graph should not necessarily be understood as a positive legal norm. In fact, in areas where such – multilaterally agreed – norms exist, unilateralism may be less called for, as states parties to the relevant agreements are expected to faithfully give effect to the norms. Unilateralism may prove to be more necessary where, as a result of political constraints, a multilateral legal solution is not forthcoming, whereas in the interest of protecting global public goods it should. Ideally, for legitimacy reasons, this interest is recognized in an informal or formal legal or political instrument, which confers some normative status on it. As it happens, given the decreasing importance of formal

---

[109] What may ultimately be decisive is whether the extraterritorial aspect of a measure has an outward-looking purpose, rather than just being 'domestically written': See Anupam Goyal, *The WTO and International Law, Towards Conciliation*, Oxford University Press (2006), p. 193.

[110] De Baere and Ryngaert, n. 8 above, pp. 401–2.

[111] Public goods are defined as non-excludable and non-rival in consumption: See Inge Kaul, 'Global Public Goods: Explaining their Underprovision' (2012) 15(3) *Journal of International Economic Law* 729, at 731.

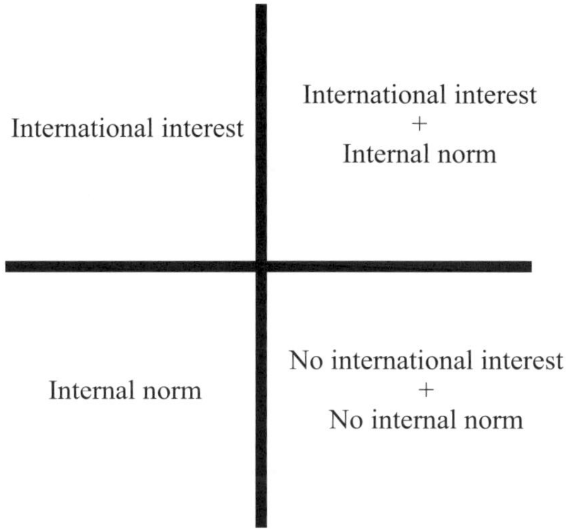

Figure 10.1

international lawmaking,[112] we have recently witnessed a rise in informal instruments that aim to protect common or global interests.[113] Thus, unilateral measures could be justified insofar as they have their basis in such 'informal' rather than formal law. In fact, a similar approach was taken by the WTO Appellate Body in the *United States – Import Prohibition of Certain Shrimp and Shrimp Products* (*US – Shrimp*) case, where it cited international environmental norms enshrined in declarations and a ministerial decision rather than in formally binding legislation, as a basis to justify unilateral trade measures aiming to provide extraterritorial environmental protection.[114] However, even where no formal or informal instrument can be identified, a unilateral assertion can

[112] Nico Krisch, 'The Decay of Consent: International Law in an Age of Global Public Goods' (2014) 1(108) *American Journal of International Law* 1, at 34.

[113] Ibid., pp. 7–8. While these informal measures might not be as effective in terms of enforcement (Kenneth W. Abbott and Duncan Snidal, 'Hard and Soft Law in International Governance' (2000) 54(3) *International Organization* 421, at 429), they can be understood as signalling recognized interests of states or the global community.

[114] Appellate Body Report, *United States – Import Prohibition of Certain Shrimp and Shrimp Products (US – Shrimp)*, WT/DS58/AB/R, adopted on 12 October 1998, paras 154–8, referring, *inter alia*, to the Marrakesh Decision on Trade and Environment, which in turn makes reference to the Rio Declaration on Environment and Development and Agenda 21.

still be justified provided that it vindicates an *interest* of the international community in confronting and regulating collective action problems arising in relation to the governance of global public goods, even if this interest has not (yet) risen to the level of an international norm. Given the scale of the global public goods challenges facing humanity, a somewhat looser interest-based rather than a slavish norm-based approach may be required, as the latter may effectively be a recipe for doing nothing.

Accordingly, where the extraterritorial aspect of a measure serves to implement an international interest or norm, as well as to safeguard the integrity of an internal interest or norm, it is presumptively permissible. The more a measure moves away from this double basis, the weaker this presumption of permissibility becomes. Thus, unilateral state action to protect purely domestic concerns should be deemed presumptively unlawful where it is neither accompanied by domestic regulation nor based on an international interest or norm. Instead, it could be considered to be a disguised form of protectionism. Legality concerns, although to a somewhat lesser extent, could also be raised over unilateral action that is based on an international interest but is not supported by concomitant domestic regulation. This may happen when a state imposes trade restrictions on foreign operators based on human rights or environmental considerations enshrined in international conventions, where internally it fails to implement and apply these conventions. Such action lacks even-handedness, and disingenuously subjects foreign operators to the international norm while exempting its own operators from its application.[115] Indeed, a legal norm could be deemed a higher threshold to reach compared with the identification of an interest since the former is scrutinized by a formal domestic lawmaking process. Here the application of these different thresholds is justified because it is in line with the general principles of jurisdiction in international law, more specifically the territorial principle, requiring states to develop a formal legal norm imposing the international interest pursued in the state's territory, prior to an extraterritorial application of such measures. Similar concerns of legitimacy could be raised over unilateral action that is based on a purely domestic norm rather than an international interest or the protection of a global public good: such action raises legitimacy concerns as it imposes on foreign nations and their operators norms that are not universally shared.

---

[115] For a discussion of the analysis of even-handedness, see AB, *EC – Seal Products*, n. 78 above, paras 115–30.

5. CONCLUDING OBSERVATIONS

Unilateral measures risk being used for protectionist purposes,[116] or being seen as imperialistic, even when pursuing international objectives. These concerns should be taken seriously, and suggest that international consensualism should be the preferred method to tackle international challenges pertaining to natural resources. Nevertheless, one has to admit that, in the face of multilateral political deadlock, international law as we traditionally conceive of it may be incapacitated in reaching an agreement to protect valuable natural resources such as biodiversity, clean air, a stable climate or rainforests. Unilateral action may then be called for as the second best alternative.

Unilateralism enables like-minded countries to strengthen their level of environmental protection without having to overcome difficulties inherent in a divided political world order. Such 'constructive unilateralism' answers to a notion of fairness, and elicits debate and cooperation among states. At the same time, unilateralism might lead to an international backlash where other states perceive it as unfair and illegitimate extraterritoriality, and for that reason refuse to further cooperate with respect to the protection of global public goods.[117] Unilateral measures with extraterritorial effect may then be at risk of defeating their own purpose.

This chapter proposes a middle way, which does justice to, on the one hand, the interests of unilaterally acting states that are bent on breaking an unjustifiable international political impasse and, on the other, the sovereign right of 'target' states to allow the autonomous determination of the level of protection regarding their own natural resources in the face of foreign 'eco-imperialism' or plain protectionism. This approach may usefully inform international regulatory practice, and possibly even judicial decision making, with respect to balancing trade and non-trade extraterritorial objectives.

In this chapter, this approach has been applied to three EU legal instruments which aim to pursue natural resource objectives, with a view to assessing the international legality of the 'extraterritorial' trade measures they contain. Of the three measures – the Timber Regulation, the Renewable Energy Directive (RED) and the Seals Regulation – the Timber Regulation seems to be the most legitimate, being the measure

---

[116] Jolene Lin, 'Governing Biofuels: A Principal-Agent Analysis of the European Union Biofuels Certification Regime and the Clean Development Mechanism' (2011) 24(1) *Journal of Environmental Law* 43, at 73.

[117] J. Mohan Rao, 'Equity in a Global Public Goods Framework', in Kaul and others, n. 92 above, p. 70.

that is most firmly embedded in both an existing international and an *internal* regulatory interest.[118] The RED, for its part, appears to be less firmly embedded in international norms or interests, and thus less legitimate. Indeed, it seems premature to conclude that an international norm exists with respect to what 'sustainable biofuels' are precisely (this is also borne out by the main biofuel producers' resistance to the EU Directive). That being said, the development of laws on the production of biofuels in different countries signals the existence of an international trend to mitigate risks associated with such production.[119] The RED's sustainability criteria contribute to this trend, which may soothe concerns over the extraterritorial aspects of the RED, and in turn allow for its justification. From a legality perspective, however, it remains somewhat problematic that the sustainability criteria of RED are not truly *embedded* in international norms or interests, but have instead been developed unilaterally – even if defensibly – by the EU.

Finally, the extraterritorial aspects of the Seals Regulation, while certainly accommodating a European consumer concern with the welfare of seals, are the most problematic of the three instruments discussed. While the international community is to a certain extent concerned about animal welfare in general,[120] there is no specific international norm relating to the protection of seals' welfare. On the contrary, the legal challenges brought against the Seals Regulation appear to suggest a divergence of opinion regarding the perceived 'immorality' of seal hunting methods, thus casting doubt on the existence of a shared understanding regarding the acceptability of such methods.[121] Since no international norm appears to exist, and only a diffuse internal norm

---

118 See above. The *internal* interest regarding the sustainable management of forestry is apparent from the 1998 EU Forest Strategy and subsequent EU-wide measures: see notes 31 and 32 above. As there is no international *definition* regarding unsustainable forestry, EU regulators could have fallen into the trap of idiosyncratically defining it and unilaterally imposing it on third countries. Wisely, they have not done so, instead deferring to the laws of the country of origin. In light of these considerations, the extraterritorial aspect of the Timber Regulation may be deemed permissible.

119 See above.

120 See above for the influence of the EU's 'five freedoms' regarding animal welfare on international discourse.

121 Note that the AB seemed to question the credibility of the moral objection to seal hunting to a certain extent: 'We found that the European Union did not show that the manner in which the EU Seal Regime treats seal products derived from IC hunts as compared to seal products derived from "commercial" hunts

based on a perceived European consensus, one may be hard-pressed to conclude that the extraterritorial aspect of the Seals Regulation might be justified.

It is hoped that the general evaluative framework proposed in this chapter, as well as its application to the selected legal instruments, may weigh on national and regional lawmaking and international dispute settlement with respect to natural resources. As far as the latter is concerned, however, we are cognizant of the limitations resulting from mandate, applicable law and party submissions.

---

can be reconciled with the objective of addressing EU public moral concerns regarding seal welfare': AB Report, *EC – Seal Products*, n. 78 above, para. 5.338.

11. Governing through trade in compliance with WTO law: a case study of the European Union Timber Regulation

Dylan Geraets and Bregt Natens*

1. INTRODUCTION

As explained by Chad Damro in this volume,[1] the European Union (EU) is a *market* power. A new generation of EU policies aiming at the provision of global public goods (and which are the subject of this edited volume), have a strong impact on trade. These measures often include conditions for access to the European markets, which is linked to adherence to certain criteria or obligations. Considering the economic importance of the EU marketplace for foreign producers, and as demonstrated by this book, measures that restrict market access are increasingly being used as governance tools. Although these policies may, at first sight, have laudable goals, they are not necessarily perceived in that way by other states. Argentina, for one, questioned the motives behind an American example of one of these policies,[2] stating that the measure 'was not necessarily intended to protect endangered species but rather to

* The authors are very grateful to Axel Marx, Marieke Koekkoek and Wolfgang Alschner for their insightful comments. Sincere thanks are also due to KLIMOS – Research Platform Climate Change and Development Cooperation. The views expressed in this chapter, as well as any errors and omissions, are solely those of the authors. This chapter builds on Dylan Geraets and Bregt Natens, 'The WTO Consistency of the European Union Timber Regulation', (2014) 48(2) *Journal of World Trade* 433–56.

[1] Chapter 2.

[2] Andrew Mitchell and Glyn Ayres, 'Out of Crooked Timber: The Consistency of Australia's Illegal Logging Prohibition Bill with the WTO Agreement' (2012) 29 *Environmental and Planning Law Journal* 462, 465.

protect domestic markets from imports'.[3] Nonetheless, even if the intentions of the legislators are benevolent, these policies also need to comply with the obligations under international (trade) law of the enacting Member of the World Trade Organization (WTO). One of the functions of the WTO is the settlement of trade disputes between its Members.[4] A Member may bring a complaint against a fellow Member if it considers that benefits accruing to it under the covered agreements are being impaired by the actions of that other Member.[5] Hence, the governance of global public goods requires attention to trade law obligations.

This chapter considers whether the EU has drafted one of these new generation policies, the EU Timber Regulation, to be compatible with the rules of the WTO. Therefore, the first part of this chapter examines the Timber Regulation and how it fits within the wider international framework of regulation aimed at preserving exhaustible natural resources, including tropical or rain forests. The second part of the chapter analyses whether the Timber Regulation complies with the relevant WTO rules. The third part draws from the analysis to provide some guidelines for future policies that aim to *govern through trade*. In the last section, preliminary evidence pertaining to the effectiveness of the Timber Regulation is assessed from the perspective of the foregoing analysis.

---

[3] WTO, Committee on Technical Barriers to Trade, Minutes of the Meeting of 5–6 November 2008, 29 January 2009, G/TBT/M/46, para. 36. See also Mitchell and Ayres, n. 2 above, 465.

[4] To that end, it shall 'administer the Understanding on Rules and Procedures Governing the Settlement of Disputes (hereinafter referred to as the "Dispute Settlement Understanding" or "DSU") in Annex 2 to [the WTO] Agreement': Marrakesh Agreement Establishing the World Trade Organization, adopted 15 April 1994, in force 1 January 1995, 1867 UNTS 154, 33 ILM 1143 (1994), Article 3.3.

[5] Therefore, any timber-exporting Member that considers that its trading opportunities are adversely affected by the Timber Regulation may file a request for consultations with the EU under Article 4.4 of the DSU (ibid). Should these consultations not lead to a 'mutually agreed solution', the complaining Member may file a request for the establishment of a Panel, which will then decide the issue. Should the Panel uphold the complaint of WTO inconsistency, the EU would be obliged to withdraw the measure. Article 3.7 DSU stipulates [in relevant part]: 'In the absence of a mutually agreed solution, the first objective of the dispute settlement mechanism is usually to secure the withdrawal of the measures concerned if these are found to be inconsistent with the provisions of any of the covered agreements.'

2. THE TIMBER REGULATION AND INTERNATIONAL TRADE LAW

On 3 March 2013, the EU Timber Regulation entered into force.[6] It aims to prevent the introduction of illegally logged timber into the market of the EU. The overarching objective of the Timber Regulation is combatting illegal logging. This phenomenon may be understood narrowly as harvesting timber without the required permits or in violation of granted permits. More broadly, it covers a wide range of illegal activities including the harvesting, transport, processing and trade of timber, and evasion of fees and taxes related thereto, which have an impact on various issues.[7] It has been pointed out that illegal logging accounts for 15–30 per cent of all forestry products worldwide and 50–90 per cent of all forestry products in key producer tropical countries.[8] Aside from damaging the environment and impacting on climate change, illegal logging also has economic effects and an impact on trade.[9] Illegal logging causes a loss of revenue for governments in timber-exporting countries, a loss of legitimate employment and an increased risk of corruption. From an economic point of view, illegal logging distorts the market because it is cheaper than legitimate logging.[10] These undesirable effects of illegal logging have clear global repercussions. However, regulating (and enforcing) timber production on a global scale has not yet yielded satisfactory results. Therefore, in addition to private certification schemes and supranational initiatives to address forest management, domestic forest programmes have been launched. Interestingly, more recently forest management has seen the emergence of instruments that verify the legality of timber, such as the Timber Regulation.[11] The crucial

---

[6] Regulation (EU) No. 995/2010 of the European Parliament and of the Council laying down the obligations of operators who place timber and timber products on the market, [2010] OJ L 295/23 (Timber Regulation).

[7] Marilyne Pereira Goncalves et al., *Justice for Forests: Improving Criminal Justice Efforts to Combat Illegal Logging* (World Bank Study, World Bank, 2012) 9–11.

[8] Christian Nellemann (ed.), *Green Carbon, Black Trade: Illegal Logging, Tax Fraud and Laundering in the World's Tropical Forests* (United Nations Environmental Programme and INTERPOL, 2012).

[9] Duncan Brack, 'Illegal Logging' (2007) Chatham House Briefing Paper 1–2.

[10] Ibid., 2.

[11] On the adequacy of legality verification, private schemes and domestic initiatives, see Ben Cashore and Michael Stone, 'Can Legality Verification Rescue Global Forest Governance? Analyzing the Potential of Public and Private

issue in this type of regulation is that, since these measures address non-economic concerns that have an impact on both domestic and foreign economic actors, it may be considered murky protectionism if the impact on foreign actors is more burdensome than the impact on domestic actors. Disciplining measures that discriminate against foreign competitors without satisfying the (strict) conditions of possible exceptions has been a central supposition at the WTO.

At the 2011 EU Trade Policy Review, a number of WTO Members expressed their concern regarding the Timber Regulation. The representative for Canada, for example, stated that the measure 'could provide an unfair competitive advantage to manufacturers of forest products in the EU compared to their international competitors' insofar it would contain labelling or traceability requirements unnecessary for consumer information that are a disproportionate burden on imports.[12] The Trade Policy Review Report places the Timber Regulation under the heading of 'measures directly affecting imports' and 'restrictions and controls', noting that 'the EU maintains unilateral import controls to attain non-economic objectives'.[13]

As the Timber Regulation covers goods (timber products), it has to fulfil the requirements set out by the General Agreement on Tariffs and Trade 1994 (GATT). The principles of market access and non-discrimination are the cornerstones of the GATT. Three obligations are most relevant in assessing the WTO consistency of the measure. First,

---

Policy Intersection to Ameliorate Forest Challenges in Southeast Asia' (2012) 18 *Forest Policy and Economics* 13, and the references there. See more generally on the regulatory framework of forest governance, including at the EU level, Jeremy Rayner, Alexander Buck and Pia Katila (eds), 'Embracing Complexity: Meeting the Challenges of International Forest Governance' (World Series Volume 28, International Union of Forest Research Organizations, 2010). According to the United Nations Climate Summit 2014 New York Declaration on Forests, legality verification is an example of policies and measures that can effectively address the problem of illegal logging.

12 WTO, Trade Policy Review Body, Trade Policy Review of the European Union, Minutes of the Meeting on 6 and 8 July 2011, 14 September 2011, WT/TPR/M/248, para. 135. Indonesia also expressed its concern with respect to the due diligence system established by the Regulation: WTO, Trade Policy Review Body, Trade Policy Review of the European Union, Minutes of the Meeting on the 6 and 8 July 2011, 31 August 2011, WT/TPR/M/248/Add.1, 364 (WTO, EU Trade Policy Review, Minutes 31 August 2011).

13 WTO, Trade Policy Review Body, Trade Policy Review of the European Union, Report by the Secretariat, WT/TPR/S/248/Rev.1, 43–4. Notably, the Regulation is not listed under 'Technical regulations and standards'.

WTO Members may not discriminate between products originating in the territories of different Members. This most-favoured nation (MFN) treatment obligation is contained in Article I:1 GATT. Second, WTO Members may not treat domestic products more favourably than like imported products. This national treatment obligation is laid down in Article III GATT. Third, WTO Members have committed themselves to the obligation not to impose prohibitions or restrictions other than duties, taxes or other charges, by virtue of Article XI GATT. In addition to these obligations, however, Article XX GATT contains a number of exceptions that may, under certain conditions, remedy an otherwise GATT-inconsistent measure.[14]

It should be stressed that international trade law in principle does not second-guess a legislator's choice to address certain issues. It merely requires that this is done in accordance with the binding rules of the WTO. Hence, this chapter does not address other crucial questions such as those of effectiveness[15] and extraterritoriality.[16]

3. KEY FEATURES OF THE EU TIMBER REGULATION FOR ITS WTO COMPLIANCE

3.1 The Timber Regulation is Part of a Larger Legal Framework

The Timber Regulation is the latest step in the EU's efforts to put a halt to illegal logging practices. The European Commission developed the Forest Law Enforcement, Governance, and Trade (FLEGT) Action Plan in 2003[17] to address 'the growing problem of illegal logging and related trade', which was named as one of the European Commission's priorities. The Action Plan has led to both a licensing agreement based on Voluntary Partnership Agreements (VPAs) and the mandatory Timber Regulation, which is to become the pinnacle in the execution of the Action Plan.

---

[14] GATT Panel Report, *United States – Section 337 of the Tariff Act of 1930*, L/6439, 36S/345, para. 5.9 (*US – Section 337 Tariff Act*).

[15] On effectiveness, see the emerging data from the sector, e.g. ITTO Market Information Service, (2014) 18 *Tropical Timber Market Report* 7, 18–22.

[16] On extraterritoriality, see e.g. Petros Mavroidis (Chapter 12, this volume) and Cedric Ryngaert and Marieke Koekkoek (Chapter 10, this volume).

[17] European Commission, 'Forest Law Enforcement, Governance and Trade (FLEGT): Proposal for an EU Action Plan', COM(2003) 251 final.

The first pillar consists of FLEGT VPAs, which are bilateral agreements between the EU and timber-exporting countries. These agreements aim to guarantee that the wood exported to the EU is legally sourced, and to support partner countries in improving their own regulation and governance of the sector.[18] Therefore, exporting countries commit themselves to establishing national licensing schemes that verify the legality of their shipments of timber and timber products to the EU. The EU has concluded six VPAs with timber-exporting countries, with six other VPAs currently under negotiation.[19] Once a VPA is in place, all covered timber and timber products exported from a partner country into the EU must in principle comply with the licensing system. Annex II of the FLEGT Regulation lists a number of categories of timber products that are to be covered by all VPAs and their corresponding Harmonized System (HS) Tariff Classification headings.[20] Individual VPAs may cover additional timber and timber products.[21]

The second pillar of the FLEGT Action Plan is the Timber Regulation. Its Preamble reiterates that illegal logging is a pervasive problem of major international concern that contributes to deforestation and forest degradation, which is responsible for about 20 per cent of global CO_2 emissions and threatens biodiversity. Moreover, it undercuts sustainable

---

[18] Council Regulation (EC) No. 2173/2005 on the establishment of a FLEGT licensing scheme for imports of timber into the European Community, [2005] OJ L 347/1. The FLEGT Regulation is implemented by Commission Regulation (EC) No. 1024/2008 laying down detailed measures for the implementation of Council Regulation (EC) No 2173/2005, [2008] OJ L 277/23.

[19] Cameroon, the Central African Republic, Ghana, Indonesia, Liberia and the Republic of Congo (Brazzaville) have signed VPAs. The Democratic Republic of Congo, Gabon, Guyana, Honduras, Malaysia and Vietnam are currently negotiating.

[20] These are: 4403 Wood in the rough, whether or not stripped of bark or sapwood, or roughly squared; 4406 Railway or tramway sleepers (cross-ties) of wood; 4407 Wood sawn or chipped lengthwise, sliced or peeled, whether or not planed, sanded or end-jointed, of a thickness exceeding 6 mm; 4408 Sheets for veneering (including those obtained by slicing laminated wood), for plywood or for other similar laminated wood and other wood, sawn lengthwise, sliced or peeled, whether or not planed, sanded, spliced or end-jointed, of a thickness not exceeding 6 mm; and 4412 Plywood, veneered panels and similar laminated wood.

[21] For example, the VPA with Cameroon also covers 4417 Tools, tool bodies, tool handles, broom or brush bodies and handles, in wood; boot or shoe lasts and trees of wood; 9403 30 Wooden furniture of a kind used in offices; 9403 40 Wooden furniture of a kind used in kitchens; 9403 50 Wooden furniture of a kind used in the bedroom; and 9403 60 Other wooden furniture.

forest management and development, and it accords a competitive disadvantage to timber that is legally logged. Furthermore, the Preamble stresses the scale of illegal logging and the urgency to combat it. In general, the Timber Regulation aims to address the economic, social and environmental impacts of illegal logging.

From the perspective of distinguishing between measures with primarily protectionist motives and measures with legitimate objectives, this presence of a larger legal framework may indicate a Member's true commitment to the objective pursued. For example, in the case of *EC – Seal Products*, in which an EU measure prohibiting the importation of seal products was scrutinized, the Panel and Appellate Body (AB) both found that the protection of seals addresses moral concerns in the EU.[22] The Panel agreed with the EU that its comprehensive regulation of animal welfare supported the conclusion that animal welfare in general,[23] and seal welfare in particular, form part of 'standards of right and wrong conduct maintained by or on behalf of [the EU]'.[24] The rationale behind this reasoning appears to be that there is much less chance of a measure having a covertly protectionist intent if a comprehensive legal framework has been adopted to address the relevant concern. The absence of such a framework may lead to the conclusion that the aim of the measure is in fact not the protection of the non-trade value at issue, but rather favouring domestic economic actors. For example, in *China – Raw Materials*, the fact that China restricted the export of domestic raw materials without 'taking steps to manage the supply of natural resources domestically' meant that it could not justify this GATT-inconsistent measure under the general exceptions contained in Article XX GATT.[25]

---

[22] Panel Report, *European Communities – Measures Prohibiting the Importation and Marketing of Seal Products*, WT/DS400/R and WT/DS401/R, adopted 18 June 2014, paras 7.405–7.410 (Panel Report, *EC – Seal Products*); Appellate Body Report, *European Communities – Measures Prohibiting the Importation and Marketing of Seal Products*, WT/DS400/AB/R and WT/DS401/AB/R, adopted 18 June 2014, paras 5.141–5.167 (Appellate Body Report, *EC – Seal Products*). The AB, however, acknowledged that the fact that the measure included an exception for seal products produced by Inuit or other indigenous communities could lead to questions about the sincerity of the EU's concern for animal welfare (para. 5.320). This, however, did not detract from the fact that animal welfare could fall within the scope of the public morals exception.

[23] For example, with regard to farm animals and ethical rules for the use of animals.

[24] Panel Report, *EC – Seal Products*, n. 22 above, paras 7.405–7.411.

[25] Panel Report, *China – Measures Related to the Exportation of Various Raw Materials*, WT/DS394/R, WT/DS395/R and WT/DS398/R, adopted 22

Consequently, the fact that the Timber Regulation forms part of a comprehensive forestry governance scheme may help it to pass WTO scrutiny.

3.2 Is the Timber Regulation a Technical Regulation?

Product safety standards and other technical regulations vary from country to country. The WTO's Agreement on Technical Barriers to Trade (TBT Agreement) aims to ensure that technical regulations and product standards do not create unnecessary obstacles to trade, whilst also ensuring that WTO Members maintain their regulatory autonomy and are free to pursue other societal objectives, such as the protection of human health and safety and the environment. As concerns the Timber Regulation, El Salvador asked why the EU did not notify the TBT Committee of the proposed Regulation. In response, the EU correctly stated that the proposal for the measure 'did not contain any technical regulations'.[26]

The TBT Agreement applies to 'technical regulations'; according to Annex 1.1 these are essentially documents which lay down product characteristics or their related processes and production methods with which compliance is mandatory. Thus, the main question is whether the Timber Regulation lays down product characteristics or related processes and production methods. In this respect, Mitchell and Ayres note that 'legality itself is not a "process or production method", particularly as legal requirements will vary from country to country', adding that 'the legality of the way in which timber is harvested is not a "related" non-physical characteristic because it does not relate to "the means of identification, the presentation or the appearance" of the product'.[27] The Timber Regulation does not lay down technical regulations, and therefore the TBT Agreement is not applicable to it. In *EC – Seal Products* the AB reversed the Panel's finding that the Seals Regulation constituted a technical regulation in the sense of Annex 1.1 of the TBT Agreement. The AB concluded that the Seals Regulation was, as such, 'not concerned

---

February 2012, paras 7.402–7.408. (*China – Raw Materials*). For a more elaborate discussion of Article XX, see below section 3.4. Of course, in this case, the justification ground on which China based its defence, Article XX (g), requires the inconsistent measures to be made effective in conjunction with restrictions on domestic production or consumption.

[26] WTO, EU Trade Policy Review, Minutes 31 August 2011, n. 12 above, 396.

[27] Mitchell and Ayres, n. 2 above, 476.

with banning the placing on the EU market of seal products'.[28] Characterizing the measure, the AB stated that 'it establishes the conditions for placing seal products on the EU market based on criteria relating to the identity of the hunter or the type or purpose of the hunt from which the product is derived'.[29] Similarly, the Timber Regulation establishes the conditions for placing timber products on the EU market based on the legality of the timber in question. As long as a measure does not lay down explicit product characteristics it is unlikely that it will qualify as a technical regulation in the sense of Annex 1.1 of the TBT Agreement. Consequently, in order to answer the question whether the Timber Regulation is in conformity with the EU's WTO obligations, one has to turn to the basic rules on trade in goods, enshrined in the General Agreement on Tariffs and Trade 1994.

3.3 A Prohibition on Placing Illegal Timber on the Market and Due Diligence Requirements

To achieve its objectives, the Timber Regulation lays down obligations for operators who place timber and timber products on the internal market.[30] Placing on the market is defined as the supply by any means, irrespective of the selling technique used, of timber or timber products for the first time on the internal market for distribution or for use in the course of a commercial activity.[31] An operator is defined as any natural or legal person that places timber or timber products on the market. An operator is to be distinguished from a trader, who is any natural or legal person who, in the course of commercial activity, sells or buys timber or timber products already on the internal market.[32] A guidance document issued by the European Commission contains more detailed definitions of terms used in the Timber Regulation.[33]

The key element of the Timber Regulation is that it prohibits the placing of illegally harvested timber or timber products from such timber

---

[28] Appellate Body Report, *EC – Seal Products*, n. 22 above, para. 5.58.

[29] Ibid.

[30] Timber Regulation, Article 2(a)–(b). Timber products covered by the Timber Regulation are listed in the Annex, with their corresponding HS Tariff Classification headings.

[31] Ibid, Article 2(c).

[32] Ibid, Article 2(d).

[33] European Commission, 'Guidance Document for the EU Timber Regulation' (2013), http://ec.europa.eu/environment/forests/pdf/Final%20Guidance%20document.pdf (accessed 6 May 2014).

on the market.[34] It is important to note that the Regulation does not prohibit *importing* illegally harvested timber as such, and hence it is not – at least not *de jure* – a border measure. However, it must be noted that, contrary to the text of the Timber Regulation, the above-mentioned guidance document uses the term *importing* rather than *placing on the market*.

Concerning all other timber and timber products, operators are subject to a due diligence obligation, which they may devise themselves, based on the framework contained in the Timber Regulation.[35] Alternatively, a monitoring organization may provide a due diligence system and grant operators a right to use it.[36] The due diligence system requires operators to keep track of information related to the marketing of timber or timber products. Furthermore, it contains risk assessment and risk mitigation procedures enabling the operator to analyse the risk of illegally harvested timber or timber products derived from such timber being placed on the market. Aside from operators, traders are also subject to obligations. They must also be able to identify throughout the supply chain: (i) the operator or traders who have supplied the timber and timber products, and (ii) where applicable, the traders to whom they have supplied timber and timber products. This traceability obligation requires the relevant information to be kept for at least five years and to be made available to the relevant authorities upon request.[37] In order to safeguard the application of the Timber Regulation, every EU Member State is to designate competent authorities, which are to check whether operators fulfil their due diligence obligations.[38] EU Member States must provide for

---

[34] Timber Regulation, Article 4.1. Hence, in essence, the Timber Regulation has important extraterritorial effects as it addresses issues and concerns that took place outside the territory of the EU. See Laurens Ankersmit, Jessica Lawrence and Gareth Davies, 'Diverging EU and WTO Perspectives on Extraterritorial Process Regulation' (2012) 21 *Minnesota Journal of International Law* 14, 59.

[35] Timber Regulation, Articles 4.2–4.3 and 6.1.

[36] Ibid, Articles 4.3, and 8. Also see Commission Delegated Regulation No. (EU) 363/2012 on the procedural rules for the recognition and withdrawal of recognition of monitoring organisations as provided for in Regulation (EU) No. 995/2010, [2012] OJ L 115/12.

[37] Timber Regulation, Article 5.

[38] Ibid., Articles 7 and 10–12. Also see European Commission Implementing Regulation (EU) 607/2012 on the detailed rules concerning the due diligence system and the frequency and nature of the checks on monitoring organisations as provided for in Regulation (EU) No. 995/2010 [2012] OJ L177/16, which stipulates, inter alia, the term within which the due diligence system shall be applied by operators, the way in which the information has to be supplied by the

penalties in the event of a violation of the due diligence obligations; these penalties are to be effective, proportionate and dissuasive.[39]

These two main obligations first raise the question whether the general obligation contained in the Timber Regulation can be considered a quantitative restriction in the sense of Article XI GATT, and thus, in effect, a *de facto* border measure. Moreover, the question whether timber or timber products can be identified as illegally logged is left up to the country of harvest and has to be made on the basis of the applicable legislation in that country, whether this is inside or outside the EU.[40] Second, this approach raises the question whether the general obligation in the Timber Regulation discriminates in a way prohibited by the GATT. Third, the exceptions to the Timber Regulation's general obligation also require scrutiny under the GATT non-discrimination rules.

3.3.1 Is the Timber Regulation a quantitative restriction?

Article XI:1 GATT prohibits measures (except duties, taxes or other charges) which restrict or prohibit (i) the importation of any product, or (ii) the exportation or sale for export of any product. The scope of Article XI GATT is very broad.[41] According to this provision, 'Members shall not forbid the importation of *any* product of *any* other Member into their markets'.[42] Article XI covers both *de jure* as well as *de facto* prohibitions and restrictions.[43] The Timber Regulation prohibits operators from placing illegally harvested timber on the market. The enforcement of this prohibition is ensured by Article 19 of the Regulation, which requires EU Member States to set up a system of effective penalties applicable to infringements of the Regulation. The Panel in *Brazil – Retreaded Tyres* held in this respect that the fact that the penalties are not administered at

operator, the way in which risk assessment and mitigation procedures have to be carried out, and the frequency and nature of checks on monitoring organizations.

[39] Timber Regulation, Article 19.

[40] Ibid., Article 2(e)–(h).

[41] Panel Report, *India – Quantitative Restrictions on Imports of Agricultural, Textile and Industrial Products*, WT/DS90/R, adopted 22 September 1999, para. 5.129 (*India – Quantitative Restrictions*); GATT Panel Report, *Japan – Trade in Semi-Conductors,* L/6309, adopted 4 May 1988, BISD 35S/116, para. 104.

[42] Panel Report, *Brazil – Measures Affecting Imports of Retreaded Tyres*, WT/DS332/R, adopted 17 December 2007, para. 7.11 (*Brazil – Retreaded Tyres*) (emphasis added).

[43] Panel Report, *Argentina – Measures Affecting the Export of Bovine Hides and the Import of Finished Leather*, WT/DS155/R, adopted 16 February 2001, paras 11.20–11.21.

the border 'does not alter their nature as a restriction on importation within the meaning of Article XI:1'.[44]

The Regulation thus implements a *de facto* prohibition on imports, such as a ban on illegally logged timber. Importers, or operators, will become very cautious about importing timber, regardless of whether it has been harvested legally or illegally, since a failure to live up to the due diligence standards could result in criminal liability. It might be argued that this is a private decision, taken by each individual operator. However, the AB stated in *Korea – Beef* that 'the intervention of some element of private choice' does not relieve a WTO Member of responsibility for the restrictive effects of a measure.[45] Charnovitz has noted that the 'illegality of importation under the law of the importing country is not a justification under WTO rules to block the importation'.[46] Consequently, the measure, insofar as it criminalizes the act of importation of illegally harvested timber, appears to be inconsistent with Article XI GATT since it constitutes a restriction on importation. In this respect it is worth pointing out that the Panel in *Colombia – Ports of Entry* held that it is not necessary to examine the actual trade effects of a measure.[47] The essential question that needs to be answered is thus whether the measure, based on its design, structure and architecture has the potential to adversely affect importation. In any event, even if the existence of a *de facto* prohibition would not be accepted by a panel, the measure qualifies as a restriction in the sense of Article XI. The Panel in *India – Quantitative Restrictions* defined the term 'restriction' as a limiting condition,[48] which led the Panel in *India – Autos* to conclude that the mere fact that there is a condition on importation is not sufficient; this condition must be limiting in nature – it must thus have a limiting effect.[49]

In sum, given the very broad scope of Article XI GATT and the way in which it has been interpreted by Panels and the AB, it is difficult for

---

[44] Panel Report, *Brazil – Retreaded Tyres*, n. 42 above, paras 7.372–7.373.

[45] Appellate Body Report, *Korea – Measures Affecting Imports of Fresh, Chilled and Frozen Beef*, WT/DS161/AB/R, WT/DS169/AB/R, adopted 10 January 2001, para. 146 (*Korea – Beef*).

[46] Steve Charnovitz, 'The World Trade Organization and Law Enforcement' (2003) 37 *Journal of World Trade* 817, 830.

[47] Panel Report, *Colombia – Indicative Prices and Restrictions on Ports of Entry*, WT/DS366/R, adopted 20 May 2009, paras 7.252–7253.

[48] Panel Report, *India – Quantitative Restrictions*, n. 41 above, para. 5.128.

[49] Panel Report, *India – Measures Affecting the Automotive Sector*, WT/DS146/R, WT/DS175/R, adopted 5 April 2002 (*India – Autos*).

legislators to avoid violating the article. This, in turn, highlights the importance of the general exceptions contained in Article XX GATT (Section 3.4 below).

3.3.2 Does the Timber Regulation discriminate between like products?

The Timber Regulation equally needs to comply with the non-discrimination obligations of Articles I and III GATT. These provisions contain respectively the MFN and national treatment obligations. The former provision requires WTO Members not to discriminate between foreign like products on the basis of their origin The latter essentially requires WTO Members not to treat foreign products less favourably than like domestic products.

The questions are therefore whether the Timber Regulation: (i) confers an advantage to certain foreign products that it does not extend immediately and unconditionally to like products of another foreign origin; and (ii) accords the illegally harvested timber less favourable treatment than it does like domestic timber. Both questions require an answer to the question as to whether illegally harvested timber is like legally harvested domestic timber. However, it must first be established whether the Timber Regulation is an internal measure or a border measure.

Is the Timber Regulation an internal measure and/or a border measure?
Article III GATT applies only to internal measures. From the Ad Note to the article it can be derived that Article III GATT would apply to border measures if the product in question fails to meet a requirement that is also applied to like domestic products.[50] As Van den Bossche notes, it is possible that one measure is both an internal measure and a border measure.[51] The Timber Regulation does not explicitly prohibit the

---

[50] Note Ad Article III: 'Any internal tax or other internal charge, or any law, regulation or requirement of the kind referred to in paragraph 1 which applies to an imported product and to the like domestic product and is collected or enforced in the case of the imported product at the time or point of importation, is nevertheless to be regarded as an internal tax or other internal charge, or a law, regulation or requirement of the kind referred to in paragraph 1, and is accordingly subject to the provisions of Article III' (emphasis added).

[51] Peter van den Bossche, The Law and Policy of the World Trade Organization (2nd edn, Cambridge University Press, 2008), 347. Van den Bossche refers to the Panel Report in India – Autos, n. 49 above, para. 7.224, where it was held that '… it therefore cannot be excluded a priori that different aspects of a measure may affect the competitive opportunities of imports in different ways, making them fall within the scope either of Article III (where

importation of illegally harvested timber; rather, it prohibits the placing on the market of such timber, thereby implying that timber that originates in the EU and was harvested illegally may also not be placed onto the market.

Are legal and illegal timber products 'like'? As set out above, in order to fall within the scope of the non-discrimination obligations, a measure must discriminate between like products. In such a case, it has to be established whether illegally logged timber and timber products are like legally logged timber and timber products.

The AB has stated that 'a determination of "likeness" under Article III:4 is, fundamentally, a determination about the nature and extent of a competitive relationship between and among products'.[52] Although the meaning of the concept 'likeness' varies according to its context, elements from the likeness test carried out under Article III:4 can equally be used to interpret likeness in the context of Article I:1 GATT.[53] In determining whether products can indeed be considered like, one has to assess four criteria: (i) physical characteristics, (ii) end use, (iii) consumer tastes and habits, and (iv) tariff classification. The physical characteristics, end uses and tariff classification of legally harvested and illegally harvested timber are essentially the same. Consumer tastes and habits are the only criterion on which an argument of *unlikeness* could reasonably be made. One might argue that consumers have a preference for legally logged timber and that they prefer to buy products that do not contain illegally harvested timber. If this preference for legally logged timber is strong enough, this might detract substantially from the competitive relationship between the two groups of products thereby making them unlike.

---

competitive opportunities on the domestic market are affected) or of Article XI (where the opportunities for importation itself, i.e. entering the market, are affected), or even that there may be, in perhaps exceptional circumstances, a potential for overlap between the two provisions, as was suggested in the case of state trading'.

52 Appellate Body Report, *EC – Measures Affecting Asbestos and Products Containing Asbestos*, WT/DS135/AB/R, adopted 5 April 2001, paras 98–9 (*EC – Asbestos*).

53 Appellate Body Report, *Japan – Taxes on Alcoholic Beverages*, WT/DS/8/AB/R, WT/DS10/AB/R, WT/DS11/AB/R, adopted 1 November 1996, paras 19–20.

Two points can be raised against a conclusion that the products are unlike. First, in the case of the Timber Regulation, illegality is determined by the legislation of the country of harvest. Consumers will often not be aware of the conditions laid down by this particular enactment. Second, as noted by Mitchell and Ayres, if the (il)legality of the timber or timber products is the only difference between two otherwise identical products, the consumer preference for legally harvested timber would not be sufficiently strong to detract substantially from the competitive relationship between the two groups of products.[54] Mitchell and Ayres therefore conclude that illegally and legally harvested timber are like products.[55]

Brack, Chandra and Kinasih oppose this conclusion as they argue that the likeness should be determined based on compliance with whatever national legislation exists, regardless of its content. It appears that in their view, products that are illegal in a certain country can never be in a competitive relationship with, and hence like, similar products originating in a country where they are legal because trade in those illegal products would be impossible as these products are unauthorized. This is exactly what the Timber Regulation does. Their point of view seems to be that when national legislation of another country determines that a certain product is illegal, the competitive relationship between that product and a similar legal product ceases to exist.[56] In that case, absent like products, there is no issue of non-discrimination under Articles I:1 or III:4 GATT. However, for the sake of argument, assuming that illegal and legal timber are indeed like products, it will now be assessed whether the Timber Regulation confers an advantage or accords less favourable treatment to like imported products.

Does the Timber Regulation confer an advantage or accord less favourable treatment? Assuming that illegally logged timber is like legally logged timber, there would be a violation of Article I:1 GATT if the Timber Regulation confers an advantage to legally logged timber that is not accorded immediately and unconditionally to like products from

---

[54] Mitchell and Ayres, n. 2 above, 468.

[55] Also see Lorand Bartels, 'WTO Law Aspects of Clean Trade', available at http://papers.ssrn.com/sol3/papers.cfm?abstract_id=2634567 (accessed 3 August 2015).

[56] Duncan Brack, Alexander Chandra and Herjuno Kinasih, 'The Australian Government's Illegal Logging Prohibition Bill: WTO Implications' (Report, International Institute for Sustainable Development Trade Knowledge Network 2012), 9.

other WTO Members. In EC – Bananas the AB held that an advantage exists where a measure creates more favourable import opportunities for certain products depending on their origin. The concept of advantage must be interpreted broadly, according to the AB in Canada – Autos.[57] In the case at hand, timber that has been legally harvested may be marketed in the EU, whereas timber that has been harvested illegally may not be placed in the internal market. Consequently, the Timber Regulation does confer an advantage to certain products.

As concerns Article III:4 GATT, the question is whether the measure accords less favourable treatment to foreign like products than it does to domestic like products. The Timber Regulation does not explicitly differentiate between domestic and imported timber. The obligations it lays down for operators and traders apply irrespectively of whether the timber is produced within the EU or in a third country. Consequently, any claim of inconsistency with respect to Article III:4 GATT would amount to an allegation of *de facto* discrimination. In *Korea – Beef*, the AB stated that less favourable treatment is established by examining whether a measure modifies the *conditions of competition* in the relevant market to the detriment of imported products.[58]

In *Dominican Republic – Cigarettes* the AB elaborated upon the term 'to the detriment of imported products' by clarifying that 'the existence of a detrimental effect on a given imported product resulting from a measure does not necessarily imply that this measure accords less favorable treatment to imports if the detrimental effect is explained *by factors or circumstances unrelated to the foreign origin of the product* …'[59] Based on this it has been argued that an inquiry into the rationale of a measure could be necessary under the less favourable treatment test of Article III:4 GATT. However, in *EC – Seal Products* the AB rejected the proposition that, similar to the position under Article 2.1 TBT Agreement, an 'additional inquiry into whether the detrimental impact on competitive opportunities for like imported products stems exclusively from a legitimate regulatory distinction' would be necessary. The AB held that 'the "treatment no less favourable" standard under Article III:4 of the GATT 1994 prohibits WTO Members from modifying

---

[57] Appellate Body Report, Canada – Certain Measures Affecting the Automotive Industry, WT/139/AB/R, WT/142/AB/R, 19 June 2000 (Canada – Autos), para. 79.

[58] Appellate Body Report, *Korea – Beef*, n. 45 above, paras 135–7.

[59] Appellate Body Report, *Dominican Republic – Measures Affecting the Importation and Internal Sale of Cigarettes*, WT/DS302/AB/R, adopted 19 May 2005, para. 96 (emphasis added).

the conditions of competition in the marketplace to the detriment of the group of imported products vis-à-vis the group of like domestic products'.[60]

However, since there is no incentive for a WTO Member that has made certain types of timber illegal within its jurisdiction to file a complaint against a Member prohibiting the importation of such illegal timber, a different comparison may be of more practical relevance. The two groups of products that must then be compared are legally harvested imported timber and legally harvested domestic timber. Considering the AB's statement in *EC – Seal Products*, what must be assessed is whether the EU Timber Regulation results in a modification of the conditions of competition to the detriment of legally harvested imported timber as compared to like domestic timber. At first glance, since the Timber Regulation applies equally to all types of timber, regardless of whether they have been produced domestically or have been imported, there does not seem to be a detrimental impact. However, there may be situations in which, for various reasons, imported products end up in a disadvantaged position in the marketplace in that new monitoring schemes would have to be set up by foreign producers, whereas such schemes are already in place in domestic production lines. In such a case, one could envisage that a WTO Panel would consider this to be a modification of the conditions of competition to the detriment of imported timber. For such a finding, however, a detailed factual inquiry would be necessary. Since this inquiry would be based on case-specific factual circumstances, such an analysis is beyond the scope of this chapter.

3.3.3 Exceptions to the general rules of the Timber Regulation

As became clear in the *EC – Seal Products* case, the exceptions to a measure may raise concerns regarding their WTO consistency. In that case, the Panel and AB found no problem with the overall measure, a ban on seal products, but decided that the measure's exceptions to the ban for indigenous communities and for marine resource management violated the non-discrimination provisions of GATT and were not justifiable under the GATT's exceptions.[61] Hence, a *more* trade restrictive, but uniformly applied, measure – a ban without exceptions – is to be preferred, because in that case the exceptions gave rise to a detrimental impact on foreign seal products vis-à-vis domestic seal products. The

---

[60] Appellate Body Report, *EC – Seal Products*, n. 22 above, para. 5.117.

[61] Panel Report, *EC – Seal Products*, n. 22 above, paras 7.600, 7.609 and 7.650.

complainants in *EC – Seal Products* did not claim that the EU seal regime *as a whole* violated Article XI GATT, but contended that the indigenous communities and marine resource management exceptions in the measure consisted of a quantitative restriction. The Panel did not agree and stated that it was the main ban, rather than the two exceptions in themselves, that was trade restrictive.[62]

In the case of the Timber Regulation, two categories of timber will automatically be considered legally harvested.[63] The first category consists of timber embedded in timber products covered by VPAs – that is, products originating in a VPA partner country and listed in the VPA. If these products comply with the requirements set out by the FLEGT Regulation and the corresponding implementing provisions, they will be considered to have been legally harvested. The second category consists of timber of tree species listed in Annex A, B and C of Council Regulation (EC) No. 338/97 (Wildlife Regulation)[64] and which complies with that Regulation and the corresponding implementing provisions. Such timber will also be considered to have been legally harvested. The tree species listed in Annexes A, B and C of the Wildlife Regulation are linked to the 1973 Convention on International Trade in Endangered Species of Wild Fauna and Flora (CITES).

CITES encompasses three appendices, each of which both contains a list of species and regulates trade.[65] Species listed in Appendix I are endangered and may only be traded subject to conditions, one of which is

---

[62] Ibid., paras 7.658–7.661.

[63] Timber Regulation, Article 3.

[64] Council Regulation (EC) No. 338/97 on the protection of species of wild fauna and flora by regulating trade therein, [1997] OJ L 61/1. The Wildlife Regulation has, in its turn, been implemented by European Commission Regulation (EC) No. 865/2006 laying down detailed rules concerning the implementation of Council Regulation (EC) No. 338/97 on the protection of species of wild fauna and flora by regulating trade therein, [2006] OJ L 166/1; European Commission Recommendation 2007/425/EC identifying a set of actions for the enforcement of Regulation (EC) No. 338/97 on the protection of species of wild fauna and flora by regulating trade therein, [2007] OC L 159/45; European Commission Implementing Regulation (EU) No. 757/2012 suspending the introduction into the Union of specimens of certain species of wild fauna and flora, [2012] OJ L 223/31; and European Commission Implementing Regulation (EU) No. 792/2012 laying down rules for the design of permits, certificates and other documents provided for in Council Regulation (EC) No. 338/97 on the protection of species of wild fauna and flora by regulating trade therein, [2012] OJ L 242/13.

[65] CITES, Washington, DC (US), adopted 3 Mar. 1973, in force 1 July 1975, 993 UNTS 243, 12 ILM 1085 (1973), Articles II:4, III, IV and V.

that the primary purpose is not commercial. Appendix II contains the large majority of protected species. In order to trade these species, an export permit must be granted. The permit will be granted only if export is not detrimental to the survival of the species – the so-called non-detriment finding – and if no laws have been violated in harvesting the species. Trade in species listed in Appendix III is subject to the condition that no laws have been violated in harvesting the species. Moreover, if a state that has listed the species in Appendix III imports the species from an exporter in a state that has not listed them, only a certificate of origin from the latter state is required for trade to be allowed.

Instead of the three categories in CITES, the Wildlife Regulation contains four categories of species, listed in Annexes A to D. For species listed in Annex A or B (all of which are CITES Appendix I and II species), some Appendix III species and some non-CITES species, the conditions for trade set out by the Wildlife Regulation are more restrictive than those prescribed by CITES. For example, an import permit is required for species listed in Annex A or B, and it is prohibited to conduct most commercial activities with regard to species listed in Annex A.

These different legality conditions under the Timber Regulation, the VPA scheme and the Wildlife Regulation may cause concern.[66] The exclusion of timber products which fall within the first exception from the application of this regulation merely serves to encourage countries to enter into VPAs. These appear to go further than the Timber Regulation,[67] and therefore would not violate the GATT non-discrimination obligations. The same can be said for timber which is listed in Annexes A to C of the Wildlife Regulation. In this case, at the very least an import notification and an export permit are required.[68] However, under the

---

66 Rosie Cooney, Stephanie van Meibom and Chin Hen Keong, 'Trading Timbers: A Comparison of Import Requirements under CITES, FLEGT and Related EU Legislation for Timber Species in Trade' (TRAFFIC/WWF, 2012) 22–4.

67 Cameroon VPA, Annex VIII, Article I.

68 It has been argued that timber species which are listed in CITES Appendix III by a country may be exported to the EU by another country, which has not listed the species in this appendix, and still benefit from the exception in Article 3. This was addressed as a loophole because a party to CITES may make unilateral changes to Appendix III: see Cooney, van Meibom and Keong, n. 66 above, 22–4. However, we believe this not to be a correct interpretation of Article 3 Timber Regulation, which refers back to Annex C of the Wildlife Regulation. There, it is stated that Annex C contains the species listed in Appendix III to CITES for which EU Member States have not made a reservation. However,

Wildlife Regulation, timber may be imported when, as concerns legality, it is not obtained in violation of the national legislation on the conservation of the species.[69] Hence, a more relaxed legal standard applies. This issue is the most pressing for species listed in Appendix III to CITES, as parties may unilaterally add timber to this appendix and when the party adds no reservations, the exception in Article 3 Timber Regulation comes into play. This may constitute a violation of GATT non-discrimination obligations.

3.4 Can the Timber Regulation be Justified by an Exception?

Measures that pursue certain policy objectives other than liberalizing trade must be balanced with WTO obligations. Therefore, GATT includes exceptions to justify measures that violate its obligations. In order to benefit from the – for these purposes most relevant – exceptions in Article XX GATT, two conditions must be fulfilled. The WTO Member maintaining the measure must establish: (i) that the measure comes within the scope of one of the policy exceptions listed in the provision; and (ii) that the measure is also consistent with the chapeau of the article.

With regard to the first step, three policy exceptions may be applicable to the Timber Regulation at first glance: (i) measures aiming to protect human, animal or plant life or health; (ii) measures necessary to secure compliance with laws or regulations which are not inconsistent with the GATT; and (iii) measures relating to the conservation of exhaustible natural resources. Subsequently, the chapeau is addressed.

3.4.1 Human, animal or plant life or health

Article XX(b) GATT contains a justification ground for measures which are necessary to protect human, animal or plant life or health. Therefore, it must first be established that the measure is *covered* by the policy objective. This was the case in *US – Gasoline*, where the Panel found that

---

listings in Appendix III to CITES are always linked to a country (e.g. 'Diospyros analamerensis (Madagascar)'). Moreover, Article II CITES states that 'Appendix III shall include all species which any Party identifies as being subject to regulation within its jurisdiction for the purpose of preventing or restricting exploitation'. Hence, we argue that the interpretation by Cooney, van Meibom and Keong is contrary to the objectives and principles of CITES, the Wildlife Regulation and the Timber Regulation. Nonetheless, if a Panel were to examine the Timber Regulation, this matter is likely to be examined from a practical perspective.

[69] Wildlife Regulation, n. 64 above, Articles 4.1(b)(i), 4.2(c), and 4.3(a).

the measure is aimed to reduce air pollution, which has an effect on human, animal and plant health.[70] The text, design, architecture and structure of the measure must underline the purpose of the protection of human, animal or plant life or health.[71] Hence, this exception does not extend to the mere side effects of a measure. The Timber Regulation aims to protect animal and plant life by protecting biodiversity, ecosystem functions and the climate system.[72] The link between illegal logging and these aims appears clear.

Second, it must be established that the measure is *necessary* to achieve the policy objective. The necessity test does not include an assessment of the appropriateness of the end sought by the measure.[73] Moreover, it is up to the Member to decide on the level of protection sought by the measure. However, taking into account the end sought and its level of protection, the question is whether the measure is necessary. The interpretation of the necessity condition arguably encompasses three factors. The first of these is the relative importance of the common interests or values that are intended to be protected by the challenged measure. Second, it is assessed whether the measure is apt to make a material contribution to the objective pursued by the measure. The third condition entails whether an alternative measure which is less trade restrictive than the measure under scrutiny is reasonably available.[74] It is up to the complainant to identify alternative measures.[75] The respondent must demonstrate that the alternative is not readily available, for example, by establishing that the alternative imposes an unduly onerous burden on the respondent or is merely theoretical.[76]

---

[70] Panel Report, *United States – Standards for Reformulated and Conventional Gasoline*, WT/DS2/R, adopted 20 May 1996, para. 6.21 (*US – Gasoline*).

[71] Panel Report, *EC – Conditions for the Granting of Tariff Preferences to Developing Countries*, WT/DS246/R, adopted 20 April 2004, paras 7.200–7.210; Panel Report, *China – Raw Materials*, n. 25 above, paras 7.498–7.516.

[72] Timber Regulation, Recital 1.

[73] Appellate Body Report, *EC – Asbestos*, n. 52 above, para. 172.

[74] Ibid., paras 161–4; GATT Panel Report, *US – Section 337 Tariff Act*, n. 14 above, para. 5.26.

[75] Appellate Body Report, *Brazil – Retreaded Tyres*, n. 42 above, para. 156.

[76] Appellate Body Report, *United States – Measures Affecting the Cross-Border Supply of Gambling and Betting Services*, WT/DS285/AB/R, adopted 20 April 2005, para. 308; Appellate Body Report, *China – Measures Affecting Trading Rights and Distribution Services for Certain Publications and Audiovisual Entertainment Products*, WT/DS363/AB/R, adopted 19 January 2010, paras 312–31.

In the case of the Timber Regulation, there appear to be few issues with the first and second factor. As concerns the third factor, it is not unthinkable that a complainant would come up with a less trade-restrictive alternative measure. An example of such an alternative, as proposed by Canada and Norway in the *EC – Seal Products* case could be a licensing or certification system.[77] As demonstrated by the Panel's finding in *EC – Seal Products* that the alternative was not reasonably available, it is not easy for the complainant to establish such an alternative. Nonetheless, it must be stressed that a Panel's analysis of the facts of the case, including information submitted by the complainant, may lead to different views regarding the necessity of the Timber Regulation.

3.4.2 Article XX(d): compliance measures

Where a measure is necessary to secure compliance with laws or regulations that are not inconsistent with the provisions of the GATT, Article XX(d) may justify a violation of a Member's WTO obligations. The design of the measure must therefore contribute to securing compliance with domestic laws or regulations, even if there is no certainty that it will.[78] The Preamble to the Timber Regulation appears to foresee this option, as it refers to illegal logging as a threat to 'the commercial viability of operators acting in accordance with applicable legislation'.[79] This indicates that the Timber Regulation aims to ensure compliance either with legislation that, for example, prevents deceptive practices[80] or, more broadly, with EU competition or consumer protection laws.[81]

As addressed in Article XX(d) GATT, the measure must be necessary to be justified under this policy exception. The legal analysis of this requirement here is almost identical to that in Article XX(b) GATT.[82]

---

[77] Panel Report, *EC – Seal Products*, n. 22 above, para. 7.639, referring back to paras 7.467–7.499.

[78] Appellate Body Report, *Mexico – Tax Measures on Soft Drinks and Other Beverages*, WT/DS308/AB/R, adopted 24 March 2006, para. 74.

[79] Timber Regulation, Recital 3.

[80] This is one of the examples listed in Article XX(d) GATT.

[81] For example, the Unfair Commercial Practices Directive: Directive 2005/29/EC of the European Parliament and of the Council of 11 May 2005 concerning unfair business-to-consumer commercial practices in the internal market, [2005] OJ L 149/22.

[82] Petros Mavroidis, *Trade in Goods* (2nd edn, Oxford University Press, 2012), 342–4; Peter Van den Bossche, *The Law and Policy of the World Trade Organization* (2nd edn, Cambridge University Press, 2008), 634.

However, when applying the necessity test regarding this policy exception to the Timber Regulation, it can be seriously questioned whether no alternative measure which is less trade restrictive than the measure under scrutiny is reasonably available to secure compliance with the mentioned laws or regulations.

3.4.3 Article XX(g): conservation of exhaustible natural resources

Article XX(g) GATT provides a justification for measures 'relating to the conservation of exhaustible natural resources if such measures are made effective in conjunction with restrictions on domestic production or consumption'. This provision has been interpreted broadly,[83] and it is safe to assume that forests would fall within the scope of exhaustible natural resources. To justify a measure under this provision, two more conditions should be fulfilled. First, for a measure to *relate to* a policy objective, there needs to be a relationship between the policy goal and the general structure and design of the measure.[84] The measure should not be 'disproportionately wide in its scope and reach in relation to the policy objective', and the means should be reasonably related to the ends.[85] The Preamble to the Timber Regulation indicates that illegal logging contributes to deforestation and forest degradation, and undermines sustainable forest management and development.[86] The structure of the measure is aimed primarily at the protection of forests without being disproportionately wide. Banning illegally logged timber would be reasonably related to the means. Second, the measure must be made effective in conjunction with restrictions on domestic production or consumption. This condition

---

[83] Panel Report, *US – Gasoline*, n. 70 above, para. 6.37; Appellate Body Report, *United States – Import Prohibition of Certain Shrimp and Shrimp Products*, WT/DS58/AB/R, adopted 6 November 1998, para. 131 (*US – Shrimp*). In the foregoing paragraphs, the AB explicitly and elaborately sets out that not only non-living resources, such as petroleum or minerals, are covered, but also living resources.

[84] Ibid, para. 137.

[85] Ibid, para. 141. Hence, the AB departed from earlier practice in which it was required that the measure was 'primarily aimed at' conserving exhaustible natural resources.

[86] Timber Regulation, Recital 3. Moreover, in the context of this policy exception, the AB referred to the fact that CITES is almost universally ratified, which, in its reasoning, indicates that the policy goal of protecting forests against illegal logging is accepted: Appellate Body Report, *US – Shrimp*, n. 83 above, para. 135. Additionally, see Chen Hin Keong, 'The Role of CITES in Combating Illegal Logging – Current And Potential' (Online Report Series 13, TRAFFIC/WWF 2006).

aims to ensure even-handedness in the application of an otherwise GATT-inconsistent measure. The 'trade restriction must operate jointly with the restrictions on domestic production or consumption', although it is not required that the trade-restrictive measure is aimed at ensuring the effectiveness of the domestic restrictions.[87] Considering that the Timber Regulation applies in the same way to domestic and foreign illegally logged timber and timber products, this condition appears to be fulfilled.

3.4.4 Article XX: chapeau

A provisionally justified measure under one of the policy exceptions in Article XX GATT must also satisfy the conditions of the chapeau of this provision, which aims to prevent abuse of the exceptions.[88] For that reason, the chapeau requires the following in the application of the measure: (i) there is no arbitrary or unjustifiable discrimination between countries where the same conditions prevail; and (ii) the measure is not a disguised restriction on international trade.[89] The term 'countries where the same conditions prevail' has been interpreted broadly as not only including other exporting countries but also including the importing country, independent of differences in trade volumes among exporting countries.[90] Consequently, in the case at hand, the Timber Regulation must apply to all timber-exporting countries and the EU itself without constituting a means of arbitrary or unjustifiable discrimination.

Although, as we have argued, the Timber Regulation may be discriminatory, the discrimination test under the chapeau requires more than what is necessary to violate Article III GATT.[91] First, the different conditions in the various Members must be taken into account as other WTO Members cannot be required to adopt an identical regulatory programme to that issued by the responding Member.[92] By making the question of legality subject to domestic laws, it seems that the EU has fulfilled this condition. Hence, the Timber Regulation is likely to pass

---

87 Appellate Body Report, *China – Raw Materials*, n. 25 above, paras 356 and 360–61.

88 Appellate Body Report, *United States – Standards for Reformulated and Conventional Gasoline*, WT/DS2/AB/R, adopted 20 May 1996, 22 (*US – Gasoline*).

89 Appellate Body Report, *US – Shrimp (Art. 21.5 – Malaysia)*, WT/DS58/AB/RW, para. 118.

90 Appellate Body Report, *US – Gasoline*, n. 88 above, 23–4; Appellate Body Report, *Brazil – Retreaded Tyres*, paras 228–9 and 250–51.

91 Appellate Body Report, *US – Gasoline*, n. 88 above, 23.

92 Appellate Body Report, *US – Shrimp*, n. 83 above, paras 164 and 177.

this test. Second, there needs to be rationale behind the discrimination that bears a relationship with and does not go against the objective of the measure provisionally justified by one of the policy goals of Article XX GATT.[93] In the case of the Timber Regulation, there appears to be a rationale that is clearly related to the objective of Articles XX(b) and (g) GATT, although it may be questioned whether this is also the case for Article XX(d) GATT. However, the exceptions to the Timber Regulation's general rule may spark inconsistency with this condition if they differentiate between countries on a basis unrelated to the purpose of the measure.[94] Article 3 of the Timber Regulation considers to have been legally harvested certain timber which either originates in VPA partners and is consistent with the FLEGT Regulation, or timber of species listed in Annex A, B or C to the Wildlife Regulation. The VPAs, in conjunction with the FLEGT Regulation, pursue an objective similar to that of the Timber Regulation.[95] The discrimination is clearly and rationally connected to the relevant policy objectives of Article XX GATT. Therefore, the discrimination results from the fact that the complex issue at hand requires multiple policy instruments at several levels – in CITES, VPAs and the Timber Regulation – in order to be WTO compliant. In this regard, the AB noted that 'certain complex public health or environmental problems may be tackled only with a comprehensive policy comprising a multiplicity of interacting measures'.[96]

The second condition of the chapeau requires that the application of the measure contain 'no disguised restriction on international trade'. This condition means that the measure should not be applied in a disguised discriminatory manner.[97] The same considerations that lead to the decision whether the measure discriminates in an arbitrary or unjustifiable manner may be taken into account in assessing whether it is a disguised restriction on trade.[98] Although factual evidence by a complainant may provide some evidence to suggest the contrary, there is little indication as to how the Timber Regulation could be a disguised barrier to trade.

---

[93] Appellate Body Report, *Brazil – Retreaded Tyres*, n. 42 above, para. 232.

[94] Appellate Body Report, *US – Gasoline*, n. 88 above, 29; Appellate Body Report, *Brazil – Retreaded Tyres*, n. 42 above, paras 227–8.

[95] See, e.g., Voluntary Partnership Agreement between the European Union and the Republic of Cameroon on forest law enforcement, governance and trade in timber and derived products to the European Union (FLEGT), [2011] OJ L 92/4 (Cameroon VPA), Articles 7–10 and Annex II.

[96] Appellate Body Report, *Brazil – Retreaded Tyres*, n. 42 above, para. 151.

[97] Appellate Body Report, *US – Gasoline*, n. 88 above, 25.

[98] Ibid, 23.

4. LESSONS FOR COMPLIANCE WITH WTO RULES

The regulatory approach taken by the EU with the Timber Regulation may well become an important technique to use the EU internal market as leverage for achieving non-trade objectives. This approach hinges upon three crucial elements: (i) ensuring non-discrimination; (ii) demanding the legality of exportation; and (iii) ensuring that the trade-restrictive effects of a particular policy form part of a wider legal framework aimed at comprehensively addressing this non-trade objective. By focusing on these elements, the EU has aimed to draft a Regulation that, even though it may have a negative impact on trade, is still in conformity with the EU's obligations as a Member of the WTO.

The first element is important since by not distinguishing between domestic and imported timber and timber products, the measure accords formally identical treatment. In doing so, the EU has, as far as possible, limited the chances of a '*de jure*' discrimination claim being brought by a WTO Member that claims to suffer from a disparate impact as a result of the Timber Regulation. Nevertheless, there is still a risk of a '*de facto*' claim being filed against the EU. Where a governmental measure modifies the conditions of competition to the detriment of the imported product vis-à-vis the like domestic product, this will result in a finding of less favourable treatment in the sense of Article III:4 GATT. Certain aspects of the Timber Regulation are prone to a challenge from a timber-exporting WTO Member on these grounds. In particular, the due diligence requirements in Article 6 of the Timber Regulation may be challenged if they cause timber operators to opt for domestically produced timber and timber products instead of imported timber. Although the chances of success of such a claim are difficult to predict *in abstracto*, this aspect of the measure potentially results in the violation of a WTO non-discrimination obligation.

Similar considerations apply to the second element of the EU's approach – namely the requirement of proof of legality of the timber or timber products that are to be placed on the internal market. Formally this part of the measure does not prohibit the importation of illegally logged timber. However, because of the way in which the measure has been drafted, the focus is on the requirement that proof of legality of the timber in question has to be provided at any given time. The aim of the drafters seems to have been to ensure that the Timber Regulation is considered as an internal measure applicable to all timber and timber products, regardless of their origin. However, although the measure may have been drafted in this way, some aspects of the measure may still result in it being qualified as a border measure, thereby leading to the applicability of Article XI GATT. This article contains the prohibition on quantitative restrictions or downright prohibitions of imports and exports. In WTO case law this prohibition has been interpreted in a broad manner, meaning that also '*de facto*' restrictions on importation are covered by the provision. Where operators become cautious of importing certain types of timber because of concerns over their legality – even where the timber may turn out to be legally harvested – this may give rise to a *de facto* restriction on importation, leading to a potential violation of Article XI GATT.

Consequently, even considering the lengths to which the EU has gone to avoid violating the core obligations of the WTO, certain aspects of the Timber Regulation might still be in breach of those obligations. This, in turn, highlights the importance of the third element of the EU's regulatory approach: the existence of a comprehensive legal framework of which the Timber Regulation forms part, which may be considered as an indication that the measure 'as such' does not serve a protectionist purpose, but rather is truly aimed at achieving a non-trade objective. This is relevant, especially in the context of the general exceptions contained in Article XX GATT. It is evident that the general policy aim (as distilled from its preamble) of the Timber Regulation falls within the scope of subparagraphs (b) and (g) of this article, for it is designed either to protect plant life or health or is aimed at the conservation of exhaustible natural resources.

In the next part of the analysis, questions such as the availability of less trade-restrictive means to achieve the desired policy objective must be addressed. It is at this stage that the place of the Timber Regulation within the comprehensive framework becomes crucial. The Timber Regulation explicitly allows the placing on the market of timber that has been harvested in accordance with the applicable legislation in the country of harvest or in accordance with the requirements of FLEGT and CITES. Consequently, it is essentially up to the exporting countries themselves to determine what can be harvested and exported. The only requirement the Timber Regulation imposes is that of traceability.

What the EU essentially has done in terms of the Timber Regulation is, in order to avoid violating core trade law obligations, outsourcing the pursuit of a non-trade objective to exporting countries by forcing these countries to, at the very least, consider the importance of sustainable forestry governance. By requiring them to present proof of the legality of harvest, timber-exporting countries are encouraged to create a forestry governance programme. Countries may also opt to join bilateral and multilateral efforts aimed at ensuring forestry conservation, such as

FLEGT (through VPAs) and CITES, in order to obtain proof of legality of the harvested timber. At the same time it is important to recognize what the EU has not done. It has not prohibited the importation of illegally logged timber, as such. The requirement to ensure the legality of the timber prior to placing it on the internal market applies to both imported to domestic timber. It has also not laid down its own technical regulations or standards that would require timber exporters to adhere to certain product criteria in order to be allowed to enter the European market. Therefore, the Timber Regulation appears to be excluded from the scope of applicability of the WTO's TBT Agreement.

By enacting the Timber Regulation in the context of a wider legal framework aimed at sustainable forest governance, the EU appears to have aimed to address a non-trade objective, whilst being mindful of the obligations it has to adhere to under the rules of the WTO. Whether the chosen measure is a WTO-consistent carrot-and-sticks approach is a question that can be answered only after an analysis of all relevant factual circumstances of the WTO Member filing the complaint. What is clear, however, is that the EU has found a way to create an incentive for timber-exporting countries to address the issue of forestry governance in a serious manner. By implementing a system of legality verification and by stipulating that timber will be considered to have been legally harvested if it has been harvested in accordance with the applicable legislation in the country of harvest, the EU seems to have focused on ensuring that timber-exporting countries take enforcement of domestic forestry legislation seriously. Whether this approach lends itself to the pursuit of other non-trade objectives should be the subject of further research.

We are, however, convinced that certain aspects of the Timber Regulation could also be applied to other types of product. One could, for example, imagine that textiles and clothing may be placed on the internal market only if they have been produced in conformity with the laws of the country of manufacture. Although this would not have a direct impact on the substance of these laws or the enforcement thereof, at the very least it would require exporting countries to think critically about labour legislation. Similarly, in the field of fisheries one could imagine a system in which exporting countries are required to prove the legality of the exported fish. In both instances there is no direct interference with the manufacturing countries' legislation and no standards are being exported. However, an incentive for good governance is created by requiring countries to ensure the legality and conformity of products with the laws applicable in their own territory.

5. PRELIMINARY EVIDENCE ON THE EFFECTIVENESS OF THE TIMBER REGULATION

Our assessment of the Timber Regulation is that it is WTO compliant, but what about its effectiveness? Is there a link between this WTO-compliant approach and effectiveness? In what way do the constraints imposed by international trade law (WTO law) force states to opt for measures that, at first sight, appear to be less effective in pursuing certain public goods? At the same time it could be considered that given these constraints – and in the absence of multilateral agreement on how to address the problem of illegal logging – the Timber Regulation is a second-best measure that ultimately aims to address the problem of illegal logging as part of a long-term approach. In this section we present some preliminary findings about the effectiveness of the Regulation. To what extent has it contributed to the goals it sets out to achieve? Are any negative side effects being reported?

Whether the Timber Regulation is considered effective or not inevitably depends on what is considered to be the main goal it aims to achieve. In the broadest sense, it aims to address the problem of illegal logging; consequently one could say that it is a successful measure if there is a decrease in illegal logging on a global scale. However, on a more narrow level, one could consider the Regulation to be effective if it results in a reduction in the importation of illegally logged timber into the EU. Between these two extremes, one could also consider the Regulation as an incentive for timber exporting countries to improve their forest management. In this sense, the aim of the EUTR could be considered more modest, in that what it hopes to achieve is a change in the mindset of those countries. Ultimately this change should result in a reduction in illegal logging, but the intermediate steps towards that goal are equally important. The idea seems to be that, rather than enforcing a particular set of standards upon timber-exporting countries, it is far more effective – in the long run at least – to offer incentives for the sustainable management of forests. Where countries ensure that they set up or implement verification and certification schemes, their access to the European timber market is guaranteed. Seen from this perspective, the Timber Regulation is a tool to foster a form of 'good governance' in timber-exporting countries. As such, it forms part of a broader scheme of 'voluntary standard initiatives and regulatory approaches' that aims to improve forest management at a global level.[99] In this respect, the spread of legality verification to countries such as Indonesia is noteworthy.[100]

Some preliminary reports from the timber industry suggest that the Timber Regulation does indeed have an impact on timber trade. In fact, even before it entered into force in March 2013, it was expected that hardwood plywood manufacturers in Malaysia, Indonesia and certain African countries would see their competitiveness in the EU market increase.[101] Because these countries had already invested heavily in legality verification, forest certification and quality assurance schemes – coupled with the fact that the supply chains in these countries are relatively straightforward – it was expected that imports from these countries would increase. At the same time, it has been reported that imports from non-VPA countries without certified supplies – such as Ivory Coast – would decrease, and that importers turn to other types of timber, sourced in countries which do have proper verification systems in place, such as Cameroon.[102] Similarly, it has been reported that some importers were no longer importing birch plywood and soft plywood made from Russian spruce veneers in China, because of inadequate legality verification procedures which may have been compromised by corruption. As a result of all of these developments, it has been suggested that there would be a consolidation in the EU timber market. Smaller companies, without the capacity to fulfil the due diligence requirements set out in the Timber Regulation were expected to stop importing directly, relying instead on larger European importers with more vertically integrated supply chains.[103] A representative of the Malaysian Timber Council was quoted as stating that 'those [tropical] countries run a higher risk of illegality, an unfounded notion that has caused some purchasers in the EU to demand almost the impossible from tropical

---

[99] Berthold Hansmann, Stefan Essel and Sophie Klose, 'Evaluation of the Interrelation between Voluntary Standard Initiatives and Regulatory Approaches Relevant to Forest Management', in Carsten Schmitz-Hoffmann et al. (eds), *Voluntary Standard Systems – A Contribution to Sustainable Development* (Springer-Verlag, 2014), 179–93.

[100] International Tropical Timber Organization (ITTO), (2014) 18(17) *Tropical Timber Market Report*, 1–15 September, 4.

[101] ITTO, (2013) 17(5) *Tropical Timber Market Report*, 1–15 March, 19.

[102] Ibid, 20.

[103] ITTO, (2013) 17(6) *Tropical Timber Market Report*, 16–31 March, 19; ITTO, (2013) 17(17) *Tropical Timber Market Report*, 1–15 September, 18.

timber supplying countries, in terms of depth and detail of chain of custody and other information'.[104]

Scientific studies suggest similar results. According to one study into the effects of the Timber Regulation on timber imports in the EU and United Kingdom, imports of tropical hardwood are decreasing. However, this study also suggests that these effects may result from ambiguity originating from the changes in the regulatory framework. Substitution and trade diversion may result from this ambiguity.[105] A study carried out at the request of the European Commission sheds further light on the impact of EU consumption patterns on deforestation. It found that 'the impact of the forestry sector on deforestation is relatively small compared to the use of agricultural products'.[106] Of course, this does not allow for any conclusions as to the effectiveness of the Timber Regulation. This finding, however, led the International Tropical Timber Organization (ITTO) to conclude that policy measures that solely target wood trade – such as the Timber Regulation – 'can play little or no role to prevent or slow deforestation', even though they 'may improve environmental and social performance in other areas'.[107]

These preliminary results suggest that the Timber Regulation does indeed have an impact on the international timber market. The question is whether it is the right measure to address the problem of illegal logging. At the same time, one has to question whether there is any real incentive for a timber-exporting country to start WTO proceedings against the EU. In addition to being costly, proceedings before the WTO could easily take up two years, a time frame within which it would be far more effective for countries and timber exporters to create a verification system which, if it complies with the conditions of the Regulation, would simply allow them to export to the EU. For these reasons, even though certain aspects of the Timber Regulation appear to be questionable from an international trade law perspective, the chances of it being challenged by a timber exporting country are slim.

---

[104] ITTO, (2013) 17(18) *Tropical Timber Market Report*, 16–30 September, 19.

[105] Alexandry Giurca, Ragnar Jonsson, Francesca Rinaldi and Hari Priyadi (2013), 'Ambiguity in Timber Trade Regarding Efforts to Combat Illegal Logging: Potential Impacts on Trade between South-East Asia and Europe' (2013) 4 *Forests* 730–50, 740.

[106] European Commission (2013), The Impact of EU Consumption on Deforestation, 190.

[107] ITTO, (2013) 17(18) *Tropical Timber Market Report*, 16–30 September, 21.

12. Reaching out for green policies – national environmental policies in the WTO legal order

Petros C. Mavroidis*

1. THE ISSUE

Members of the World Trade Organization (WTO) retain sovereignty over the design of domestic policies, such as environmental policies, as long as such instruments are not used for protectionist purposes. In regulating their own market, however, nations often influence the behaviour of third parties: a 'demanding' environmental policy will keep goods that do not meet the set standard away from the market. The jurisdictional issue thus becomes important, and yet the WTO does not discuss jurisdictional rules at all. Jurisdictional rules, nevertheless, are central to the effectiveness of any trade agreement. Consider a world consisting of two countries that can trade. Each government has access to one type of domestic policy instrument (taxes) and to one trade instrument (tariffs).[1] Taxes can only be levied on economic activities, such as the production, sale and consumption of goods. Tax policies are perfectly enforceable, so any tax that is levied may also be collected without administrative costs, regardless of where the activity occurs. When setting its policies, each government is concerned only with the interests of its nationals.

Assume, first, that there are absolutely no jurisdictional restrictions on permissible policies.[2] The exact tax/tariff schemes that the countries

* For many helpful comments on previous drafts, I am indebted to Jagdish Bhagwati, Henrik Horn, Rob Howse, Mike Gerrard, Alan O. Sykes and Mark Wu.

1 This example is from Horn and Mavroidis (2008).

2 Economics literature does not pay particular attention to the legal aspects of this issue, although it typically discusses the pros and cons of the extraterritorial application of laws: compare, e.g., Nordhaus (2013), Keith (2013), Hamilton (2013) and, for a more 'pragmatic' discussion, Sabin (2013).

would choose in the absence of any form of policy coordination with other countries would depend on the particular circumstances. Yet since governments have the opportunity to tax any activity occurring in this hypothetical world, they would typically find it profitable to tax foreign as well as domestic activities. What is clear is that, since governments often disregard foreign interests when deciding on their tax schemes, the possibility of taxing foreign activities would introduce beggar-thy-neighbour-like features into the tax schemes. An agreement binding border instruments would in all likelihood have no impact at all, absent jurisdictional rules: in this world, there would be no need to use trade instruments, since the possibility to tax foreign activities directly offers a more attractive means for beggar-thy-neighbour behaviour.

Suppose next that the agreement on tariffs is coupled with a national treatment type of provision that restricts tax treatment of products in the domestic territory. It is hard, in general, to say whether such an agreement would have any impact at all, but the opportunity would still remain to tax activities taking place in the foreign economy. As a result, very little, if anything, would be achieved through this agreement.

As a final case, suppose instead that the agreement on tariffs and quotas is coupled with a jurisdictional rule prohibiting taxation of activities in the foreign country. In contrast to the previous two examples, this agreement is likely to have some impact. Note, however, that the 'trade part' of this agreement is immaterial since the outcome is likely to be the same, even if the bindings of the trade instruments were omitted. This will be the case since, absent restrictions on domestic policies, the importing country can use production subsidies and consumption taxes to mimic trade barriers.[3] In order to ensure that an agreed tariff reduction is meaningful, it must therefore at the very least be accompanied by some form of restriction on the use of domestic policies.

The point we want to make through this abstract reasoning is that the trading rules must be supported by jurisdictional rules in order to have any impact. The trading nations were fully aware of this issue. They attempted to address the 'loophole' in the original contract through the Working Party on Border Tax Adjustments, which we discuss in Section 2. Alas, their efforts were not crowned with success. Section 3 discusses in some detail the case law – which emerges against a background of

---

[3] For instance, a production subsidy (which is a negative tax) and a consumption tax of equal magnitude (levied on the domestic as well as the imported product) can do a perfect job of mimicking a tariff of this magnitude.

absence of agreement on jurisdiction between WTO Members – concerning the jurisdictional ambit of unilaterally defined environmental policies. Section 4 recaps the conclusions.

2. THE DISCIPLINE ON ENVIRONMENTAL POLICIES

2.1 The Law

The GATT[4] leaves discretion over internal (domestic) instruments to its WTO Members, although they are not entirely free to determine them to their liking: WTO Members may unilaterally define their environmental policy, but must apply it in non-discriminatory manner (over all imported and domestic 'like' goods). The GATT is, in this sense, a 'negative integration' scheme in that no common policies are established. Environmental policies must respect these rules.

The GATT also contains in Article XX a loophole out of (at least formally) any other provision in the agreement. For a measure coming within the purview of this provision to be GATT-inconsistent, it must not amount to 'arbitrary or unjustifiable discrimination and/or a disguised restriction on trade'. Standing WTO case law has made it clear that the WTO judge will review only the means used and not the ends pursued (provided, of course, that the ends pursued figure in the list in Article XX GATT).[5] The test for legal consistency differs depending on the objective sought. The measure has to be 'necessary' in order to achieve some of the listed policy objectives, and it can simply 'relate to' the protection of others.

2.2 Jurisdiction (in Public International Law)

The absence of agreement within the WTO does not mean that jurisdiction is not regulated at all. Bargaining solutions can emerge regarding the allocation of jurisdiction. What we care about here, though, are the rules applicable when no bargaining solutions have been included in an

---

4 GATT stands for General Agreement on Tariffs and Trade (adopted 15 April 1994, in force 1 January 1995, 1867 UNTS 187, 33 ILM 1153 (1994), the agreement that regulates trade in goods, and comes within the ambit of the WTO. Grossman, Horn and Mavroidis (2013) discuss the basic features of non-discrimination in the GATT.

5 For confirmation, see Appellate Body Report, *Brazil – Measures Affecting Imports of Retreaded Tyres*, WT/DS332/AB/R, adopted 17 December 2007.

agreement: let us call them the 'default rules' concerning allocation of jurisdiction. There are two bases for prescriptive jurisdiction – territoriality and nationality – which may be summarized as follows:

(a) The rules apply in situations where:
  (i) we are neither in the realm of 'universal jurisdiction' (defined as cases where all nations have right to intervene, e.g. terrorism);
  (ii) nor has a bargaining solution (international agreement) been negotiated.

(b) A state may lawfully exercise prescriptive jurisdiction:[6]
  (i) on all activities occurring in its own territory (territoriality principle);
  (ii) over its nationals, even for acts, omissions committed outside its territory (nationality principle).

2.3 The Hierarchy between Territoriality and Nationality

In the case of an activity occurring in the territory of Home and its 'effects' are felt in the territory of Foreign, or if the effects are spread over different states, all affected states are, in principle, competent to exercise (prescriptive)[7] jurisdiction and regulate the behaviour that is affecting them (effects doctrine). In this case, public international law provides principles (comity) that aim to avoid the cumulative exercise of jurisdiction, whereas bargaining solutions frequently occur as well. In the event of 'conflict' between the two bases conferring jurisdiction,[8] the

---

[6] There are other bases which, exceptionally, might be relevant, such as the passive protective principle, whereby a state may claim jurisdiction on activities occurring outside its jurisdiction *and* aimed at one of its nationals. However, this basis is of no interest for this chapter. By the same token, there is widespread acknowledgement of the protective principle, which enables states to exercise jurisdiction against activity occurring outside its territory aimed at its national security, and there is special jurisdiction for activities occurring aboard vessels, aircraft and spacecraft: neither of these two bases is of direct relevance to this chapter.

[7] As opposed to enforcing their own rules, which they might or might not be in position to do: e.g. what to do against a foreign cartel that has no assets in the market where it practises supra-competitive prices?

[8] Indeed, from early on it has been accepted that states may not regulate in an extraterritorial manner. Viewed from this perspective the (ongoing) discussion on the nature of international law (whereby we distinguish between those that take the view that, absent permissive international rules, no unilateral exercise of

territoriality principle prevails.[9] The hierarchy between territoriality and nationality is well documented. In its often discussed *Lotus*[10] judgment, the Permanent Court of International Justice (PCIJ) said as much:

> Now the first and foremost restriction imposed by international law upon a State is that – failing the existence of a permissive rule to the contrary- it may not exercise its power in any form in the territory of another State. In this sense jurisdiction is certainly territorial; it cannot be exercised by a State outside its territory except by virtue of a permissive rule derived from international custom or from a convention.[11]

The same principle had been adopted earlier by domestic courts. Justice Holmes, for example, proclaimed in the early twentieth century:

> [T]the general and almost universal rule is that the character of an act as lawful or unlawful must be determined wholly by the law of the country where the act is done.[12]

---

jurisdiction is permissible, and those who take the opposite view, that is, that international law can impose limits only to the exercise of unilateral jurisdiction) is futile. No matter what the starting point is, it will inevitably as is the case, at least with respect to many transactions of interest to this chapter, that more than one jurisdiction will, in principle, legitimately believe that they can exercise jurisdiction. See on this point, Dunoff (2005) and Buxbaum (2006).

[9] The interpretation of the term 'conflict' is crucial here and there is asymmetric practice across states on this score: some will interpret it in a very strict manner and understand conflict as a situation where the individual concerned cannot simultaneously comply with the legislation of two (or more) states. Others have adopted a looser standard: this is where the *comity* principle kicks in; some states will weigh their interest to regulate a particular transaction and will give in (to another state), if they judge that another state has more of an interest to regulate, even if the individual concerned could, in theory at least, comply with both regimes.

[10] *France v Turkey*, Judgment No. 9, September 7, 1927, PCIJ Reports, 1928, Series A, No 10.

[11] Ibid., pp. 18–19. On this score, see also Parrish (2007) and Bradley and Goldsmith (2006, pp. 625ff).

[12] See *American Banana Co. v United Fruit Co.* 213 US 347, 356–9 (1909). US courts have recently refused to extend jurisdiction to foreigners challenging the consistency of actions by Swiss companies with US antitrust law: see *F. Hoffman La Roche Ltd v Empagran SA*, 542 US 155, 164 (2004); see, on this score, Klevorick and Sykes (2007).

This does not mean that problems cannot arise: it could be that the penalty imposed by the state that exercises jurisdiction invoking nationality is different from that of the state exercising jurisdiction on territoriality; in such cases, it could be that both states might wish to exercise jurisdiction in a *cumulative* manner. We can use the facts in *Lotus* by way of illustration: a Frenchman shoots from a French vessel (considered to be French territory) and kills a Turkish citizen on Turkish soil; the act takes place in France, its effects are felt in Turkey. The question arises as to who has jurisdiction in such a case? State practice first, and international courts later, have distinguished between *objective* and *subjective* territoriality. The former refers to jurisdiction for any act occurring within the national territory as circumscribed by the geographic frontiers, the effects of which are also felt within this territory. The latter covers cases where the effects of an act occurring *outside* the national geographic frontiers are felt *within* it (cases where there are, in other words, *transboundary effects*). In this latter case, jurisdiction to adjudicate on the transaction is allocated to both Turkey and France, unless they agree either on comity grounds or through an agreement they have signed to defer to one or the other.

2.4 The Effects Doctrine (and its Discontents)

Jurisdiction based Institute's on the effects doctrine is not uncontested. We read, for example, from the American Law prominent restatement of *Foreign Relations Law of the United States* (the *Restatement)*:[13]

> The effects principle is not controversial with respect to acts such as shooting or even sending libelous publications across a boundary. It is generally accepted with respect to liability for injury in the state from products made outside the state and introduced into its stream of commerce. *Controversy has arisen as a result of economic regulation* by the US and others, particularly through competition laws, *on the basis of economic effect in their territory*, when the conduct was lawful where carried out. This Restatement takes the position that a state may exercise jurisdiction based on effects in the state, when the effect or intended effect is substantial and the exercise of jurisdiction is reasonable under § 403.

[13] See *Restatement of the Law, Third, Foreign Relations Law of the United States* (American Law Institute, 1990) p. 238 (emphasis added). The *Restatement* is considered to be an authentic description of international law practice, and it is routinely cited in judgments of the highest courts around the world. It has thus exercised a *de facto* persuasive effect on courts in the United States and around the world.

A threshold issue is the magnitude of the effects that suffice for the effects doctrine to be applicable. The *Restatement* takes the view that, at the very least, a jurisdiction must demonstrate *substantial*, *direct* and *foreseeable* effects upon its territory.[14] Absent similar effects, countries may not legitimately exercise jurisdiction. What exactly 'substantial, direct and foreseeable' means is unclear. The most authoritative guide to their interpretation is state practice and the decisions of international courts, as well as awards of arbitral bodies on this question.

State practice provides us, alas, with incoherent responses: there are states which liberally assert jurisdiction, and states which are more conservative in this respect.[15] The lack of clarity in the default rules is exemplified, for example, in the divergent views of Kramer (1995) and Lowenfeld (1995) regarding the manner in which the US Supreme Court addressed the jurisdictional issue in the highly contentious *Hartford Inc.* case. This provoked the disapproval of the United Kingdom government, which held the view that it alone had the right to prescribe jurisdiction over this particular transaction. State practice, nevertheless, is not always inconsistent: for example, at the time the *Restatement* was written, it is true that there was no unanimity across nations as to the application of the effects doctrine in antitrust issues. The situation is different today, with the application of the effects doctrine by the European Union (EU) and the United States in several high-profile competition cases during the last two decades.[16]

2.5 Overlapping Jurisdictions

It stems from the above that it is quite possible that more than one state may exercise prescriptive jurisdiction by virtue of the territoriality principle. In this case, one can envisage several outcomes.

---

[14] Ibid., pp. 244ff.

[15] For example, the US has often been criticized for its policy in this respect – in the fields of both human rights and international business transactions – for asserting jurisdiction in too liberal a manner: see Lowenfeld (1995).

[16] See the extensive analysis in Mavroidis and Neven (1999), and also Colangelo (2007).

2.5.1 Cumulative application

One possibility is the cumulative application of different legal regimes. There is, strictly speaking, nothing *legally* wrong with assigning jurisdiction concurrently to several sovereignties.[17] For instance, assume that stealing is punished with five years in prison in Home and seven years in Foreign. An individual who is convicted in both jurisdictions could spend two years in Foreign, having already spent five years in Home. However, it is easy to see that assigning jurisdiction to more than one state with divergent laws has potentially serious drawbacks. The fact that courts or administrations in two or more countries will be involved in the decision making will lead to duplication of transaction costs. More importantly perhaps, the outcome of the combined regulation will typically not be optimal from any country's point of view. In the example above, Home might consider the additional two years of jail term excessive. It could also be the case that the party involved is unable to comply simultaneously with two decisions because they are contradictory.

As a consequence of its many drawbacks, the assignment of overlapping jurisdictions is discouraged, although the cumulative application of regulations does occur quite often in practice.

2.5.2 Comity

A second possibility is that all but one state refrain from exercising jurisdiction, a solution that is often referred to as *comity*. This is most likely the case in situations where there is agreement that one state clearly has more of an interest to regulate a particular transaction or activity than other states which could also have legitimately exercised prescriptive jurisdiction; the *Restatement* expresses support for this option.[18] Reasonable exercise of jurisdiction will also be called for when the effects of an activity are 'felt' across various territories; the *Restatement* acknowledges as much.[19] It is not easy though, to codify what should be considered reasonable exercise of prescriptive jurisdiction. Roughly, under a 'reasonableness standard' states will either – through unilateral action (comity) or through a negotiated settlement – conclude that some of them should not exercise jurisdiction over a particular transaction and let others do so. Considerations comprise, *but are not necessarily limited to*, the following:[20]

---

17 This was largely the solution in the often discussed *Lotus* judgment by the PCIJ: *France v Turkey*, n. 10 above.

18 Ibid., p. 247.

19 Ibid., p. 250.

20 Ibid., pp. 244ff.

(i) the link of the activity with another state (nationality or territoriality, in the sense that there are *direct, substantial and foreseeable* effects with another jurisdiction);
(ii) the importance of regulating the activity to another state;
(iii) the existence of justified (legitimate) expectations;
(iv) the importance of the regulation to the international system;
(v) the manner in which such transactions have been prescribed in prior relevant state practice.

The *Restatement* also provides an example of what could be considered an unreasonable exercise of jurisdiction:

> … regulation by the United States of the labor relations of a foreign vessel that regularly calls on the United States may be unreasonable; regulation of the vessel's safety standards may not be unreasonable.[21]

The intuition here seems to be that, absent respect for strict safety standards on the foreign vessel, an accident might occur in US territory, or an environmental hazard that might have an impact (on US territory as well). The link with the US territory seems less strong where, for example, workers on the foreign vessel receive wages below the statutory minimum reserved for the corresponding job when performed on US territory by workers legally employed in the US.[22] As suggested above, a field (for example, antitrust)-specific evaluation is warranted given that practice has developed in asymmetric manner across fields.[23] Comity happens quite rarely in practice, however, because there is often disagreement as to which state should be the one designated to regulate. Take the example of an international merger between companies originating in Home and Foreign. Assume that 30 per cent of their sales are in the market of Home, 25 per cent in Foreign, 35 per cent in Third, and 10 per

---

[21] Ibid., p. 246.

[22] This is a very interesting example. We will return to it when we discuss the applicability of our discussion here to environmental disputes.

[23] One probable explanation is that, whereas there is an emerging worldwide consensus as to what should be the criteria for antitrust intervention, this is hardly the case in other fields of regulatory activity. Most competition regimes understand the role of antitrust as the means to promote rivalry in a given market, using consumer welfare as proxy to measure whether rivalry indeed exists. This quasi-uniformity concerning the substantive criteria for antitrust intervention probably explains the worldwide acceptance of the *effects* doctrine in this field: after all, the importing state is the one that suffers (in consumer welfare terms) from, say, monopolistic prices of a foreign cartel.

cent in Fourth. Should Third and Fourth desist simply because Home and Foreign companies are foreign, or should Third exercise jurisdiction, being the country with the largest sales? How should the antitrust authorities of Home and Foreign behave? Should both Home and Foreign regulate this transaction? Should one of them desist and, if yes, on what grounds should it desist? What if the new merged entity will have a monopoly in Foreign, but no such thing in Home?

2.5.3 Bargaining solutions

The third possible solution in the case of overlapping jurisdictions is an international agreement. For instance, the *Restatement* points to this option:

> When neither state has a clearly strong interest, states often attempt to eliminate the conflict so as to reduce international friction and avoid putting those who are the object of the regulations in a difficult situation.[24]

When two states search for a bargaining solution to address a jurisdictional ambiguity, they can allocate jurisdiction between them to their liking, to the extent that they do not interfere with the jurisdictional space of a third state.

Parrish (2009) points out that there has been an explosion of extraterritorial cases in copyright, securities regulation, trademarks and trade names, intellectual property, corporate law and governance, bankruptcy, tax, criminal law, civil rights and labour laws,[25] which has not been accompanied by a clarification of the legal framework within which prescriptive jurisdiction should operate. The discussion so far points to an elaborate framework regarding the allocation of jurisdiction in public international law, which, nonetheless, does not always allocate jurisdiction to one sovereignty.

---

[24] *Restatement*, n. 13 above, p. 247.

[25] There is abundant literature on this issue: Vagts (2003), Avi-Yonah (2003) and Baumgartner (2004) provide a very adequate synthesis.

3. INTO THE WTO RING: WHO CAN DO WHAT?

3.1 Commercial and Environmental Externalities

The WTO Agreement[26] was not created in a legal vacuum. The only reasonable interpretation is that countries, when signing the Agreement, did so with the expectation that the default rules indeed are applicable. Otherwise, important institutions (like national treatment, as we noted above) could not be meaningfully applied. Two types of externality arise when national policies are applied:

- (negative) commercial externalities arise when lax environmental policies in the exporting country provide its exporters with a competitive advantage at the perceived expense of the government of the importing country;
- 'physical' transboundary externalities arise from lax environmental policies and might take the form of, say, acid rain.

They should not be treated in the same way. The fundamental reason for arguing for differential treatment goes back to the basic purpose of the agreement. The GATT/WTO is an agreement to regulate commercial relations between WTO Members. Hence, WTO Members should be assumed to have accepted the resulting commercial externalities from unilaterally pursued policies, to the extent these are not caught by the non-discrimination provisions. As a result, the default rules do not apply in the case of commercial externalities. In particular, the effects doctrine cannot be invoked to give a country the right to regulate against such an effect.

The WTO is not meant to regulate physical environmental externalities, however, and therefore it cannot be argued that WTO Members have agreed to accept transboundary physical externalities. Consequently, in the absence of other agreements – MEAs, for instance – the default rules apply and should allow affected WTO Members to react. The very purpose of the GATT is to harmonize conditions of competition *within* and not *across* markets. Societies make different choices as to the level of taxation, the level of environmental protection, the level of antitrust enforcement, and so on. All such choices affect trade, even if only

---

[26] Agreement Establishing the World Trade Organization, Marrakesh (Morocco), adopted 15 April 1994, in force 1 January 1995, 1867 UNTS 154, 33 ILM 1143 (1994).

remotely so. By signing the GATT (and then the WTO), trading partners have accepted that they will conduct trade on the basis of such differences. When they wanted to address some of them, they did so explicitly: the antidumping provisions are a very appropriate illustration here. Nonetheless, this does not mean that whenever there is silence there is acceptance of the other's practices. This is precisely where the default rules kick in: Article XX GATT explicitly allows WTO Members to deviate from their obligations in order to protect, *inter alia*, animal life. To do that, however, they must have jurisdiction over such animal life. In the same way that WTO Members cannot tax income of foreigners made abroad, they cannot, in principle, protect foreign animal life. To do that, they must show a nexus with their own jurisdiction (for example, that a change in the ecological equilibrium affects all nations). To accept the opposite would lead us to absurd results such as Home taxing the income of Foreign nationals made in Foreign. In a nutshell, unless the default rules have been observed, the GATT cannot function, at the very least not in accordance with its intended function – that is, as an instrument to promote trade liberalization through negative integration. All this should be considered settled. Why however, did not the trading nations try to address jurisdictional issues when they realized how their actions could affect others? They did. Although not the central focus of the exercise, the Working Party (WP) on Border Tax Adjustments (BTA) did *de facto* address the issue of jurisdictional ambit.

3.2 The Working Party on Border Tax Adjustments

Paragraph 4 of the report of the WP on BTA defines 'border tax adjustments' as:[27]

> any fiscal measures which put into effect, in whole or in part, the destination principle (i.e. which enable exported products to be relieved of some or all of the tax charged in the exporting country in respect of similar domestic products sold to consumers on the home market and which enable imported products sold to consumers to be charged with some or all of the tax charged in the importing country in respect of similar domestic products.)[28,29]

---

[27] GATT Working Party Report, *Border Tax Adjustments*, L/3464, adopted 2 December 1970, BISD 18S/97 (WPBTA Report). This was the agreed definition at the time the report was being negotiated. Since, as we have argued in Horn and Mavroidis (2010), this report should be understood as a *decision* by the GATT contracting parties, it is part of the GATT 1994 – i.e. an agreed definition.

[28] The *destination* principle was taken over from bilateral agreements negotiated in the 1930s, such as the agreement of 6 May 1936 between the United

The WP was established following a request by the US. In the 1960s and 1970s, there was considerable concern in the US about the impact of European indirect taxes, such as value added taxes (VAT) on international trade. European economies were becoming more competitive in this period, and the US felt this was the case because its tax system (indirect taxation) allowed them to profit from tax havens around the world. The narrow question before the WP regarded the GATT consistency of practices by the GATT contracting parties where the customs tariff was adjusted by the amount of an internal tax already imposed on domestic production. The wider issue was the perceived imbalance regarding the attitude of the GATT towards direct and indirect taxation. The WP report reflects agreement on some measures and disagreement on many others. The extent of the agreement is reflected in the following paragraph:

> The Working Party concluded that there was convergence of views to the effect that taxes directly levied on products were eligible for tax adjustment. Examples of such taxes comprised specific excise duties, sales taxes and cascade taxes and the tax on value added. It was agreed that the TVA, regardless of its technical construction (fractioned collection), was equivalent in this respect to a tax levied directly – a retail or sales tax. Furthermore, the Working Party concluded that there was convergence of views to the effect that certain taxes that were not directly levied on products were not eligible for tax adjustment. Examples of such taxes comprised social security charges whether on employers or employees and payroll taxes.[30]

Security charges, as well as payroll taxes, thus escape the purview of Article III GATT, in the sense that the importing state (Foreign) could not, for example, raise the level of payroll taxes applied by the exporter (Home) to its own. By the same token, Home (if its payroll taxes were lower) could not adjust them to the level of Foreign when exporting there. There was a divergence of views regarding the eligibility for

---

States and France: see WPBTA Report, ibid., Annex, § 10. See also Irwin, Mavroidis and Sykes (2008).

[29] Some discussion regarding precisely which taxes should come within the purview of Article III GATT had already occurred even during the negotiation stage. At the Havana Conference, for example, the following view was reflected: '[N]either income taxes nor import duties fall within the scope of Art 18 (of the Havana Charter – Art III of the GATT) which is concerned solely with internal taxes on goods': WPBTA Report, ibid., Annex, § 12. These were the words of the UK delegate, one of the key delegations in the drafting of Article III GATT: see Irwin, Mavroidis and Sykes (2008) and the corresponding discussion on 'property rights on the GATT'.

[30] WPBTA Report, n. 27 above, § 14.

adjustment of 'taxes occultes' and some other taxes, such as property taxes. The scarcity of complaints with respect to either of these two taxes, however, persuaded negotiators to stop discussing them any further:[31]

> The Working Party noted that there was a divergence of views with regard to the eligibility for adjustment of certain categories of tax and that these could be subdivided into:
>
> (a) 'Taxes occultes', which the OECD defined as consumption taxes on capital equipment, auxiliary materials and services used in the transportation and production of other taxable goods. Taxes on advertising, energy, machinery and transport were among the more important taxes which might be involved. It appeared that adjustment was not normally made for taxes occultes except in countries having a cascade tax;
> (b) Certain other taxes, such as property taxes, stamp duties and registration duties … which are not generally considered eligible for tax adjustment. Most countries do not make adjustments for such taxes, but a few do as a few do for the payroll taxes and employers' social security charges referred to in the last sentence of paragraph 14.
>
> It was generally felt that while this area of taxation was unclear, its importance – as indicated by the scarcity of complaints reported in connexion with adjustment of taxes occultes – was not such as to justify further examination.

Finally, there was agreement between negotiators that some taxes, such as 'cascade taxes',[32] were eligible for adjustment, though the modalities for adjusting them were not clear:[33]

> The Working Party noted that there were some taxes which, while generally considered eligible for adjustment, presented a problem because of the difficulty in some cases of calculating exactly the amount of compensation. Examples of such difficulties were encountered in cascade taxes. For adjustment, countries operating cascade systems usually resorted to calculating average rates of rebate for categories of products rather than calculating the actual tax levied on a particular product. It was noted, however, that most cascade tax systems were to be replaced by TVA systems, and that therefore the area in which such problems occurred was diminishing. Other examples included composite goods which, on export, contained ingredients for which the Working Party agreed in principle it was administratively sensible and sufficiently accurate to rebate by average rates for a given class of goods.

---

[31] Ibid., § 15.

[32] A cascade tax is a turnover tax which is applied at every stage of the production process.

[33] WPBTA Report, n. 27 above, § 16.

The preceding analysis supports the conclusion that the WP on BTAs did not manage to resolve all ambiguities and disagreements regarding tax adjustability. Disagreements between trading partners regarding similar issues continued to persist and some of them found their way into GATT/WTO adjudication. Notoriously, the US subsequently enacted legislation on the Domestic International Sales Corporation (DISC) and the Foreign Sales Corporation (FSC),[34] both of which were condemned, the first by a GATT Panel, the second by a WTO Panel and the Appellate Body (AB).[35] Nevertheless, there was agreement in the WP concerning at least some of the taxes. It is unclear whether the final report should be regarded as a decision by the Contracting Parties, and thus comes under the purview of Art. 1(b)(iv) GATT 1994, or whether it is part of the GATT acquis, and thus comes within the purview of Article XVI of the Agreement Establishing the WTO.[36] No matter how it is classified, the WP report will have legal significance: if it comes under the former it should be regarded as binding on all WTO Members, whereas if it comes under the latter it should be regarded as creating legitimate expectations that WTO practice will be guided by it. It seems that the better arguments lie with the view that the WP report should come under Article 1(b)(iv) GATT 1994. After all, the WP was not convened to adjudicate a dispute between two GATT contracting parties; it was asked to discuss the treatment of tax adjustments in general. In subsequent practice, a number of WTO Panel and AB reports have referred to this report, without classifying it either as part and parcel of Article 1(b)(iv) GATT 1994 or under Article XVI WTO Agreement.[37,38]

---

[34] The FSC dispute is the 'successor' dispute to the DISC dispute. US – DISC, its GATT predecessor, was adjudicated during the GATT years. At stake was US tax legislation on Domestic International Sales Corporations. In brief, a US company that qualified as a DISC company would not be subjected to US federal income tax on its current or retained export earnings. Following a complaint, the Panel found that the US tax legislation constituted an export subsidy and was thus inconsistent with Article XVI GATT: see GATT Docs BISD 23S/98 and 28S/114. See also the very thorough analysis of the case by Jackson (1978).

[35] On the overall stance of adjudicating bodies with respect to BTAs, see Bhagwati and Mavroidis (2007) and Demaret and Stewardson (1994).

[36] For a detailed discussion of this issue, see Mavroidis (2008).

[37] See, e.g., Panel Report, *Japan – Taxes on Alcoholic Beverages*, WT/DS8/R, WT/DS10/R, WT/DS11/R, adopted 1 November 1996; and Appellate Body Report, *Japan – Taxes on Alcoholic Beverages*, WT/DS8/AB/R, WT/DS10/AB/R, WT/DS11/AB/R, adopted 1 November 1996.

3.3 Jurisdictional Issues in GATT Case Law

The preceding analysis points to a narrow agreement regarding jurisdiction in the GATT/WTO. Against this background, how have Panels dealt with jurisdictional issues brought before them? We turn to this issue in what follows.

3.3.1 *US – Canadian Tuna*[39]

This dispute, which is the closest we have got to discuss jurisdictional issues in the GATT/WTO dispute settlement practice, has been surprisingly overlooked in literature. Canadian authorities seized US vessels and arrested US fishermen who were fishing within the 200 miles of the Canadian coast.[40] In response, the US government, as per section 205 of the US Fishery Conservation & Management Act (1976), blocked all imports of Canadian albacore tuna into its market. Canada and the US consulted, without success, and Canada submitted its dispute to a Panel. Subsequently, agreement was reached whereby the US government agreed to lift the embargo. The Canadian government, nonetheless, did not wish to suspend the Panel's proceedings. In its view, the very existence of section 205 constituted enough of a threat that similar behaviour could be repeated in the future; it thus requested the Panel to continue its proceedings and judge whether the US measure based on section 205 was not GATT-inconsistent.[41]

The Canadian claim was that the US measure violated, *inter alia*, Article XI GATT. The US government sought to justify its measure by invoking Article XX(g) GATT, arguing that its measures sought to

---

[38] Grossman (1980) examined to what extent indirect taxes, like the VAT, were origin-neutral. He asserted the trade neutrality of uniform indirect taxes under both the origin and destination principles, and re-examined their validity in the context of a world with trade in intermediate goods. He showed that a uniform general sales tax is trade-neutral under the destination principle, but trade-distorting under the origin principle; a 'stage of processing' value added tax is non-distorting under either border tax adjustment principle.

[39] GATT Panel Report, United States – Prohibition of Imports of Tuna and Tuna Products from Canada, L/5198, adopted 22 February 1982, BISD 29S/91.

[40] According to customary international law, codified in the Convention on the Law of the Sea (UNCLOS III), the 200-mile zone signals the exclusive economic zone that foreign countries may not exploit without the consent of the coastal state having right to it.

[41] The Panel should have adjudicated this as an 'as such' claim – that is, as a claim against the US statute itself and not against the measure that it gave rise to, since the measure ceased to exist before the Panel was established.

conserve an exhaustible natural resource. Canada did not dispute that tuna was an exhaustible natural resource, but argued that the US measures at hand had not been aimed at conserving tuna. They were meant rather to be a response to the seizure of US fishing boats by Canadian authorities, since the US government and another (un-named) state were the only two states which did not recognize the 200-mile Exclusive Economic Zone (EEZ) that every other nation member of the UN system recognized as conferring exclusive economic rights to the coastal state.

On paper, it seems that this Panel would unavoidably have been led to address the jurisdictional issue – that is, whether the GATT allows a country to regulate a common resource outside its border. Yet it declined to do so. It found the US measure to be in violation of Article XX(g) GATT in that the US government had taken no accompanying measures with the aim of restricting the fishing of albacore tuna by US fishermen. The Panel emphasized that its findings were intended to address the trade issue only, and that they should not be understood as an attempt to also discuss the fisheries issue (which also involved a jurisdictional issue).[42]

3.3.2 *US – Tuna (Mexico)*[43]

In this case, the US banned imports of tuna originating in Mexico on the ground that its production process did not conform to the US process. By not using special (purse seine) nets, Mexican fishermen were accidentally taking the life of, for US standards, an unacceptably large number of dolphins. The jurisdictional issue here could be described as follows. Through its regulation of the conditions of sale for tuna to its own market, the US government imposed a production process requirement not only on domestic fishermen but also on Mexican fishermen. The US was hence *de facto* regulating a production process with which Mexican fishermen had to comply if they wished to export to the US market. Mexico did not attack the right of the US government to regulate this transaction; it challenged the consistency of the US measure with Article XI GATT on the basis that the US had imposed an import ban. The US government did not present any arguments to rebut the claim that Article XI GATT had been violated. Instead, it sought justification of its measures under Article XX(b) GATT, which allows WTO Members to

---

[42] GATT Panel Report, *US – Canadian Tuna*, n. 39 above, § 4.16.

[43] GATT Panel Report, United States – Restrictions on Imports of Tuna, DS21/R, DS21/R, 3 September 1991, unadopted, BISD 39S/155.

justify violations of the GATT if they can demonstrate that their measure is necessary to protect human, animal or plant life or health.

The Panel did not put into question the need, as perceived by the US government, to regulate the fishing of tuna in order to save dolphins. The Panel rejected, nonetheless, the particular way in which the fishing regulation was passed. In the Panel's view, the US government had no basis to act *unilaterally* in this context. In the Panel's thinking, were WTO Members to be allowed to act unilaterally, the result would be a world where a plethora of national regulations would make it quite onerous to trade. Hence, in this Panel's view, any unilaterally defined environmental policy is GATT-inconsistent, precisely because it has been unilaterally (as opposed to multilaterally) defined.

3.3.3 *US – Tuna (EEC)*[44]

The facts of this case are strikingly similar to those in *US – Tuna (Mexico)*. The only difference is that in this case the US measure was applied to intermediary nations that were importing only to re-export tuna fished in an environmentally unfriendly manner. The European Community (EC) and the Netherlands (on behalf of the Netherlands Antilles) challenged the consistency of the US measure and prevailed on the same grounds as Mexico did in the case described immediately above.

3.4 WTO Case Law

We will distinguish between cases which directly concern disputes over the use of environmental protection, and cases which concern disputes over the use of domestic instruments other than environmental policies. However, since all domestic instruments (environmental included) fall within the same legal discipline (Article III GATT), the WTO jurisprudence under this provision is at least potentially relevant to environmental disputes. There are four cases within the former class: *US – Gasoline*, *US – Shrimp*, *EC – Approval and Marketing of Biotech Products*, and *Brazil – Re-treaded Tyres*.

[44] GATT Panel Report, United States – Restrictions on Imports of Tuna, DS29/R, 16 June 1994, unadopted.

3.4.1 *US – Gasoline*[45]

This case concerned a US measure which provided for different methodologies to be applied to domestic and foreign products in order to calculate the composition and emission effects of gasoline products sold in the US market. The US alleged that the rationale for the law was the protection of the environment. The Panel and the AB first determined that environmental protection came within the ambit of Article III GATT (more recently, the Panel report on *EC – Approval and Marketing of Biotech Products* has confirmed this view – see 3.4.3 below). They then found the measure to be inconsistent with the GATT because of its discriminatory aspect (different methodologies), and that it could not be justified through recourse to Article XX GATT. In the AB's view, the measure at hand amounted to a disguised restriction on trade. The AB also held that the US had failed to consider the costs involved for the complainants to comply with the regulation, and that it should have sought a bargaining solution instead of unilaterally imposing its policies in this context.

The jurisdictional issue could be described as follows. The US maintained that it had the right to regulate the conditions under which gasoline products would be sold within its territory in that environmental externalities in the production of gasoline products abroad could affect also its territory, assuming that the said externalities were of transboundary nature. The US thus exercised its prescriptive jurisdiction to this effect. The complainants argued that the US legislation was discriminatory in that it was introducing two different baselines to calculate the pollution created by activities undertaken domestically and in the foreign territory. The complainants prevailed under Article III GATT. Neither the Panel nor the AB addressed the jurisdictional issue at all. The AB, nonetheless, emphasized the relevance of public international law for adjudication in the WTO.

3.4.2 *US – Shrimp*[46]

The facts in this case are also strikingly similar to those in *US – Tuna (Mexico)* (3.3.2. above). The difference is that the products concerned

---

[45] Panel Report, United States – Standards for Reformulated and Conventional Gasoline, WT/DS2/R, adopted 20 May 1996; Appellate Body Report, United States – Standards for Reformulated and Conventional Gasoline, WT/DS2/AB/R, adopted 20 May 1996.

[46] Panel Report, United States – Import Prohibition of Certain Shrimp and Shrimp Products, WT/DS58/R and Corr.1, adopted 6 November 1998; Appellate

were shrimps and sea turtles rather than tuna and dolphins.[47] The US government had adopted a statute whereby sales of shrimps in the US market were conditioned upon the prior demonstration that a particular production process had been followed, which restricted the number of sea turtles that were accidentally being caught.[48]

The jurisdictional issue is the same as that in *US – Tuna (Mexico)*. The US government was regulating access to its territory (market) only, but imposed obligations on two sets of nationals, domestic and foreign, effectively regulating a production process that foreigners had to observe, assuming they had an interest in exporting to the US market. The Panel and the AB reached opposite conclusions on the substance of the dispute. We will reflect only the latter, since the AB has the legal power to overturn a Panel's findings.[49] The AB decision is a sea change when viewed against the background of the Panel report on *US – Tuna (Mexico)*. In an oft-quoted passage, reproduced below, the AB held that the US government had the right to unilaterally define its environmental policy, provided that it observed the statutory requirements reflected in the GATT (on this occasion, the requirements embedded in Article XX(g) GATT – that the challenged measure related to the conservation of exhaustible natural resources and was applied in a non-discriminatory manner). In other words, in the absence of transfer of sovereignty to the international plane, WTO Members remain free to regulate their market unilaterally, provided that they respect the relevant GATT disciplines.[50] This case law has been consistently reproduced ever since.[51] As a result,

---

Body Report, United States – Import Prohibition of Certain Shrimp and Shrimp Products, WT/DS58/AB/R, adopted 6 November 1998.

47 See Howse and Neven (2007) for an economic-*cum*-legal of core features of this dispute, and Howse and Regan (2000) and Howse (2002) for discussion of, e.g., jurisdictional aspects.

48 The US fishermen were using turtle excluding devices (TEDs), a rather cheap device that allows sea turtles to swim out in the event that they are caught. Initially, the US government requested that all foreign traders wishing to sell to the US market should demonstrate that their traded shrimps were fished using TEDs. Following multilateral rulings to this effect, the US government then accepted that not only TEDs, but any device of comparable efficiency, could be legitimately employed.

49 See WTO, Understanding on Rules and Procedures Governing the Settlement of Disputes (DSU), Article 17.13.

50 Appellate Body Report, *US – Shrimp*, n. 46 above, § 121.

51 See, e.g., Appellate Body Report, *United States – Import Prohibition of Certain Shrimp and Shrimp Products – Recourse to Article 21.5 of the DSU by Malaysia*, WT/DS58/AB/RW, adopted 21 November 2001 in §§ 137–8.

it is now uncontested, as a matter of jurisprudential finding, that Article XX GATT condones regulatory diversity.

Having established the right of the US government to regulate this transaction in a unilateral manner, the AB went on to find that, while the US measure was necessary in the sense of Article XX GATT, it was being applied in a discriminatory manner and thus violated the chapeau of this provision. Following corrective measures, the US government was eventually exonerated from all liability under the multilateral rules. The AB did not pronounce on the jurisdictional reach of the US measure. The reason why this issue did not come up was probably because the measure was allegedly designed to protect sea turtles, which migrate through US waters. The AB found that there was 'sufficient nexus' between the US interest to regulate and the litigated transaction:

> We do not pass upon the question of whether there is an implied jurisdictional limitation in Article XX(g), and if so, the nature or extent of that limitation. We note only that in the specific circumstances of the case before us, there is a sufficient nexus between the migratory and endangered marine populations involved and the United States for purposes of Article XX(g).[52]

The legal implications of this important passage are not entirely clear. One possible reading is that the AB effectively held that the killing of sea turtles by, for example, Malaysian shrimp fishermen physically affected the US environment by reducing the turtle population in the US.

3.4.3 *EC – Approval and Marketing of Biotech Products*[53]

This Panel Report confirmed that environmental policies come within the ambit of Article III GATT. It also dealt with the legal impact of multilateral trade agreements (MEAs) in the WTO legal order. The issue before the Panel was whether the EC regime for approval of genetically modified organisms (GMOs) was consistent with a number of provisions of the GATT and the SPS Agreement.[54] The EC had argued that its system of approval was, *inter alia*, necessary to protect the environment. The Panel agreed that similar policies come within the purview of Article III GATT. The EC had also argued that its challenged measures were fully justified by the Cartagena Protocol on Biosafety, an instrument

---

52 Appellate Body Report, *US – Shrimp*, n. 46 above, § 134.

53 Panel Reports, European Communities – Measures Affecting the Approval and Marketing of Biotech Products, WT/DS291/R/WT/DS292/R/WT/DS293/R, Add.1 to Add.9, and Corr.1, adopted 21 November 2006.

54 WTO, Agreement on the Application of Sanitary and Phytosanitary Measures.

which had been ratified by 142 states. The Panel took the view that since the totality of WTO Members had not ratified this instrument, it was legally irrelevant. This report was not appealed against so the AB had no opportunity to pronounce on this aspect.[55]

3.4.4 *Brazil – Retreaded Tyres*[56]

This is the most recent case to deal with environmental protection. Brazil imposed an import embargo on retreaded tyres, but not on new tyres. The argument for the differential treatment was that retreaded tyres have a shorter life span than new tyres and, consequently, represent more of an environmental concern. On the other hand, the embargo on retreaded tyres was not non-discriminatory. Brazil accepted retreaded tyres from its MERCOSUR partners. The Panel criticized Brazil on the ground that its environmental policy did not respect the chapeau of Article XX GATT, holding that the Brazilian measure amounted to a disguised restriction on trade (and thus violated the requirements of the chapeau of Article XX GATT). The AB, while modifying some of the conclusions, essentially upheld this finding. However, neither the Panel nor the AB discussed the permissibility of the jurisdictional reach of the Brazilian measure. This is less of a concern compared with other cases as the environmental externality that Brazil claimed to be regulating would be borne, in all likelihood, by Brazil alone.

3.4.5 *EC – Asbestos*[57]

Based on scientific evidence, France enacted legislation banning sales into its market of construction material that contained asbestos. Canada challenged the consistency of the measure with Article III GATT. In its view, asbestos-containing and asbestos-free construction material should be awarded the same regulatory treatment since they are like products. The Panel agreed with Canada that the contested measure violated Article

---

[55] Mavroidis (2008), however, looking at the manner in which WTO adjudicating bodies have been looking on extra-WTO law, takes a pessimistic view on this score, arguing that the overall record of the AB shows a tendency to close the door to extra-WTO law rather than to open it.

[56] Panel Report, Brazil – Measures Affecting Imports of Retreaded Tyres, WT/DS332/R, adopted 17 December 2007; Appellate Body Report, Brazil – Retreaded Tyres, WWT/DS332/AB/R, adopted 17 December 2007.

[57] Panel Report, European Communities – Measures Affecting Asbestos and Asbestos-Containing Products, WT/DS135/R and Add.1, adopted 5 April 2001; Appellate Body Report, European Communities – Measures Affecting Asbestos and Asbestos-Containing Products, WT/DS135/AB/R, adopted 5 April 2001.

III GATT, but exonerated it under Article XX GATT as being necessary to protect human life. The AB overturned the Panel's findings and held that France's measures were consistent with Article III GATT. In its view, 'reasonable consumers', if presented with a choice between the two types of product, would not view them as 'like' because of the health hazard to which the product containing asbestos gave rise. Since the two products were unlike, there could be no violation of Article III GATT.[58] The 'reasonable consumer' is a fictitious person who is endowed with what the AB sees as 'reasonable' preferences.[59] Some observers have interpreted the *EC – Asbestos* ruling as opening the door to a wider interpretation whereby consumer preferences are decisive, regardless of whether the perceived differences are reflected in the physical properties of the product.[60,61]

The jurisdictional issue in *EC – Asbestos* could be described as follows. France, by imposing the sales ban on asbestos-containing construction material, regulates the *effect* of the consumption of such material in its domestic market. At the same time, it indirectly regulates the production in Canada, forcing Canadian producers to reduce or redirect some of their production. To see that there is a jurisdictional issue involved here, note that France could have achieved the same (or at least a similar) outcome by regulating production in Canada rather than consumption in France. Since economically the outcomes are about the same, and the regulation of Canadian producers clearly involves a jurisdictional issue, so also implicitly does the regulation of consumption in France. Yet, once again, in the absence of specific claims to this effect, neither the Panel nor the AB explicitly addressed the jurisdictional issue.

3.4.6 *EC – Tariff Preferences*[62]

The EC provided Pakistani textiles exports with preferences in addition to those granted to Indian exporters under its Generalised System of

---

[58] See Horn and Weiler (2007) for a critical discussion, not of the outcome of the dispute, but of the adjudicating bodies' reasoning in arriving there.

[59] In many civil law countries a similar construction exists.

[60] It seems likely that consumer preferences are less decisive in cases adjudicated under the SPS Agreement.

[61] It should be noted, nonetheless, that the AB did not have any empirical evidence before it. It should also be noted that it requested none.

[62] Panel Report, European Communities – Conditions for the Granting of Tariff Preferences to Developing Countries, WT/DS246/R, adopted 20 April 2004; Appellate Body Report, European Communities – Conditions for the Granting of Tariff Preferences to Developing Countries, WT/DS246/AB/R, adopted 20 April 2004.

Preferences (GSP). Overruling the Panel, the AB found nothing wrong with the EC scheme, provided that it was relying on *objective criteria*. The term 'objective criteria' was not defined by the AB.[63] The EC policy, of course, affected production choices in Pakistan, but the AB did not even ask whether this aspect of the EC measure could be considered as extraterritorial.

4. CONCLUDING REMARKS

The case law discussed above could be summarized as follows:

(a) Cases where a WTO Member aims to redress a situation that will occur in its market if importation takes place (a local consumption hazard): *EC – Asbestos, EC – Approval and Marketing of Biotech Products, Brazil – Retreaded Tyres*.
(b) Cases where a WTO Member aims to redress a situation that has occurred outside its territory – that is, in the territory of the exporting state – but which affects the complainant state (a trans-boundary production externality): *US – Tuna (Mexico), US – Tuna (EEC), US – Canadian Tuna, US – Shrimp, US – Gasoline*.
(c) Cases where a WTO Member aims to redress a situation that, prima facie at least, is not linked to either a production or a consumption externality: in this vein, a WTO Member aims to compensate those trading partners that, in its view, adopt sound policies by contributing (through preferential tariffs) to the costs that such policies might entail: *EC – Tariff Preferences*.

In none of the cases presented above did the complainant raise any jurisdictional claims. In the absence of specific claims to this effect, Panels did not address this issue either. At least implicitly, they have accepted that when the WTO Member was regulating access to its market, it was lawfully exercising jurisdiction. The absence of claims concerning jurisdiction naturally raises the question whether Panels could examine the jurisdictional reach of a WTO Member's measures *ex officio* – that is, even in the absence of a specific claim to this effect. WTO Panels are not keen to address issues that have not been explicitly referred to them; nor are they likely to tinker light-heartedly with domestic policies, especially if they are considered 'sensitive' issues in

[63] Grossman and Sykes (2005) are also critical of the fact that the AB did not interpret this term any further.

the form of important societal choices: since *EC – Asbestos* the AB has consistently held this line. This would lead us to the view that, not only in cases where physical (environmental) externalities are at stake, but also when 'moral' externalities (for example, disapproval by Home of Foreign's environmental attitude and corresponding action, even if the environmental hazard is local in Foreign and not transboundary) have provided the basis for regulatory intervention, Panels might be willing to defer to non-discriminatory measures.

BIBLIOGRAPHY

Avi-Yonah, Ruben (2003), 'National Regulation of Multinational Enterprises: an Essay on Comity, Extraterritoriality and Harmonization', *Columbia Journal of Transnational Law*, **5**: 17–57.

Baumgartner, Samuel P. (2004), 'Is Transnational Litigation Different?', *University of Pennsylvania Journal of International Economic Law*, **25**: 1297–381.

Bhagwati, Jagdish and Petros C. Mavroidis (2007), 'Is Action against US Exports for Failure to Sign the Kyoto-Protocol WTO Legal?', *World Trade Review*, **6**: 299–310.

Bradley, Curtis and Jack Goldsmith (2006), *Foreign Relations Law: Cases and Materials*, 2nd edn, Sandy, UT: Aspen Press.

Buxbaum, Hannah L. (2006), 'Transnational Regulatory Litigation', *Virginia Journal of International Law*, **46**: 251–98.

Colangelo, Anthony J. (2007), 'Constitutional Limits on Extraterritorial Jurisdiction: Terrorism and the Intersection of National and International Law', *Harvard Journal of International Law*, **48**: 121–65.

Démaret, Paul and Raoul Stewardson (1994), 'Border Tax Adjustments under GATT and EC Law and General Implications for Environmental Taxes', *Journal of World Trade*, **28**: 5–65.

Dunoff, Jeffrey (2005), 'Lotus Eaters: The Varietals Dispute, the SPS Agreement, and WTO Dispute Resolution', in George Bermann and Petros C. Mavroidis (eds), *Trade and Health in the WTO*, Cambridge: Cambridge University Press.

Grossman, Gene M. (1980), 'Border Tax Adjustments: Do they Distort Trade?', *Journal of International Economics*, **10**: 117–28.

Grossman, Gene M., Henrik Horn and Petros C. Mavroidis (2013), 'Domestic Instruments', in Henrik Horn and Petros C. Mavroidis (eds), *Legal and Economic Principles of World Trade Law*, The American Law Institute Reporters' Studies on WTO Law, New York: Cambridge University Press, pp. 205–345

Grossman, Gene M. and Alan Sykes (2005), 'A Preference for Development: the Law and Economics of GSP', *World Trade Review* **4**: 41–68.

Hamilton, Clive (2013), *Earthmasters*, New Haven, CT, USA and London, UK: Yale University Press.

Horn, Henrik and Petros C. Mavroidis (2008), 'The Permissible Reach of National Environmental Policies', *Journal of World Trade*, **42**: 1107–78.

Horn, Henrik and Petros C. Mavroidis (2010), 'Climate Change and the WTO: Legal Issues Concerning Border Tax Adjustments', *Japanese Yearbook of International Law*, **53**: 19–40.

Horn, Henrik and Joseph H.H. Weiler (2007), 'EC – Asbestos', in Henrik Horn and Petros C. Mavroidis (eds), *The American Law Institute Reporters' Studies on WTO Case Law – Legal and Economic Analysis*, Cambridge: Cambridge University Press.

Howse, Robert L. (2002), 'The Appellate Body's Rulings in the Shrimps/Turtles Case: a New Legal Baseline for the Trade and Environment Debate', *Columbia Journal of Environmental Law*, **27**: 491–521.

Howse, Robert L. and Damien J. Neven (2007), 'US – Shrimp', in Henrik Horn and Petros C. Mavroidis (eds), *The American Law Institute Reporters' Studies on WTO Case Law – Legal and Economic Analysis*, Cambridge: Cambridge University Press.

Howse, Robert L. and Donald Regan (2000), 'The Product/Process Distinction: an Illusory Basis for Disciplining "Unilateralism" in Trade Policy', *European Journal of International Law*, **11**: 249–83.

Irwin, Douglas A., Petros C. Mavroidis and Alan O. Sykes (2008), *The Genesis of the GATT*, Cambridge: Cambridge University Press.

Jackson, John H. (1978), 'The Crumbling Institutions of the Liberal Trade Regime', *Journal of World Trade*, **12**: 93–106.

Keith, David (2013), *A Case for Climate Engineering*, Cambridge, MA: The MIT Press.

Klevorick Alan K. and Alan O. Sykes (2007), 'United States Courts and the Optimal Deterrence of International Cartels: a Welfarist Perspective on Empagran', in Eleanor M. Fox and Daniel A. Crane (eds), *Antitrust Stories*, New York: Foundation Press, pp. 361–93.

Kramer, Larry (1995), 'Extra-territorial Application of Antitrust Law after the *Insurance Antitrust Case*: a Reply to Professors Lowenfeld and Trimble', *American Journal of International Law*, **89**: 750–58.

Lowenfeld, Andreas F. (1995), 'Conflict, Balancing of Interests, and the Exercise of Jurisdiction to Prescribe: Reflections on the *Insurance Antitrust Case*', *American Journal of International Law*, **89**: 42–53.

Mavroidis, Petros C. (2008), 'No Outsourcing of Law? WTO Law as Practised by WTO Courts', *American Journal of International Law*, **102**: 421–74.

Mavroidis, Petros C. and Damien J. Neven (1999), 'Application of Laws: a Law and Economics Analysis', in *Mélanges Offerts à Michel Waelbroeck*, Bruxelles: PUB, pp. 1297–325.

Nordhaus, William (2013), *The Climate Casino*, New Haven, CT, USA and London, UK: Yale University Press.

Parrish, Austen L. (2009), 'Reclaiming International Law from Extraterritoriality', *Minnesota Law Review*, **93**: 815–74.

Sabin, Paul (2013), *The Bet*, New Haven, CT, USA and London, UK: Yale University Press.

Vagts, Detlev F. (2003), 'Extraterritoriality and the Corporate Governance Law', *American Journal of International Law*, **97**: 289–99.

13. Just sue the bastards? An assessment of the alternative to negative harmonization of regulatory priorities

Geert van Calster

1. INTRODUCTION

In this contribution I summarily, and largely in essay style, review the state of, and challenges to, the main alternative to negative harmonization of regulatory priorities. I introduce the concepts of regulatory autonomy, 'negative' and 'positive' harmonization; I highlight the shortcomings in the approach of the European Union (EU or Union) (the EU often being hailed as having the better approach to the issues under consideration); I review the achievements of both negative and positive harmonization at the level of the World Trade Organization (WTO); and I end with succinct references to similar issues in mega-free trade agreements (FTAs).

2. 'REGULATORY AUTONOMY' IN TRADE AGREEMENTS

Trade and regulatory law collide where barriers to trade are established in the name of regulatory, non-trade priorities. The usual suspects among these latter priorities are environmental protection, public health and consumer protection, although the list is by definition endless. Indeed, the unpredictable character of what at some point in time might emerge as requiring protection, even if the protective measures clash with free trade, is what prompted the European Court of Justice (ECJ) to develop its case law on the 'rule of reason'. This case law supplemented the EEC Treaty-sanctioned exceptions to free trade, with a judge-invented regime protecting newer, modern societal values which the Treaty drafters did not or could not anticipate.

Any modern (post 1940s) trade agreement in principle respects 'regulatory autonomy'. That is to say, all self-respecting trade agreements allow their states' signatories to give priority to regulatory concerns over and above free trade, subject to conditions to avoid abuse. The application of these conditions then leads to discussion and to so-called 'Trade and … [complete with the relevant regulatory interest]' disputes.

Tension between these signatory states over the use of regulatory autonomy may be the result of diverging regulatory responses to environmental etc. problems, and discussion as to whether the other's response is effective in addressing the concern at hand. Especially for regulatory concerns of a truly international kind (such as climate change, the protection of the ozone layer and the oceans), states may indeed have a genuine regulatory goal in mind when they complain about another state's actions. It is, however, more common for a state to suggest that a particular regulatory response in fact amounts to disguised protectionism (rather than arguing that it is insufficient in meeting its regulatory goal): in those cases, the complaining state often does not itself have a regime aimed at protecting the same regulatory value.

3. 'REGULATORY AUTONOMY', 'NEGATIVE' AND 'POSITIVE' HARMONIZATION

Systems of 'deep integration', such as the EU, combine negative with positive harmonization. 'Negative harmonization' is said to occur when trade barriers are dismantled by the intervention of a dispute settlement mechanism (a Panel, or a court of some kind and denomination). This dispute settlement mechanism applies a set of rules, typically formulated as prohibitions: 'Thou shall not hinder the free movement of [goods, capital, services …]'. The mechanism is called 'negative' because: (i) it requires a breach of the rules, which is then disciplined; (ii) it is necessarily ad hoc: litigation against an individual measure is required to trigger the court's intervention; and (iii) most importantly, because suspicion (not in fact always supported by data) has always been that this type of court intervention triggers downwards harmonization or a 'race to the bottom': the phenomenon whereby states that have been, or are in fear of being, rebuked by the relevant court, lower their regulatory standards, triggering a general incentive not to raise the regulatory bar.

This is where 'positive' harmonization comes in. It comes in many forms and degrees of intensity, but it may be summarized as follows.

Using some kind of legislative procedure, it proactively harmonizes the non-trade regulatory standard across the Members of the trading community concerned. Having provided a debated and agreed regulatory floor (sometimes also a ceiling) across the trade community, it takes away the temptation and justification for unilateral action.

Various contributions in this volume address the legality, under international trade law, of national measures that address regulatory concerns.[1] This is therefore not the focus of my contribution. Rather, using the EU's positive harmonization agenda (and accomplishments, as well as shortcomings) as a benchmark, I review the positive harmonization potential, and achievements, in the international community.

4. THE EU: A SHINING EXAMPLE?

Through its harmonization process, the EU has established an extensive set of common EU regulatory laws. Taken together, EU law covers many if not all of the regulatory areas which, at the WTO level, cause tension among Members. Such positive harmonization achievements have no equivalent in the WTO: this is common knowledge (see also further). However, the EU's approach is not a panacea, as I further outline below.

The crucial advantage of positive harmonization is that it ought to counter states' incentives to introduce measures unilaterally. WTO 'trade and' practice has been dogged by unilateral action. Positive harmonization could counter this.

There is merit in examining the EU's approach of regulatory autonomy, even though obviously one needs to be aware of the chalk-and-cheese element in the comparison. Wherever comparisons are made between regional arrangements, such as the EU, and the international trade system spearheaded by the WTO, a word of caution is appropriate. Each of these systems, of course, operates within its own context. The EU's trade policy is embedded in the overall goals of the Union. Even though internal market principles, including the 'four freedoms', stood at the cradle of the European Communities, the Treaties have always aimed for more than merely economic objectives. One of the challenges of the GATT/WTO today is precisely the identification of its agenda. These agreements are fundamentally pure trade agreements, and the integration

---

[1] See also G. van Calster and D. Prévost, (eds), *Research Handbook on Environment, Health and the WTO* (Cheltenham, UK and Northampton, MA, USA: Edward Elgar Publishing, 2013).

of values such as environmental and social protection obliges them to assess their 'mission'.

Some of the provisions of the original Treaty establishing the European Economic Community were almost literally copied from the 1947 General Agreement on Tariffs and Trade (GATT). Article III:4 and 5 GATT prohibits protectionism in the application of internal regulatory measures; Article XI GATT prohibits quantitative restrictions; the original Articles 9, 12, 30 and 34 EEC[2] prohibit tariffs, quantitative restrictions, and other measures which directly or indirectly, actually or potentially, hinder trade.

Article XX GATT secures domestic policy autonomy, provided national measures do not involve arbitrary discrimination, are not disguised restrictions on trade, and meet the specific conditions of the subparagraphs, which contain a closed list of legitimate policy objectives. The original Article 36 EC secures domestic policy autonomy, provided the measures concerned further the policy goals enumerated in that article, do not involve arbitrary discrimination or disguised restrictions on trade, and meet the conditions of the proportionality test (including necessity).

While the texts may be similar or in places even identical, little is to be learnt from merely comparing the application of these texts by the ECJ and the WTO dispute settlement institutions respectively. It is probably more relevant to study the mechanisms behind developments in both policy and case law.

Despite the inherent difficulty of having to compare two substantially different sets of international law, and notwithstanding the caution expressed below in section 4, the experience of the EU is a useful reference for the WTO. Clearly, if regulatory autonomy issues are to be resolved successfully, a great deal of cooperation will have to be realized between the trade and the regulatory community. The EU is 'lucky' in that its agenda includes both trade and the various regulatory policies. The WTO, by contrast, clearly has no immediate regulatory agenda. Its rules do, however, equally clearly, have a high impact on non-trade regulation. Arguably, in light of this impact, the absence of clear regulatory policies in its mandate obliges the WTO to broker a successful partnership on 'trade and ...' issues with the international regulatory community.

---

[2] Previously Articles 9, 12, 30 and 34 EC. Various Treaty amendments have led to a general renumbering of these Articles.

Three arguments figure strongly in commentators' caution in comparing the EU and the GATT set-up.[3] Firstly, the GATT has far more limited *ratione materiae*. GATT had set trade liberalization as its goal, while even in the original EC social cohesion and regional redistribution of wealth, among others, figured alongside economic development as the Communities' purpose. Secondly, GATT's institutional structure – and, in particular, the weaknesses of its dispute settlement provisions (which make it more of a political/diplomatic instrument than a legal one) – have prevented 'creative lawmaking'. Finally, the homogeneity among EC Member States was already far greater than that among GATT Members.

In the WTO, the first two arguments arguably no longer hold. Firstly, even though such issues as environmental protection and social cohesion are not among the WTO's aims, the WTO Agreement nevertheless has formally recognized the need for these considerations to be taken into account in the further liberalization of international trade. Secondly, the dispute settlement provisions of the WTO are, of course, far more advanced than those of the GATT, including the provision that Panel and Appellate Body Reports are deemed to be accepted unless rejected by unanimity. It is only the third argument which may reflect a reality that is still in place. For instance, one of the elements of the ECJ's 'mutual recognition' jurisprudence[4] is the requirement that Member States recognize each other's measures which serve the protection of the interest concerned, when adopting stricter rules or in the absence of Union harmonization. This includes, for instance, the existence of adequate health and sanitary inspections in the exporting Member State. This represents an application of good faith, mutual confidence and quasi-federal loyalty, which is not justified in the WTO (see also below, in the discussion on judicial activism at section 6.1. below).

One crucial characteristic of the EU, which is a precondition for making its harmonization programme a success, is its supranational nature. Through the doctrine of the supremacy of Union law and the direct effect of some of its provisions, EU law penetrates directly into the legal regimes of the Member States. The WTO remains a classic instrument of international diplomacy, with no equivalent in most of its Members of the direct effect doctrine: very few WTO Members accept

---

[3] See, e.g., P. Demaret, 'TREMs, Multilateralism and the GATT', in J. Cameron, P. Demaret and D. Geradin (eds), *Trade and the Environment: The Search for Balance* (London: Cameron May, 1994), pp. 52–68, at 65.

[4] Which, subject to exceptions, foresees that Member States are obliged to allow the marketing, on their territory, of products manufactured in accordance with the laws and regulations of the 'home' Member State.

that WTO provisions may be called upon directly by private parties in dispute settlement proceedings in their national courts.

5. A WORD OF CAUTION ON THE EU'S LEADING ROLE

In theory, where EU harmonization has been set in place through 'secondary law',[5] regulatory action of its Member States must comply with these provisions rather than with the Treaty's regime of exceptions to free trade rules. As states all follow the same rulebook, the 'Trade and …' debate ought to be resolved. However, for a variety of reasons, in practice there are several instances where this overall ambition has not quite worked.

5.1 The Issue of 'Pre-emption' or 'Occupation of the Field', and Pre-emption Cut Off by the 'Environmental Guarantee'

It is established case law[6] that recourse to the exceptions of Article 36 of the Treaty on the Functioning of the European Union (TFEU) (the exceptions Article which allows for infringements of the free movement of goods) and/or of the 'rule of reason' is no longer possible where Union law has *exhaustively* harmonized the national legislation at issue. National measures derogating from the harmonized regime are then said to be 'pre-empted' by the Union initiative, which 'occupies the field'. The underlying assumption is that the protection of the interests caught under Article 36 and under the 'rule of reason' is guaranteed by Member States' approval (via the legislative procedure and voting requirements) of the measures concerned. The keyword is 'exhaustive'. The EU's regime must have laid down a complete regulatory mechanism for the issues under consideration. Where it deals only with partial elements of a regime, and/or one that is not considered to rule out national initiative in

---

[5] 'Primary law' is the body of rules included (mainly) in the EU Treaties. Secondary law is adopted through the legislative procedures detailed in the Treaties.

[6] See e.g. Case 227/82, *Van Bennekom* [1983] ECR 388, at para. 15; Case C-347/89, *Freistaat Bayern v Eurim-Pharm GmbH* [1991] ECR I-1747, at para. 26. Controversially applied in Case C-1/96, *The Queen v Minister of Agriculture, Fisheries and Food, ex parte Compassion in World Farming Ltd* [1998] ECR I-1251 (*Compassion*). See G. Van Calster, 'Export Restrictions – A Watershed for Article 30' (2000) 25 *European Law Review* 335–52.

the area, Member States may continue to regulate provided they do not exceed the limits of that regulatory autonomy under primary law. Confused? Readers should be: the ins and outs of the complex regime of pre-emption and exhaustion wrong-foots many a practitioner and national official. This is compounded by the fact that there is no such thing as an 'exhaustion clause' in secondary law. EU secondary law does not say in so many words whether it is exhaustive or not: one has to detect it, taking clues from the wording of the text, its preparatory history and preparatory works – with, of course, the Court of Justice being the final judge of the exhaustive (or not) character.

It is also noteworthy that the underlying assumption of pre-emption no longer holds where legislation is based upon Article 192 TFEU (the environmental legal basis) or Article 114 TFEU (harmonization in the framework of the internal market) in the light of the (albeit conditional) room for Member States to introduce permanent deviations from the legislation at issue. These Articles grant Member States the conditional right to introduce stricter measures, in particular, for reasons of environmental protection or occupational health and safety, and they serve as a permanent (albeit strictly regulated) hurdle to pre-emption.[7]

5.2 The Use of Minimum Harmonization Creates an Anchor Point for Many a Discussion

Section 5.1 discussed whether Member States may take measures protecting regulatory measures in a stricter way than proscribed by secondary law: that is, whether they can call upon the Treaty's protection of non-trade regulatory interests even where there has been positive harmonization. In many areas, however, discussion centres around the question whether Member States have even achieved reaching the goals identified by those laws.

The harmonization model used in the EU positively encourages lots of discussion on whether Member States abide by its requirements. In many regulatory areas (food law being a notable, if partial, exception), harmonization in the EU uses the so-called 'minimum harmonization' model, which leaves quite a lot of wriggle room (and hence room for discussion) even following legislative intervention.

---

[7] See also G. Van Calster, 'Green Unilateralism – The European Commission and the Environmental Guarantee of Article 95 EC' (2000) 9 *European Environmental Law Review* 232–6. (Note that Article 95 EC is a predecessor of the current Article 114 TFEU.)

During an initial period, EU legislators attempted to effectively replace national law with European law in areas relevant to the internal market (the so-called 'total harmonization' approach). The requirement of unanimity for approval of such secondary legislation, as it then existed, proved to make consensus on many, even technical issues, all but impossible. The need to change tack was made all the more urgent following the ECJ's finding in *Cassis de Dijon*,[8] in which it held that the free movement of goods articles of the Treaty effectively impose mutual recognition of national product requirements. What followed was both a Treaty change in the requirement of unanimity (the introduction of qualified majority voting, in the Single European Act) and a change in the general approach to harmonization, now dubbed the 'New Approach':[9] rather than exhausting itself in detail, a Directive now sets out general principles.

Where suitable (in particular, when it comes to product standards; far less frequently for process standards), these are further detailed in technical standards developed by the relevant standardization bodies, under mandate of the European Commission. However, these eventual standards, even where they do exist, are never obligatory. Rather, they are an optional means for manufacturers to enjoy free movement more easily (and, as noted, they do not have an equivalent in areas where the EU has harmonized the levels of regulatory protection in production *processes*, as opposed to *products*, and even less of an equivalent in the services, as opposed to the goods, sector).

Finally, an important feature which defines minimum harmonization is the use of a regulatory floor. Once the floor is met, products originating anywhere can travel freely within the EU. However, Member States are free to impose stricter conditions upon their own industry, and there is no identity of regulation between the various Member States: only a guarantee of minimum protection.

Whether a particular Member State has properly enacted the minimum floor in its national laws is often a first point of debate (particularly in the environmental sector, which has the highest rate of infringement proceedings for non-implementation and non-compliance in the ECJ). A subsequent level of complication arises as a result of so-called 'safeguard clauses' in the legislation itself. These are provisions negotiated by

---

[8] Case 120/78, *Rewe-Zentrale AG v Bundesmonopolverwaltung für Branntwein* [1979] ECR 649.

[9] See, in particular, Communication of the Commission to the Council on the New Approach in Technical Harmonization, COM(85) 19, adopted by the Council in its Resolution of 7 May 1985, [1985] OJ C 136/1.

(typically a group of) Member States and which provide for exceptions to the unified regime which the legislation entails. Such exceptions are often subject to conditions (often even Commission approval) and they are typically also time-limited.

In summary, if readers are confused after reading sections 5.1 and 5.2, I have them exactly where I want them to be (and indeed where Member States often are). Far from providing a high level of certainty, the EU's prima facie very promising use of positive harmonization hides many layers of complexity. This is not to say that positive harmonization in the EU is a failure; rather, that it is a continuous process of adaptation and fine tuning, which requires a heavy legislative and executive machinery under the control of the courts.

5.3 PPMs and Free Movement of Goods

A further illustration of the unfinished nature of the EU's harmonization approach is that, until quite recently, the ECJ has not had to deal with cases involving product distinctions based on processes and production methods (PPMs) in the area of trade in goods. PPMs are a long-running staple part of the regulatory autonomy debate in the WTO. PPMs in the general sense are all ways in which a product is being produced. If that method of production is not reflected in the final product, the PPM concerned is referred to as an 'n-PR PPM'. For reasons outside the scope of this chapter, PPMs in general and n-PR PPMs in particular are something of an obsession in the legal debate on regulatory autonomy in the WTO.

In the first cases in which the ECJ was asked to address PPMs – in particular, *Lomas*[10] and *Compassion*[11] (but also in *Dusseldorp*)[12] – the ECJ effectively avoided having to tackle the PPM issue by confining the

---

10 Case C-5/94, *The Queen v Ministry of Agriculture, Fisheries and Food, ex parte Hedley Lomas (Ireland) Ltd* [1996] ECR I-2553. See my review in G. van Calster (1996) 3 *Columbia Journal of European Law* 132–45, available at http://www.cjel.net/print/3_1-van-calster.

11 *Compassion*, n. 6 above.

12 Case C-203/96, *Chemische Afvalstoffen Dusseldorp and Others v VROM* [1998] ECR I-4075. See my review in G. van Calster, 'Court Criticises Restrictions on Free Movement of Waste' (1999) 24(2) *European Law Review* 181, 183.

analysis to the rather complex theory behind pre-emption and harmonization (reviewed above, section 5.1). The judgments concerned provoked controversy and led to scepticism in the regulatory community, just as the two *Tuna/Dolphin* cases did within the context of the GATT.[13]

The Court had, however, previously considered the PPM issue in its case law on what is now Article 110 TFEU: the core article on tax discrimination (effectively the EU counterpart of GATT Article III:2). In according Member States room for manoeuvre to discriminate between products on the basis of regulatory priorities, the ECJ simply dismissed any relevance for the non-product v product-incorporated issue, focusing instead on arbitrary discrimination and the legitimacy of a regulatory priority, judged on the basis of the EU's own non-trade regulatory priorities and on international law.[14]

Most recently, the non-product-related n-PR PPM issue came to the fore in the ECJ's case law on national incentive schemes for domestically produced renewable energy. In *Vindkraft* and in *Essent*, the Court insists on transparent and non-discriminatory market-based instruments being required to justify the market infringement of the national schemes at issue under the Treaty's free movement of goods rules, again not being preoccupied with the n-PR PPM issue per se.[15]

5.4 Can Member States be 'Too' Non-Trade Friendly? ECJ Review of the Level of Protection

The ECJ has not unequivocally indicated that it sees itself fit to judge the very level of regulatory protection sought by Member States in the absence of EU harmonization. Most judgments would seem to indicate that it does not; however, the jury is out (see, for instance, the Opinion of the AG in *Danish Bottles*[16]).

---

[13] GATT Panel Report, *United States – Restrictions on Imports of Tuna*, DS21/R, DS21/R, 3 September 1991, unadopted, BISD 39S/155 (*US – Tuna (Mexico)*); GATT Panel Report, *United States – Restrictions on Imports of Tuna*, DS29/R, 16 June 1994, unadopted *(US – Tuna (EEC))*.

[14] See G. van Calster, 'Topsy-Turvy: the European Court of Justice and Border (Energy) Tax Adjustments – Should the World Trade Organization Follow Suit?', in *Critical Issues in International Environmental Taxation*, Vol. 2 (London: Richmond Law and Tax, 2003), pp. 311–41.

[15] See my review: G. van Calster, 'Climate Change and Renewable Energy as a Super Trump for EU Trade Law. All Essent Clear' (2014) 1 *Renewable Energy Law and Policy Review* 60–66.

[16] Case 302/86, *Commission v Denmark* [1988] ECR 4607.

The ECJ does not suggest a weighing and balancing test such as that proposed (granted, somewhat fuzzily) by the WTO Appellate Body,[17] among others, in the light of the Treaty's integration principle. However, cases involving the precautionary principle suggest a lot of sympathy for generally giving (in particular) environmental protection, public health and occupational health and safety the benefit of the doubt when it comes to their impact on trade: in other words, the ECJ is not generally minded to rebuke Member States for being 'too' regulatory friendly (again, only outside the context of harmonization).

5.5 Are Extraterritorial Measures Allowed?

The ECJ has not unequivocally decided whether Member States may take unilateral initiatives to protect the environment in other Member States. This 'extraterritoriality' issue has been at the centre of a majority of the trade and environment discussions in the WTO.[18] It was debated in the *Tuna/Dolphin* cases, references to it were made in *Shrimp/Turtle*,[19] and had the EU's Leghold Trap Regulation[20] ever been brought before the WTO, it would have been crucial again. (In the similar and later *EU – Seal Products* case,[21] the EU – as readers will know – pulled the 'public morals' card, which pre-empted a discussion of the extraterritoriality issue).

The European Court, by contrast, did not address the issue in either *Scottish Grouse*,[22] *Lomas*, *Compassion*, or *Dusseldorp*, even though all

---

17 See my critical review in G. van Calster, '*Faites vos jeux* – Regulatory Autonomy and the World Trade Organization after *Brazil Tyres*' (2008) 20(1) *Journal of Environmental Law* 121–36.

18 See C. Ryngaert and M. Koekkoek (Chapter 10, this volume) and P. Mavroidis (Chapter 12, this volume).

19 Panel Report, *United States – Import Prohibition of Certain Shrimp and Shrimp Products*, WT/DS58/R and Corr.1, adopted 6 November 1998; Appellate Body Report, *United States – Import Prohibition of Certain Shrimp and Shrimp Products*, WT/DS58/AB/R, adopted 6 November 1998.

20 Council Regulation No. 3254/91 of 4 November 1991 prohibiting the use of leghold traps in the Community and the introduction into the Community of pelts and manufactured goods of certain wild animal species originating in countries which catch them by means of leghold traps or trapping methods which do not meet international humane trapping standards, OJ [1991] L308/1.

21 Appellate Body Report, *EC – Measures Prohibiting the Importation and Marketing of Seal Products*, WT/DS400/AB/R, adopted 18 June 2014.

22 Case C-169/89, *Criminal Proceedings against Gourmetterie Van den Burg* [1990] ECR I-2143.

these could be taken to involve some degree of extraterritoriality. In two cases involving the Waste Shipments Regulation (WSR), Regulation 1013/2006,[23] the Court did hold that that Regulation allows for objections to shipments of waste, within strict conditions, if the Member State of dispatch considers that the environment or the occupational health and safety of those having to handle the waste would not be sufficiently protected by the standards applicable in the state of destination. In *EU – Wood Trading*[24] the ECJ was of the view that the objectives to protect health and environment, which the Union legislature targets with the WSR, could be compromised if shipments of waste between Member States were not perceived in their entirety – that is to say, from the point of departure of the waste in the state of dispatch to the end of its processing in the state of destination. In *Pedersen*[25] it clarified the potential to call upon stricter standards in the Member State of dispatch in order to refuse shipment. The Court first of all held that the WSR implies that the authorities, in assessing the risks which recovery of waste carried out in the state of destination would entail for human health and the environment, may take account of all relevant criteria in that regard, including those which are in force in the state of dispatch, even if they are stricter than those of the state of destination, and provided they are intended to avoid those risks. The authorities of dispatch cannot, however, be bound by the criteria of their state if such criteria are no more apt to avoid those risks than those of the state of destination. Moreover, opposition by the authority of dispatch on the basis of its national waste recovery standards to a shipment can only be lawful in so far as those standards, in compliance with the principle of proportionality, are apt to attain the objectives pursued, which are intended to prevent risks for human health and the environment, and do not go beyond what is necessary to attain them.[26]

These cases, judged within the specific context of the WSR, do not divulge an overall view of the ECJ on the legality of extraterritorial measures.

---

[23] Regulation (EC) No. 1013/2006 on shipments of waste, [2006] OJ L 190/1.

[24] Case C-277/02, *EU-Wood-Trading GmbH v Sonderabfall-Management-Gesellschaft Rheinland-Pfalz mbH* [2004] ECR I-11957.

[25] Case C-215/04, *Marius Pedersen A/S v Miljostyrelsen* [2006] ECR I-01465.

[26] More details on those cases in G. van Calster, *Handbook of EU Waste Law* (Oxford: Oxford University Press, 2015).

6. 'NEGATIVE HARMONIZATION' – THE ROLE OF WTO DISPUTE SETTLEMENT

6.1 The WTO and Judicial Activism

Is the WTO dispute settlement mechanism equipped to play the crucial role which the ECJ has played? The role of the ECJ in addressing trade and environment concerns in the EU has been crucial. The ECJ has not confined itself to a textual interpretation of Community, and later Union, law. It has followed a proactive approach, moving the issues forward in what it perceived as being the best interest of the Union.

GATT and WTO dispute settlement Panels and the WTO Appellate Body (AB) have traditionally stuck to a literal and textual interpretation of the Agreement, and arguably continue to do so. A good recent illustration are the *China – Raw Materials* and *China – Rare Earth* cases.[27] In that debate, on the room for manoeuvre for a new WTO Member in the context of its regulatory autonomy, both Panels and the AB could have developed arguments related to a WTO 'constitutional body' of law (in response to a technical point on China's Protocol of Accession), but failed to do so.

Contrasting the debate on 'green' Border Tax Adjustment,[28] within both the EC/EU and in the WTO, may serve as a good example of the very different overall approach of the respective dispute settlement institutions. The current Article 110 TFEU (previously Article 90 EC), which regulates the internal taxation regime of Member States where it has an effect on Union trade (much like GATT's Article III), is rigid in its conception. However, in the light of the overall slow progress in tax harmonization and the sensitivity of national fiscal legislation, the ECJ has allowed Member States considerable leeway under Article 110. It has held that Union law does not restrict the freedom of each Member State to lay down tax arrangements which differentiate between certain products on the basis of objective criteria, such as the nature of the raw materials used or the production processes employed. Such differentiation is considered compatible with Union economic law if it is: (i) based on objective criteria, such as the nature of the raw materials used or the

[27] See, *inter alia*, G. van Calster, 'China, Minerals Export, Raw Materials and Rare Earth Materials: A Perfect Storm for World Trade Organisation Dispute Settlement', (2013) 22(1) *RECIEL* 117–22.

[28] Border Tax Adjustment refers to aligning exported and imported goods from the point of view of taxation, leading to rebates of the imposition of domestically levied taxes.

production processes employed; (ii) if it pursues economic or social policy objectives which are themselves compatible with the requirements of the Treaty and secondary law; and (iii) if it avoids any form of discrimination, direct or indirect, with regard to imports from other Member States or any form of protection of domestic products.

This jurisprudence-based exception applies even to products which are 'similar' (the EU term for 'like') within the meaning of Article 110 TFEU. The Court's emphasis on the absence of any discrimination, direct or indirect, in respect of imported produce, or any form of protection of domestic products, is considered to be a safeguard against abuse.

This example of judicial activism remains in stark contrast with a similar debate in the WTO, namely that of 'like products'. The like product issue is not the only area where judicial activism is possible in the WTO. A renewed emphasis on the Headnote of GATT's Article XX, in particular, could well increase the role of the dispute settlement Panels, and lead them from a purely textual interpretation of the Agreement to a more teleological approach. The Appellate Body report in *Shrimp/Turtle* has often been quoted for its 'evolutionary' approach: it stated, in particular, that the interpretation of the term 'exhaustible natural resources' is not static but evolutionary); however, case law since then, in my view, has not exactly given WTO Members the clarity they require in seeking to comply with WTO expectations.

One understandable concern with judicial activism in the WTO is the 'slippery slope' argument.[29] The moment the WTO dispute settlement mechanism decides to take a proactive stance in, say, the Trade and Environment issue, could have ramifications, for instance, for the debate on social clauses and all other 'Trade and …' issues. The argument continues that even if the GATT may be able to cope with an important part of the Trade and Environment issue through the normal application of non-discrimination rules – so much so that Article XX need not even be invoked[30] – extending GATT rules and concepts beyond product characteristics 'might open the risk of GATT allowing potential import restrictions based on thousands of societal and economic characteristics

---

[29] That is, the 'difficulty of a quasi "judicial" body consisting of three experts making an interpretation which could have extensive ramifications (by the operation of informal precedent and analogy) beyond the specific environmental cases': J. Jackson, 'Greening the GATT: Trade Rules and Environmental Policy', in J. Cameron, P. Demaret and D. Geradin (eds), *Trade and the Environment: The Search for Balance* (London: Cameron May, 1994), pp. 39–51, at 43 (prior to the installation of the WTO's Dispute Settlement Body (DSB)).

[30] Ibid.

of the exporting', and indeed the importing nation. In other words, the argument goes that after decades of trade liberalization, states would be allowed once again to retire into national values.

6.2 A Victim of its Own Success

A number of features of the WTO dispute settlement mechanism attract 'Trade and …' disputes. In environmental disputes, in particular, even if a conflict includes states that are all parties to a multilateral environmental agreement (MEA), for instance, these states often prefer to take recourse to the WTO dispute settlement system. Outside the MEA context, one alternative would be the International Court of Justice, which created a special chamber for international environmental disputes in 1993, but which so far has failed to attract the most high-profile cases.

The WTO dispute settlement process presents considerable attractions to quarrelling states. These attractions are well reported. Firstly, the WTO Agreements, including GATT, result in a comprehensive set of altogether rather clear rules. Most MEAs include framework obligations only, the precise content of which is moulded during Conferences of the Parties, Resolutions, Working Party Reports and the like, the exact status and interaction of which is far from clear. Furthermore and crucially, WTO dispute settlement proceedings are fast, subject to a clear set of rules, and enforceable.

Moreover, WTO dispute settlement now makes a much greater effort at taking binding international regulatory law more or less fully into account. The importance of the WTO abandoning legal isolationism has been emphasized throughout the agreements and in dispute settlement practice. WTO dispute settlement Panels, and the AB, have emphasized that the WTO Dispute Settlement Understanding (DSU) obliges them to apply any binding rule of public international law between the Members. The DSU and the Vienna Convention on the Law of Treaties enable WTO Members to adhere to a variety of international regulatory agreements.

Crucially, the further elaboration and clarification of international regulatory law would serve the settlement of 'Trade and …' disputes in the GATT/WTO.

7. ROOM FOR 'POSITIVE HARMONIZATION' WITHIN THE WTO

The introduction of common minimum standards within the WTO framework is not untested. The TRIPS Agreement, for instance, has introduced comprehensive obligations for the protection of private property rights by requiring substantive minimum standards for the availability, scope, use and protection of intellectual property rights. At the time the Uruguay Round Agreements were signed, Ministers recognized that the TRIPS Agreement could serve as an approach that could also be used to harmonize domestic policy in other areas. The WTO Agreement itself, in Article III states that:

> the WTO shall provide the forum for the negotiations among its Members concerning their multilateral trade relations in matters dealt with under the [WTO Agreements]. The WTO may also provide a forum for further negotiations among its Members concerning their multilateral trade relations, and a framework for the implementation of the results of these negotiations, as may be decided by the Ministerial Conference.

There is therefore arguably a mandate for the WTO to step into a wide range of issues with a trade impact, including the coordination of environmental harmonization efforts.

Of course, to the extent that harmonization is realized, this will not *ipso facto* mean that all regulatory unilateralism will be ruled out and no more disputes will arise. For instance, in the area of food and feed, even if international harmonization is realized, the SPS Agreement expressly authorizes Members to maintain higher standards (linked to a set of appropriate conditions). The Preamble to that Agreement, furthermore, expressly notes that harmonization is to be advanced without, however, requiring Members to change their appropriate level of protection of human, animal or plant life or health.

Harmonization techniques are plentiful. The most basic distinction is between 'mutual recognition', whereby states accept each other's standards in a given area as being equivalent, as opposed to some form of true 'harmonization' – alignment – of the different national standards. Harmonization in a few well-defined areas could exceed the procedural and methodological level. The improvement in transparency procedures could serve as an interim solution for part of the tensions caused by the development of national, regional and multilateral regulatory solutions.

It is clear that if positive harmonization is to form part of resolving the 'Trade and …' debate at the WTO level, it will *not* be realized by the WTO itself. Rather, the WTO should take proper account of the developments in other international fora, such as the United Nations Environment Programme, the International Standards Organization and the Food and Agriculture Organization. The provisions of the TBT Agreement could in this respect serve as an example (albeit also of slow progress). The creation of one global super-regulatory forum (or even one such forum per regulatory issue), where the gradual coordination and harmonization of environmental policies would take place, is arguably neither feasible nor warranted. A realistic alternative is the establishment of a set of international agreements for specific regulatory topics. One needs to be realistic, though, in one's expectations of these large international negotiations. In the environmental field, for instance, the greatest successes have been reached through singular, technically undisputed environmental threats (such as the threat to the ozone layer). These are a far cry from multifaceted challenges, such as climate change.

8. MEGA-FTAs AND THEIR REGULATORY AGENDA

As part of the current range of alternatives for enhancing international trade, many WTO Members are pursuing not just ever more regional FTAs, but also so-called 'mega-FTAs'. These are more extensive not so much in terms of the products and services which they intend to, or do, cover, but rather in the type of cooperation they envisage. The ambition of all of these is to reach some kind of regulatory coordination which can only be described as attempts at positive harmonization, albeit in varying levels of intensity.

The most prominent of such attempts are, of course, the current negotiations between the EU and the United States to create a Transatlantic Trade and Investment Partnership (TTIP). Both the European Commission and the US have repeatedly announced that TTIP will only be called a success to the extent that its regulatory coordination efforts will be successful. (The more traditional elements of trade liberalization of the agreement are considered to be more obviously realistic).

As regulatory priorities arguably reflect core societal values,[31] these negotiations, led by trade officials, have not failed to attract heavy criticism on both sides of the Atlantic. It is also clear, however, that at the very least, whether or not the talks will ultimately be successful, they have already led to increased transparency and understanding of each other's regulatory process.[32]

---

[31] See also G. van Calster, 'Risk Regulation, EU Law and Emerging Technologies: Smother or Smooth?' (2008) 2(1) *NanoEthics* 61–71.

[32] See, e.g., the following review for DG Trade: R. Parker and A. Alemanno, *Towards Effective Regulatory Co-operation under TTIP: a Comparative Overview of the EU and US Legislative and regulatory systems*, May 2014, available at http://goo.gl/7xRqAj (accessed 12 December 2014).

The development of ambitious regulatory coordination agendas in mega-FTAs arguably reflects a lack of belief that any real harmonization effort can be reached in truly international negotiations.

9. CONCLUSION

It is very much this author's view that blaming the 'Trade and …' conundrum on the lack of room within the WTO for regulatory considerations is all too easy and wrong. There is a striking lack of unity among the international regulatory community when it comes to dealing with some of even the most pressing regulatory problems.

Consequently, managing the different regulatory responses of states is of the utmost importance. This will require some degree of harmonization, whether via the principle of mutual recognition or some degree of 'true' harmonization.

14. Conclusion: possibilities and limitations of governing *through* trade

Jan Wouters, Axel Marx, Dylan Geraets and Bregt Natens

1. INTRODUCTION

This volume started by noting the current stalemate in multilateral negotiations and its effect on the creation of traditional international law. Indeed, several observers posit that traditional international law is stagnating. As Joost Pauwelyn, Ramses Wessel and Jan Wouters (2014) argue, formal international law is stagnating in terms of both quantity and quality, and is increasingly superseded by informal international lawmaking in which rules and standards are developed and enforced by non-state actors on a global scale (see also Marx, 2011; Büthe and Mattli, 2011). As argued in the Introduction, besides the emergence and proliferation of different forms of informal lawmaking (Pauwelyn, Wessel and Wouters, 2012; Büthe and Mattli, 2011; Marx and Wouters, 2015), another form of international policy making is rapidly expanding: *governance through trade* (Meunier and Nicolaïdis, 2006; Hafner-Burton, 2013; Damro, Chapter 2, this volume). This concept entails that countries are exercising power through their trade policies in order to promote non-trade objectives. This especially includes, as elaborated in this volume, the provision of global public goods (Croquet (Chapter 6), Bartels (Chapter 4), Leal-Arcas and Wilmarth (Chapter 5), Geraets and Natens (Chapter 11), Ryngaert and Koekkoek (Chapter 10)) and the promotion of good governance (Bartels (Chapter 4), Yap (Chapter 9), Beke and Hachez (Chapter 8), Marx and Soares (Chapter 7)).

The European Union (EU or Union) is a particularly interesting case of governance through trade. In comparison to other major trading blocks, it is very active in the pursuit of this form of policy making. Although not a state, the EU possesses exclusive competence for its common commercial policy. Moreover, the Union is a major trading power on a global scale. The latter is captured by the idea of Market Power Europe (MPE), proposed by Chad Damro. According to the idea of MPE, the EU should be seen as exercising power 'through the externalization of its social and economic agendas' (Damro, 2012, p. 696). There is externalization of such norms when the EU induces other actors to behave, says Damro, 'in a way that generally satisfies or conforms to the EU's market-related policies and regulatory measures'. It does so on the basis of characteristics of its internal market: market size, high levels of regulatory capacity and domestic pressure groups favouring externalization. The centrality of the Common Commercial Policy in the EU's international presence links MPE to trade policy. The policies addressed in this volume are prime examples of how MPE externalizes certain non-trade objectives, such as human rights and sustainable development. How this idea is grounded and anchored in the constitutional foundations of the EU has been further elaborated by Joris Larik. Larik explains the explicit link between the EU's foreign trade policy and good global governance from the perspective of the objectives enshrined in the Treaty on European Union (TEU) and the Treaty on the Functioning of European Union (TFEU). The treaty objectives articulated in Articles 3(5) and 21 TEU and 205–207(1) TFEU are 'for all practical purposes … not to be seen as strict rules which can be either respected or violated. Rather, it is more appropriate to conceive of them as "optimization requirements"'. Such optimization requirements imply that their objective is realized to the greatest extent possible, in the given legal and factual constellation. Larik goes on to argue that, despite the weak legal force of the EU's constitutional mandate to foster good global governance *through* trade policy and despite the width of such obligations, there are a number of examples of trade-related measures through which the EU seeks to implement the objectives of good global governance. These examples are discussed further in other contributions to this volume. What are the possibilities and limitations of this approach, and how effective is it? In this concluding chapter we aim to bring together some of the main insights on the limitations and possibilities of this approach.

It is still early days to make a full assessment of the instruments used to govern *through* trade, since many of them continue to develop and will change over time. A comparison between different free trade agreements is a case in point (see, for example, Marx and Soares, Chapter 7, this volume). Such continuous 'adaptation by doing' is part of a broader governance approach, which is often referred to as 'reflexive governance' (Brousseau, Dedeurwaerdere and Siebenhüner, 2012) or experimentalist governance (Zeitlin, 2015). A key characteristic of this type of governance is that the objectives of a specific policy pursued through a specific policy instrument are, by definition, a 'moving target', which changes continuously. This makes it more difficult to assess this form of governance in terms of its effectiveness, as the effectiveness benchmarks are continually moving and can be very diverse, depending on the perspective. For example, as Dylan Geraets and Bregt Natens note in their chapter (Chapter 11), there are several ways to assess the effectiveness of the EU Timber Regulation (EUTR). First, most narrowly, effectiveness could be measured in terms of the degree to which the EUTR reduces the import of illegally logged timber into the EU. Second, the effectiveness of the measure can be assessed in relation to the decrease in illegal logging activities on a global scale. Indeed, a measure like the EUTR may cause several substitution effects, which result in different trade flows that do not necessarily reduce illegal logging. Illegal loggers may well decide to export to other countries. Third, and more in line with the experimentalist governance literature, effectiveness can also be assessed in terms of the incentives that the EUTR provides to timber-exporting countries to engage in governance change – that is, towards sustainable forest management. The example of the EUTR thus illustrates that the dimensions on the basis of which an effectiveness assessment is conducted are diverse and will differ from one instrument to the other.

2. ASSESSING GOVERNANCE *THROUGH* TRADE ON THREE DIMENSIONS

Notwithstanding these limitations, the different contributions to this volume offer several insights that shed light on what the current generation of governance *through* trade instruments can achieve. Moreover, the contributions also indicate their limitations. In addressing the potential and limitations of these instruments, we identify and discuss three dimensions which are important in different degrees to the various instruments: (i) legality, (ii) consistency, and (iii) effectiveness.

2.1 The Legality of Governance through Trade Instruments

A first dimension, mostly relevant for unilateral governance *through* trade instruments (regulatory initiatives), concerns the 'legality' of such instruments. Legality may be defined in narrow terms with reference to specific legal agreements, or in broader terms in relation to the *acquis* of international law. Assessing legality in a narrow sense entails conducting an in-depth assessment of the degree to which specific instruments are in accordance with particular international legal instruments. A specific assessment in the context of trade governance is to evaluate whether, mostly unilateral, regulatory measures are in accordance with international trade law. The broader approach also assesses the degree to which regulatory measures are in accordance with international law, yet it also examines whether such measures are capable of further enforcing *other* instruments of international law. This approach to assessing legality represents in a way an assessment of the legitimacy of these instruments. Here, the assessment starts from the underlying assumption that measures that are in conformity with international law – and therefore are based on norms resulting from prior agreement between actors at the international level – are more legitimate, since they are less prone to contestation. Such norms can be expected to reflect some kind of consensus in (a larger part of) the international community. In a way it represents a unilateral enforcement of a multilateral agreement (Scott, 2013). Therefore, where domestic regulatory measures with external effects are designed with the idea of adhering to norms laid down in international law in mind, they are not only more likely to possess a higher degree of strict legality, but they might also be considered to be more legitimate. The increased legitimacy of these domestic regulatory measures, based on the international legality of the norms they reflect, might make them more acceptable for third countries. In turn, the legality and legitimacy of the instruments contributes to their effectiveness. Several contributions to this book contain an in-depth analysis of the issue of legality in a narrow and a broad sense.

As may be expected, considering the focus on governance through *trade*, international trade law is the focus of the legality assessment in several contributions to this book. The World Trade Organization (WTO) plays a crucial role in determining the extent to which its Members are free to pursue other societal objectives. However, when it comes to internal policies that have an extraterritorial effect, the WTO agreements are silent on the issue of jurisdiction. Petros Mavroidis (Chapter 12) examines the 'jurisdictional ambit' of national policies, in light of the obligations WTO Members are under, by analysing a number of WTO disputes. Before doing so, he assesses the concept of jurisdiction in public international law to determine to what extent it might be relevant in the context of the WTO. Mavroidis identifies three types of measure that have come under WTO scrutiny: (i) disputes in which a WTO Member has taken a measure that aims to redress a situation that occurs if importation takes place; (ii) disputes involving 'transboundary production externalities'; and (iii) situations in which a WTO Member aims to compensate those trading partners which adopt, in the view of the regulating Member, sound policies by contributing (through preferential tariffs) to the costs that such policies might entail. However, in none of the disputes examined did the complaining party raise any jurisdictional claim. Mavroidis concludes that in the absence of claims to that effect, WTO panels appear to be unwilling to address jurisdictional arguments '*ex officio*'. He finds that they (increasingly) appear to be willing to give deference to non-discriminatory measures. In that sense, WTO panels are unlikely to 'tinker with' domestic policies.

Dylan Geraets and Bregt Natens (Chapter 11) turn to a specific case study and examine the consistency of the EUTR with the law of the WTO. The EUTR conditions access to the European timber market, requiring the provision of proof of legality of the timber in question. As such, timber-exporting WTO Members may consider the measure to be trade restrictive, potentially prompting them to initiate a WTO dispute against the EU. The examination of the WTO consistency of the EUTR involves an assessment of the core principles of the WTO, namely non-discrimination and market access. Geraets and Natens find that – although a practical examination of all the relevant evidence would be required – the EUTR appears to be inconsistent with at least two provisions of the General Agreement on Tariffs and Trade 1994 (GATT 1994). However, given the way in which the EUTR has been designed – and the way in which it forms part of 'a wider legal framework' that aims to address the same non-trade objective (that is, the prevention of illegal logging), the measure appears to be justifiable under the general exceptions of Article XX of the GATT 1994. In addition to their legality assessment *sensu stricto*, Geraets and Natens provide some preliminary findings on the effectiveness of the EUTR in the first year of its operation. Their case study illustrates the importance of taking international norms into account in designing (unilateral) regulatory measures. Doing so might not only increase the strict legality of such measures, but also their legitimacy in the eyes of third states. As a result, the analysis of the EUTR makes for an interesting contribution to the assessment of legality in a broad sense. To determine whether timber is harvested legally, the timber laws of the country of harvest are to be respected. Therefore, the determination of 'legality' refers back to domestic timber laws. In combination with being based on international forest governance norms, the EUTR thereby strengthens its legality in both a narrow and a broader sense.

Similar conclusions are reached by Geert van Calster (Chapter 13), who assesses the state of – and challenges to – the alternatives to the negative harmonization of regulatory priorities. Van Calster begins by setting out the inherent tension between trade liberalization and other societal values. In the next part of his contribution he defines the concepts of 'regulatory autonomy', 'positive harmonization' and 'negative harmonization'. After examining the EU's track record in the field of positive harmonization – having compared it with the inherently different structure and objectives of the WTO – van Calster proceeds with an analysis of the instances in which the positive harmonization approach of the EU has not worked quite so well. In a penultimate part, he discusses the role that the WTO's dispute settlement mechanism has played with respect to the issue of negative harmonization. Contrary to the Court of Justice of the European Union (CJEU), WTO Panels and the Appellate Body (AB) have stuck to a literal and textual interpretation of the organization's founding document, the WTO Agreement. The CJEU has taken up a role than can be described as 'activist', which is not the case for the WTO dispute settlement system. Nevertheless, WTO Panels and the AB can take other international agreements into account when interpreting WTO agreements. Indeed, as also noted by Mavroidis, the WTO Agreement was not created in a legal vacuum but rather in a situation where public international law applies. Therefore, the default rules of dealing with physical (and possibly moral) externalities – that is, territoriality and nationality as bases for prescriptive jurisdiction – should be applied in WTO dispute settlement. Consequently, van Calster argues, the further elaboration and clarification of international regulatory law would serve the settlement of 'Trade and …' disputes in the WTO.

Besides compatibility with specific international agreements, governance *through* trade measures also aim to induce the compliance of third states with a wider set of agreements. This form of legality in the broad sense can specifically be seen in the case for the EU's Generalised System of Preferences + (GSP+) scheme, which, as noted, explicitly requires compliance with certain international treaties as a condition for obtaining preferential tariff treatment. As James Yap shows in his chapter (Chapter 9), the EU's GSP programme is a multi-tiered arrangement, with each tier offering different degrees of benefits. At the highest tier of benefits is the Everything But Arms (EBA) scheme. Beneficiary countries designated under this scheme receive duty-free, quota-free access to the European market for all products other than from arms and ammunition. This treatment is only granted to the group of 49 least developed countries (LDCs) as defined by the United Nations. Other countries receive more limited trade privileges under the least preferential tier – the ordinary GSP scheme. More advanced developing countries such as China, India, Nigeria and the Philippines fall within this category. However, between these two levels of benefits there is a third tier that operates differently from the other two: the trade privileges granted under the scheme, called GSP+, are contingent upon continued adherence to a set of conditions, including compliance with a list of 27 key international conventions. These include treaties relating to human rights, labour rights, the environment and governance. To benefit, countries must, in addition to complying with the aforementioned treaties, be considered 'vulnerable'. This yardstick is measured on the basis of trade parameters, which establish the country's degree of integration in international trade, specifically in relation to trading with the EU.

On a more aggregated level, Cedric Ryngaert and Marieke Koekkoek (Chapter 10) propose an analytical tool for a legality assessment *sensu lato* of unilateral measures which govern *through* trade. Their approach involves a determination of the degree to which measures are in conformity with existing international rules. The greater the extent to which a measure is grounded or embedded in existing global policy objectives, the more likely it is that the measure could be considered to be 'presumptively permissible'. As Ryngaert and Koekkoek note:

> Where the protection of domestic trade interests may only be incidental to the protection of global interests, such as the protection of natural resources, 'extraterritorial' levelling of the regulatory playing field may be considered to be legitimate, even in the face of international protest, especially where the global interests to be furthered have a normative basis in international legal or political instruments (footnotes omitted).

They apply their newly suggested approach to three EU legal instruments that are all aimed at the pursuit of natural resource objectives: the EUTR, the EU Renewable Energy Directive (RED) and the EU Seals Regulation. In assessing the extent to which the three instruments are 'embedded in international norms or interests', Ryngaert and Koekkoek find that the concerns addressed by the EUTR appear to be embedded in international norms or interests, rendering this measure to be the most legitimate of the three. The legitimacy or legality of the RED and the Seals Regulation is more questionable, given the lack of international norms on the issues addressed by these measures.

2.2 Consistency of Governance *through* Trade Instruments

A second dimension concerns the consistency of measures used to govern through trade. The idea here is that the potential of governance *through* trade measures is limited when the measures are inconsistent or even contradictory. At the same time, where individual measures or multifaceted policies are generally consistent, the chances of these measures or policies working effectively are greatly increased. What consistency exactly entails is currently subject to debate and no generally accepted definition exists (Marangoni and Raube, 2014). Throughout the various contributions in the volume different approaches to assessing consistency are proposed.

Chad Damro (Chapter 2) combines insights from legal scholarship and political science to clarify the challenges identified in both disciplines with respect to assessing consistency in the EU's trade policy. According to Damro, the core of the problem is that 'any action that appears to be the promotion of one general non-trade objective may at the same time contradict or be inconsistent with the promotion of other general non-trade objectives'. In order to test the MPE hypothesis, the consistency of three types of EU measure is examined from the perspective of the MPE approach. The first two types of trade policy – free trade agreements (FTAs) and GSP(+) – are autonomous initiatives that include broad and general non-trade objectives ('civilian ends or norms'). The third type of autonomous initiative – EU Regulations and Directives – is characterized by a narrower objective, resulting in a more 'operational character'. Therefore, according to Damro, all three types of EU measures fit well within an MPE-approach, since they are in effect, specific examples of the EU's market-related policies and regulatory measures. Importantly, from the perspective of consistency, Damro argues that horizontal consistency – that is, consistency between different instruments or policies – in the externalization of non-trade objectives is not necessary. Such horizontal consistency is impossible considering the breadth of the EU's foreign policy objectives. What is crucial is that the overarching objective of good global governance must be realized in the EU's foreign trade policy 'as far as possible', which does not necessarily require full horizontal consistency. Nonetheless, this does not do away with the fact that, in practice, horizontal inconsistency can create problems. However, the MPE approach 'removes the [analytical[complications' that arise from the pitfall of inconsistency. From the perspective of MPE, 'all that matters is whether the EU does or does not externalize the specific [...] market-related policy or regulatory measure. If it does, then the EU has exercised its power of externalization'.

In contrast to the assessment of horizontal consistency, the chapters by Lorand Bartels (Chapter 4), Nicolas Croquet (Chapter 6), and Rafael Leal-Arcas and Catherine Wilmarth (Chapter 5) highlight that a lack of consistency *within* a governance through trade instrument (that is, internal consistency) is problematic.

First, Bartels focuses on the internal consistency of EU FTAs in respect of the human rights and sustainable development obligations they contain. Human rights obligations have featured in EU FTAs for a long time, but 'sustainable development' chapters (which contain obligations relating to labour and environmental standards) have only been introduced as recently as 2008. Bartels observes that the human rights obligations and the obligations relating to labour standards (as part of the sustainable development chapter) may overlap. However, since the sustainable development chapters are not subject to dispute settlement proceedings, the same state conduct may be subject to different types of provision on implementation and remedies. This lack of internal consistency is far from desirable as a matter of policy, and probably even as a matter of law. Arguably, Bartels concludes, the EU may even act contrary to Article 21 TEU by treating human rights so differently, depending on their precise location within the FTA.

Second, as part of his assessment of climate change norms in the EU-Korea FTA, Nicolas Croquet analyses the issue of internal consistency through the internal or 'horizontal coherence' clause that is included in the agreement. Such a clause is designed to enable a harmonious and consistent interpretation of the various objectives underpinning the treaty. In the particular context of the FTA, Chapter 13 on the environmental governance framework should be read in light of the trade-furthering objective of the FTA. More concretely, in Croquet's view, the focus on internal consistency requires parties to the FTA to liberalize trade in environmental goods and services as much as possible within the bounds set by the treaty's substantive trade provisions.

Third, looking ahead in the field of trade policy and sustainable development, Leal-Arcas and Wilmarth express their hopes that the negotiations for the Transatlantic Trade and Investment Partnership (TTIP) take consistency seriously, since consistency and mutual supportiveness are crucial for achieving the objective of sustainable development.

2.3 Effectiveness of Governance *through* Trade Instruments

The third dimension focuses more specifically on the impact of trade measures through which states attempt to contribute to global governance. Effectiveness can be approached from different angles of incidence. On the basis of the contributions two approaches can be identified. A first angle of incidence is to look at the language used in the instruments and assess whether these contain specific (legal) commitments, or rather general ones (Mamic, 2004). If commitments are specific, they can be followed by a specific action (such as fines and trade suspensions). If commitments are rather general, it is difficult to assess compliance with them. Consequently, it is also difficult to adopt appropriate action where concerns arise with respect to the compliance with commitments. This is, in essence, the approach taken by Bartels, Croquet, and Leal-Arcas and Wilmarth (Chapters 4, 6 and 5, respectively). Bartels finds that whereas the human rights provisions in EU FTAs are legally effective in the sense that they are quite specific (at least for some agreements – see also Chapter 7 for some examples), the sustainable development provisions are less clear. It is notable that human rights clauses in EU FTAs create the possibility of unilateral enforcement. In the event that one party does not adhere to its human rights obligations at the domestic level, the other party may unilaterally adopt 'appropriate measures' under the agreement, most notably the suspension of the agreement. However, in practice, the EU's use of these possibilities 'falls far short in virtually all respects of what is legally possible'. With regard to sustainable development, the EU does not have the possibility of suspending the agreement (unless it denounces the entire agreement). According to Bartels, this dichotomy, which is also evident from the implementation of the provisions in question, does not make sense and leaves much to be desired.

The lack of clear commitments, and hence the resulting limitations on action, are also highlighted in the contributions by Leal-Arcas and Wilmarth (Chapter 5), on the one hand, and Croquet (Chapter 6), on the other. Croquet analyses the EU-Korea FTA, the first of what have been dubbed 'new generation' FTAs, specifically in relation to the specificity of the commitments on climate change. In order to distinguish between 'soft' and 'hard' provisions, Croquet compares the climate change provisions in the *trade* agreement with the climate change provisions in the EU-Korea *political* agreement. Based on this comparison, he assesses the possibility of spillover effects between the two agreements. He finds marked differences. Contrary to Bartels' (Chapter 4) findings on sustainable development, Croquet considers the climate change provisions in the EU-Korea FTA to be quite 'hard'. The difference in assessment partially results from the benchmark used: Bartels compares environmental provisions with human rights provisions, while Croquet compares climate change provisions contained in two different agreements. Croquet then develops a hard–soft law normativity continuum to accurately assess how precise certain provisions are. High soft law normativity, or low soft law normativity, can be derived from the generality of the provisions, their looseness, and their policy-oriented and conditional language. In order to strengthen the climate change provisions in the political agreement, the main poles of climate change policy – notably energy efficiency, renewable energy and greenhouse gas reductions – should be tackled more directly and less through *renvoi* or through a requirement of further cooperation.

In contrast to Croquet, and more in line with Bartels, Leal-Arcas and Wilmarth take a more sceptical approach towards the specificity of sustainable development provisions in trade agreements. The authors start by explaining how the effectiveness of sustainable development provisions is crucial in FTAs. Because such agreements are, or may be, globally standard-setting for sustainable development, they focus on the negotiations for 'mega-regional' FTAs, namely the Trans-Pacific Partnership (TPP) between Pacific Rim countries, and the Transatlantic Trade and Investment Partnership (TTIP) between the EU and the United States. However, scrutiny of the available information related to, *inter alia*, the scope, enforcement and implementation provisions of the sustainable development provisions indicates that, disappointingly, the negotiations are not promising. The information available on the TPP shows that sustainable development objectives set out by the sustainable development chapter are 'merely aspirational'. Crucially, the enforcement mechanism for the sustainable development chapter is severely lacking. Moreover, there is no binding dispute settlement mechanism for these provisions. In the TTIP negotiations, aspirational statements concerning the proposed enforceability of relevant provisions have been made by the EU and the US, but it remains too early to assess whether they can be put into practice.

A second angle of incidence to address effectiveness is to zoom in more directly on the effects which governing *through* trade measures are generating. As noted above, these effects can take several forms. In the case of the EUTR, preliminary reports from the timber industry suggest that legality verification schemes are spreading globally, and the EU Regulation is generating an impact in terms of governance reform in the forest sector. This might be an indication of the effectiveness of the EUTR and similar measures, such as the Australian Illegal Logging Prohibition Bill and the United States' Lacey Act. However, more generally, empirical evidence on the impact of these unilateral and bilateral trade measures is still very much missing. In respect of labour rights, a recent report by the International Labour Organization (ILO) (ILO, 2013), canvassing all recent trade agreements, noted that there is almost no empirical material available to assess the effect of the integration of labour rights in trade agreements on the protection of these rights. It is in this area that Axel Marx and Jadir Soares (Chapter 7) aim to make a first contribution. Their exploratory study starts from agreements containing strong and specific language on two particular labour rights – namely freedom of association and collective bargaining. Subsequently, they assess whether an impact for 13 countries – with whom the EU has concluded a trade agreement with strong provisions on labour rights – can be identified. Their results show no clear evidence that trade agreements that include labour provisions result in increased protection of freedom of association and collective bargaining. On the contrary, they find a steady decline in the protection of these two core labour rights. This is not to argue that these provisions have no effect at all. Indeed, the authors do not have any information as to what might have happened without the inclusion of labour provisions in trade agreements. Further case-based research is required to complement these findings in order to assess the impact of the trade agreements. However, the results do indicate that significant violations of these rights occur in the countries under investigation.

Given those results, it may be surprising that so few countries are suspended from the GSP+ scheme. Suspension from the scheme could be considered as one indicator for the strength of the enforcement of GSP+ and hence, its effectiveness (see Ostrom (2005) for a discussion of the link between enforcement and effectiveness). Freedom of association and collective bargaining rights, analysed in Chapter 7 by Marx and Soares, are part of the ILO Declaration on Fundamental Principles and Rights at Work, which also covers the elimination of all forms of forced or compulsory labour, the effective abolition of child labour, the elimination of discrimination and respect for employment and occupation. The ILO Declaration is part of the GSP+ package and hence the violation of these rights is a ground for suspending the trade privilege. So far, however, there has been only one suspension on the basis of violations of such rights: the suspension of the GSP+ trade preference system with Belarus (EU Regulation 1933/2006; see also Yap, 2013). More generally, GSP+ benefits have been suspended in only three cases – Myanmar, Sri Lanka and Belarus – which could indicate the EU's reluctance to enforce the commitments. This reluctance to use the suspension mechanism does not necessarily indicate a lack of effectiveness, but rather a specific policy strategy. This point is stressed by James Yap in his assessment of whether the Rana Plaza tragedy in Bangladesh should have given rise to a GSP+ suspension (Chapter 9). He finds that the threat of withdrawing benefits from Bangladesh, in combination with the actual withdrawal of certain trade benefits by the US and media attention, has led to slow but noticeable changes in labour rights protection. Hence, effectively suspending benefits may be more detrimental than threatening to do so, considering the continuous pressure that can be exerted in the latter situation.

Chapter 8 by Beke and Hachez also contains an in-depth case study (of Burma/Myanmar) on the suspension of the GSP scheme in order to identify the conditions under which this scheme works best. They analyse whether GSP conditionality is likely to induce change in beneficiary countries and what happens when preferential access is suspended. They conclude that the case study on Burma tends to show that the threat of withdrawal is not a very powerful tool to induce change in beneficiary countries to comply with the set of international treaty rules that GSP aims to promote. The authors argue that the effect of the withdrawal of trade preferences will be rather low if they are an isolated action which is not complemented by other economic and political sanctions, trade measures from other key trading partners and support from the private sector. If those conditions are not met, it is likely that the regime in question will be able to continue to operate as usual and to divert its trade flows towards other regions and other actors. Hence, the GSP system is expected to hold the most potential in respect of countries for whom the EU is the main trading partner.

3. CONCLUSION

Joanne Scott (2013) labelled the EU a 'contingent unilateralist' which is willing to pursue autonomous international action when multilateralism fails. This approach is exemplified in its governance *through* trade policies. As discussed in the introductory chapter to this volume, several authors in recent years have indeed identified trade policy as a key area to pursue non-trade objectives. This field of research is becoming increasingly relevant for scholars focusing on non-multilateral forms of global governance. Through this volume we aimed to contribute to this research strand by assessing the different governance *through* trade policies which the EU is pursuing in an in-depth manner. Where these policies will lead the EU in terms of international cooperation is still an open-ended question. Nico Krisch (2014) recently observed that these new forms of international rule-making increasingly side-line international law and use hierarchy, especially by major players in international politics, to enforce specific objectives. It is obvious that in these trade policies, hierarchy and power play a very important role. The concept of using trade policy to pursue non-trade objectives is based on the idea of unbalanced power relations in which one party uses its power to induce changes in another sovereign state. Market Power Europe, as a concept, clearly exemplifies this and the many contributions in this book show how such an approach operates in practice. Whether this side-lines existing international law is another issue which is not fully supported by the contributions to this volume. Several of the governance *through* trade instruments do not necessarily aim to complement or substitute existing international law, but rather to strengthen it through other forms of enforcement. Indeed, GSP, non-trade paragraphs in bilateral trade agreements and unilateral regulatory measures often explicitly refer to a whole body of existing international law, such as ILO conventions, human rights conventions and climate change agreements. What governance *through* trade adds is a link between these international commitments and trade measures that is enacted in the case of non-compliance. In theory, this approach holds significant potential to further pursue compliance with international rules on good governance and global public goods, such as the protection of the environment and human rights. Whether this approach will succeed needs to be further analysed. Indeed, the contributions in this volume point to significant gaps in our understanding of the impact of these policies in the target 'recipient' countries. Closing these gaps will require significant research efforts which will focus not only on legal and institutional changes in countries but also on the practical implications for firms, natural resource managers, and similar.

The various contributions to this volume also identified some potential limitations, especially in negotiated agreements, which often result in rather vague commitments on, for example, environmental governance. Whether these limitations constitute structural barriers for effective governance *through* trade policy is unclear, especially in a context in which developing countries not only negotiate trade agreements with the EU, the US, Canada or Australia (countries likely to include human rights, environmental and other conditions in trade agreements) but also with emerging economic powers such as China, India and Brazil. The effects of this changing context is another area on which future research could focus. Finally, in the context of negotiated trade agreements, research should focus also on the effect of the integration of non-trade objectives in such agreements. Trade agreements are negotiated primarily with the purpose of facilitating trade and to stimulate economic growth; integrating other objectives might influence these primary objectives. Scholars have long debated the issue of a potential trade-off between social, human rights and environmental protection, on the one hand, and enhancing economic globalization through trade, on the other. As indicated in the introduction to this volume, we do not engage in this debate as many measures are too recent to conduct a thorough analysis. Nonetheless, the issue remains important and policy makers should focus on the question of how and to what extent the integration of non-trade objectives in trade agreements influences (or not) trade objectives and trade negotiations.

The results of this future research, as well as the conclusions of this volume, should enable policy makers to acquire a better understanding of the possibilities and limitations of using trade as a foreign policy instrument. The EU, in designing measures that fall within the concept of governing *through* trade, appears to be well aware of the legal constraints arising from international treaties, such as the WTO agreements. For example, the way in which EU measures, such as the EUTR, are designed, reflects efforts to contribute to global efforts aimed at addressing illegal logging. At the same time, the measures are designed in a way that is aimed at fulfilling the EU's obligations under the law of the WTO. However, there is still a knowledge gap when it comes to anticipating – and measuring – the effectiveness of governance through trade instruments, as indicated above. At the same time, the importance of the coherence of the wider group of governing through trade instruments should not be underestimated. Where these instruments are generally coherent, this will often increase their effectiveness. We consider that governing *through* trade is of increasing importance in a world characterized by a decline in multilateral initiatives. However, in order to ensure that this 'instrumental' approach to trade delivers its full potential, it needs to be coherent. This search for coherence can take different institutional forms and can be translated into different coordination mechanisms. These would not only bring together actors from the policy units concerned, but also from adjacent units who focus on issues such as climate change, human rights, development cooperation and external action. Moreover, the EU is well-advised to monitor and assess the impact of these different initiatives in order to assess their effectiveness.

This volume had the ambition of delving further into one new form of global governance, namely governing *through* trade, with a specific focus on the policies of the EU. Throughout its contributions it has become clear that governing through trade occurs via different instruments. With the expansion of trade, the importance for other countries of the European market on a global scale, and the continued search of the EU to influence the international political agenda, governing *through* trade will continue to be an important global governance tool of the EU.

REFERENCES

Brousseau, E., T. Dedeurwaerdere and B. Siebenhüner (2012), *Reflexive Governance for Global Public Goods*, Cambridge, MA: The MIT Press.

Büthe, T. and W. Mattli (2011), *The New Global Rulers: The Privatization of Regulation in the World Economy*, Princeton, NJ: Princeton University Press.

Damro, C. (2012), 'Market Power Europe', *Journal of European Public Policy*, **19** (5), 682–99.

Hafner-Burton, E. (2005), 'Trading Human Rights: How Preferential Trade Agreements Influence Government Repression', *International Organization*, **59** (3), 593–629.

Hafner-Burton, E. (2013), *Making Human Rights a Reality*, Princeton, NJ: Princeton University Press.

International Labour Organization (ILO) (2013), *Social Dimensions of Free Trade Agreements*, International Institute for Labour Studies, Geneva: ILO.

Krisch, N. (2014), 'The Decay of Consent: International Law in an Age of Global Public Goods', *The American Journal of International Law*, **108** (1), 1–40.

Mamic, I. (2004), *Implementing Codes of Conduct. How Businesses Manage Social Performance in Global Supply Chains*, Geneva: ILO.

Marangoni, A.C. and K. Raube (2014), 'Virtue or Vice? The Coherence of the EU's External Policies', *Journal of European Integration*, **36** (5), 473–89, DOI:10.1080/07036337.2014.883505

Marx, A. (2011), 'Global Governance and the Certification Revolution', in D. Levi-Faur (ed.), *Handbook of the Politics of Regulation*, Cheltenham, UK and Northampton, MA, USA: Edward Elgar Publishing.

Marx, A. and J. Wouters (2015), 'Competition and Cooperation in the Market of Voluntary Standards Sustainability Standards', in P. Delimatsis (ed.), *International Standardization – Law, Economics and Politics*, Cambridge: Cambridge University Press.

Marx, A., J. Soares and W. Van Acker (2015), 'The Protection of International Labour Rights. A Longitudinal Analysis of the Protection of the Rights of Freedom of Association and Collective Bargaining over 30 years in 73 Countries', in A. Marx, J. Wouters, G. Rayp and L. Beke (eds), *Global Governance and Labour Rights*, Cheltenham, UK and Northampton, MA, USA: Edward Elgar Publishing.

Marx, A., M. Maertens, J. Swinnen and J. Wouters (eds) (2012), *Global Governance and Private Standards. Interdisciplinary Perspectives*, Cheltenham, UK and Northampton, MA, USA: Edward Elgar Publishing.

Meunier, S. and K. Nicolaïdis (2006) 'The European Union as a Conflicted Trade Power', *Journal of European Public Policy*, **13** (6), 906–25.

Ostrom, E. (2005), *Understanding Institutional Diversity*, Princeton, NJ: Princeton University Press.

Pauwelyn, J., R. Wessel and J. Wouters (2012), *Informal International Lawmaking*, Oxford: Oxford University Press.

Pauwelyn, J., R. Wessel and J. Wouters (2014), 'When Structures Become Shackles: Stagnation and Dynamics in International Lawmaking', *European Journal of International Law*, **25**, 733–63.

Scott, J. (2013), 'Contingent Unilateralism – International Aviation in the European Emissions Trading Scheme', in B. van Vooren, S. Blockmans and J. Wouters (eds), *The EU's Role in Global Governance: The Legal Dimension*, Oxford: Oxford University Press.

Yap, J. (2013), 'Beyond "Don't Be Evil": The European Union GSP+ Trade Preference Scheme and the Incentivisation of the Sri Lankan Garment Industry to Foster Human Rights', *European Law Journal*, **19** (2), 293–301.

Zeitlin, J. (2015) 'Introduction: Theoretical Framework and Research Agenda', in J. Zeitlin, *Extending Experimentalist Governance? The European Union and Transnational Regulation*, Oxford: Oxford University Press.

Index